THE **COMPLETE WORKS** OF **SWAMI VIVEKANANDA**

VOLUME IV

Discovery Publisher

2018, Discovery Publisher

No part of this book may be reproduced in any form or by any electronic or mechanical means including information storage and retrieval systems, without permission in writing from the publisher.

Author: Swami Vivekananda

616 Corporate Way
Valley Cottage, New York, 10989
www.discoverypublisher.com
edition@discoverypublisher.com
facebook.com/discoverypublisher
twitter.com/discoverypb

New York • Paris • Dublin • Tokyo • Hong Kong

TABLE OF CONTENTS

Volume IV — 2

Addresses on Bhakti-Yoga — 3

THE PREPARATION — 4
THE FIRST STEPS — 7
THE TEACHER OF SPIRITUALITY — 12
THE NEED OF SYMBOLS — 17
THE CHIEF SYMBOLS — 20
THE ISHTA — 25

Lectures and Discourses — 32

THE RAMAYANA — 34
Delivered at the Shakespeare Club, Pasadena, California, January 31, 1900

THE MAHABHARATA — 40
Delivered at the Shakespeare Club, Pasadena, California, February 1, 1900

THOUGHTS ON THE GITA — 50

THE STORY OF JADA BHARATA — 54
Delivered in California

THE STORY OF PRAHLADA — 56
Delivered in California

THE GREAT TEACHERS OF THE WORLD — 58
Delivered at the Shakespeare Club, Pasadena, California, February 3, 1900

ON LORD BUDDHA — 64
Delivered in Detroit

CHRIST, THE MESSENGER — 65
Delivered at Los Angeles, California, 1900

MY MASTER — 72

INDIAN RELIGIOUS THOUGHT — 86
Delivered under the auspices of tile Brooklyn Ethical Society, in the Art Gallery of tile Pouch Mansion, Clinton Avenue, Brooklyn, U.S.A.

THE BASIS FOR PSYCHIC OR SPIRITUAL RESEARCH — 88

ON ART IN INDIA — 90

IS INDIA A BENIGHTED COUNTRY? — 90

THE CLAIMS OF RELIGION — 93
Sunday, 5th January

CONCENTRATION — 99
Delivered at the Washington Hall, San Francisco, on March 16, 1900

MEDITATION — 103
Delivered at the Washington Hall, San Francisco, April 3, 1900

THE PRACTICE OF RELIGION — 107
Delivered at Alameda, California, on April 18, 1900

Writings: Prose — 114

IS THE SOUL IMMORTAL? — 116
"None has power to destroy the unchangeable."

REINCARNATION — 117
"Both you and I have passed through many births; you know them not, I know them all."

ON DR. PAUL DEUSSEN — 124

ON PROFESSOR MAX MÜLLER — 126

SKETCH OF THE LIFE OF PAVHARI BABA — 128

ARYANS AND TAMILIANS — 134

THE SOCIAL CONFERENCE ADDRESS — 137

INDIA'S MESSAGE TO THE WORLD — 139
Syllabus — 139
Introduction — 141

STRAY REMARKS ON THEOSOPHY — 143

REPLY TO THE ADDRESS OF THE MAHARAJA OF KHETRI — 144
India — The Land of Religion — 144

REPLY TO THE MADRAS ADDRESS — 149

A MESSAGE OF SYMPATHY TO A FRIEND — 159

WHAT WE BELIEVE IN — 160

OUR DUTY TO THE MASSES — 162

REPLY TO THE CALCUTTA ADDRESS — 163

TO MY BRAVE BOYS — 164

A PLAN OF WORK FOR INDIA	165
FUNDAMENTALS OF RELIGION	167

Writings: Poems — 174

KALI THE MOTHER	176
ANGELS UNAWARES	177
TO THE AWAKENED INDIA	180
REQUIESCAT IN PACE	183
HOLD ON YET A WHILE, BRAVE HEART	184
NIRVANASHATKAM, ON SIX STANZAS ON NIRVANA	185
THE SONG OF THE SANNYÂSIN	187
PEACE	191

Translation: Prose — 194

THE PROBLEM OF MODERN INDIA AND ITS SOLUTION	196
RAMAKRISHNA: HIS LIFE AND SAYINGS	200
THE PARIS CONGRESS OF THE HISTORY OF RELIGIONS	205
KNOWLEDGE: ITS SOURCE AND ACQUIREMENT	209
MODERN INDIA	212

Translated from a Bengali contribution to the Udbodhana, March 1899

THE EDUCATION THAT INDIA NEEDS	231
OUR PRESENT SOCIAL PROBLEMS	234

Translation: Poems — 238

TO A FRIEND — 240
Rendered from a Bengali poem composed by Swami Vivekananda

THE HYMN OF CREATION — 245
Rendered from Bengali

THE HYMN OF SAMADHI — 247
Rendered from Bengali

A HYMN TO THE DIVINE MOTHER — 248
अम्बास्तोत्रम्।

A HYMN TO SHIVA — 252

A HYMN TO THE DIVINITY OF SHRI RAMAKRISHNA — 255

"AND LET SHYAMA DANCE THERE" — 258
Rendered from Bengali

A SONG I SING TO THEE — 263
Rendered from Bengali

THE **COMPLETE WORKS** OF SWAMI VIVEKANANDA

VOLUME IV

ADDRESSES ON BHAKTI-YOGA

THE PREPARATION

The best definition given of Bhakti-Yoga is perhaps embodied in the verse: "May that love undying which the non-discriminating have for the fleeting objects of the senses never leave this heart of mine — of me who seek after Thee!" We see what a strong love men, who do not know any better, have for sense-objects, for money, dress, their wives, children, friends, and possessions. What a tremendous clinging they have to all these things! So in the above prayer the sage says, "I will have that attachment, that tremendous clinging, only to Thee." This love, when given to God, is called Bhakti. Bhakti is not destructive; it teaches us that no one of the faculties we have has been given in vain, that through them is the natural way to come to liberation. Bhakti does not kill out our tendencies, it does not go against nature, but only gives it a higher and more powerful direction. How naturally we love objects of the senses! We cannot but do so, because they are so real to us. We do not ordinarily see anything real about higher things, but when a man has seen something real beyond the senses, beyond the universe of senses, the idea is that he can have a strong attachment, only it should be transferred to the object beyond the senses, which is God. And when the same kind of love that has before been given to sense-objects is given to God, it is called Bhakti. According to the sage Râmânuja, the following are the preparations for getting that intense love.

The first is Viveka. It is a very curious thing, especially to people of the West. It means, according to Ramanuja, "discrimination of food". Food contains all the energies that go to make up the forces of our body and mind; it has been transferred, and conserved, and given new directions in my body, but my body and mind have nothing essentially different from the food that I ate. Just as the force and matter we find in the material world become body and mind in us, so, essentially, the difference between body and mind and the food we eat is only in manifestation. It being so, that out of the material particles of our food we construct the instrument of thought, and that from the finer forces lodged in these particles we manufacture thought itself, it naturally follows, that both this thought and the instrument will be modified by the food we take. There are certain kinds of food that produce a certain change in the mind; we see it every day. There are other sorts which produce a change in the body, and in the long run have a tremendous effect on the mind. It is a great thing to learn; a good deal of the misery we suffer is occasioned by the food we take. You find that after a heavy and indigestible meal it is very hard to control the mind; it is running, running all the time. There are certain foods which are exciting; if you eat such food, you find that you cannot control the mind. It is obvious that after drinking a large quantity of wine, or other alcoholic beverage, a man finds that his mind would not be controlled; it runs away from his control.

According to Ramanuja, there are three things in food we must avoid. First, there is Jâti, the nature, or species of the food, that must be considered. All exciting food should be avoided, as meat, for instance; this should not be taken because it is by its very nature impure. We can get it only by taking the life of another. We get pleasure for a moment, and another creature has to give up its life to give us that pleasure. Not only so, but we demoralise other human beings. It would be rather better if every man who eats meat killed the animal himself; but, instead of doing so, society gets a class of persons to do that business for them, for doing which, it hates them. In England no butcher can serve on a jury, the idea being that he is cruel by nature. Who makes him cruel? Society. If we did not eat beef and mutton, there would be no butchers. Eating meat is only allowable for people who do very hard work, and who are not going to be Bhaktas; but if you are going to be Bhaktas, you should avoid meat. Also, all exciting foods, such as onions, garlic, and all evil-smelling food, as "sauerkraut". Any food that has been standing for days, till its condition is changed, any food whose natural juices have been almost dried ups any food that is malodorous, should be avoided.

The next thing that is to be considered as regards food is still more intricate to Western minds — it is what is called Âshraya, i.e. the person from whom it comes This is rather a mysterious theory of the Hindus. The idea is that each man has a certain aura round him, and whatever thing he touches, a part of his character, as it were, his influence, is left on it. It is supposed that a man's character emanates from him, as it were, like a physical force, and whatever he touches is affected by it. So we must take care who touches our food when it is cooked; a wicked or immoral person must not touch it. One who wants to be a Bhakta must not dine with people whom he knows to be very wicked, because their infection will come through the food.

The other form of purity to be observed is Nimitta, or instruments. Dirt and dust must not be in food. Food should not be brought from the market and placed on the table unwashed. We must be careful also about the saliva and other secretions. The lips ought never, for instance, to be touched with the fingers. The mucous membrane is the most delicate part of the body, and all tendencies are conveyed very easily by the saliva. Its contact, therefore, is to be regarded as not only offensive, but dangerous. Again, we must not eat food, half of which has been eaten by someone else. When these things are avoided in food, it becomes pure; pure food brings a pure mind, and in a pure mind is a constant memory of God.

Let me tell you the same thing as explained by another commentator, Shankarâchârya, who takes quite another view. This word for food, in Sanskrit, is derived from the root, meaning to gather. Âhâra means "gathered in". What is his explanation? He says, the passage that when food is pure the mind will become pure really means that lest we become subject to the senses we should avoid the following: First as to attachment; we must not be extremely attached to anything excepting God. See everything, do everything, but be not attached. As soon as extreme attachment comes, a man loses himself, he is no more master of himself, he is a slave. If a woman is tremendously attached to a man, she becomes a slave to that man. There is no use in being a slave. There are higher things in this world than becoming a slave to a human being. Love and do good to everybody, but do not become a slave. In the first place, attachment degenerates us, individually, and in the second place, makes us extremely selfish. Owing to this failing, we want to injure others to do good to those we love. A good many of the wicked deeds done in this world are really done through attachment to certain persons. So all attachment excepting that for good works should be avoided; but love should be given to everybody. Then as to jealousy. There should be no jealousy in regard to objects of the senses; jealousy is the root of all evil, and a most difficult thing to conquer. Next, delusion. We always take one thing for another, and act upon that, with the result that we bring misery upon ourselves. We take the bad for the good. Anything that titillates our nerves for a moment we think; as the highest good, and plunge into it immediately, but find, when it is too late, that it has given us a tremendous blow. Every day, we run into this error, and we often continue in it all our lives. When the senses, without being extremely attached, without jealousy, or without delusion, work in the world, such work or collection of impressions is called pure food, according to Shankaracharya. When pure food is taken, the mind is able to take in objects and think about them without attachment, jealousy or delusion; then the mind becomes pure, and then there is constant memory of God in that mind.

It is quite natural for one to say that Shankara's meaning is the best, but I wish to add that one should not neglect Ramanuja's interpretation either. It is only when you take care of the real material food that the rest will come. It is very true that mind is the master, but very few of us are not bound by the senses. We are all controlled by matter; and as long as we are so controlled, we must take material aids; and then, when we have become strong, we can eat or drink anything we like. We have to follow Ramanuja in taking care about food and drink; at the same time we must also take care about our mental food. It is very easy to take care about material food, but mental work must go along with it; then gradually our spiritual self will become stronger and stronger, and the physical self less assertive. Then will food hurt you no more. The great danger is that every man wants to jump at the highest ideal, but jumping is not the way. That ends only in a fall. We are bound down here, and we have to break our chains slowly. This is called Viveka, discrimination.

The next is called Vimoka, freedom from desires. He who wants to love God must get rid of extreme desires, desire nothing except God. This world is good so far as it helps one to go to the higher world. The objects of the senses are good so far as they help us to attain higher objects. We always forget that this world is a means to an end, and not an end itself. If this were the end we should be immortal here in our physical body; we should never die. But we see people every moment dying around us, and yet, foolishly, we think we shall never die; and from that conviction we come to think that this life is the goal. That is the case with ninety-nine per cent of us. This notion should be given up at once. This world is good so far as it is a means to perfect ourselves; and as soon as it has ceased to be so, it is evil. So wife, husband, children, money and learning, are good so long as they help us forward; but as soon as they cease to do that, they are nothing but evil. If the wife help us to attain God, she is a good wife; so with a husband or a child. If money help a man to do good to others, it is of some value; but if not, it is simply a mass of evil, and the sooner it is got rid of, the better.

The next is Abhyâsa, practice. The mind should always go towards God. No other things have any right to withhold it. It should continuously think of God, though this is a very hard task; yet it can be done by persistent practice. What we are now is the result of our past practice. Again, practice makes us what we shall be. So practice the other way; one sort of turning round has brought us this way, turn the other way and get out of it as soon as you can. Thinking of the senses has brought us down here — to cry one moment, to rejoice the next, to be at the mercy of every breeze, slave to everything. This is shameful, and yet we call ourselves spirits. Go the other way, think of God; let the mind not think of any physical or mental enjoyment, but of God alone. When it tries to think of anything else, give it a good blow, so that it may turn round and think of God. As oil poured from one vessel to another falls in an unbroken line, as chimes coming from a distance fall upon the ear as one continuous sound, so should the mind flow towards God in one continuous stream. We should not only impose this practice on the mind, but the senses too should be employed. Instead of hearing foolish things, we must hear about God; instead of talking foolish words, we must talk of God. Instead of reading foolish books, we must read good ones which tell of God.

The greatest aid to this practice of keeping God in memory is, perhaps, music. The Lord says to Nârada, the great teacher of Bhakti, "I do not live in heaven, nor do I live in the heart of the Yogi, but where My devotees sing My praise, there am I". Music has such tremendous power over the human mind; it brings it to concentration in a moment. You will find the dull, ignorant, low, brute-like human beings, who never steady their mind for a moment at other times, when they hear attractive music, immediately become charmed and concentrated. Even the minds of animals, such as dogs, lions, cats, and serpents, become charmed with music.

The next is Kriyâ, work — doing good to others. The memory of God will not come to the selfish man. The more we come out and do good to others, the more our hearts will be purified, and God will be in them. According to our scriptures, there are five sorts of work, called the fivefold sacrifice. First, study. A man must study every day something holy and good. Second, worship of God, angels, or saints, as it may be. Third, our duty to our forefathers. Fourth, our duty to human beings. Man has no right to live in a house himself, until he builds for the poor also, or for anybody who needs it. The householder's house should be open to everybody that is poor and suffering; then he is a real householder. If he builds a house only for himself and his wife to enjoy, he will never be a lover of God. No man has the right to cook food only for himself; it is for others, and he should have what remains. It is a common practice in India that when the season's produce first comes into the market, such as strawberries or mangoes, a man buys some of them and gives to the poor. Then he eats of them; and it is a very good example to follow in this country. This training will make a man unselfish, and at the same time, be an excellent object-lesson to his wife and children. The Hebrews in olden times used to give the first fruits to God. The first of everything should go to the poor; we have only a right to what remains. The poor are God's representatives; anyone that suffers is His representative. Without giving, he who eats and enjoys eating, enjoys sin. Fifth, our duty to the lower animals. It is diabolical to say that all animals are created for men to be killed and used in any way man likes. It is the devil's gospel, not God's. Think how diabolical it is to cut them up to see whether a nerve quivers or not, in a certain part of the body. I am glad that in our country such things are not countenanced by the Hindus, whatever encouragement they may get from the foreign government they are under. One portion of the food cooked in a household belongs to the animals also. They should be given food every day; there ought to be hospitals in every city in this country for poor, lame, or blind horses, cows, dogs, and cats, where they should be fed and taken care of.

Then there is Kalyâna, purity, which comprises the following: Satya, truthfulness. He who is true, unto him the God of truth comes. Thought, word, and deed should be perfectly true. Next Ârjava, straightforwardness, rectitude. The word means, to be simple, no crookedness in the heart, no double-dealing. Even if it is a little harsh, go straightforward, and not crookedly. Dayâ, pity, compassion. Ahimsâ, not injuring any being by thought, word, or deed. Dâna, charity. There is no higher virtue than charity. The lowest man is he whose hand draws in, in receiving; and he is the highest man whose hand goes out in giving. The hand was made to give always. Give the last bit of bread you have even if you are starving. You will be free in a moment if you starve yourself to death by giving to another. Immediately you will be perfect, you will become God. People who have children are bound already. They cannot give away. They want to enjoy their children, and they must pay for it. Are there not enough children in the world? It is only selfishness which says, "I'll have a child for myself".

The next is Anavasâda — not desponding, cheerfulness. Despondency is not religion, whatever else it may be. By being pleasant always and smiling, it takes you nearer to God, nearer than any prayer. How can those minds that are gloomy and dull love? If they talk of love, it is false; they want to hurt others. Think of the fanatics; they make the longest faces, and all their religion is to fight against others in word and act. Think of what they have done in the past, and of what they would do now if they were given a free hand. They would deluge the whole world in blood tomorrow if it would bring them power. By worshipping power and making long faces, they lose every bit of love from their hearts. So the man who always feels miserable will never come to God. It is not religion, it is diabolism to say, "I am so miserable." Every man has his own burden to bear. If you are miserable, try to be happy, try to conquer it.

God is not to be reached by the weak. Never be weak. You must be strong; you have infinite strength within you. How else will you conquer anything? How else will you come to God? At the same time you must avoid excessive merriment, Uddharsha, as it is called. A mind in that state never becomes calm; it becomes fickle. Excessive merriment will always be followed by sorrow. Tears and laughter are near kin. People so often run from one extreme to the other. Let the mind be cheerful, but calm. Never let it run into excesses, because every excess will be followed by a reaction.

These, according to Ramanuja, are the preparations for Bhakti.

THE FIRST STEPS

The philosophers who wrote on Bhakti defined it as extreme love for God. Why a man should love God is the question to be solved; and until we understand that, we shall not be able to grasp the subject at all. There are two entirely different ideals of life. A man of any country who has any religion knows that he is a body and a spirit also. But there is a great deal of difference as to the goal of human life.

In Western countries, as a rule, people lay more stress on the body aspect of man; those philosophers who wrote on Bhakti in India laid stress on the spiritual side of man; and this difference seems to be typical of the Oriental and Occidental nations. It is so even in common language. In England, when speaking of death it is said, a man gave up his ghost; in India, a man gave up his body. The one idea is that man is a body and has a soul; the other that man is a soul and has a body. More intricate problems arise out of this. It naturally follows that the ideal which holds that man is a body and has a soul lays all the stress on the body. If you ask why man lives, you will be told it is to enjoy the senses, to enjoy possessions and wealth. He cannot dream of anything beyond even if he is told of it; his idea of a future life would be a continuation of this enjoyment. He is very sorry that it cannot continue all the time here, but he has to depart; and he thinks that somehow or other he will go to some place where the same thing will be renewed. He will have the same enjoyments, the same senses, only heightened and strengthened. He wants to worship Cod, because God is the means to attain this end. The goal of his life is enjoyment of sense-objects, and he comes to know there is a Being who can give him a very long lease of these enjoyments, and that is why he worships God.

On the other hand the Indian idea is that God is the goal of life; there is nothing beyond God, and the sense-enjoyments are simply something through which we are passing now in the hope of getting better things. Not only so; it would be disastrous and terrible if man had nothing but sense-enjoyments. In our everyday life we find that the less the sense-enjoyments, the higher the life of the man. Look at the dog when he eats. No man ever ate with the same satisfaction. Observe the pig giving grunts of satisfaction as he eats; it is his heaven, and if the greatest archangel came and looked on, the pig would not even notice him. His whole existence is in his eating. No man was ever born who could eat that way. Think of the power of hearing in the lower animals, the power of seeing; all their senses are highly developed. Their enjoyment of the senses is extreme; they become simply mad with delight and pleasure. And the lower the man also, the more delight he finds in the senses. As he gets higher, the goal becomes reason and love. In proportion as these faculties develop, he loses the power of enjoying the senses.

For illustration's sake, if we take for granted that a certain amount of power is given to man, and that can be spent either on the body, or the mind, or the spirit, then all the powers spent on any one of these leaves just so much less to be expended on the others. The ignorant or savage races have much stronger sensual faculties than the civilised races, and this is, in fact, one of the lessons we learn from history that as a nation becomes civilised the nerve organisation becomes finer, and they become physically weaker. Civilise a savage race, and you will find the same thing; another barbarian race comes up and conquers it. It is nearly always the barbarian race that conquers. We see then that if we desire only to have sense-enjoyments all the time, we degrade ourselves to the brute state. A man does not know what he is asking for when he says, he wants to go to a place where his sense-enjoyments will be intensified; that he can only have by going down to the brutes.

So with men desiring a heaven full of sense-pleasures. They are like swine wallowing in the mire of the senses, unable to see anything beyond. This sense-enjoyment is what they want, and the loss of it is the loss of heaven to them. These can never be Bhaktas in the highest sense of the word; they can never be true lovers of God. At the same time, though this lower ideal be followed for a time, it will also in course of time change, each man will find that there is something higher, of which he did not know, and so this clinging to life and to things of the senses will gradually die away. When I was a little boy at school, I had a fight with another schoolfellow about some sweetmeats, and he being the stronger boy snatched them from my hand. I remember the feeling I had; I thought that boy was the most wicked boy ever born, and that as soon as I grew strong enough I would punish him; there was no punishment sufficient for his wickedness. We have both grown up now, and we are fast friends. This world is full of babies to whom eating and drinking, and all these little cakes are everything. They will dream of these cakes, and their idea of future life is where these cakes will be plentiful. Think of the American Indian who believes that his future life will be in a place which is a very good hunting ground. Each one of us has an idea of a heaven just as we want it to be; but in course of time, as we grow older and see higher things, we catch higher glimpses beyond. But let us not dispense with our ideas of future life in the ordinary way of modern times, by not believing in anything — that is destruction. The agnostic who thus destroys everything is mistaken, the Bhakta sees higher. The agnostic does not want to go to heaven, because he has none; while the Bhakta does not want to go to heaven, because he thinks it is child's play. What he wants is God.

What can be a higher end than God? God Himself is the highest goal of man; see Him, enjoy Him. We can never conceive anything higher, because God is perfection. We cannot conceive of any higher enjoyment than that of love, but this word love has different meanings. It does not mean the ordinary selfish love of the world; it is blasphemy to call that love. The love for our children and our wives is mere animal love; that love which is perfectly unselfish is the only love, and that is of God. It is a very difficult thing to attain to. We are passing through all these different loves — love of children, father, mother, and so forth. We slowly exercise the faculty of love; but in the majority of cases we never learn anything from it, we become bound to one step, to one person. In some cases men come out of this bondage. Men are ever running after wives and wealth and fame in this world; sometimes they are hit very hard on the head, and they find out what this world really is. No one in this world can really love anything but God. Man finds out that human love is all hollow. Men cannot love though they talk of it. The wife says she loves her husband and kisses him; but as soon as he dies, the first thing she thinks about is the bank account, and what she shall do the next day. The husband loves the wife; but when she becomes sick and loses her beauty, or becomes haggard, or makes a mistake, he ceases to care for her. All the love of the world is hypocrisy and hollowness.

A finite subject cannot love, nor a finite object be loved. When the object of the love of a man is dying every moment, and his mind also is constantly changing as he grows, what eternal love can you expect to find in the world? There cannot be any real love but in God: why then all these loves? These are mere stages. There is a power behind impelling us forward, we do not know where to seek for the real object, but this love is sending us forward in search of it. Again and again we find out our mistake. We grasp something, and find it slips through our fingers, and then we grasp something else. Thus on and on we go, till at last comes light; we come to God, the only One who loves. His love knows no change and is ever ready to take us in. How long would any of you bear with me if I injured you? He in whose mind is no anger, hatred, or envy, who never loses his balance, dies, or is born, who is he but God? But the path to God is long and difficult, and very few people attain Him. We are all babies struggling. Millions of people make a trade of religion. A few men in a century attain to that love of God, and the whole country becomes blessed and hallowed. When a son of God appears, a whole country becomes blessed. It is true that few such are born in any one century in the whole world, but all should strive to attain that love of God. Who knows but you or I may be the next to attain? Let us struggle therefore.

We say that a wife loves her husband. She thinks that her whole soul is absorbed in him: a baby comes and half of it goes out to the baby, or more. She herself will feel that the same love of husband does not exist now. So with the father. We always find that when more intense objects of love come to us, the previous love slowly vanishes. Children at school think that some of their schoolfellows are the dearest beings that they have in life, or their fathers or mothers are so; then comes the husband or wife, and immediately the old feeling disappears, and the new love becomes uppermost. One star arises, another bigger one comes, and then a still bigger one, and at last the sun comes, and all the lesser lights vanish. That sun is God. The stars are the smaller loves. When that Sun bursts upon him, a man becomes mad what Emerson calls "a God-intoxicated man". Man becomes transfigured into God, everything is merged in that one ocean of love. Ordinary love is mere animal attraction. Otherwise why is the distinction between the sexes? If one kneels before an image, it is dreadful idolatry; but if one kneels before husband or wife, it is quite permissible!

The world presents to us manifold stages of love. We have first to clear the ground. Upon our view of life the whole theory of love will rest. To think that this world is the aim and end of life is brutal and degenerating. Any man who starts in life with that idea degenerates himself He will never rise higher, he will never catch this glimpse from behind, he will always be a slave to the senses. He will struggle for the dollar that will get him a few cakes to eat. Better die than live that life. Slaves of this world, slaves of the senses, let us rouse ourselves; there is something higher than this sense-life. Do you think that man, the Infinite Spirit was born to be a slave to his eyes, his nose, and his ears? There is an Infinite, Omniscient Spirit behind that can do everything, break every bond; and that Spirit we are, and we get that power through love. This is the ideal we must remember. We cannot, of course, get it in a day. We may fancy that we have it, but it is a fancy after all; it is a long, long way off. We must take man where he stands, and help him upwards. Man stands in materialism; you and I are materialists. Our talking about God and Spirit is good; but it is simply the vogue in our society to talk thus: we have learnt it parrot-like and repeat it. So we have to take ourselves where we are as materialists, and must take the help of matter and go on slowly until we become real spiritualists, and feel ourselves spirits, understand the spirit, and find that this world which we call the infinite is but a gross external form of that world which is behind.

But something besides that is necessary. You read in the Sermon on the Mount, "Ask, and it shall be given (to) you; seek, and ye shall find; knock, and it shall be opened unto you." The difficulty is, who seeks, who wants? We all say we know God. One man writes a book to disprove God, another to prove Him. One man thinks it his duty to prove Him all his life; another, to disprove Him, and he goes about to teach man there is no God. What is the use of writing a book either to prove or disprove God? What does it matter to most people whether there is a God or not? The majority of men work just like a machine with no thought of God and feeling no need of Him. Then one day comes Death and says, "Come." The man says, "Wait a little, I want a little more time. I want to see my son grow a little bigger." But Death says, "Come at once." So it goes on. So goes poor John. What shall we say to poor John? He never found anything in which God was the highest; perhaps he was a pig in the past, and he is much better as a man. But there are some who get a little awakening. Some misery comes, someone whom we love most dies, that upon which we had bent our whole soul, that for which we had cheated the whole world and perhaps our own brother, that vanishes, and a blow comes to us. Perhaps a voice comes in our soul and asks, "What after this?" Sometimes death comes without a blow, but such cases are few. Most of us, when anything slips through our fingers, say, "What next?" How we cling to the senses! You have heard of a drowning man clutching at a straw; a man will clutch at a straw first, and when it fails, he will say someone must help him. Still people must, as the English phrase goes, "sow their wild oats", before they can rise to higher things.

Bhakti is a religion. Religion is not for the many, that is impossible. A sort of knee-drill, standing up and sitting down, may be suited for the many; but religion is for the few. There are in every country only a few hundreds who can be, and will be religious. The others cannot be religious, because they will not be awakened, and they do not want to be. The chief thing is to want God. We want everything except God, because our ordinary wants are supplied by the external world; it is only when our necessities have gone beyond the external world that we want a supply from the internal, from God.

So long as our needs are confined within the narrow limits of this physical universe, we cannot have any need for God; it is only when we have become satiated with everything here that we look beyond for a supply. It is only when the need is there that the demand will come. Have done with this child's play of the world as soon as you can, and then you will feel the necessity of something beyond the world, and the first step in religion will come.

There is a form of religion which is fashionable. My friend has much furniture in her parlour; it is the fashion to have a Japanese vase, so she must have one even if it costs a thousand dollars. In the same way she will have a little religion and join a church. Bhakti is not for such. That is not want. Want is that without which we cannot live. We want breath, we want food, we want clothes; without them we cannot live. When a man loves a woman in this world, there are times when he feels that without her he cannot live, although that is a mistake. When a husband dies, the wife thinks she cannot live without him; but she lives all the same. This is the secret of necessity: it is that without which we cannot live; either it must come to us or we die. When the time comes that we feel the same about God, or in other words, we want something beyond this world, something above all material forces, then we may become Bhaktas. What are our little lives when for a moment the cloud passes away, and we get one glimpse from beyond, and for that moment all these lower desires seem like a drop in the ocean? Then the soul grows, and feels the want of God, and must have Him.

The first step is: What do we want? Let us ask ourselves this question every day, do we want God? You may read all the books in the universe, but this love is not to be had by the power of speech, not by the highest intellect, not by the study of various sciences. He who desires God will get Love, unto him God gives Himself. Love is always mutual, reflective. You may hate me, and if I want to love you, you repulse me. But if I persist, in a month or a year you are bound to love me. It is a wellknown psychological phenomenon. As the loving wife thinks of her departed husband, with the same love we must desire the Lord, and then we will find God, and all books and the various sciences would not be able to teach us anything. By reading books we become parrots; no one becomes learned by reading books. If a man reads but one word of love, he indeed becomes learned. So we want first to get that desire.

Let us ask ourselves each day, "Do we want God?" When we begin to talk religion, and especially when we take a high position and begin to teach others, we must ask ourselves the same question. I find many times that I don't want God, I want bread more. I may go mad if I don't get a piece of bread; many ladies will go mad if they don't get a diamond pin, but they do not have the same desire for God; they do not know the only Reality that is in the universe. There is a proverb in our language — If I want to be a hunter, I'll hunt the rhinoceros; if I want to be a robber, I'll rob the king's treasury. What is the use of robbing beggars or hunting ants? So if you want to love, love God. Who cares for these things of the world? This world is utterly false; all the great teachers of the world found that out; there is no way out of it but through God. He is the goal of our life; all ideas that the world is the goal of life are pernicious. This world and this body have their own value, a secondary value, as a means to an end; but the world should not be the end. Unfortunately, too often we make the world the end and God the means. We find people going to church and saying, "God, give me such and such; God, heal my disease." They want nice healthy bodies; and because they hear that someone will do this work for them, they go and pray to Him. It is better to be an atheist than to have such an idea of religion. As I have told you, this Bhakti is the highest ideal; I don't know whether we shall reach it or not in millions of years to come, but we must make it our highest ideal, make our senses aim at the highest. If we cannot get to the end, we shall at least come nearer to it. We have slowly to work through the world and the senses to reach God.

THE TEACHER OF SPIRITUALITY

Every soul is destined to be perfect, and every being, in the end, will attain to that state. Whatever we are now is the result of whatever we have been or thought in the past; and whatever we shall be in the future will be the result of what we do or think now. But this does not preclude our receiving help from outside; the possibilities of the soul are always quickened by some help from outside, so much so that in the vast majority of cases in the world, help from outside is almost absolutely necessary. Quickening influence comes from outside, and that works upon our own potentialities; and then the growth begins, spiritual life comes, and man becomes holy and perfect in the end. This quickening impulse which comes from outside cannot be received from books; the soul can receive impulse only from another soul, and from nothing else. We may study books all our lives, we may become very intellectual, but in the end we find we have not developed at all spiritually. It does not follow that a high order of intellectual development always shows an equivalent development of the spiritual side of man; on the other hand, we find cases almost every day where the intellect has become very highly developed at the expense of the spirit.

Now in intellectual development we can get much help from books, but in spiritual development, almost nothing. In studying books, sometimes we are deluded into thinking that we are being spiritually helped; but if we analyse ourselves, we shall find that only our intellect has been helped, and not the spirit. That is the reason why almost everyone of us can speak most wonderfully on spiritual subjects, but when the time of action comes, we find ourselves so woefully deficient. It is because books cannot give us that impulse from outside. To quicken the spirit, that impulse must come from another soul.

That soul from which this impulse comes is called the Guru, the teacher; and the soul to which the impulse is conveyed is called the disciple, the student. In order to convey this impulse, in the first place, the soul from which it comes must possess the power of transmitting it, as it were, to another; and in the second place, the object to which it is transmitted must be fit to receive it. The seed must be a living seed, and the field must be ready ploughed; and when both these conditions are fulfilled, a wonderful growth of religion takes place. "The speaker of religion must be wonderful, so must the hearer be"; and when both of these are really wonderful, extraordinary, then alone will splendid spiritual growth come, and not otherwise. These are the real teachers, and these are the real students. Besides these, the others are playing with spirituality — just having a little intellectual struggle, just satisfying a little curiosity — but are standing only on the outward fringe of the horizon of religion. There is some value in that; real thirst for religion may thus be awakened; all comes in course of time. It is a mysterious law of nature that as soon as the field is ready the seed must come, as soon as the soul wants religion, the transmitter of religious force must come. "The seeking sinner meeteth the seeking Saviour." When the power that attracts in the receiving soul is full and ripe, the power which answers to that attraction must come.

But there are great dangers in the way. There is the danger to the receiving soul of mistaking its momentary emotion for real religious yearning. We find that in ourselves. Many times in our lives, somebody dies whom we loved; we receive a blow; for a moment we think that this world is slipping between our fingers, and that we want something higher, and that we are going to be religious. In a few days that wave passes away, and we are left stranded where we were. We often times mistake such impulses for real thirst after religion, but so long as these momentary emotions are thus mistaken, that continuous, real want of the soul will not come, and we shall not find the "transmitter".

So when we complain that we have not got the truth, and that we want it so much, instead of complaining, our first duty ought to be to look into our own souls and find whether we really want it. In the vast majority of cases we shall find that we are not fit; we do not want; there was no thirst after the spiritual.

There are still more difficulties for the "transmitter". There are many who, though immersed in ignorance, yet, in the pride of their hearts, think they know everything, and not only do not stop there, but offer to take others on their shoulders, and thus "the blind leading the blind, they both fall into the ditch". The world is full of these; everyone wants to be a teacher, every beggar wants to make a gift of a million dollars. Just as the latter is ridiculous, so are these teachers.

How are we to know a teacher then? In the first place, the sun requires no torch to make it visible. We do not light a candle to see the sun. When the sun rises, we instinctively become aware of its rising; and when a teacher of men comes to help us, the soul will instinctively know that it has found the truth. Truth stands on its own evidences; it does not require any other testimony to attest it; it is self-effulgent. It penetrates into the inmost recesses of our nature, and the whole universe stands up and says, "This is Truth." These are the very great teachers, but we can get help from the lesser ones also; and as we ourselves are not always sufficiently intuitive to be certain of our judgment of the man from whom we receive, there ought to be certain tests. There are certain conditions necessary in the taught, and also in the teacher.

The conditions necessary in the taught are purity, a real thirst after knowledge, and perseverance. No impure soul can be religious; that is the one great condition; purity in every way is absolutely necessary. The other condition is a real thirst after knowledge. Who wants? That is the question. We get whatever we want — that is an old, old law. He who wants, gets. To want religion is a very difficult thing, not so easy as we generally think. Then we always forget that religion does not consist in hearing talks, or in reading books, but it is a continuous struggle, a grappling with our own nature, a continuous fight till the victory is achieved. It is not a question of one or two days, of years, or of lives, but it may be hundreds of lifetimes, and we must be ready for that. It may come immediately, or it may not come in hundreds of lifetimes; and we must be ready for that. The student who sets out with such a spirit finds success.

In the teacher we must first see that he knows the secret of the scriptures. The whole world reads scriptures — Bibles, Vedas, Korans, and others; but they are only words, external arrangement, syntax, the etymology, the philology, the dry bones of religion. The teacher may be able to find what is the age of any book, but words are only the external forms in which things come. Those who deal too much in words and let the mind run always in the force of words lose the spirit. So the teacher must be able to know the spirit of the scriptures. The network of words is like a huge forest in which the human mind loses itself and finds no way out. The various methods of joining words, the various methods of speaking a beautiful language, the various methods of explaining the dicta of the scriptures, are only for the enjoyment of the learned. They do not attain perfection; they are simply desirous to show their learning, so that the world may praise them and see that they are learned men. You will find that no one of the great teachers of the world went into these various explanations of texts; on their part there is no attempt at "text-torturing", no saying, "This word means this, and this is the philological connection between this and that word." You study all the great teachers the world has produced, and you will see that no one of them goes that way. Yet they taught, while others, who have nothing to teach, will take up a word and write a three-volume book on its origin and use. As my Master used to say, what would you think of men who went into a mango orchard and busied themselves in counting the leaves and examining the colour of the leaves, the size of the twigs, the number of branches, and so forth, while only one of them had the sense to begin to eat the mangoes? So leave this counting of leaves and twigs and this note-taking to others. That work has its own value in its proper place, but not here in the spiritual realm. Men never become spiritual through such work; you have never once seen a strong spiritual man among these "leaf-counters". Religion is the highest aim of man, the highest glory, but it does not require "leaf-counting". If you want to be a Christian, it is not necessary to know whether Christ was born in Jerusalem or Bethlehem or just the exact date on which he pronounced the Sermon on the Mount; you only require to feel the Sermon on the Mount. It is not necessary to read two thousand words on when it was delivered. All that is for the enjoyment of the learned. Let them have it; say amen to that. Let us eat the mangoes.

The second condition necessary in the teacher is that he must be sinless. The question was once asked me in England by a friend, "Why should we look to the personality of a teacher? We have only to judge of what he says, and take that up." Not so. If a man wants to teach me something of dynamics or chemistry or any other physical science, he may be of any character; he can still teach dynamics or any other science. For the knowledge that the physical sciences require is simply intellectual and depends on intellectual strength; a man can have in such a case a gigantic intellectual power without the least development of his soul. But in the spiritual sciences it is impossible from first to last that there can be any spiritual light in that soul which is impure. What can such a soul teach? It knows nothing. Spiritual truth is purity. "Blessed are the pure in heart, for they shall see God". In that one sentence is the gist of all religions. If you have learnt that, all that has been said in the past and all that it is possible to say in the future, you have known; you need not look into anything else, for you have all that is necessary in that one sentence; it could save the world, were all the other scriptures lost. A vision of God, a glimpse of the beyond never comes until the soul is pure. Therefore in the teacher of spirituality, purity is the one thing indispensable; we must see first what he is, and then what he says. Not so with intellectual teachers; there we care more for what he says than what he is. With the teacher of religion we must first and foremost see what he is, and then alone comes the value of the words, because he is the transmitter. What will he transmit, if he has not flat spiritual power in him? To give a simile: If a heater is hot, it can convey heat vibrations, but if not, it is impossible to do so. Even so is the case with the mental vibrations of the religious teacher which he conveys to the mind of the taught. It is a question of transference, and not of stimulating only our intellectual faculties. Some power, real and tangible, goes out from the teacher and begins to grow in the mind of the taught. Therefore the necessary condition is that the teacher must be true.

The third condition is motive. We should see that he does not teach with any ulterior motive, for name, or fame, or anything else, but simply for love, pure love for you. When spiritual forces are transmitted from the teacher to the taught, they can only be conveyed through the medium of love; there is no other medium that can convey them. Any other motive, such as gain or name, would immediately destroy the conveying medium; therefore all must be done through love. One who has known God can alone be a teacher. When you see that in the teacher these conditions are fulfilled, you are safe; if they are not fulfilled, it is unwise to accept him. There is a great risk, if he cannot convey goodness, of his conveying wickedness sometimes. This must be guarded against; therefore it naturally follows that we cannot be taught by anybody and everybody.

The preaching of sermons by brooks and stones may be true as a poetical figure but no one can preach a single grain of truth until he has it in himself. To whom do the brooks preach sermons? To that human soul only whose lotus of life has already opened. When the heart has been opened, it can receive teaching from the brooks or the stones — it can get some religious teaching from all these; but the unopened heart will see nothing but brooks and rolling stones. A blind man may come to a museum, but he comes and goes only; if he is to see, his eyes must first be opened. This eye-opener of religion is the teacher. With the teacher, therefore, our relationship is that of ancestor and descendant; the teacher is the spiritual ancestor, and the disciple is the spiritual descendant. It is all very well to talk of liberty and independence, but without humility, submission, veneration, and faith, there will not be any religion. It is a significant fact that where this relation still exists between the teacher and the taught, there alone gigantic spiritual souls grow; but in those who have thrown it off religion is made into a diversion. In nations and churches where this relation between teacher and taught is not maintained spirituality is almost an unknown quantity. It never comes without that feeling; there is no one to transmit and no one to be transmitted to, because they are all independent. Of whom can they learn? And if they come to learn, they come to buy learning. Give me a dollar's worth of religion; cannot I pay a dollar for it? Religion cannot be got that way!

There is nothing higher and holier than the knowledge which comes to the soul transmitted by a spiritual teacher. If a man has become a perfect Yogi it comes by itself, but it cannot be got in books. You may go and knock your head against the four corners of the world, seek in the Himalayas, the Alps, the Caucasus, the Desert of Gobi or Sahara, or the bottom of the sea, but it will not come until you find a teacher. Find the teacher, serve him as a child, open your heart to his influence, see in him God manifested. Our attention should be fixed on the teacher as the highest manifestation of God; and as the power of attention concentrates there, the picture of the teacher as man will melt away; the frame will vanish, and the real God will be left there. Those that come to truth with such a spirit of veneration and love — for them the Lord of truth speaks the most wonderful words. "Take thy shoes from off thy feet, for the place whereon thou standest is holy ground". Wherever His name is spoken, that place is holy. How much more so is a man who speaks His name, and with what veneration ought we to approach a man out of whom come spiritual truths! This is the spirit in which we are to be taught. Such teachers are few in number, no doubt, in this world, but the world is never altogether without them. The moment it is absolutely bereft of these, it will cease to be, it will become a hideous hell and will just drop. These teachers are the fair flowers of human life and keep the world going; it is the strength that is manifested from these hearts of life that keeps the bounds of society intact.

Beyond these is another set of teachers, the Christs of the world. These Teachers of all teachers represent God Himself in the form of man. They are much higher; they can transmit spirituality with a touch, with a wish, which makes even the lowest and most degraded characters saints in one second. Do you not read of how they used to do these things? They are not the teachers about whom I was speaking; they are the Teachers of all teachers, the greatest manifestations of God to man; we cannot see God except through them. We cannot help worshipping them, and they are the only beings we are bound to worship.

No man hath "seen" God but as He is manifested in the Son. We cannot see God. If we try to see Him, we make a hideous caricature of God. There is an Indian story that an ignorant man was asked to make an image of the God Shiva, and after days of struggle he made an image of a monkey. So whenever we attempt to make an image of God, we make a caricature of Him, because we cannot understand Him as anything higher than man so long as we are men. The time will come when we transcend our human nature and know Him as He is; but so long as we are men we must worship Him in man. Talk as we may, try as we may, we cannot see God except as a man. We may deliver great intellectual speeches, become very great rationalists, and prove that these tales of God as all nonsense, but let us come to practical common sense. What is behind this remarkable intellect? Zero, nothing, simply so much froth. When next you hear a man delivering great intellectual lectures against this worship of God, get hold of him and ask him what is his idea of God, what he means by "omnipotence", and "omniscience", and "omnipresent love", and so forth, beyond the spelling of the words. He means nothing, he cannot formulate an idea, he is no better than the man in the street who has not read a single book. That man in the street, however, is quiet and does not disturb the world, while the other man's arguments cause disturbance. He has no actual perception, and both are on the same plane.

Religion is realisation, and you must make the sharpest distinction between talk and realisation. What you perceive in your soul is realisation. Man has no idea of the Spirit, he has to think of it with the forms he has before him. He has to think of the blue skies, or the expansive fields, or the sea, or something huge. How else can you think of God? So what are you doing in reality? You are talking of omnipresence, and thinking of the sea. Is God the sea? A little more common sense is required. Nothing is so uncommon as common sense, the world is too full of talk. A truce to all this frothy argument of the world. We are by our present constitution limited and bound to see God as man. If the buffaloes want to worship God, they will see Him as a huge buffalo. If a fish wants to worship God, it will have to think of Him as a big fish. You and I, the buffalo, the fish, each represents so many different vessels. All these go to the sea to be filled with water according to the shape of each vessel. In each of these vessels is nothing but water. So with God. When men see Him, they see Him as man, and the animals as animal — each according to his ideal. That is the only way you can see Him; you have to worship Him as man, because there is no other way out of it. Two classes of men do not worship God as man — the human brute who has no religion, and the Paramahamsa (highest Yogi) who has gone beyond humanity, who has thrown off his mind and body and gone beyond the limits of nature. All nature has become his Self. He has neither mind nor body, and can worship God as God, as can a Jesus or a Buddha. They did not worship God as man. The other extreme is the human brute. You know how two extremes look alike. Similar is the case with the extreme of ignorance and the other extreme of knowledge; neither of these worships anybody. The extremely ignorant do not worship God, not being developed enough to feel the need for so doing. Those that have attained the highest knowledge also do not worship God — having realised and become one with God. God never worships God. Between these two poles of existence, if anyone tells you he is not going to worship God as man, take care of him. He is an irresponsible talker, he is mistaken; his religion is for frothy thinkers, it is intellectual nonsense.

Therefore it is absolutely necessary to worship God as man, and blessed are those races which have such a "God-man" to worship. Christians have such a God-man in Christ; therefore cling close to Christ; never give up Christ. That is the natural way to see God; see God in man. All our ideas of God are concentrated there. The great limitation Christians have is that they do not heed other manifestations of God besides Christ. He was a manifestation of God; so was Buddha; so were some others, and there will be hundreds of others. Do not limit God anywhere. Pay all the reverence that you think is due to God, to Christ; that is the only worship we can have. God cannot be worshipped; He is the immanent Being of the universe. It is only to His manifestation as man that we can pray. It would be a very good plan, when Christians pray, to say, "in the name of Christ". It would be wise to stop praying to God, and only pray to Christ. God understands human failings and becomes a man to do good to humanity. "Whenever virtue subsides and immorality prevails, then I come to help mankind", says Krishna. He also says, "Fools, not knowing that I, the Omnipotent and Omnipresent God of the universe, have taken this human form, deride Me and think that cannot be." Their minds have been clouded with demoniacal ignorance, so they cannot see in Him the Lord of the universe. These great Incarnations of God are to be worshipped. Not only so, they alone can be worshipped; and on the days of their birth, and on the days when they went out of this world, we ought to pay more particular reverence to them. In worshipping Christ I would rather worship Him just as He desires; on the day of His birth I would rather worship Him by fasting than by feasting — by praying. When these are thought of, these great ones, they manifest themselves in our souls, and they make us like unto them. Our whole nature changes, and we become like them.

But you must not mix up Christ or Buddha with hobgoblins flying through the air and all that sort of nonsense. Sacrilege! Christ coming into a spiritualistic seance to dance! I have seen that presence in this country. It is not in that way that these manifestations of God come. The very touch of one of them will be manifest upon a man; when Christ touches, the whole soul of man will change, that man will be transfigured just as He was. His whole life will be spiritualised; from every pore of his body spiritual power will emanate. What were the great powers of Christ in miracles and healing, in one of his character? They were low, vulgar things that He could not help doing because He was among vulgar beings. Where was this miracle-making done? Among the Jews; and the Jews did not take Him. Where was it not done? In Europe. The miracle-making went to the Jews, who rejected Christ, and the Sermon on the Mount to Europe, which accepted Him. The human spirit took on what was true and rejected what was spurious. The great strength of Christ is not in His miracles or His healing. Any fool could do those things. Fools can heal others, devils can heal others. I have seen horrible demoniacal men do wonderful miracles. They seem to manufacture fruits out of the earth. I have known fools and diabolical men tell the past, present, and future. I have seen fools heal at a glance, by the will, the most horrible diseases. These are powers, truly, but often demoniacal powers. The other is the spiritual power of Christ which will live and always has lived - an almighty, gigantic love, and the words of truth which He preached. The action of healing men at a glance is forgotten, but His saying, "Blessed are the pure in heart", that lives today. These words are a gigantic magazine of power — inexhaustible. So long as the human mind lasts, so long as the name of God is not forgotten, these words will roll on and on and never cease to be. These are the powers Jesus taught, and the powers He had. The power of purity; it is a definite power. So in worshipping Christ, in praying to Him, we must always remember what we are seeking. Not those foolish things of miraculous display, but the wonderful powers of the Spirit, which make man free, give him control over the whole of nature, take from him the badge of slavery, and show God unto him.

THE NEED OF SYMBOLS

Bhakti is divided into two portions. One is called Vaidhi, formal or ceremonial; the other portion is called Mukhyâ, supreme. The word Bhakti covers all the ground between the lowest form of worship and the highest form of life. All the worship that you have seen in any country in the world, or in any religion, is regulated by love. There is a good deal that is simple ceremony; there is also a good deal which, though not ceremony, is still not love, but a lower state. Yet these ceremonies are necessary. The external part of Bhakti is absolutely necessary to help the soul onward. Man makes a great mistake when he thinks that he can at once jump to the highest state. If a baby thinks he is going to be an old man in a day, he is mistaken; and I hope you will always bear in mind this one ideal, that religion is neither in books, nor in intellectual consent, nor in reasoning. Reason, theories, documents, doctrines, books, religious ceremonies, are all helps to religion: religion itself consists in realisation. We all say, "There is a God." Have you seen God? That is the question. You hear a man say, "There is God in heaven." You ask him if he has seen Him, and if he says he has, you would laugh at him and say he is a maniac. With most people religion is a sort of intellectual assent and goes no further than a document. I would not call it religion. It is better to be an atheist than to have that sort of religion. Religion does not depend on our intellectual assent or dissent. You say there is a soul. Have you seen the soul? How is it we all have souls and do not see them? You have to answer the question and find out the way to see the soul. If not, it is useless to talk of religion. If any religion is true, it must be able to show us the soul and show us God and the truth in ourselves. If you and I fight for all eternity about one of these doctrines or documents, we shall never come to any conclusion. People have been fighting for ages, and what is the outcome? Intellect cannot reach there at all. We have to go beyond the intellect; the proof of religion is in direct perception. The proof of the existence of this wall is that we see it; if you sat down and argued about its existence or non-existence for ages, you could never come to any conclusion; but directly you see it, it is enough. If all the men in the world told you it did not exist, you would not believe them, because you know that the evidence of your own eyes is superior to that of all the doctrines and documents in the world.

To be religious, you have first to throw books overboard. The less you read of books, the better for you; do one thing at a time. It is a tendency in Western countries, in these modern times, to make a hotchpotch of the brain; all sorts of unassimilated ideas run riot in the brain and form a chaos without ever obtaining a chance to settle down and crystallise into a definite shape. In many cases it becomes a sort of disease, but this is not religion. Then some want a sensation. Tell them about ghosts and people coming from the North Pole or any other remote place, with wings or in any other form, and that they are invisibly present and watching over them, and make them feel uncanny, then they are satisfied and go home; but within twenty-four hours they are ready for a fresh sensation. This is what some call religion. This is the way to the lunatic asylum, and not to religion. The Lord is not to be reached by the weak, and all these weird things tend to weakness. Therefore go not near them; they only make people weak, bring disorder to the brain, weaken the mind, demoralise the soul, and a hopeless muddle is the result. You must bear in mind that religion does not consist in talk, or doctrines, or books, but in realisation; it is not learning, but 'being. Everybody knows, "Do not steal", but what of it? That man has really known who has not stolen. Everybody knows, "Do not injure others", but of what value is it? Those who have not done so have realised it, they know it and have built their character on it. Religion is realising; and I will call you a worshipper of God when you have become able to realise the Idea. Before that it is the spelling of the weird, and no more. It is this power of realisation that makes religion. No amount of doctrines or philosophies or ethical books, that you may have stuffed into your brain, will matter much, only what you are and what you have realised. So we have to realise religion, and this realisation of religion is a long process. When men hear of something very high and wonderful, they all think they will get that, and never stop for a moment to consider that they will have to work their way up to it; they all want to jump there. If it is the highest, we are for it. We never stop to consider whether we have the power, and the result is that we do not do anything. You cannot take a man with a pitchfork and push him up there; we all have to work up gradually. Therefore the first part of religion is Vaidhi Bhakti, the lower phase of worship.

What are these lower phases of worship? They are various. In order to attain to the state where we can realise, we must pass through the concrete — just as you see children learn through the concrete first — and gradually come to the abstract. If you tell a baby that five times two is ten, it will not understand; but if you bring ten things and show how five times two is ten, it will understand. Religion is a long, slow process. We are all of us babies here; we may be old, and have studied all the books in the universe, but we are all spiritual babies. We have learnt the doctrines and dogmas, but realised nothing in our lives. We shall have to begin now in the concrete, through forms and words, prayers and ceremonies; and of these concrete forms there will be thousands; one form need not be for everybody. Some may be helped by images, some may not. Some require an image outside, others one inside the brain. The man who puts it inside says, "I am a superior man. When it is inside it is all right; when it is outside, it is idolatry, I will fight it." When a man puts an image in the form of a church or a temple, he thinks it is holy; but when it is in a human form, he objects to it!

So there are various forms through which the mind will take this concrete exercise; and then, step by step, we shall come to the abstract understanding, abstract realisation. Again, the same form is not for everyone; there is one form that will suit you, and another will suit somebody else, and so on. All forms, though leading to the same goal, may not be for all of us. Here is another mistake we generally make. My ideal does not suit you; and why should I force it on you? My fashion of building churches or reading hymns does not suit you; why should I force it on you? Go into the world and every fool will tell you that his form is the only right one, that every other form is diabolical, and he is the only chosen man ever born in the universe. But in fact, all these forms are good and helpful. Just as there are certain varieties in human nature, so it is necessary that there should be an equal number of forms in religion; and the more there are, the better for the world. If there are twenty forms of religion in the world, it is very good; if there are four hundred, so much the better — there will be the more to choose from. So we should rather be glad when the number of religions and religious ideas increase and multiply, because they will then include every man and help mankind more. Would to God that religions multiplied until every man had his own religion, quite separate from that of any other! This is the idea of the Bhakti-Yogi.

The final idea is that my religion cannot be yours, or yours mine. Although the goal and the aim are the same, yet each one has to take a different road, according to the tendencies of his mind; and although these roads are various, they must all be true, because they lead to the same goal. It cannot be that one is true and the rest not. The choosing of one's own road is called in the language of Bhakti, Ishta, the chosen way.

Then there are words. All of you have heard of the power of words, how wonderful they are! Every book — the Bible, the Koran, and the Vedas — is full of the power of words. Certain words have wonderful power over mankind. Again, there are other forms, known as symbols. Symbols have great influence on the human mind. But great symbols in religion were not created indefinitely. We find that they are the natural expressions of thought. We think symbolically. All our words are but symbols of the thought behind, and different people have come to use different symbols without knowing the reason why. It was all behind, and these symbols are associated with the thoughts; and as the thought brings the symbol outside, so the symbol, on the contrary, can bring the thought inside. So one portion of Bhakti tells about these various subjects of symbols and words and prayers. Every religion has prayers, but one thing you must bear in mind — praying for health or wealth is not Bhakti, it is all Karma or meritorious action. Praying for any physical gain is simply Karma, such as a prayer for going to heaven and so forth. One that wants to love God, to be a Bhakta, must discard all such prayers. He who wants to enter the realms of light must first give up this buying and selling this "shopkeeping" religion, and then enter the gates. It is not that you do not get what you pray for; you get everything, but such praying is a beggar's religion. "Foolish indeed is he who, living on the banks of the Ganga, digs a little well for water. A fool indeed is the man who, coming to a mine of diamonds, seeks for glass beads." This body will die some time, so what is the use of praying for its health again and again? What is there in health and wealth? The wealthiest man can use and enjoy only a little portion of his wealth. We can never get all the things of this world; and if not, who cares? This body will go, who cares for these things? If good things come, welcome; if they go away, let them go. Blessed are they when they come, and blessed are they when they go. We are striving to come into the presence of the King of kings. We cannot get there in a beggar's dress. Even if we wanted to enter the presence of an emperor, should we be admitted? Certainly not. We should be driven out. This is the Emperor of emperors, and in these beggar's rags we cannot enter. Shopkeepers never have admission there; buying and selling have no place there. As you read in the Bible, Jesus drove the buyers and sellers out of the Temple. Do not pray for little things. If you seek only bodily comforts, where is the difference between men and animals? Think yourselves a little higher than that.

So it goes without saying that the first task in becoming a Bhakta is to give up all desires of heaven and other things. The question is how to get rid of these desires. What makes men miserable? Because they are slaves, bound by laws, puppets in the hand of nature, tumbled about like playthings. We are continually taking care of this body that anything can knock down; and so we are living in a constant state of fear. I have read that a deer has to run on the average sixty or seventy miles every day, because it is frightened. We ought to know that we are in a worse plight than the deer. The deer has some rest, but we have none. If the deer gets grass enough it is satisfied, but we are always multiplying our wants.

It is a morbid desire with us to multiply our wants. We have become so unhinged and unnatural that nothing natural will satisfy us. We are always grasping after morbid things, must have unnatural excitement — unnatural food, drink, surroundings, and life. As to fear, what are our lives but bundles of fear? The deer has only one class of fear, such as that from tigers, wolves, etc. Man has the whole universe to fear.

How are we to free ourselves from this is the question. Utilitarians say, "Don't talk of God and hereafter; we don't know anything of these things, let us live happily in this world." I would be the first to do so if we could, but the world will not allow us. As long as you are a slave of nature, how can you? The more you struggle, the more enveloped you become. You have been devising plans to make you happy, I do not know for how many years, but each year things seem to grow worse. Two hundred years ago in the old world people had few wants; but if their knowledge increased in arithmetical progression, their wants increased in geometrical progression. We think that in salvation at least our desires will be fulfilled, so we desire to go to heaven. This eternal, unquenchable thirst! Always wanting something! When a man is a beggar, he wants money. When he has money, he wants other things, society; and after that, something else. Never at rest. How are we to quench this? If we get to heaven, it will only increase desire. If a poor man gets rich, it does not quench his desires, it is only like throwing butter on the fire, increasing its bright flames. Going to heaven means becoming intensely richer, and then desire comes more and more. We read of many human things in heaven in the different Bibles of the world; they are not always very good there; and after all, this desire to go to heaven is a desire after enjoyment. This has to be given up. It is too little, too vulgar a thing for you to think of going to heaven. It is just the same as thinking, I will become a millionaire and lord it over people. There are many of these heavens, but through them you cannot gain the right to enter the gates of religion and love.

THE CHIEF SYMBOLS

There are two Sanskrit words, Pratika and Pratimâ. Pratika means coming towards, nearing. In all countries you find various grades of worship. In this country, for instance, there are people who worship images of saints, there are people who worship certain forms and symbols. Then there are people who worship different beings who are higher than men, and their number is increasing very rapidly — worshippers of departed spirits. I read that there are something like eight millions of them here. Then there are other people who worship certain beings of higher grade — the angels, the gods, and so forth. Bhakti-Yoga does not condemn any one of these various grades, but they are all classed under one name, Pratika. These people are not worshipping God, but Pratika, something which is near, a step towards God. This Pratika worship cannot lead us to salvation and freedom; it can only give us certain particular things for which we worship them. For instance, if a man worships his departed ancestors or departed friends, he may get certain powers or certain information from them. Any particular gift that is got from these objects of worship is called Vidyâ, particular knowledge; but freedom, the highest aim, comes only by worship of God Himself. Some Orientalists think, in expounding the Vedas, that even the Personal God Himself is a Pratika. The Personal God may be a Pratika, but the Pratikas are neither the Personal nor Impersonal God. They cannot be worshipped as God. So it would be a great mistake if people thought that by worshipping these different Pratikas, either as angels, or ancestors, or Mahâtmâs (holy men, saints), etc., or departed spirits, they could ever reach to freedom. At best they can only reach to certain powers, but God alone can make us free. But because of that they are not to be condemned, their worship produces some result. The man who does not understand anything higher may get some power, some enjoyment, by the worship of these Pratikas; and after a long course of experience, when he will be ready to come to freedom, he will of his own accord give up the Pratikas.

Of these various Pratikas the most prevalent form is the worship of departed friends. Human nature — personal love, love for our friends — is so strong in us that when they die, we wish to see them once more — clinging on to their forms. We forget that these forms while living were constantly changing, and when they die, we think they become constant, and that we shall see them so. Not only so, but if I have a friend or a son who has been a scoundrel, as soon as he dies, I begin to think he is the saintliest person in existence; he becomes a god. There are people in India who, if a baby dies, do not burn it, but bury it and build a temple over it; and that little baby becomes the god of that temple. This is a very prevalent form of religion in many countries, and there are not wanting philosophers who think this has been the origin of all religions. Of course they cannot prove it. We must remember, however, that this worship of Pratikas can never bring us to salvation or to freedom.

Secondly, it is very dangerous. The danger is that these Pratikas, "nearing-stages", so far as they lead us on to a further stage, are all right; but the chances are ninety-nine to one that we shall stick to the Pratikas all our lives. It is very good to be born in a church, but it is very bad to die there. To make it clearer, it is very good to be born in a certain sect and have its training — it brings out our higher qualities; but in the vast majority of cases we die in that little sect, we never come out or grow. That is the great danger of all these worships of Pratikas. One says that these are all stages which one has to pass, but one never gets out of them; and when one becomes old, one still sticks to them. If a young man does not go to church, he ought to be condemned. But if an old man goes to church, he also ought to be condemned; he has no business with this child's play any more; the church should have been merely a preparation for something higher. What business has he any more with forms and Pratikas and all these preliminaries?

Book worship is another strong form of this Pratika, the strongest form. You find in every country that the book becomes the God. There are sects in my country who believe that God incarnates and becomes man, but even God incarnate as man must conform to the Vedas, and if His teachings do not so conform, they will not take Him. Buddha is worshipped by the Hindus, but if you say to them, "If you worship Buddha, why don't you take His teachings?" they will say, because they, the Buddhists, deny the Vedas. Such is the meaning of book worship. Any number of lies in the name of a religious book are all right. In India if I want to teach anything new, and simply state it on my own authority, as what I think, nobody will come to listen to me; but if I take some passage from the Vedas, and juggle with it, and give it the most impossible meaning, murder everything that is reasonable in it, and bring out my own ideas as the ideas that were meant by the Vedas, all the fools will follow me in a crowd. Then there are men preaching a sort of Christianity that would frighten the ordinary Christian out of his wits; but they say, "This is what Jesus Christ meant", and many come round them. People do not want anything new, if it is not in the Vedas or the Bible It is a case of nerves: when you hear a new and striking thing, you are startled; or when you see a new thing, you are startled; it is constitutional. It is much more so with thoughts. The mind has been running in ruts, and to take up a new idea is too much of a strain; so the idea has to be put near the ruts, and then we slowly take it. It is a good policy, but bad morality. Think of the mass of incongruities that reformers, and what you call the liberal preachers, pour into society today. According to Christian Scientists, Jesus was a great healer; according to the Spiritualists, He was a great psychic; according to the Theosophists, He was a Mahâtmâ. All these have to be deduced from the same text. There is a text in the Vedas which says, "Existence (Sat) alone existed, O beloved, nothing else existed in the beginning". Many different meanings are given to the word Sat in this text. The Atomists say the word meant "atoms", and out of these atoms the world has been produced. The Naturalists say it meant "nature", and out of nature everything has come. The Shunyavâdins (maintainers of the Void) say it meant "nothing", "zero", and out of nothing everything has been produced. The Theists say it meant "God", and the Advaitists say it was "Absolute Existence", and all refer to the same text as their authority.

These are the defects of book worship. But there is, on the other hand, a great advantage in it: it gives strength. All religious sects have disappeared excepting those that have a book. Nothing seems to kill them. Some of you have heard of the Parsees. They were the ancient Persians, and at one time there were about a hundred millions of them. The majority of them were conquered by the Arabs, and converted to Mohammedanism. A handful fled from their persecutors with their book, which is still preserving them. A book is the most tangible form of God. Think of the Jews; if they had not had a book, they would have simply melted into the world. But that keeps them up; the Talmud keeps them together, in spite of the most horrible persecution. One of the great advantages of a book is that it crystallises everything in tangible and convenient form, and is the handiest of all idols. Just put a book on an altar and everyone sees it; a good book everyone reads. I am afraid I may be considered partial. But, in my opinion books have produced more evil than good. They are accountable for many mischievous doctrines. Creeds all come from books, and books are alone responsible for the persecution and fanaticism in the world. Books in modern times are making liars everywhere. I am astonished at the number of liars abroad in every country.

The next thing to be considered is the Pratima, or image, the use of images. All over the world you will find images in some form or other. With some, it is in the form of a man, which is the best form. If I wanted to worship an image I would rather have it in the form of a man than of an animal, or building, or any other form. One sect thinks a certain form is the right sort of image, and another thinks it is bad. The Christian thinks that when God came in the form of a dove it was all right, but if He comes in the form of a fish, as the Hindus say, it is very wrong and superstitious. The Jews think if an idol be made in the form of a chest with two angels sitting on it, and a book on it, it is all right, but if it is in the form of a man or a woman, it is awful. The Mohammedans think that when they pray, if they try to form a mental image of the temple with the Caaba, the black stone in it, and turn towards the west, it is all right, but if you form the image in the shape of a church it is idolatry. This is the defect of image-worship. Yet all these seem to be necessary stages.

In this matter it is of supreme importance to think what we ourselves believe. What we have realised, is the question. What Jesus, or Buddha, or Moses did is nothing to us, unless we too do it for ourselves. It would not satisfy our hunger to shut ourselves up in a room and think of what Moses ate, nor would what Moses thought save us. My ideas are very radical on these points. Sometimes I think that I am right when I agree with all the ancient teachers, at other times I think they are right when they agree with me. I believe in thinking independently. I believe in becoming entirely free from the holy teachers; pay all reverence to them, but look at religion as an independent research. I have to find my light, just as they found theirs. Their finding the light will not satisfy us at all. You have to become the Bible, and not to follow it, excepting as paying reverence to it as a light on the way, as a guide-post, a mark: that is all the value it has. But these images and other things are quite necessary. You may try to concentrate your mind, or even to project any thought. You will find that you naturally form images in your mind. You cannot help it. Two sorts of persons never require any image — the human animal who never thinks of any religion, and the perfected being who has passed through these stages. Between these two points all of us require some sort of ideal, outside and inside. It may be in the form of a departed human being, or of a living man or woman. This is clinging to personality and bodies, and is quite natural. We are prone to concretise. How could we be here if we did not concretise? We are concreted spirits, and so we find ourselves here on this earth. Concretisation has brought us here, and it will take us out. Going after things of the senses has made us human beings, and we are bound to worship personal beings, whatever we may say to the contrary. It is very easy to say "Don't be personal"; but the same man who says so is generally most personal. His attachment for particular men and women is very strong; it does not leave him when they die, he wants to follow them beyond death. That is idolatry; it is the seed, the very cause of idolatry; and the cause being there it will come out in some form. Is it not better to have a personal attachment to an image of Christ or Buddha than to an ordinary man or woman? In the West, people say that it is bad to kneel before images, but they can kneel before a woman and say, "You are my life, the light of my eyes, my soul." That is worse idolatry. What ifs this talk about my soul my life? It will soon go away. It is only sense-attachment. It is selfish love covered by a mass of flowers. Poets give it a good name and throw lavender-water and all sorts of attractive things over it. Is it not better to kneel before a statue of Buddha or the Jina conqueror and say, "Thou art my life"? I would rather do that.

There is another sort of Pratika which is not recognised in Western countries, bout is taught in our books. This teaches the worship of mind as God. Anything that is worshipped as God is a stage, a nearing, as it were. An example of this is the method of showing the fine star known as Arundhati, near the group Pleiades. One is shown a big star near to it, and when he has fixed his attention on this and has come to know it, he is shown a finer and still nearer star; and when he has fixed his attention on that, he is led up to Arundhati. So all these various Pratikas and Pratimas lead to God. The worship of Buddha and of Christ constitute a Pratika. A drawing near to the worship of God. But this worship of Buddha and of Christ will not save a man, he must go beyond them to Him who manifested Himself as Jesus Christ, for God alone can give us freedom. There are even some philosophers who say these should he regarded as God; they are not Pratikas, but God Himself. However, we can take all these different Pratikas, these different stages of approach, and not be hurt by them: but if we think while we are worshipping them that we are worshipping God, we are mistaken. If a man worships Jesus Christ, and thinks he will be saved by that, he is mistaken entirely. If a man thinks that by worshipping an idol or the ghosts or spirits of the departed he will be saved, he is entirely mistaken. We may worship anything by seeing God in it, if we can forget the idol and see God there. We must not project any image upon God. But we may fill any image with that Life which is God. Only forget the image, and you are right enough — for "Out of Him comes everything". He is everything. We may worship a picture as God, but not God as the picture. God in the picture is right, but the picture as God is wrong. God in the image is perfectly right. There is no danger there. This is the real worship of God. But the image-God is a mere Pratika.

The next great thing to consider in Bhakti is the "word", the Nâmashakti, the power of the name. The whole universe is composed of name and form. Whatever we see is either a compound of name and form, or simply name with form which is a mental image. So, after all, there is nothing that is not name and form. We all believe God to be without form or shape, but as soon as we begin to think of Him, He acquires both name and form The Chitta is like the calm lake, thoughts being like waves upon this Chitta — and name and form are the normal ways in which these waves arise; no wave can rise without name and form. The uniform cannot be thought of; it is beyond thought; as soon as it becomes thought and matter, it must have name and form. We cannot separate these. It is said in many books that God created the universe out of the Word. Shabdabrahman, in Sanskrit, is the Christian theory of the Word. An old Indian theory, it was taken to Alexandria by Indian preachers and was planted there. Thus the idea of the Word and the Incarnation became fixed there.

There is deep meaning in the thought that God created everything out of the Word. God Himself being formless, this is the best way to describe the projection of forms, or the creation. The Sanskrit word for creation is Srishti, projection. What is meant by "God created things out of nothing"? The universe is projected out of God. He becomes the universe, and it all returns to Him, and again it proceeds forth, and again returns. Through all eternity it will go on in that way. We have seen that the projection of anything in the mind cannot be without name and form. Suppose the mind to be perfectly calm, entirely without thought; nevertheless, as soon as thought begins to rise it will immediately take name and form. Every thought has a certain name and a certain form. In the same way the very fact of creation, the very fact of projection is eternally connected with name and form. Thus we find that every idea that man has, or can have, must be connected with a certain name or word as its counterpart. This being so, it is quite natural to suppose that this universe is the outcome of mind, just as your body is the outcome of your idea — your idea, as it were, made concrete and externalised. If it be true, moreover, that the whole universe is built on the same plan, then, if you know the manner in which one atom is built, you can understand how the whole universe is built. If it is true that in you, the body forms the gross part outside and the mind forms the fine part inside, and both are eternally inseparable, then, when you cease to have the body, you will cease to have the mind also. When a man's brain is disturbed, his ideas also get disturbed, because they are but one, the finer and the grosser parts. There are not two such things as matter and mind. As in a high column of air there are dense and rarefied strata of one and the same element air, so it is with the body; it is one thing throughout, layer on layer, from grosser to finer. Again, the body is like the finger nails. As these continue growing even when they are cut, so from our subtle ideas grows body after body. The finer a thing the more persistent it is; we find that always. The grosser it is the less persistent. Thus, form is the grosser and name the finer state of a single manifesting power called thought. But these three are one; it is the Unity and the Trinity, the three degrees of existence of the same thing. Finer, more condensed, and most condensed. Wherever the one is, the others are there also. Wherever name is, there is form and thought.

It naturally follows that if the universe is built upon the same plan as the body, the universe also must have the same divisions of form, name, and thought. The "thought" is the finest part of the universe, the real motive power. The thought behind our body is called soul, and the thought behind the universe is called God. Then after that is the name, and last of all is the form which we see and feel. For instance, you are a particular person, a little universe in this universe, a body with a particular form; then behind that a name, John or Jane, and behind that again a thought; similarly there is this whole universe, and behind that is the name, what is called the "Word" in all religions, and behind that is God. The universal thought is Mahat, as the Sânkhyas call it, universal consciousness. What is that name? There must be some name. The world is homogeneous, and modern science shows beyond doubt that each atom is composed of the same material as the whole universe. If you know one lump of clay you know the whole universe. Man is the most representative being in the universe, the microcosm, a small universe in himself. So in man we find there is the form, behind that the name, and behind that the thought, the thinking being. So this universe must be on exactly the same plan. The question is: What is that name? According to the Hindus that word is Om. The old Egyptians also believed that. The Katha Upanishad says, "That, seeking which a man practices Brahmacharya, I will tell you in short what that is, that is Om. ... This is Brahman, the Immutable One, and is the highest; knowing this Immutable One, whatever one desires one gets."

This Om stands for the name of the whole universe, or God. Standing midway between the external world and God, it represents both. But then we can take the universe piecemeal, according to the different senses, as touch, as colour, as taste, and in various other ways. In each case we can make of this universe millions of universes from different standpoints, each of which will be a complete universe by itself, and each one will have a name, and a form, and a thought behind. These thoughts behind are Pratikas. Each of them has a name. These names of sacred symbols are used in Bhakti-Yoga. They have almost infinite power. Simply by repetition of these words we can get anything we desire, we can come to perfection. But two things are necessary. "The teacher must be wonderful, so also must be the taught", says the Katha Upanishad. Such a name must come from a person to whom it has descended through right succession. From master to disciple, the spiritual current has been coming; from ancient times, bearing its power. The person from whom such a word comes is called a Guru, and the person to whom it goes is called Shishya, the disciple. When the word has been received in the regular way, and when it has been repeated, much advance has been made in Bhakti-Yoga. Simply by the repetition of that word will come even the highest state of Bhakti. "Thou hast so many names. Thou understandest what is meant by them all these names are Thine, and in each is Thine infinite power; there is neither time nor place for repeating these names, for all times and places are holy. Thou art so easy, Thou art so merciful, how unfortunate am I, that I have no love for Thee!"

THE ISHTA

The theory of Ishta, which I briefly referred to before, is a subject requiring careful attention because with a proper understanding of this, all the various religions of the world can be understood. The word Ishta is derived from the root Ish, to desire, choose. The ideal of all religions, all sects, is the same — the attaining of liberty and cessation of misery. Wherever you find religion, you find this ideal working in one form or other. Of course in lower stages of religion it is not so well expressed; but still, well or ill-expressed, it is the one goal to which every religion approaches. All of us want to get rid of misery; we are struggling to attain to liberty — physical, mental, spiritual. This is the whole idea upon which the world is working. Through the goal is one and the same, there may be many ways to reach it, and these ways are determined by the peculiarities of our nature. One man's nature is emotional, another's intellectual, another's active, and so forth. Again, in the same nature there may be many subdivisions. Take for instance love, with which we are specially concerned in this subject of Bhakti. One man's nature has a stronger love for children; another has it for wife, another for mother, another for father, another for friends. Another by nature has love for country, and a few love humanity in the broadest sense; they are of course very few, although everyone of us talks of it as if it were the guiding motive power of our lives. Some few sages have experienced it. A few great souls among mankind feel this universal love, and let us hope that this world will never be without such men.

We find that even in one subject there are so many different ways of attaining to its goal. All Christians believe in Christ; but think, how many different explanations they have of him. Each church sees him in a different light, from different standpoints. The Presbyterian's eyes are fixed upon that scene in Christ's life when he went to the money-changers; he looks on him as a fighter. If you ask a Quaker, perhaps he will say, "He forgave his enemies." The Quaker takes that view, and so on. If you ask a Roman Catholic, what point of Christ's life is the most pleasing to him, he, perhaps, will say, "When he gave the keys to Peter". Each sect is bound to see him in its own way.

It follows that there will be many divisions and subdivisions even of the same subject. Ignorant persons take one of these subdivisions and take their stand upon it, and they not only deny the right of every other man to interpret the universe according to his own light, but dare to say that others are entirely wrong, and they alone are right. If they are opposed, they begin to fight. They say that they will kill any man who does not believe as they believe, just as the Mohammedans do. These are people who think they are sincere, and who ignore all others. But what is the position we want to take in this Bhakti-Yoga? Not only that we would not tell others that they are wrong, but that we would tell them that they are right — all of these who follow their own ways. That way, which your nature makes it absolutely necessary for you to take, is the right way. Each one of us is born with a peculiarity of nature as the result of our past existence. Either we call it our own reincarnated past experience or a hereditary past; whatever way we may put it, we are the result of the past – that is absolutely certain, through whatever channels that past may have come. It naturally follows that each one of us is an effect, of which our past has been the cause; and as such, there is a peculiar movement, a peculiar train, in each one of us; and therefore each one will have to find way for himself.

This way, this method, to which each of us is naturally adapted, is called the "chosen way". This is the theory of Ishta, and that way which is ours we call our own Ishta. For instance, one man's idea of God is that He is the omnipotent Ruler of the universe. His nature is perhaps such. He is an overbearing man who wants to rule everyone; he naturally finds God an omnipotent Ruler. Another man, who was perhaps a schoolmaster, and severe, cannot see any but a just God, a God of punishment, and so on Each one sees God according to his own nature; and this vision, conditioned by our own nature, is our Ishta. We have brought ourselves to a position where we can see that vision of God, and that alone; we cannot see any other vision. You will perhaps sometimes think of the teaching of a man that it is the best and fits you exactly, and the next day you ask one of your friends to go and hear him; but he comes away with the idea that it was the worst teaching he had ever heard. He is not wrong, and it is useless to quarrel with him. The teaching was all right, but it was not fitted to that man. To extend it a little further, we must understand that truth seen from different standpoints can be truth, and yet not the same truth.

This would seem at first to be a contradiction in terms, but we must remember that an absolute truth is only one, while relative truths are necessarily various. Take your vision of this universe, for instance. This universe, as an absolute entity, is unchangeable, and unchanged, and the same throughout. But you and I and everybody else hear and see, each one his own universe. Take the sun. The sun is one; but when you and I and a hundred other people stand at different places and look at it, each one of us sees a different sun. We cannot help it. A very little change of place will change a man's whole vision of the sun. A slight change in the atmosphere will make again a different vision. So, in relative perception, truth always appears various. But the Absolute Truth is only one. Therefore we need not fight with others when we find they; are telling something about religion which is not exactly according to our view of it. We ought to remember that both of us may be true, though apparently contradictors. There may be millions of radii converging towards the same centre in the sun. The further they are from the centre, the greater is the distance between any two. But as they all meet at the centre, all difference vanishes. There is such a centre, which is the absolute goal of mankind. It is God. We are the radii. The distances between the radii are the constitutional limitations through which alone we can catch the vision of God. While standing on this plane, we are bound each one of us to have a different view of the Absolute Reality; and as such, all views are true, and no one of us need quarrel with another. The only solution lies in approaching the centre. If we try to settle our differences by argument or quarrelling, we shall find that we can go on for hundreds of years without coming to a conclusion. History proves that. The only solution is to march ahead and go towards the centre; and the sooner we do that the sooner our differences will vanish.

This theory of Ishta, therefore, means allowing a man to choose his own religion. One man should not force another to worship what he worships. All attempts to herd together human beings by means of armies, force, or arguments, to drive them pell-mell into the same enclosure and make them worship the same God have failed and will fail always, because it is constitutionally impossible to do so. Not only so, there is the danger of arresting their growth. You scarcely meet any man or woman who is not struggling for some sort of religion; and how many are satisfied, or rather how few are satisfied! How few find anything! And why? Simply because most of them go after impossible tasks. They are forced into these by the dictation of others. For instance, when I am a child, my father puts a book into my hand which says God is such and such. What business has he to put that into my mind? How does he know what way I would develop? And being ignorant of my constitutional development, he wants to force his ideas on my brain, with the result that my growth is stunted. You cannot make a plant grow in soil unsuited to it. A child teaches itself. But you can help it to go forward in its own way. What you can do is not of the positive nature, but of the negative. You can take away the obstacles, but knowledge comes out of its own nature. Loosen the soil a little, so that it may come out easily. Put a hedge round it; see that it is not killed by anything, and there your work stops. You cannot do anything else. The rest is a manifestation from within its own nature. So with the education of a child; a child educates itself. You come to hear me, and when you go home, compare what you have learnt, and you will find you have thought out the same thing; I have only given it expression. I can never teach you anything: you will have to teach yourself, but I can help you perhaps in giving expression to that thought.

So in religion — more so — I must teach myself religion. What right has my father to put all sorts of nonsense into my head? What right has my master or society to put things into my head? Perhaps they are good, but they may not be my way. Think of the appalling evil that is in the world today, of the millions and millions of innocent children perverted by wrong ways of teaching. How many beautiful things which would have become wonderful spiritual truths have been nipped in the bud by this horrible idea of a family religion, a social religion, a national religion, and so forth. Think of what a mass of superstition is in your head just now about your childhood's religion, or your country's religion, and what an amount of evil it does, or can do. Man does not know what a potent power lies behind each thought and action. The old saying is true that, "Fools rush in where angels fear to tread." This should be kept in view from the very first. How? By this belief in Ishta. There are so many ideals; I have no right to say what shall be your ideal, to force any ideal on you. My duty should be to lay before you all the ideals I know of and enable you to see by your own constitution what you like best, and which is most fitted to you. Take up that one which suits you best and persevere in it. This is your Ishta, your special ideal.

We see then that a congregational religion can never be. The real work of religion must be one's own concern. I have an idea of my own, I must keep it sacred and secret, because I know that it need not be your idea. Secondly, why should I create a disturbance by wanting to tell everyone what my idea is? Other people would come and fight me. They cannot do so if I do not tell them; but if I go about telling them what my ideas are, they will all oppose me. So what is the use of talking about them? This Ishta should be kept secret, it is between you and God. All theoretical portions of religion can be preached in public and made congregational, but higher religion cannot be made public. I cannot get ready my religious feelings at a moment's notice. What is the result of this mummery and mockery? It is making a joke of religion, the worst of blasphemy. The result is what you find in the churches of the present day. How can human beings stand this religious drilling? It is like soldiers in a barrack. Shoulder arms, kneel down, take a book, all regulated exactly. Five minutes of feeling, five minutes of reason, five minutes of prayer, all arranged beforehand. These mummeries have driven out religion. Let the churches preach doctrines, theories, philosophies to their hearts' content, but when it comes to worship, the real practical part of religion, it should be as Jesus says, "When thou prayest, enter into thy closet, and when thou hast shut thy door, pray to thy Father which is in secret"

This is the theory of Ishta. It is the only way to make religion meet practically the necessities of different constitutions, to avoid quarrelling with others, and to make real practical progress in spiritual life. But I must warn you that you do not misconstrue my words into the formation of secret societies. If there were a devil, I would look for him within a secret society — as the invention of secret societies. They are diabolical schemes. The Ishta is sacred, not secret. But in what sense? Why should I not speak of my Ishta to others? Because it is my own most holy thing. It may help others, but how do I know that it will not rather hurt them? There may be a man whose nature is such that he cannot worship a Personal God, but can only worship as an Impersonal God his own highest Self. Suppose I leave him among you, and he tells you that there is no Personal God, but only God as the Self in you or me. You will be shocked. His idea is sacred, but not secret. There never was a great religion or a great teacher that formed secret societies to preach God's truths. There are no such secret societies in India. Such things are purely Western in idea, and merely foisted upon India. We never knew anything about them. Why indeed should there be secret societies in India? In Europe, people were not allowed to talk a word about religion that did not agree with the views of the Church. So they were forced to go about amongst the mountains in hiding and form secret societies, that they might follow their own kind of worship. There was never a time in India when a man was persecuted for holding his own views on religion. There were never secret religious societies in India, so any idea of that sort you must give up at once. These secret societies always degenerate into the most horrible things. I have seen enough of this world to know what evil they cause, and how easily they slide into free love societies and ghost societies, how men play into the hands of other men or women, and how their future possibilities of growth in thought and act are destroyed, and so on. Some of you may be displeased with me for talking in this way, but I must tell you the truth. Perhaps only half a dozen men and women will follow me in all my life; but they will be real men and women, pure and sincere, and I do not want a crowd. What can crowds do? The history of the world was made by a few dozens, whom you can count on your fingers, and the rest were a rabble. All these secret societies and humbugs make men and women impure, weak and narrow; and the weak have no will, and can never work. Therefore have nothing to do with them. All this false love of mystery should be knocked on the head the first time it comes into your mind. No one who is the least impure will ever become religious. Do not try to cover festering sores with masses of roses. Do you think you can cheat God? None can. Give me a straightforward man or woman; but Lord save me from ghosts, flying angels, and devils. Be common, everyday, nice people.

There is such a thing as instinct in us, which we have in common with the animals, a reflex mechanical movement of the body. There is again a higher form of guidance, which we call reason, when the intellect obtains facts and then generalises them. There is a still higher form of knowledge which we call inspiration, which does not reason, but knows things by flashes. That is the highest form of knowledge. But how shall we know it from instinct? That is the great difficulty. Everyone comes to you, nowadays, and says he is inspired, and puts forth superhuman claims. How are we to distinguish between inspiration and deception? In the first place, inspiration must not contradict reason. The old man does not contradict the child, he is the development of the child. What we call inspiration is the development of reason. The way to intuition is through reason. Instinctive movements of your body do not oppose reason. As you cross a street, how instinctively you move your body to save yourself from the cars. Does your mind tell you it was foolish to save your body that way? It does not. Similarly, no genuine inspiration ever contradicts reason. Where it does it is no inspiration. Secondly, inspiration must be for the good of one and all, and not for name or fame, or personal gain. It should always be for the good of the world, and perfectly unselfish. When these tests are fulfilled, you are quite safe to take it as inspiration. You must remember that there is not one in a million that is inspired, in the present state of the world. I hope their number will increase. We are now only playing with religion. With inspiration we shall begin to have religion. Just as St. Paul says, "For now we see through a glass darkly, but then face to face." But in the present state of the world they are few and far between who attain to that state; yet perhaps at no other period were such false claims made to inspiration, as now. It is said that women have intuitive faculties, while men drag themselves slowly upward by reason. Do not believe it. There are just as many inspired men as women, though women have perhaps more claim to peculiar forms of hysteria and nervousness. You had better die as an unbeliever than be played upon by cheats and jugglers. The power of reasoning was given you for use. Show then that you have used it properly. Doing so, you will be able to take care of higher things.

We must always remember that God is Love. "A fool indeed is he who, living on the banks of the Ganga, seeks to dig a little well for water. A fool indeed is the man who, living near a mine of diamonds, spends his life in searching for beads of glass." God is that mine of diamonds. We are fools indeed to give up God for legends of ghosts or flying hobgoblins. It is a disease, a morbid desire. It degenerates the race, weakens the nerves and the brain, living in incessant morbid fear of hobgoblins, or stimulating the hunger for wonders; all these wild stories about them keep the nerves at an unnatural tension — a slow and sure degeneration of the race. It is degeneration to think of giving up God, purity, holiness, and spirituality, to go after all this nonsense! Reading other men's thoughts! If I must read everyone else's thoughts for five minutes at a time I shall go crazy. Be strong and stand up and seek the God of Love. This is the highest strength. What power is higher than the power of purity? Love and purity govern the world. This love of God cannot be reached by the weak; therefore, be not weak, either physically, mentally, morally or spiritually. The Lord alone is true. Everything else is untrue; everything else should be rejected for the salve of the Lord. Vanity of vanities, all is vanity. Serve the Lord and Him alone.

LECTURES AND DISCOURSES

THE RAMAYANA

*Delivered at the Shakespeare Club,
Pasadena, California, January 31, 1900*

There are two great epics in the Sanskrit language, which are very ancient. Of course, there are hundreds of other epic poems. The Sanskrit language and literature have been continued down to the present day, although, for more than two thousand years, it has ceased to be a spoken language. I am now going to speak to you of the two most ancient epics, called the Râmâyana and the Mahâbhârata. They embody the manners and customs, the state of society, civilisation, etc., of the ancient Indians. The oldest of these epics is called Ramayana, "The Life of Râma". There was some poetical literature before this — most of the Vedas, the sacred books of the Hindus, are written in a sort of metre — but this book is held by common consent in India as the very beginning of poetry.

The name of the poet or sage was Vâlmiki. Later on, a great many poetical stories were fastened upon that ancient poet; and subsequently, it became a very general practice to attribute to his authorship very many verses that were not his. Notwithstanding all these interpolations, it comes down to us as a very beautiful arrangement, without equal in the literatures of the world.

There was a young man that could not in any way support his family. He was strong and vigorous and, finally, became a highway robber; he attacked persons in the street and robbed them, and with that money he supported his father, mother, wife, and children. This went on continually, until one day a great saint called Nârada was passing by, and the robber attacked him. The sage asked the robber, "Why are you going to rob me? It is a great sin to rob human beings and kill them. What do you incur all this sin for?" The robber said, "Why, I want to support my family with this money." "Now", said the sage, "do you think that they take a share of your sin also?" "Certainly they do," replied the robber. "Very good," said the sage, "make me safe by tying me up here, while you go home and ask your people whether they will share your sin in the same way as they share the money you make." The man accordingly went to his father, and asked, "Father, do you know how I support you?" He answered, "No, I do not." "I am a robber, and I kill persons and rob them." "What! you do that, my son? Get away! You outcast! "He then went to his mother and asked her, "Mother, do you know how I support you?" "No," she replied. "Through robbery and murder." "How horrible it is!" cried the mother. "But, do you partake in my sin?" said the son. "Why should I? I never committed a robbery," answered the mother. Then, he went to his wife and questioned her, "Do you know how I maintain you all?" "No," she responded. "Why, I am a highwayman," he rejoined, "and for years have been robbing people; that is how I support and maintain you all. And what I now want to know is, whether you are ready to share in my sin." "By no means. You are my husband, and it is your duty to support me."

The eyes of the robber were opened. "That is the way of the world — even my nearest relatives, for whom I have been robbing, will not share in my destiny." He came back to the place where he had bound the sage, unfastened his bonds, fell at his feet, recounted everything and said, "Save me! What can I do?" The sage said, "Give up your present course of life. You see that none of your family really loves you, so give up all these delusions. They will share your prosperity; but the moment you have nothing, they will desert you. There is none who will share in your evil, but they will all share in your good. Therefore worship Him who alone stands by us whether we are doing good or evil. He never leaves us, for love never drags down, knows no barter, no selfishness."

Then the sage taught him how to worship. And this man left everything and went into a forest. There he went on praying and meditating until he forgot himself so entirely that the ants came and built ant-hills around him and he was quite unconscious of it. After many years had passed, a voice came saying, "Arise, O sage! " Thus aroused he exclaimed, "Sage? I am a robber!" "No more 'robber'," answered the voice, "a purified sage art thou. Thine old name is gone. But now, since thy meditation was so deep and great that thou didst not remark even the ant-hills which surrounded thee, henceforth, thy name shall be Valmiki — 'he that was born in the ant-hill'." So, he became a sage.

And this is how he became a poet. One day as this sage, Valmiki, was going to bathe in the holy river Ganga, he saw a pair of doves wheeling round and round, and kissing each other. The sage looked up and was pleased at the sight, but in a second an arrow whisked past him and killed the male dove. As the dove fell down on the ground, the female dove went on whirling round and round the dead body of its companion in grief. In a moment the poet became miserable, and looking round, he saw the hunter. "Thou art a wretch," he cried, "without the smallest mercy! Thy slaying hand would not even stop for love!" "What is this? What am I saying?" the poet thought to himself, "I have never spoken in this sort of way before." And then a voice came: "Be not afraid. This is poetry that is coming out of your mouth. Write the life of Rama in poetic language for the benefit of the world." And that is how the poem first began. The first verse sprang out of pits from the mouth of Valmiki, the first poet. And it was after that, that he wrote the beautiful Ramayana, "The Life of Rama".

There was an ancient Indian town called Ayodhyâ — and it exists even in modern times. The province in which it is still located is called Oudh, and most of you may have noticed it in the map of India. That was the ancient Ayodhya. There, in ancient times, reigned a king called Dasharatha. He had three queens, but the king had not any children by them. And like good Hindus, the king and the queens, all went on pilgrimages fasting and praying, that they might have children and, in good time, four sons were born. The eldest of them was Rama.

Now, as it should be, these four brothers were thoroughly educated in all branches of learning. To avoid future quarrels there was in ancient India a custom for the king in his own lifetime to nominate his eldest son as his successor, the Yuvarâja, young king, as he is called.

Now, there was another king, called Janaka, and this king had a beautiful daughter named Sitâ. Sita was found in a field; she was a daughter of the Earth, and was born without parents. The word "Sita" in ancient Sanskrit means the furrow made by a plough. In the ancient mythology of India you will find persons born of one parent only, or persons born without parents, born of sacrificial fire, born in the field, and so on — dropped from the clouds as it were. All those sorts of miraculous birth were common in the mythological lore of India.

Sita, being the daughter of the Earth, was pure and immaculate. She was brought up by King Janaka. When she was of a marriageable age, the king wanted to find a suitable husband for her.

There was an ancient Indian custom called Svayamvara, by which the princesses used to choose husbands. A number of princes from different parts of the country were invited, and the princess in splendid array, with a garland in her hand, and accompanied by a crier who enumerated the distinctive claims of each of the royal suitors, would pass in the midst of those assembled before her, and select the prince she liked for her husband by throwing the garland of flowers round his neck. They would then be married with much pomp and grandeur.

There were numbers of princes who aspired for the hand of Sita; the test demanded on this occasion was the breaking of a huge bow, called Haradhanu. All the princes put forth all their strength to accomplish this feat, but failed. Finally, Rama took the mighty bow in his hands and with easy grace broke it in twain. Thus Sita selected Rama, the son of King Dasharatha for her husband, and they were wedded with great rejoicings. Then, Rama took his bride to his home, and his old father thought that the time was now come for him to retire and appoint Rama as Yuvaraja. Everything was accordingly made ready for the ceremony, and the whole country was jubilant over the affair, when the younger queen Kaikeyi was reminded by one of her maidservants of two promises made to her by the king long ago. At one time she had pleased the king very much, and he offered to grant her two boons: "Ask any two things in my power and I will grant them to you," said he, but she made no request then. She had forgotten all about it; but the evil-minded maidservant in her employ began to work upon her jealousy with regard to Rama being installed on the throne, and insinuated to her how nice it would be for her if her own son had succeeded the king, until the queen was almost mad with jealousy. Then the servant suggested to her to ask from the king the two promised boons: one would be that her own son Bharata should be placed on the throne, and the other, that Rama should be sent to the forest and be exiled for fourteen years.

Now, Rama was the life and soul of the old king and when this wicked request was made to him, he as a king felt he could not go back on his word. So he did not know what to do. But Rama came to the rescue and willingly offered to give up the throne and go into exile, so that his father might not be guilty of falsehood. So Rama went into exile for fourteen years, accompanied by his loving wife Sita and his devoted brother Lakshmana, who would on no account be parted from him.

The Aryans did not know who were the inhabitants of these wild forests. In those days the forest tribes they called "monkeys", and some of the so-called "monkeys", if unusually strong and powerful, were called "demons".

So, into the forest, inhabited by demons and monkeys, Rama, Lakshmana, and Sita went. When Sita had offered to accompany Rama, he exclaimed, "How can you, a princess, face hardships and accompany me into a forest full of unknown dangers!" But Sita replied, "Wherever Rama goes, there goes Sita. How can you talk of 'princess' and 'royal birth' to me? I go before you!" So, Sita went. And the younger brother, he also went with them. They penetrated far into the forest, until they reached the river Godâvari. On the banks of the river they built little cottages, and Rama and Lakshmana used to hunt deer and collect fruits. After they had lived thus for some time, one day there came a demon giantess. She was the sister of the giant king of Lanka (Ceylon). Roaming through the forest at will, she came across Rama, and seeing that he was a very handsome man, she fell in love with him at once. But Rama was the purest of men, and also he was a married man; so of course he could not return her love. In revenge, she went to her brother, the giant king, and told him all about the beautiful Sita, the wife of Rama.

Rama was the most powerful of mortals; there were no giants or demons or anybody else strong enough to conquer him. So, the giant king had to resort to subterfuge. He got hold of another giant who was a magician and changed him into a beautiful golden deer; and the deer went prancing round about the place where Rama lived, until Sita was fascinated by its beauty and asked Rama to go and capture the deer for her. Rama went into the forest to catch the deer, leaving his brother in charge of Sita. Then Lakshmana laid a circle of fire round the cottage, and he said to Sita, "Today I see something may befall you; and, therefore, I tell you not to go outside of this magic circle. Some danger may befall you if you do." In the meanwhile, Rama had pierced the magic deer with his arrow, and immediately the deer, changed into the form of a man, died.

Immediately, at the cottage was heard the voice of Rama, crying, "Oh, Lakshmana, come to my help!" and Sita said, "Lakshmana, go at once into the forest to help Rama!" "That is not Rama's voice," protested Lakshmana. But at the entreaties of Sita, Lakshmana had to go in search of Rama. As soon as he went away, the giant king, who had taken the form of a mendicant monk, stood at the gate and asked for alms. "Wait awhile," said Sita, "until my husband comes back and I will give you plentiful alms." "I cannot wait, good lady," said he, "I am very hungry, give me anything you have." At this, Sita, who had a few fruits in the cottage, brought them out. But the mendicant monk after many persuasions prevailed upon her to bring the alms to him, assuring her that she need have no fear as he was a holy person. So Sita came out of the magic circle, and immediately the seeming monk assumed his giant body, and grasping Sita in his arms he called his magic chariot, and putting her therein, he fled with the weeping Sita. Poor Sita! She was utterly helpless, nobody, was there to come to her aid. As the giant was carrying her away, she took off a few of the ornaments from her arms and at intervals dropped them to the grounds

She was taken by Râvana to his kingdom, Lanka, the island of Ceylon. He made peals to her to become his queen, and tempted her in many ways to accede to his request. But Sita who was chastity itself, would not even speak to the giant; and he to punish her, made her live under a tree, day and night, until she should consent to be his wife.

When Rama and Lakshmana returned to the cottage and found that Sita was not there, their grief knew no bounds. They could not imagine what had become of her. The two brothers went on, seeking, seeking everywhere for Sita, but could find no trace of her. After long searching, they came across a group of "monkeys", and in the midst of them was Hanumân, the "divine monkey". Hanuman, the best of the monkeys, became the most faithful servant of Rama and helped him in rescuing Sita, as we shall see later on. His devotion to Rama was so great that he is still worshipped by the Hindus as the ideal of a true servant of the Lord. You see, by the "monkeys" and "demons" are meant the aborigines of South India.

So, Rama, at last, fell in with these monkeys. They told him that they had seen flying through the sky a chariot, in which was seated a demon who was carrying away a most beautiful lady, and that she was weeping bitterly, and as the chariot passed over their heads she dropped one of her ornaments to attract their attention. Then they showed Rama the ornament. Lakshmana took up the ornament, and said, "I do not know whose ornament this is." Rama took it from him and recognised it at once, saying, "Yes, it is Sita's." Lakshmana could not recognise the ornament, because in India the wife of the elder brother was held in so much reverence that he had never looked upon the arms and the neck of Sita. So you see, as it was a necklace, he did not know whose it was. There is in this episode a touch of the old Indian custom. Then, the monkeys told Rama who this demon king was and where he lived, and then they all went to seek for him.

Now, the monkey-king Vâli and his younger brother Sugriva were then fighting amongst themselves for the kingdom. The younger brother was helped by Rama, and he regained the kingdom from Vali, who had driven him away; and he, in return, promised to help Rama. They searched the country all round, but could not find Sita. At last Hanuman leaped by one bound from the coast of India to the island of Ceylon, and there went looking all over Lanka for Sita, but nowhere could he find her.

You see, this giant king had conquered the gods, the men, in fact the whole world; and he had collected all the beautiful women and made them his concubines. So, Hanuman thought to himself, "Sita cannot be with them in the palace. She would rather die than be in such a place." So Hanuman went to seek for her elsewhere. At last, he found Sita under a tree, pale and thin, like the new moon that lies low in the horizon. Now Hanuman took the form of a little monkey and settled on the tree, and there he witnessed how giantesses sent by Ravana came and tried to frighten Sita into submission, but she would not even listen to the name of the giant king.

Then, Hanuman came nearer to Sita and told her how he became the messenger of Rama, who had sent him to find out where Sita was; and Hanuman showed to Sita the signet ring which Rama had given as a token for establishing his identity. He also informed her that as soon as Rama would know her whereabouts, he would come with an army and conquer the giant and recover her. However, he suggested to Sita that if she wished it, he would take her on his shoulders and could with one leap clear the ocean and get back to Rama. But Sita could not bear the idea, as she was chastity itself, and could not touch the body of any man except her husband. So, Sita remained where she was. But she gave him a jewel from her hair to carry to Rama; and with that Hanuman returned.

Learning everything about Sita from Hanuman, Rama collected an army, and with it marched towards the southernmost point of India. There Rama's monkeys built a huge bridge, called Setu-Bandha, connecting India with Ceylon. In very low water even now it is possible to cross from India to Ceylon over the sand-banks there.

Now Rama was God incarnate, otherwise, how could he have done all these things? He was an Incarnation of God, according to the Hindus. They in India believe him to be the seventh Incarnation of God.

The monkeys removed whole hills, placed them in the sea and covered them with stones and trees, thus making a huge embankment. A little squirrel, so it is said, was there rolling himself in the sand and running backwards and forwards on to the bridge and shaking himself. Thus in his small way he was working for the bridge of Rama by putting in sand. The monkeys laughed, for they were bringing whole mountains, whole forests, huge loads of sand for the bridge — so they laughed at the little squirrel rolling in the sand and then shaking himself. But Rama saw it and remarked: "Blessed be the little squirrel; he is doing his work to the best of his ability, and he is therefore quite as great as the greatest of you." Then he gently stroked the squirrel on the back, and the marks of Rama's fingers, running lengthways, are seen on the squirrel's back to this day.

Now, when the bridge was finished, the whole army of monkeys, led by Rama and his brother entered Ceylon. For several months afterwards tremendous war and bloodshed followed. At last, this demon king, Ravana, was conquered and killed; and his capital, with all the palaces and everything, which were entirely of solid gold, was taken. In faraway villages in the interior of India, when I tell them that I have been in Ceylon, the simple folk say, "There, as our books tell, the houses are built of gold." So, all these golden cities fell into the hands of Rama, who gave them over to Vibhishana, the younger brother of Ravana, and seated him on the throne in the place of his brother, as a return for the valuable services rendered by him to Rama during the war.

Then Rama with Sita and his followers left Lanka. But there ran a murmur among the followers. "The test! The test!" they cried, "Sita has not given the test that she was perfectly pure in Ravana's household. "Pure! she is chastity itself" exclaimed Rama. "Never mind! We want the test," persisted the people. Subsequently, a huge sacrificial fire was made ready, into which Sita had to plunge herself. Rama was in agony, thinking that Sita was lost; but in a moment, the God of fire himself appeared with a throne upon his head, and upon the throne was Sita. Then, there was universal rejoicing, and everybody was satisfied.

Early during the period of exile, Bharata, the younger brother had come and informed Rama, of the death of the old king and vehemently insisted on his occupying the throne. During Rama's exile Bharata would on no account ascend the throne and out of respect placed a pair of Rama's wooden shoes on it as a substitute for his brother. Then Rama returned to his capital, and by the common consent of his people he became the king of Ayodhya.

After Rama regained his kingdom, he took the necessary vows which in olden times the king had to take for the benefit of his people. The king was the slave of his people, and had to bow to public opinion, as we shall see later on. Rama passed a few years in happiness with Sita, when the people again began to murmur that Sita had been stolen by a demon and carried across the ocean. They were not satisfied with the former test and clamoured for another test, otherwise she must be banished.

In order to satisfy the demands of the people, Sita was banished, and left to live in the forest, where was the hermitage of the sage and poet Valmiki. The sage found poor Sita weeping and forlorn, and hearing her sad story, sheltered her in his Âshrama. Sita was expecting soon to become a mother, and she gave birth to twin boys. The poet never told the children who they were. He brought them up together in the Brahmachârin life. He then composed the poem known as Ramayana, set it to music, and dramatised it.

The drama, in India, was a very holy thing. Drama and music are themselves held to be religion. Any song — whether it be a love-song or otherwise — if one's whole soul is in that song, one attains salvation, one has nothing else to do. They say it leads to the same goal as meditation.

So, Valmiki dramatised "The Life of Rama", and taught Rama's two children how to recite and sing it.

There came a time when Rama was going to perform a huge sacrifice, or Yajna, such as the old kings used to celebrate. But no ceremony in India can be performed by a married man without his wife: he must have the wife with him, the Sahadharmini, the "co-religionist" — that is the expression for a wife. The Hindu householder has to perform hundreds of ceremonies, but not one can be duly performed according to the Shâstras, if he has not a wife to complement it with her part in it.

Now Rama's wife was not with him then, as she had been banished. So, the people asked him to marry again. But at this request Rama for the first time in his life stood against the people. He said, "This cannot be. My life is Sita's." So, as a substitute, a golden statue of Sita was made, in order that the ceremony could be accomplished. They arranged even a dramatic entertainment, to enhance the religious feeling in this great festival. Valmiki, the great sage-poet, came with his pupils, Lava and Kusha, the unknown sons of Rama. A stage had been erected and everything was ready for the performance. Rama and his brothers attended with all his nobles and his people — a vast audience. Under the direction of Valmiki, the life of Rama was sung by Lava and Kusha, who fascinated the whole assembly by their charming voice and appearance. Poor Rama was nearly maddened, and when in the drama, the scene of Sita's exile came about, he did not know what to do. Then the sage said to him, "Do not be grieved, for I will show you Sita." Then Sita was brought upon the stage and Rama delighted to see his wife. All of a sudden, the old murmur arose: "The test! The test!" Poor Sita was so terribly overcome by the repeated cruel slight on her reputation that it was more than she could bear. She appealed to the gods to testify to her innocence, when the Earth opened and Sita exclaimed, "Here is the test", and vanished into the bosom of the Earth. The people were taken aback at this tragic end. And Rama was overwhelmed with grief.

A few days after Sita's disappearance, a messenger came to Rama from the gods, who intimated to him that his mission on earth was finished and he was to return to heaven. These tidings brought to him the recognition of his own real Self. He plunged into the waters of Sarayu, the mighty river that laved his capital, and joined Sita in the other world.

This is the great, ancient epic of India. Rama and Sita are the ideals of the Indian nation. All children, especially girls, worship Sita. The height of a woman's ambition is to be like Sita, the pure, the devoted, the all-suffering! When you study these characters, you can at once find out how different is the ideal in India from that of the West. For the race, Sita stands as the ideal of suffering. The West says, "Do! Show your power by doing." India says, "Show your power by suffering." The West has solved the problem of how much a man can have: India has solved the problem of how little a man can have. The two extremes, you see. Sita is typical of India — the idealised India. The question is not whether she ever lived, whether the story is history or not, we know that the ideal is there. There is no other Paurânika story that has so permeated the whole nation, so entered into its very life, and has so tingled in every drop of blood of the race, as this ideal of Sita. Sita is the name in India for everything that is good, pure and holy — everything that in woman we call womanly. If a priest has to bless a woman he says, "Be Sita!" If he blesses a child, he says "Be Sita!" They are all children of Sita, and are struggling to be Sita, the patient, the all-suffering, the ever-faithful, the ever-pure wife. Through all this suffering she experiences, there is not one harsh word against Rama. She takes it as her own duty, and performs her own part in it. Think of the terrible injustice of her being exiled to the forest! But Sita knows no bitterness. That is, again, the Indian ideal. Says the ancient Buddha, "When a man hurts you, and you turn back to hurt him, that would not cure the first injury; it would only create in the world one more wickedness." Sita was a true Indian by nature; she never returned injury.

Who knows which is the truer ideal? The apparent power and strength, as held in the West, or the fortitude in suffering, of the East?

The West says, "We minimise evil by conquering it." India says, "We destroy evil by suffering, until evil is nothing to us, it becomes positive enjoyment." Well, both are great ideals. Who knows which will survive in the long run? Who knows which attitude will really most benefit humanity? Who knows which will disarm and conquer animality? Will it be suffering, or doing?

In the meantime, let us not try to destroy each other's ideals. We are both intent upon the same work, which is the annihilation of evil. You take up your method; let us take up our method. Let us not destroy the ideal. I do not say to the West, "Take up our method." Certainly not. The goal is the same, but the methods can never be the same. And so, after hearing about the ideals of India, I hope that you will say in the same breath to India, "We know, the goal, the ideal, is all right for us both. You follow your own ideal. You follow your method in your own way, and Godspeed to you!" My message in life is to ask the East and West not to quarrel over different ideals, but to show them that the goal is the same in both cases, however opposite it may appear. As we wend our way through this mazy vale of life, let us bid each other Godspeed.

THE MAHABHARATA

Delivered at the Shakespeare Club, Pasadena, California, February 1, 1900

The other epic about which I am going to speak to you this evening, is called the Mahâbhârata. It contains the story of a race descended from King Bharata, who was the son of Dushyanta and Shakuntalâ. Mahâ means great, and Bhârata means the descendants of Bharata, from whom India has derived its name, Bhârata. Mahabharata means Great India, or the story of the great descendants of Bharata. The scene of this epic is the ancient kingdom of the Kurus, and the story is based on the great war which took place between the Kurus and the Panchâlas. So the region of the quarrel is not very big. This epic is the most popular one in India; and it exercises the same authority in India as Homer's poems did over the Greeks. As ages went on, more and more matter was added to it, until it has become a huge book of about a hundred thousand couplets. All sorts of tales, legends and myths, philosophical treatises, scraps of history, and various discussions have been added to it from time to time, until it is a vast, gigantic mass of literature; and through it all runs the old, original story. The central story of the Mahabharata is of a war between two families of cousins, one family, called the Kauravas, the other the Pândavas — for the empire of India.

The Aryans came into India in small companies. Gradually, these tribes began to extend, until, at last, they became the undisputed rulers of India and then arose this fight to gain the mastery, between two branches of the same family. Those of you who have studied the Gitâ know how the book opens with a description of the battlefield, with two armies arrayed one against the other. That is the war of the Mahabharata.

There were two brothers, sons of the emperor. The elder one was called Dhritarâshtra, and the other was called Pându. Dhritarashtra, the elder one, was born blind. According to Indian law, no blind, halt, maimed, consumptive, or any other constitutionally diseased person, can inherit. He can only get a maintenance. So, Dhritarashtra could not ascend the throne, though he was the elder son, and Pandu became the emperor.

Dhritarashtra had a hundred sons, and Pandu had only five. After the death of Pandu at an early age, Dhritarashtra became king of the Kurus and brought up the sons of Pandu along with his own children. When they grew up they were placed under the tutorship of the great priestwarrior, Drona, and were well trained in the various material arts and sciences befitting princes. The education of the princes being finished, Dhritarashtra put Yudhishthira, the eldest of the sons of Pandu, on the throne of his father. The sterling virtues of Yudhishthira and the valour and devotion of his other brothers aroused jealousies in the hearts of the sons of the blind king, and at the instigation of Duryodhana, the eldest of them, the five Pandava brothers were prevailed upon to visit Vâranâvata, on the plea of a religious festival that was being held there. There they were accommodated in a palace made under Duryodhana's instructions, of hemp, resin, and lac, and other inflammable materials, which were subsequently set fire to secretly. But the good Vidura, the step-brother of Dhritarashtra, having become cognisant of the evil intentions of Duryodhana and his party, had warned the Pandavas of the plot, and they managed to escape without anyone's knowledge. When the Kurus saw the house was reduced to ashes, they heaved a sigh of relief and thought all obstacles were now removed out of their path. Then the children of Dhritarashtra got hold of the kingdom. The five Pandava brothers had fled to the forest with their mother, Kunti. They lived there by begging, and went about in disguise giving themselves out as Brâhmana students. Many were the hardships and adventures they encountered in the wild forests, but their fortitude of mind, and strength, and valour made them conquer all dangers. So things went on until they came to hear of the approaching marriage of the princess of a neighbouring country.

I told you last night of the peculiar form of the ancient Indian marriage. It was called Svayamvara, that is, the choosing of the husband by the princess. A great gathering of princes and nobles assembled, amongst whom the princess would choose her husband. Preceded by her trumpeters and heralds she would approach, carrying a garland of flowers in her hand. At the throne of each candidate for her hand, the praises of that prince and all his great deeds in battle would be declared by the heralds. And when the princess decided which prince she desired to have for a husband, she would signify the fact by throwing the marriage-garland round his neck. Then the ceremony would turn into a wedding. King Drupada was a great king, king of the Panchalas, and his daughter, Draupadi, famed far and wide for her beauty and accomplishments, was going to choose a hero.

At a Svayamvara there was always a great feat of arms or something of the kind. On this occasion, a mark in the form of a fish was set up high in the sky; under that fish was a wheel with a hole in the centre, continually turning round, and beneath was a tub of water. A man looking at the reflection of the fish in the tub of water was asked to send an arrow and hit the eye of the fish through the Chakra or wheel, and he who succeeded would be married to the princess. Now, there came kings and princes from different parts of India, all anxious to win the hand of the princess, and one after another they tried their skill, and every one of them failed to hit the mark.

You know, there are four castes in India: the highest caste is that of the hereditary priest, the Brâhmana; next is the caste of the Kshatriya, composed of kings and fighters; next, the Vaishyas, the traders or businessmen, and then Shudras, the servants. Now, this princess was, of course, a Kshatriya, one of the second caste.

When all those princes failed in hitting the mark, then the son of King Drupada rose up in the midst of the court and said: "The Kshatriya, the king caste has failed; now the contest is open to the other castes. Let a Brahmana, even a Shudra, take part in it; whosoever hits the mark, marries Draupadi."

Among the Brahmanas were seated the five Pandava brothers. Arjuna, the third brother, was the hero of the bow. He arose and stepped forward. Now, Brahmanas as a caste are very quiet and rather timid people. According to the law, they must not touch a warlike weapon, they must not wield a sword, they must not go into any enterprise that is dangerous. Their life is one of contemplation, study, and control of the inner nature. Judge, therefore, how quiet and peaceable a people they are. When the Brahmanas saw this man get up, they thought this man was going to bring the wrath of the Kshatriyas upon them, and that they would all be killed. So they tried to dissuade him, but Arjuna did not listen to them, because he was a soldier. He lifted the bow in his hand, strung it without any effort, and drawing it, sent the arrow right through the wheel and hit the eye of the fish.

Then there was great jubilation. Draupadi, the princess, approached Arjuna and threw the beautiful garland of flowers over his head. But there arose a great cry among the princes, who could not bear the idea that this beautiful princess who was a Kshatriya should be won by a poor Brahmana, from among this huge assembly of kings and princes. So, they wanted to fight Arjuna and snatch her from him by force. The brothers had a tremendous fight with the warriors, but held their own, and carried off the bride in triumph.

The five brothers now returned home to Kunti with the princess. Brahmanas have to live by begging. So they, who lived as Brahmanas, used to go out, and what they got by begging they brought home and the mother divided it among them. Thus the five brothers, with the princess, came to the cottage where the mother lived. They shouted out to her jocosely, "Mother, we have brought home a most wonderful alms today." The mother replied, "Enjoy it in common, all of you, my children." Then the mother seeing the princess, exclaimed, "Oh! what have I said! It is a girl!" But what could be done! The mother's word was spoken once for all. It must not be disregarded. The mother's words must be fulfilled. She could not be made to utter an untruth, as she never had done so. So Draupadi became the common wife of all the five brothers.

Now, you know, in every society there are stages of development. Behind this epic there is a wonderful glimpse of the ancient historic times. The author of the poem mentions the fact of the five brothers marrying the same woman, but he tries to gloss it over, to find an excuse and a cause for such an act: it was the mother's command, the mother sanctioned this strange betrothal, and so on. You know, in every nation there has been a certain stage in society that allowed polyandry — all the brothers of a family would marry one wife in common. Now, this was evidently a glimpse of the past polyandrous stage.

In the meantime, the brother of the princess was perplexed in his mind and thought: "Who are these people? Who is this man whom my sister is going to marry? They have not any chariots, horses, or anything. Why, they go on foot!" So he had followed them at a distance, and at night overheard their conversation and became fully convinced that they were really Kshatriyas. Then King Drupada came to know who they were and was greatly delighted.

Though at first much objection was raised, it was declared by Vyâsa that such a marriage was allowable for these princes, and it was permitted. So the king Drupada had to yield to this polyandrous marriage, and the princess was married to the five sons of Pandu.

Then the Pandavas lived in peace and prosperity and became more powerful every day. Though Duryodhana and his party conceived of fresh plots to destroy them, King Dhritarashtra was prevailed upon by the wise counsels of the elders to make peace with the Pandavas; and so he invited them home amidst the rejoicings of the people and gave them half of the kingdom. Then, the five brothers built for themselves a beautiful city, called Indraprastha, and extended their dominions, laying all the people under tribute to them. Then the eldest, Yudhishthira, in order to declare himself emperor over all the kings of ancient India, decided to perform a Râjasuya Yajna or Imperial Sacrifice, in which the conquered kings would have to come with tribute and swear allegiance, and help the performance of the sacrifice by personal services. Shri Krishna, who had become their friend and a relative, came to them and approved of the idea. But there alas one obstacle to its performance. A king, Jarâsandha by name, who intended to offer a sacrifice of a hundred kings, had eighty-six of them kept as captives with him. Shri Krishna counselled an attack on Jarasandha. So he, Bhima, and Arjuna challenged the king, who accepted the challenge and was finally conquered by Bhima after fourteen days, continuous wrestling. The captive kings were then set free.

Then the four younger brothers went out with armies on a conquering expedition, each in a different direction, and brought all the kings under subjection to Yudhishthira. Returning, they laid all the vast wealth they secured at the feet of the eldest brother to meet the expenses of the great sacrifice.

So, to this Rajasuya sacrifice all the liberated kings came, along with those conquered by the brothers, and rendered homage to Yudhishthira. King Dhritarashtra and his sons were also invited to come and take a share in the performance of the sacrifice. At the conclusion of the sacrifice, Yudhishthira was crowned emperor, and declared as lord paramount. This was the sowing of the future feud. Duryodhana came back from the sacrifice filled with jealousy against Yudhishthira, as their sovereignty and vast splendour and wealth were more than he could bear; and so he devised plans to effect their fall by guile, as he knew that to overcome them by force was beyond his power. This king, Yudhishthira, had the love of gambling, and he was challenged at an evil hour to play dice with Shakuni, the crafty gambler and the evil genius of Duryodhana. In ancient India, if a man of the military caste was challenged to fight, he must at any price accept the challenge to uphold his honour. And if he was challenged to play dice, it was a point of honour to play, and dishonourable to decline the challenge. King Yudhishthira, says the Epic, was the incarnation of all virtues. Even he, the great sage-king, had to accept the challenge. Shakuni and his party had made false dice. So Yudhishthira lost game after game, and stung with his losses, he went on with the fatal game, staking everything he had, and losing all, until all his possessions, his kingdom and everything, were lost. The last stage came when, under further challenge, he had no other resources left but to stake his brothers, and then himself, and last of all, the fair Draupadi, and lost all. Now they were completely at the mercy of the Kauravas, who cast all sorts of insults upon them, and subjected Draupadi to most inhuman treatment. At last through the intervention of the blind king, they got their liberty, and were asked to return home and rule their kingdom. But Duryodhana saw the danger and forced his father to allow one more throw of the dice in which the party which would lose, should retire to the forests for twelve years, and then live unrecognised in a city for one year; but if they were found out, the same term of exile should have to be undergone once again and then only the kingdom was to be restored to the exiled. This last game also Yudhishthira lost, and the five Pandava brothers retired to the forests with Draupadi, as homeless exiles. They lived in the forests and mountains for twelve years. There they performed many deeds of virtue and valour, and would go out now and then on a long round of pilgrimages, visiting many holy places. That part of the poem is very interesting and instructive, and various are the incidents, tales, and legends with which this part of the book is replete. There are in it beautiful and sublime stories of ancient India, religious and philosophical. Great sages came to see the brothers in their exile and narrated to them many telling stories of ancient India, so as to make them bear lightly the burden of their exile. One only I will relate to you here.

There was a king called Ashvapati. The king had a daughter, who was so good and beautiful that she was called Sâvitri, which is the name of a sacred prayer of the Hindus. When Savitri grew old enough, her father asked her to choose a husband for herself. These ancient Indian princesses were very independent, you see, and chose their own princely suitors.

Savitri consented and travelled in distant regions, mounted in a golden chariot, with her guards and aged courtiers to whom her father entrusted her, stopping at different courts, and seeing different princes, but not one of them could win the heart of Savitri. They came at last to a holy hermitage in one of those forests that in ancient India were reserved for animals, and where no animals were allowed to be killed. The animals lost the fear of man — even the fish in the lakes came and took food out of the hand. For thousands of years no one had killed anything therein. The sages and the aged went there to live among the deer and the birds. Even criminals were safe there. When a man got tired of life, he would go to the forest; and in the company of sages, talking of religion and meditating thereon, he passed the remainder of his life.

Now it happened that there was a king, Dyumatsena, who was defeated by his enemies and was deprived of his kingdom when he was struck with age and had lost his sight. This poor, old, blind king, with his queen and his son, took refuge in the forest and passed his life in rigid penance. His boy's name was Satyavân.

It came to pass that after having visited all the different royal courts, Savitri at last came to this hermitage, or holy place. Not even the greatest king could pass by the hermitages, or Âshramas as they were called, without going to pay homage to the sages, for such honour and respect was felt for these holy men. The greatest emperor of India would be only too glad to trace his descent to some sage who lived in a forest, subsisting on roots and fruits, and clad in rags. We are all children of sages. That is the respect that is paid to religion. So, even kings, when they pass by the hermitages, feel honoured to go in and pay their respects to the sages. If they approach on horseback, they descend and walk as they advance towards them. If they arrive in a chariot, chariot and armour must be left outside when they enter. No fighting man can enter unless he comes in the manner of a religious man, quiet and gentle.

So Savitri came to this hermitage and saw there Satyavan, the hermit's son, and her heart was conquered. She had escaped all the princes of the palaces and the courts, but here in the forest-refuge of King Dyumatsena, his son, Satyavan, stole her heart.

When Savitri returned to her father's house, he asked her, "Savitri, dear daughter, speak. Did you see anybody whom you would like to marry " Then softly with blushes, said Savitri, "Yes, father." "What is the name of the prince?" "He is no prince, but the son of King Dyumatsena who has lost his kingdom — a prince without a patrimony, who lives a monastic life, the life of a Sannyasin in a forest, collecting roots and herbs, helping and feeding his old father and mother, who live in a cottage."

On hearing this the father consulted the Sage Nârada, who happened to be then present there, and he declared it was the most ill-omened choice that was ever made. The king then asked him to explain why it was so. And Narada said, "Within twelve months from this time the young man will die." Then the king started with terror, and spoke, "Savitri, this young man is going to die in twelve months, and you will become a widow: think of that! Desist from your choice, my child, you shall never be married to a short-lived and fated bridegroom." "Never mind, father; do not ask me to marry another person and sacrifice the chastity of mind, for I love and have accepted in my mind that good and brave Satyavan only as my husband. A maiden chooses only once, and she never departs from her troth." When the king found that Savitri was resolute in mind and heart, he complied. Then Savitri married prince Satyavan, and she quietly went from the palace of her father into the forest, to live with her chosen husband and help her husband's parents. Now, though Savitri knew the exact date when Satyavan was to die, she kept it hidden from him. Daily he went into the depths of the forest, collected fruits and flowers, gathered faggots, and then came back to the cottage, and she cooked the meals and helped the old people. Thus their lives went on until the fatal day came near, and three short days remained only. She took a severe vow of three nights' penance and holy fasts, and kept her hard vigils. Savitri spent sorrowful and sleepless nights with fervent prayers and unseen tears, till the dreaded morning dawned. That day Savitri could not bear him out of her sight, even for a moment. She begged permission from his parents to accompany her husband, when he went to gather the usual herbs and fuel, and gaining their consent she went. Suddenly, in faltering accents, he complained to his wife of feeling faint, "My head is dizzy, and my senses reel, dear Savitri, I feel sleep stealing over me; let me rest beside thee for a while." In fear and trembling she replied, "Come, lay your head upon my lap, my dearest lord." And he laid his burning head in the lap of his wife, and ere long sighed and expired. Clasping him to her, her eyes flowing with tears, there she sat in the lonesome forest, until the emissaries of Death approached to take away the soul of Satyavan. But they could not come near to the place where Savitri sat with the dead body of her husband, his head resting in her lap. There was a zone of fire surrounding her, and not one of the emissaries of Death could come within it. They all fled back from it, returned to King Yama, the God of Death, and told him why they could not obtain the soul of this man.

Then came Yama, the God of Death, the Judge of the dead. He was the first man that died — the first man that died on earth — and he had become the presiding deity over all those that die. He judges whether, after a man has died, he is to be punished or rewarded. So he came himself. Of course, he could go inside that charmed circle as he was a god. When he came to Savitri, he said, "Daughter, give up this dead body, for know, death is the fate of mortals, and I am the first of mortals who died. Since then, everyone has had to die. Death is the fate of man." Thus told, Savitri walked off, and Yama drew the soul out. Yama having possessed himself of the soul of the young man proceeded on his way. Before he had gone far, he heard footfalls upon the dry leaves. He turned back. "Savitri, daughter, why are you following me? This is the fate of all mortals." "I am not following thee, Father," replied Savitri, "but this is, also, the fate of woman, she follows where her love takes her, and the Eternal Law separates not loving man and faithful wife." Then said the God of Death, "Ask for any boon, except the life of your husband." "If thou art pleased to grant a boon, O Lord of Death, I ask that my father-in-law may be cured of his blindness and made happy." "Let thy pious wish be granted, duteous daughter." And then the King of Death travelled on with the soul of Satyavan. Again the same footfall was heard from behind. He looked round. "Savitri, my daughter, you are still following me?" "Yes my Father; I cannot help doing so; I am trying all the time to go back, but the mind goes after my husband and the body follows. The soul has already gone, for in that soul is also mine; and when you take the soul, the body follows, does it not?" "Pleased am I with your words, fair Savitri. Ask yet another boon of me, but it must not be the life of your husband." "Let my father-in-law regain his lost wealth and kingdom, Father, if thou art pleased to grant another supplication." "Loving daughter," Yama answered, "this boon I now bestow; but return home, for living mortal cannot go with King Yama." And then Yama pursued his way. But Savitri, meek and faithful still followed her departed husband. Yama again turned back. "Noble Savitri, follow not in hopeless woe." "I cannot choose but follow where thou takest my beloved one." "Then suppose, Savitri, that your husband was a sinner and has to go to hell. In that case goes Savitri with the one she loves?" "Glad am I to follow where he goes be it life or death, heaven or hell," said the loving wife. "Blessed are your words, my child, pleased am I with you, ask yet another boon, but the dead come not to life again." "Since you so permit me, then, let the imperial line of my father-in-law be not destroyed; let his kingdom descend to Satyavan's sons." And then the God of Death smiled. "My daughter, thou shalt have thy desire now: here is the soul of thy husband, he shall live again. He shall live to be a father and thy children also shall reign in due course. Return home. Love has conquered Death! Woman never loved like thee, and thou art the proof that even I, the God of Death, am powerless against the power of the true love that abideth!"

This is the story of Savitri, and every girl in India must aspire to be like Savitri, whose love could not be conquered by death, and who through this tremendous love snatched back from even Yama, the soul of her husband.

The book is full of hundreds of beautiful episodes like this. I began by telling you that the Mahabharata is one of the greatest books in the world and consists of about a hundred thousand verses in eighteen Parvans, or volumes.

To return to our main story. We left the Pandava brothers in exile. Even there they were not allowed to remain unmolested from the evil plots of Duryodhana; but all of them were futile.

A story of their forest life, I shall tell you here. One day the brothers became thirsty in the forest. Yudhishthira bade his brother, Nakula, go and fetch water. He quickly proceeded towards the place where there was water and soon came to a crystal lake, and was about to drink of it, when he heard a voice utter these words: "Stop, O child. First answer my questions and then drink of this water." But Nakula, who was exceedingly thirsty, disregarded these words, drank of the water, and having drunk of it, dropped down dead. As Nakula did not return, King Yudhishthira told Sahadeva to seek his brother and bring back water with him. So Sahadeva proceeded to the lake and beheld his brother lying dead. Afflicted at the death of his brother and suffering severely from thirst, he went towards the water, when the same words were heard by him: "O child, first answer my questions and then drink of the water." He also disregarded these words, and having satisfied his thirst, dropped down dead. Subsequently, Arjuna and Bhima were sent, one after the other, on a similar quest; but neither returned, having drunk of the lake and dropped down dead. Then Yudhishthira rose up to go in search of his brothers. At length, he came to the beautiful lake and saw his brothers lying dead. His heart was full of grief at the sight, and he began to lament. Suddenly he heard the same voice saying, "Do not, O child, act rashly. I am a Yaksha living as a crane on tiny fish. It is by me that thy younger brothers have been brought under the sway of the Lord of departed spirits. If thou, O Prince, answer not the questions put by me even thou shalt number the fifth corpse. Having answered my questions first, do thou, O Kunti's son, drink and carry away as much as thou requires"." Yudhishthira replied, "I shall answer thy questions according to my intelligence. Do thou ask met" The Yaksha then asked him several questions, all of which Yudhishthira answered satisfactorily. One of the questions asked was: "What is the most wonderful fact in this world?" "We see our fellow-beings every moment falling off around us; but those that are left behind think that they will never die. This is the most curious fact: in face of death, none believes that he will die! " Another question asked was: "What is the path of knowing the secret of religion?" And Yudhishthira answered, "By argument nothing can be settled; doctrines there are many; various are the scriptures, one part contradicting the other. There are not two sages who do not differ in their opinions. The secret of religion is buried deep, as it were, in dark caves. So the path to be followed is that which the great ones have trodden." Then the Yaksha said, "I am pleased. I am Dharma, the God of Justice in the form of the crane. I came to test you. Now, your brothers, see, not one of them is dead. It is all my magic. Since abstention from injury is regarded by thee as higher than both profit and pleasure, therefore, let all thy brothers live, O Bull of the Bharata race." And at these words of the Yaksha, the Pandavas rose up.

Here is a glimpse of the nature of King Yudhishthira. We find by his answers that he was more of a philosopher, more of a Yogi, than a king.

Now, as the thirteenth year of the exile was drawing nigh, the Yaksha bade them go to Virâta's kingdom and live there in such disguises as they would think best.

So, after the term of the twelve years' exile had expired, they went to the kingdom of Virata in different disguises to spend the remaining one year in concealment, and entered into menial service in the king's household. Thus Yudhishthira became a Brâhmana courtier of the king, as one skilled in dice; Bhima was appointed a cook; Arjuna, dressed as a eunuch, was made a teacher of dancing and music to Uttarâ, the princess, and remained in the inner apartments of the king; Nakula became the keeper of the king's horses; and Sahadeva got the charge of the cows; and Draupadi, disguised as a waiting-woman, was also admitted into the queen's household. Thus concealing their identity the Pandava brothers safely spent a year, and the search of Duryodhana to find them out was of no avail. They were only discovered just when the year was out.

Then Yudhishthira sent an ambassador to Dhritarashtra and demanded that half of the kingdom should, as their share, be restored to them. But Duryodhana hated his cousins and would not consent to their legitimate demands. They were even willing to accept a single province, nay, even five villages. But the headstrong Duryodhana declared that he would not yield without fight even as much land as a needle's point would hold. Dhritarashtra pleaded again and again for peace, but all in vain. Krishna also went and tried to avert the impending war and death of kinsmen, so did the wise elders of the royal court; but all negotiations for a peaceful partition of the kingdom were futile. So, at last, preparations were made on both sides for war, and all the warlike nations took part in it.

The old Indian customs of the Kshatriyas were

observed in it. Duryodhana took one side, Yudhishthira the other. From Yudhishthira messengers were at once sent to all the surrounding kings, entreating their alliance, since honourable men would grant the request that first reached them. So, warriors from all parts assembled to espouse the cause of either the Pandavas or the Kurus according to the precedence of their requests; and thus one brother joined this side, and the other that side, the father on one side, and the son on the other. The most curious thing was the code of war of those days; as soon as the battle for the day ceased and evening came, the opposing parties were good friends, even going to each other's tents; however, when the morning came, again they proceeded to fight each other. That was the strange trait that the Hindus carried down to the time of the Mohammedan invasion. Then again, a man on horseback must not strike one on foot; must not poison the weapon; must not vanquish the enemy in any unequal fight, or by dishonesty; and must never take undue advantage of another, and so on. If any deviated from these rules he would be covered with dishonour and shunned. The Kshatriyas were trained in that way. And when the foreign invasion came from Central Asia, the Hindus treated the invaders in the self-same way. They defeated them several times, and on as many occasions sent them back to their homes with presents etc. The code laid down was that they must not usurp anybody's country; and when a man was beaten, he must be sent back to his country with due regard to his position. The Mohammedan conquerors treated the Hindu kings differently, and when they got them once, they destroyed them without remorse.

Mind you, in those days — in the times of our story, the poem says — the science of arms was not the mere use of bows and arrows at all; it was magic archery in which the use of Mantras, concentration, etc., played a prominent part. One man could fight millions of men and burn them at will. He could send one arrow, and it would rain thousands of arrows and thunder; he could make anything burn, and so on — it was all divine magic. One fact is most curious in both these poems — the Ramayana and the Mahabharata — along with these magic arrows and all these things going on, you see the cannon already in use. The cannon is an old, old thing, used by the Chinese and the Hindus. Upon the walls of the cities were hundreds of curious weapons made of hollow iron tubes, which filled with powder and ball would kill hundreds of men. The people believed that the Chinese, by magic, put the devil inside a hollow iron tube, and when they applied a little fire to a hole, the devil came out with a terrific noise and killed many people.

So in those old days, they used to fight with magic arrows. One man would be able to fight millions of others. They had their military arrangements and tactics: there were the foot soldiers, termed the Pâda; then the cavalry, Turaga; and two other divisions which the moderns have lost and given up — there was the elephant corps — hundreds and hundreds of elephants, with men on their backs, formed into regiments and protected with huge sheets of iron mail; and these elephants would bear down upon a mass of the enemy — then, there were the chariots, of course (you have all seen pictures of those old chariots, they were used in every country). These were the four divisions of the army in those old days.

Now, both parties alike wished to secure the alliance of Krishna. But he declined to take an active part and fight in this war, but offered himself as charioteer to Arjuna, and as the friend and counsellor of the Pandavas while to Duryodhana he gave his army of mighty soldiers.

Then was fought on the vast plain of Kurukshetra the great battle in which Bhisma, Drona, Karna, and the brothers of Duryodhana with the kinsmen on both sides and thousands of other heroes fell. The war lasted eighteen days. Indeed, out of the eighteen Akshauhinis of soldiers very few men were left. The death of Duryodhana ended the war in favour of the Pandavas. It was followed by the lament of Gândhâri, the queen and the widowed women, and the funerals of the deceased warriors.

The greatest incident of the war was the marvellous and immortal poem of the Gitâ, the Song Celestial. It is the popular scripture of India and the loftiest of all teachings. It consists of a dialogue held by Arjuna with Krishna, just before the commencement of the fight on the battle-field of Kurukshetra. I would advise those of you who have not read that book to read it. If you only knew how much it has influenced your own country even! If you want to know the source of Emerson's inspiration, it is this book, the Gita. He went to see Carlyle, and Carlyle made him a present of the Gita; and that little book is responsible for the Concord Movement. All the broad movements in America, in one way or other, are indebted to the Concord party.

The central figure of the Gita is Krishna. As you worship Jesus of Nazareth as God come down as man so the Hindus worship many Incarnations of God. They believe in not one or two only, but in many, who have come down from time to time, according to the needs of the world, for the preservation of Dharma and destruction of wickedness. Each sect has one, and Krishna is one of them. Krishna, perhaps, has a larger number of followers in India than any other Incarnation of God. His followers hold that he was the most perfect of those Incarnations. Why? "Because," they say, "look at Buddha and other Incarnations: they were only monks, and they had no sympathy for married people. How could they have? But look at Krishna: he was great as a son, as a king, as a father, and all through his life he practiced the marvellous teachings which he preached." "He who in the midst of the greatest activity finds the sweetest peace, and in the midst of the greatest calmness is most active, he has known the secret of life." Krishna shows the way how to do this — by being non-attached: do everything but do not get identified with anything. You are the soul, the pure, the free, all the time; you are the Witness. Our misery comes, not from work, but by our getting attached to something. Take for instance, money: money is a great thing to have, earn it, says Krishna; struggle hard to get money, but don't get attached to it. So with children, with wife, husband, relatives, fame, everything; you have no need to shun them, only don't get attached. There is only one attachment and that belongs to the Lord, and to none other. Work for them, love them, do good to them, sacrifice a hundred lives, if need be, for them, but never be attached. His own life was the exact exemplification of that.

Remember that the book which delineates the life of Krishna is several thousand years old, and some parts of his life are very similar to those of Jesus of Nazareth. Krishna was of royal birth; there was a tyrant king, called Kamsa, and there was a prophecy that one would be born of such and such a family, who would be king. So Kamsa ordered all the male children to be massacred. The father and mother of Krishna were cast by King Kamsa into prison, where the child was born. A light suddenly shone in the prison and the child spoke saying, "I am the Light of the world, born for the good of the world." You find Krishna again symbolically represented with cows — "The Great Cowherd," as he is called. Sages affirmed that God Himself was born, and they went to pay him homage. In other parts of the story, the similarity between the two does not continue.

Shri Krishna conquered this tyrant Kamsa, but he never thought of accepting or occupying the throne himself. He had nothing to do with that. He had done his duty and there it ended.

After the conclusion of the Kurukshetra War, the great warrior and venerable grandsire, Bhishma, who fought ten days out of the eighteen days' battle, still lay on his deathbed and gave instructions to Yudhishthira on various subjects, such as the duties of the king, the duties of the four castes, the four stages of life, the laws of marriage, the bestowing of gifts, etc., basing them on the teachings of the ancient sages. He explained Sânkhya philosophy and Yoga philosophy and narrated numerous tales and traditions about saints and gods and kings. These teachings occupy nearly one-fourth of the entire work and form an invaluable storehouse of Hindu laws and moral codes. Yudhishthira had in the meantime been crowned king. But the awful bloodshed and extinction of superiors and relatives weighed heavily on his mind; and then, under the advice of Vyasa, he performed the Ashvamedha sacrifice.

After the war, for fifteen years Dhritarashtra dwelt in peace and honour, obeyed by Yudhishthira and his brothers. Then the aged monarch leaving Yudhishthira on the throne, retired to the forest with his devoted wife and Kunti, the mother of the Pandava brothers, to pass his last days in asceticism.

Thirty-six years had now passed since Yudhishthira regained his empire. Then came to him the news that Krishna had left his mortal body. Krishna, the sage, his friend, his prophet, his counsellor, had departed. Arjuna hastened to Dwârâka and came back only to confirm the sad news that Krishna and the Yâdavas were all dead. Then the king and the other brothers, overcome with sorrow, declared that the time for them to go, too, had arrived. So they cast off the burden of royalty, placed Parikshit, the grandson of Arjuna, on the throne, and retired to the Himalayas, on the Great Journey, the Mahâprasthâna. This was a peculiar form of Sannyâsa. It was a custom for old kings to become Sannyâsins. In ancient India, when men became very old, they would give up everything. So did the kings. When a man did not want to live any more, then he went towards the Himalayas, without eating or drinking and walked on and on till the body failed. All the time thinking of God, be just marched on till the body gave way.

Then came the gods, the sages, and they told King Yudhishthira that he should go and reach heaven. To go to heaven one has to cross the highest peaks of the Himalayas. Beyond the Himalayas is Mount Meru. On the top of Mount Meru is heaven. None ever went there in this body. There the gods reside. And Yudhishthira was called upon by the gods to go there.

So the five brothers and their wife clad themselves in robes of bark, and set out on their journey. On the way, they were followed by a dog. On and on they went, and they turned their weary feet northward to where the Himalayas lifts his lofty peaks, and they saw the mighty Mount Meru in front of them. Silently they walked on in the snow, until suddenly the queen fell, to rise no more. To Yudhishthira who was leading the way, Bhima, one of the brothers, said, "Behold, O King, the queen has fallen." The king shed tears, but he did not look back. "We are going to meet Krishna," he says. "No time to look back. March on." After a while, again Bhima said, "Behold, our brother, Sahadeva has fallen." The king shed tears; but paused not. "March on," he cried.

One after the other, in the cold and snow, all the four brothers dropped down, but unshaken, though alone, the king advanced onward. Looking behind, he saw the faithful dog was still following him. And so the king and the dog went on, through snow and ice, over hill and dale, climbing higher and higher, till they reached Mount Meru; and there they began to hear the chimes of heaven, and celestial flowers were showered upon the virtuous king by the gods. Then descended the chariot of the gods, and Indra prayed him, "Ascend in this chariot, greatest of mortals: thou that alone art given to enter heaven without changing the mortal body." But no, that Yudhishthira would not do without his devoted brothers and his queen; then Indra explained to him that the brothers had already gone thither before him.

And Yudhishthira looked around and said to his dog, "Get into the chariot, child." The god stood aghast. "What! the dog?" he cried. "Do thou cast off this dog! The dog goeth not to heaven I Great King, what dost thou mean? Art thou mad? Thou, the most virtuous of the human race, thou only canst go to heaven in thy body." "But he has been my devoted companion through snow and ice. When all my brothers were dead, my queen dead, he alone never left me. How can I leave him now?" "There is no place in heaven for men with dogs. He has to be left behind. There is nothing unrighteous in this." "I do not go to heaven," replied the king, "without the dog. I shall never give up such a one who has taken refuge with me, until my own life is at an end. I shall never swerve from righteousness, nay, not even for the joys of heaven or the urging of a god." "Then," said Indra, "on one condition the dog goes to heaven. You have been the most virtuous of mortals and he has been a dog, killing and eating animals; he is sinful, hunting, and taking other lives. You can exchange heaven with him. "Agreed," says the king. "Let the dog go to heaven."

At once, the scene changed. Hearing these noble words of Yudhishthira, the dog revealed himself as Dharma; the dog was no other than Yama, the Lord of Death and Justice. And Dharma exclaimed, "Behold, O King, no man was ever so unselfish as thou, willing to exchange heaven with a little dog, and for his sake disclaiming all his virtues and ready to go to hell even for him. Thou art well born, O King of kings. Thou hast compassion for all creatures, O Bhârata, of which this is a bright example. Hence, regions of undying felicity are thine! Thou hast won them, O King, and shine is a celestial and high goal."

Then Yudhishthira, with Indra, Dharma, and other gods, proceeds to heaven in a celestial car. He undergoes some trials, bathes in the celestial Ganga, and assumes a celestial body. He meets his brothers who are now immortals, and all at last is bliss.

Thus ends the story of the Mahabharata, setting forth in a sublime poem the triumph of virtue and defeat of vice.

In speaking of the Mahabharata to you, it is simply impossible for me to present the unending array of the grand and majestic characters of the mighty heroes depicted by the genius and master-mind of Vyasa. The internal conflicts between righteousness and filial affection in the mind of the god-fearing, yet feeble, old, blind King Dhritarashtra; the majestic character of the grandsire Bhishma; the noble and virtuous nature of the royal Yudhishthira, and of the other four brothers, as mighty in valour as in devotion and loyalty; the peerless character of Krishna, unsurpassed in human wisdom; and not less brilliant, the characters of the women — the stately queen Gandhari, the loving mother Kunti, the ever-devoted and all-suffering Draupadi — these and hundreds of other characters of this Epic and those of the Ramayana have been the cherished heritage of the whole Hindu world for the last several thousands of years and form the basis of their thoughts and of their moral and ethical ideas. In fact, the Ramayana and the Mahabharata are the two encyclopaedias of the ancient Aryan life and wisdom, portraying an ideal civilisation which humanity has yet to aspire after.

THOUGHTS ON THE GITA

During his sojourn in Calcutta in 1897, Swami Vivekananda used to stay for the most part at the Math, the headquarters of the Ramakrisnna Mission, located then at Alambazar. During this time several young men, who had been preparing themselves for some time previously, gathered round him and took the vows of Brahmacharya and Sannyâsa, and Swamiji began to train them for future work, by holding classes on the Gitâ and Vedanta, and initiating them into the practices of meditation. In one of these classes he talked eloquently in Bengali on the Gita. The following is the translation of the summary of the discourse as it was entered in the Math diary:

The book known as the Gita forms a part of the Mahâbhârata. To understand the Gita properly, several things are very important to know. First, whether it formed a part of the Mahabharata, i.e. whether the authorship attributed to Veda-Vyâsa was true, or if it was merely interpolated within the great epic; secondly, whether there was any historical personality of the name of Krishna; thirdly, whether the great war of Kurukshetra as mentioned in the Gita actually took place; and fourthly, whether Arjuna and others were real historical persons.

Now in the first place, let us see what grounds there are for such inquiry. We know that there were many who went by the name of Veda-Vyasa; and among them who was the real author of the Gita — the Bâdarâyana Vyasa or Dvaipâyana Vyasa? "Vyasa" was only a title. Anyone who composed a new Purâna was known by the name of Vyasa, like the word Vikramâditya, which was also a general name. Another point is, the book, Gita, had not been much known to the generality of people before Shankarâchârya made it famous by writing his great commentary on it. Long before that, there was current, according to many, the commentary on it by Bodhâyana. If this could be proved, it would go a long way, no doubt, to establish the antiquity of the Gita and the authorship of Vyasa. But the Bodhayana Bhâshya on the Vedânta Sutras — from which Râmânuja compiled his Shri-Bhâshya, which Shankaracharya mentions and even quotes in part here and there in his own commentary, and which was so greatly discussed by the Swami Dayânanda — not a copy even of that Bodhayana Bhashya could I find while travelling throughout India. It is said that even Ramanuja compiled his Bhashya from a worm-eaten manuscript which he happened to find. When even this great Bodhayana Bhashya on the Vedanta-Sutras is so much enshrouded in the darkness of uncertainty, it is simply useless to try to establish the existence of the Bodhayana Bhashya on the Gita. Some infer that Shankaracharya was the author of the Gita, and that it was he who foisted it into the body of the Mahabharata.

Then as to the second point in question, much doubt exists about the personality of Krishna. In one place in the Chhândogya Upanishad we find mention of Krishna, the son of Devaki, who received spiritual instructions from one Ghora, a Yogi. In the Mahabharata, Krishna is the king of Dwârakâ; and in the Vishnu Purâna we find a description of Krishna playing with the Gopis. Again, in the Bhâgavata, the account of his Râsalilâ is detailed at length. In very ancient times in our country there was in vogue an Utsava called Madanotsava (celebration in honour of Cupid). That very thing was transformed into Dola and thrust upon the shoulders of Krishna. Who can be so bold as to assert that the Rasalila and other things connected with him were not similarly fastened upon him? In ancient times there was very little tendency in our country to find out truths by historical research. So any one could say what he thought best without substantiating it with proper facts and evidence. Another thing: in those ancient times there was very little hankering after name and fame in men. So it often happened that one man composed a book and made it pass current in the name of his Guru or of someone else. In such cases it is very hazardous for the investigator of historical facts to get at the truth. In ancient times they had no knowledge whatever of geography; imagination ran riot. And so we meet with such fantastic creations of the brain as sweet-ocean, milk-ocean, clarified-butter-ocean, curd-ocean, etc! In the Puranas, we find one living ten thousand years, another a hundred thousand years! But the Vedas say, शतायुर्वै पुरुषः — "Man lives a hundred years." Whom shall we follow here? So, to reach a correct conclusion in the case of Krishna is well-nigh impossible.

It is human nature to build round the real character of a great man all sorts of imaginary superhuman attributes. As regards Krishna the same must have happened, but it seems quite probable that he was a king. Quite probable I say, because in ancient times in our country it was chiefly the kings who exerted themselves most in the preaching of Brahma-Jnâna. Another point to be especially noted here is that whoever might have been the author of the Gita, we find its teachings the same as those in the whole of the Mahabharata. From this we can safely infer that in the age of the Mahabharata some great man arose and preached the Brahma-Jnâna in this new garb to the then existing society. Another fact comes to the fore that in the olden days, as one sect after another arose, there also came into existence and use among them one new scripture or another. It happened, too, that in the lapse of time both the sect and its scripture died out, or the sect ceased to exist but its scripture remained. Similarly, it was quite probable that the Gita was the scripture of such a sect which had embodied its high and noble ideas in this sacred book.

Now to the third point, bearing on the subject of the Kurukshetra War, no special evidence in support of it can be adduced. But there is no doubt that there was a war fought between the Kurus and the Panchâlas. Another thing: how could there be so much discussion about Jnâna, Bhakti, and Yoga on the battle-field, where the huge army stood in battle array ready to fight, just waiting for the last signal? And was any shorthand writer present there to note down every word spoken between Krishna and Arjuna, in the din and turmoil of the battle-field? According to some, this Kurukshetra War is only an allegory. When we sum up its esoteric significance, it means the war which is constantly going on within man between the tendencies of good and evil. This meaning, too, may not be irrational.

About the fourth point, there is enough ground

of doubt as regards the historicity of Arjuna and others, and it is this: Shatapatha Brâhmana is a very ancient book. In it are mentioned somewhere all the names of those who were the performers of the Ashvamedha Yajna: but in those places there is not only no mention, but no hint even of the names of Arjuna and others, though it speaks of Janamejaya, the son of Parikshit who was a grandson of Arjuna. Yet in the Mahabharata and other books it is stated that Yudhishthira, Arjuna, and others celebrated the Ashvamedha sacrifice.

One thing should be especially remembered here, that there is no connection between these historical researches and our real aim, which is the knowledge that leads to the acquirement of Dharma. Even if the historicity of the whole thing is proved to be absolutely false today, it will not in the least be any loss to us. Then what is the use of so much historical research, you may ask. It has its use, because we have to get at the truth; it will not do for us to remain bound by wrong ideas born of ignorance. In this country people think very little of the importance of such inquiries. Many of the sects believe that in order to preach a good thing which may be beneficial to many, there is no harm in telling an untruth, if that helps such preaching, or in other words, the end justifies the means. Hence we find many of our Tantras beginning with, "Mahâdeva said to Pârvati". But our duty should be to convince ourselves of the truth, to believe in truth only. Such is the power of superstition, or faith in old traditions without inquiry into its truth, that it keeps men bound hand and foot, so much so, that even Jesus the Christ, Mohammed, and other great men believed in many such superstitions and could not shake them off. You have to keep your eye always fixed on truth only and shun all superstitions completely.

Now it is for us to see what there is in the Gita. If we study the Upanishads we notice, in wandering through the mazes of many irrelevant subjects, the sudden introduction of the discussion of a great truth, just as in the midst of a huge wilderness a traveller unexpectedly comes across here and there an exquisitely beautiful rose, with its leaves, thorns, roots, all entangled. Compared with that, the Gita is like these truths beautifully arranged together in their proper places — like a fine garland or a bouquet of the choicest flowers. The Upanishads deal elaborately with Shraddhâ in many places, but hardly mention Bhakti. In the Gita, on the other hand, the subject of Bhakti is not only again and again dealt with, but in it, the innate spirit of Bhakti has attained its culmination.

Now let us see some of the main points discussed in the Gita. Wherein lies the originality of the Gita which distinguishes it from all preceding scriptures? It is this: Though before its advent, Yoga, Jnana, Bhakti, etc. had each its strong adherents, they all quarrelled among themselves, each claiming superiority for his own chosen path; no one ever tried to seek for reconciliation among these different paths. It was the author of the Gita who for the first time tried to harmonise these. He took the best from what all the sects then existing had to offer and threaded them in the Gita. But even where Krishna failed to show a complete reconciliation (Samanvaya) among these warring sects, it was fully accomplished by Ramakrishna Paramahamsa in this nineteenth century.

The next is, Nishkâma Karma, or work without desire or attachment. People nowadays understand what is meant by this in various ways. Some say what is implied by being unattached is to become purposeless. If that were its real meaning, then heartless brutes and the walls would be the best exponents of the performance of Nishkama Karma. Many others, again, give the example of Janaka, and wish themselves to be equally recognised as past masters in the practice of Nishkama Karma! Janaka (lit. father) did not acquire that distinction by bringing forth children, but these people all want to be Janakas, with the sole qualification of being the fathers of a brood of children! No! The true Nishkama Karmi (performer of work without desire) is neither to be like a brute, nor to be inert, nor heartless. He is not Tâmasika but of pure Sattva. His heart is so full of love and sympathy that he can embrace the whole world with his love. The world at large cannot generally comprehend his all-embracing love and sympathy.

The reconciliation of the different paths of Dharma, and work without desire or attachment — these are the two special characteristics of the Gita.

Let us now read a little from the second chapter.

सञ्जय उवाच॥

तं तथा कृपयाविष्टमश्रुपूर्णाकुलेक्षणम् ।
विषीदन्तमिदं वाक्यमुवाच मधुसूदनः ॥१॥

श्रीभगवानुवाच ॥

कुतस्त्वा कश्मलमिदं विषमे समुपस्थितम् ।
अनार्यजुष्टमस्वर्ग्यमकीर्तिकरमर्जुन ॥२॥

क्लैब्यं मा स्म गमः पार्थ नैतत्त्वय्युपपद्यते ।
क्षुद्रं हृदयदौर्बल्यं त्यक्त्वोत्तिष्ठ परंतप ॥३॥

"Sanjaya said:

To him who was thus overwhelmed with pity and sorrowing, and whose eyes were dimmed with tears, Madhusudana spoke these words.

The Blessed Lord said:

In such a strait, whence comes upon thee, O Arjuna, this dejection, un-Aryan-like, disgraceful, and contrary to the attainment of heaven?

Yield not to unmanliness, O son of Prithâ! Ill doth it become thee. Cast off this mean faint-heartedness and arise, O scorcher of thine enemies!"

In the Shlokas beginning with तं तथा कृपयाविष्ट, how poetically, how beautifully, has Arjuna's real position been painted! Then Shri Krishna advises Arjuna; and in the words क्लैब्यं मा स्म गमः पार्थ etc., why is he goading Arjuna to fight? Because it was not that the disinclination of Arjuna to fight arose out of the overwhelming predominance of pure Sattva Guna; it was all Tamas that brought on this unwillingness. The nature of a man of Sattva Guna is, that he is equally calm in all situations in life — whether it be prosperity or adversity. But Arjuna was afraid, he was overwhelmed with pity. That he had the instinct and the inclination to fight is proved by the simple fact that he came to the battle-field with no other purpose than that. Frequently in our lives also such things are seen to happen. Many people think they are Sâttvika by nature, but they are really nothing but Tâmasika. Many living in an uncleanly way regard themselves as Paramahamsas! Why? Because the Shâstras say that Paramahamsas live like one inert, or mad, or like an unclean spirit. Paramahamsas are compared to children, but here it should be understood that the comparison is one-sided. The Paramahamsa and the child are not one and non-different. They only appear similar, being the two extreme poles, as it were. One has reached to a state beyond Jnana, and the other has not got even an inkling of Jnana. The quickest and the gentlest vibrations of light are both beyond the reach of our ordinary vision; but in the one it is intense heat, and in the other it may be said to be almost without any heat. So it is with the opposite qualities of Sattva and Tamas. They seem in some respects to be the same, no doubt, but there is a world of difference between them. The Tamoguna loves very much to array itself in the garb of the Sattva. Here, in Arjuna, the mighty warrior, it has come under the guise of Dayâ (pity).

In order to remove this delusion which had overtaken Arjuna, what did the Bhagavân say? As I always preach that you should not decry a man by calling him a sinner, but that you should draw his attention to the omnipotent power that is in him, in the same way does the Bhagavan speak to Arjuna. नैतत्त्वय्युपपद्यते — "It doth not befit thee!" "Thou art Atman imperishable, beyond all evil. Having forgotten thy real nature, thou hast, by thinking thyself a sinner, as one afflicted with bodily evils and mental grief, thou hast made thyself so — this doth not befit thee!" — so says the Bhagavan: क्लैब्यं मा स्म गमः पार्थ — Yield not to unmanliness, O son of Pritha. There is in the world neither sin nor misery, neither disease nor grief; if there is anything in the world which can be called sin, it is this — 'fear'; know that any work which brings out the latent power in thee is Punya (virtue); and that which makes thy body and mind weak is, verily, sin. Shake off this weakness, this faintheartedness! क्लैब्यं मा स्म गमः पार्थ। — Thou art a hero, a Vira; this is unbecoming of thee."

If you, my sons, can proclaim this message to the world — क्लैब्यं मा स्म गमः पार्थ नैतत्त्वय्युपपद्यते — then all this disease, grief, sin, and sorrow will vanish from off the face of the earth in three days. All these ideas of weakness will be nowhere. Now it is everywhere — this current of the vibration of fear. Reverse the current: bring in the opposite vibration, and behold the magic transformation! Thou art omnipotent — go, go to the mouth of the cannon, fear not.

Hate not the most abject sinner, fool; not to his exterior. Turn thy gaze inward, where resides the Paramâtman. Proclaim to the whole world with trumpet voice, "There is no sin in thee, there is no misery in thee; thou art the reservoir of omnipotent power. Arise, awake, and manifest the Divinity within!"

If one reads this one Shloka — क्लैब्यं मा स्म गमः पार्थ नैतत्त्वय्युपपद्यते । क्षुद्रं हृदयदौर्बल्यं त्यक्त्वोत्तिष्ठ परंतप॥ — one gets all the merits of reading the entire Gita; for in this one Shloka lies imbedded the whole Message of the Gita.

THE STORY OF JADA BHARATA

Delivered in California

There was a great monarch named Bharata. The land which is called India by foreigners is known to her children as Bhârata Varsha. Now, it is enjoined on every Hindu when he becomes old, to give up all worldly pursuits — to leave the cares of the world, its wealth, happiness, and enjoyments to his son — and retire into the forest, there to meditate upon the Self which is the only reality in him, and thus break the bonds which bind him to life. King or priest, peasant or servant, man or woman, none is exempt from this duty: for all the duties of the householder — of the son, the brother, the husband, the father, the wife, the daughter, the mother, the sister — are but preparations towards that one stage, when all the bonds which bind the soul to matter are severed asunder for ever.

The great king Bharata in his old age gave over his throne to his son, and retired into the forest. He who had been ruler over millions and millions of subjects, who had lived in marble palaces, inlaid with gold and silver, who had drunk out of jewelled cups — this king built a little cottage with his own hands, made of reeds and grass, on the banks of a river in the Himalayan forests. There he lived on roots and wild herbs, collected by his own hands, and constantly meditated upon Him who is always present in the soul of man. Days, months, and years passed. One day, a deer came to drink water near by where the royal sage was meditating. At the same moment, a lion roared at a little distance off. The deer was so terrified that she, without satisfying her thirst, made a big jump to cross the river. The deer was with young, and this extreme exertion and sudden fright made her give birth to a little fawn, and immediately after she fell dead. The fawn fell into the water and was being carried rapidly away by the foaming stream, when it caught the eyes of the king. The king rose from his position of meditation and rescuing the fawn from the water, took it to his cottage, made a fire, and with care and attention fondled the little thing back to life. Then the kindly sage took the fawn under his protection, bringing it up on soft grass and fruits. The fawn thrived under the paternal care of the retired monarch, and grew into a beautiful deer. Then, he whose mind had been strong enough to break away from lifelong attachment to power, position, and family, became attached to the deer which he had saved from the stream. And as he became fonder and fonder of the deer, the less and less he could concentrate his mind upon the Lord. When the deer went out to graze in the forest, if it were late in returning, the mind of the royal sage would become anxious and worried. He would think, "Perhaps my little one has been attacked by some tiger — or perhaps some other danger has befallen it; otherwise, why is it late?"

Some years passed in this way, but one day death came, and the royal sage laid himself down to die. But his mind, instead of being intent upon the Self, was thinking about the deer; and with his eyes fixed upon the sad looks of his beloved deer, his soul left the body. As the result of this, in the next birth he was born as a deer. But no Karma is lost, and all the great and good deeds done by him as a king and sage bore their fruit. This deer was a born Jâtismara, and remembered his past birth, though he was bereft of speech and was living in an animal body. He always left his companions and was instinctively drawn to graze near hermitages where oblations were offered and the Upanishads were preached.

After the usual years of a deer's life had been spent, it died and was next born as the youngest son of a rich Brahmin. And in that life also, he remembered all his past, and even in his childhood was determined no more to get entangled in the good and evil of life. The child, as it grew up, was strong and healthy, but would not speak a word, and lived as one inert and insane, for fear of getting mixed up with worldly affairs. His thoughts were always on the Infinite, and he lived only to wear out his past Prârabdha Karma. In course of time the father died, and the sons divided the property among themselves; and thinking that the youngest was a dumb, good-for-nothing man, they seized his share. Their charity, however, extended only so far as to give him enough food to live upon. The wives of the brothers were often very harsh to him, putting him to do all the hard work; and if he was unable to do everything they wanted, they would treat him very unkindly. But he showed neither vexation nor fear, and neither did he speak a word. When they persecuted him very much, he would stroll out of the house and sit under a tree, by the hour, until their wrath was appeased, and then he would quietly go home again.

One day; when the wives of the brothers had treated him with more than usual unkindness, Bharata went out of the house, seated himself under the shadow of a tree and rested. Now it happened that the king of the country was passing by, carried in a palanquin on the shoulders of bearers. One of the bearers had unexpectedly fallen ill, and so his attendants were looking about for a man to replace him. They came upon Bharata seated under a tree; and seeing he was a strong young man, they asked him if he would take the place of the sick man in bearing the king's palanquin. But Bharata did not reply. Seeing that he was so able-bodied, the king's servants caught hold of him and placed the pole on his shoulders. Without speaking a word, Bharata went on. Very soon after this, the king remarked that the palanquin was not being evenly carried, and looking out of the palanquin addressed the new bearer, saying "Fool, rest a while; if thy shoulders pain thee, rest a while." Then Bharata laying the pole of the palanquin down, opened his lips for the first time in his life, and spoke, "Whom dost thou, O King, call a fool? Whom dost thou ask to lay down the palanquin? Who dost thou say is weary? Whom dost thou address as 'thou'? If thou meanest, O King, by the word 'thee' this mass of flesh, it is composed of the same matter as thine; it is unconscious, and it knoweth no weariness, it knoweth no pain. If it is the mind, the mind is the same as thine; it is universal. But if the word 'thee' is applied to something beyond that, then it is the Self, the Reality in me, which is the same as in thee, and it is the One in the universe. Dost thou mean, O King, that the Self can ever be weary, that It can ever be tired, that It can ever be hurt? I did not want, O King — this body did not want — to trample upon the poor worms crawling on the road, and therefore, in trying to avoid them, the palanquin moved unevenly. But the Self was never tired; It was never weak; It never bore the pole of the palanquin: for It is omnipotent and omnipresent." And so he dwelt eloquently on the nature of the soul, and on the highest knowledge, etc. The king, who was proud of his learning, knowledge, and philosophy, alighted from the palanquin, and fell at the feet of Bharata, saying, "I ask thy pardon, O mighty one, I did not know that thou wast a sage, when I asked thee to carry me." Bharata blessed him and departed. He then resumed the even tenor of his previous life. When Bharata left the body, he was freed for ever from the bondage of birth.

THE STORY OF PRAHLADA

Delivered in California

Hiranyakashipu was the king of the Daityas. The Daityas, though born of the same parentage as the Devas or gods, were always, at war with the latter. The Daityas had no part in the oblations and offerings of mankind, or in the government of the world and its guidance. But sometimes they waxed strong and drove all the Devas from the heaven, and seized the throne of the gods and ruled for a time. Then the Devas prayed to Vishnu, the Omnipresent Lord of the universe, and He helped them out of their difficulty. The Daityas were driven out, and once more the gods reigned. Hiranyakashipu, king of the Daityas, in his turn, succeeded in conquering his cousins, the Devas, and seated himself on the throne of the heavens and ruled the three worlds — the middle world, inhabited by men and animals; the heavens, inhabited by gods and godlike beings; and the nether world, inhabited by the Daityas. Now, Hiranyakashipu declared himself to be the God of the whole universe and proclaimed that there was no other God but himself, and strictly enjoined that the Omnipotent Vishnu should have no worship offered to Him anywhere; and that all the worship should henceforth be given to himself only.

Hiranyakashipu had a son called Prahlâda. Now, it so happened, that this Prahlada from his infancy was devoted to God. He showed indications of this as a child; and the king of the Daityas, fearing that the evil he wanted to drive away from the world would crop up in his own family, made over his son to two teachers called Shanda and Amarka, who were very stern disciplinarians, with strict injunctions that Prahlada was never to hear even the name of Vishnu mentioned. The teachers took the prince to their home, and there he was put to study with the other children of his age. But the little Prahlada, instead of learning from his books, devoted all the time in teaching the other boys how to worship Vishnu. When the teachers found it out, they were frightened, for the fear of the mighty king Hiranyakashipu was upon them, and they tried their best to dissuade the child from such teachings. But Prahlada could no more stop his teaching and worshipping Vishnu than he could stop breathing. To clear themselves, the teachers told the terrible fact to the king, that his son was not only worshipping Vishnu himself, but also spoiling all the other children by teaching them to worship Vishnu.

The monarch became very much enraged when he heard this and called the boy to his presence. He tried by gentle persuasions to dissuade Prahlada from the worship of Vishnu and taught him that he, the king, was the only God to worship. But it was to no purpose. The child declared, again and again, that the Omnipresent Vishnu, Lord of the universe, was the only Being to be worshipped — for even he, the king, held his throne only so long as it pleased Vishnu. The rage of the king knew no bounds, and he ordered the boy to be immediately killed. So the Daityas struck him with pointed weapons; but Prahlad's mind was so intent upon Vishnu that he felt no pain from them.

When his father, the king, saw that it was so, he became frightened but, roused to the worst passions of a Daitya, contrived various diabolical means to kill the boy. He ordered him to be trampled under foot by an elephant. The enraged elephant could not crush the body any more than he could have crushed a block of iron. So this measure also was to no purpose. Then the king ordered the boy to be thrown over a precipice, and this order too was duly carried out; but, as Vishnu resided in the heart of Prahlada, he came down upon the earth as gently as a flower drops upon the grass. Poison, fire, starvation, throwing into a well, enchantments, and other measures were then tried on the child one after another, but to no purpose. Nothing could hurt him in whose heart dwelt Vishnu.

At last, the king ordered the boy to be tied with mighty serpents called up from the nether worlds, and then cast to the bottom of the ocean, where huge mountains were to be piled high upon him, so that in course of time, if not immediately, he might die; and he ordered him to be left in this plight. Even though treated in this manner, the boy continued to pray to his beloved Vishnu: "Salutation to Thee, Lord of the universe. Thou beautiful Vishnu!" Thus thinking and meditating on Vishnu, he began to feel that Vishnu was near him, nay, that He was in his own soul, until he began to feel that he was Vishnu, and that he was everything and everywhere.

As soon as he realised this, all the snake bonds snapped asunder; the mountains were pulverised, the ocean upheaved, and he was gently lifted up above the waves, and safely carried to the shore. As Prahlada stood there, he forgot that he was a Daitya and had a mortal body: he felt he was the universe and all the powers of the universe emanated from him; there was nothing in nature that could injure him; he himself was the ruler of nature. Time passed thus, in one unbroken ecstasy of bliss, until gradually Prahlada began to remember that he had a body and that he was Prahlada. As soon as he became once more conscious of the body, he saw that God was within and without; and everything appeared to him as Vishnu.

When the king Hiranyakashipu found to his horror that all mortal means of getting rid of the boy who was perfectly devoted to his enemy, the God Vishnu, were powerless, he was at a loss to know what to do. The king had the boy again brought before him, and tried to persuade him once more to listen to his advice, through gentle means. But Prahlada made the same reply. Thinking, however, that these childish whims of the boy would be rectified with age and further training, he put him again under the charge of the teachers, Shanda and Amarka, asking them to teach him the duties of the king. But those teachings did not appeal to Prahlada, and he spent his time in instructing his schoolmates in the path of devotion to the Lord Vishnu.

When his father came to hear about it, he again became furious with rage, and calling the boy to him, threatened to kill him, and abused Vishnu in the worst language. But Prahlada still insisted that Vishnu was the Lord of the universe, the Beginningless, the Endless, the Omnipotent and the Omnipresent, and as such, he alone was to be worshipped. The king roared with anger and said: "Thou evil one, if thy Vishnu is God omnipresent, why doth he not reside in that pillar yonder?" Prahlada humbly submitted that He did do so. "If so," cried the king, "let him defend thee; I will kill thee with this sword." Thus saying the king rushed at him with sword in hand, and dealt a terrible blow at the pillar. Instantly thundering voice was heard, and lo and behold, there issued forth from the pillar Vishnu in His awful Nrisimha form — half-lion, half-man! Panic-stricken, the Daityas ran away in all directions; but Hiranyakashipu fought with him long and desperately, till he was finally overpowered and killed.

Then the gods descended from heaven and offered hymns to Vishnu, and Prahlada also fell at His feet and broke forth into exquisite hymns of praise and devotion. And he heard the Voice of God saying, "Ask, Prahlada ask for anything thou desires"; thou art My favourite child; therefore ask for anything thou mayest wish." And Prahlada choked with feelings replied, "Lord, I have seen Thee. What else can I want? Do thou not tempt me with earthly or heavenly boons." Again the Voice said: "Yet ask something, my son." And then Prahlada replied, "That intense love, O Lord, which the ignorant bear to worldly things, may I have the same love for Thee; may I have the same intensity of love for Thee, but only for love's sake!"

Then the Lord said, "Prahlada, though My intense devotees never desire for anything, here or hereafter, yet by My command, do thou enjoy the blessings of this world to the end of the present cycle, and perform works of religious merit, with thy heart fixed on Me. And thus in time, after the dissolution of thy body, thou shalt attain Me." Thus blessing Prahlada, the Lord Vishnu disappeared. Then the gods headed by Brahma installed Prahlada on the throne of the Daityas and returned to their respective spheres.

THE GREAT TEACHERS OF THE WORLD

Delivered at the Shakespeare Club, Pasadena, California, February 3, 1900

The universe, according to the theory of the Hindus, is moving in cycles of wave forms. It rises, reaches its zenith, then falls and remains in the hollow, as it were, for some time, once more to rise, and so on, in wave after wave and fall after fall. What is true of the universe is true of every part of it. The march of human affairs is like that. The history of nations is like that: they rise and they fall; after the rise comes a fall, again out of the fall comes a rise, with greater power. This motion is always going on. In the religious world the same movement exists. In every nation's spiritual life, there is a fall as well as a rise. The nation goes down, and everything seems to go to pieces. Then, again, it gains strength, rises; a huge wave comes, sometimes a tidal wave — and always on the topmost crest of the wave is a shining soul, the Messenger. Creator and created by turns, he is the impetus that makes the wave rise, the nation rise: at the same time, he is created by the same forces which make the wave, acting and interacting by turns. He puts forth his tremendous power upon society; and society makes him what he is. These are the great world-thinkers. These are the Prophets of the world, the Messengers of life, the Incarnations of God.

Man has an idea that there can be only one religion, that there can be only one Prophet, and that there can be only one Incarnation; but that idea is not true. By studying the lives of all these great Messengers, we find that each, as it were, was destined to play a part, and a part only; that the harmony consists in the sum total and not in one note. As in the life of races — no race is born to alone enjoy the world. None dare say no. Each race has a part to play in this divine harmony of nations. Each race has its mission to perform, its duty to fulfil. The sum total is the great harmony.

So, not any one of these Prophets is born to rule the world for ever. None has yet succeeded and none is going to be the ruler for ever. Each only contributes a part; and, as to that part, it is true that in the long run every Prophet will govern the world and its destinies.

Most of us are born believers in a personal religion. We talk of principles, we think of theories, and that is all right; but every thought and every movement, every one of our actions, shows that we can only understand the principle when it comes to us through a person. We can grasp an idea only when it comes to us through a materialised ideal person. We can understand the precept only through the example. Would to God that all of us were so developed that we would not require any example, would not require any person. But that we are not; and, naturally, the vast majority of mankind have put their souls at the feet of these extraordinary personalities, the Prophets, the Incarnations of God — Incarnations worshipped by the Christians, by the Buddhists, and by the Hindus. The Mohammedans from the beginning stood against any such worship. They would have nothing to do with worshipping the Prophets or the Messengers, or paying any homage to them; but, practically, instead of one Prophet, thousands upon thousands of saints are being worshipped. We cannot go against facts! We are bound to worship personalities, and it is good. Remember that word from your great Prophet to the query: "Lord, show us the Father", "He that hath seen me hath seen the Father." Which of us can imagine anything except that He is a man? We can only see Him in and through humanity. The vibration of light is everywhere in this room: why cannot lie see it everywhere? You have to see it only in that lamp. God is an Omnipresent Principle — everywhere: but we are so constituted at present that we can see Him, feel Him, only in and through a human God. And when these great Lights come, then man realises God. And they come in a different way from what we come. We come as beggars; they come as Emperors. We come here like orphans, as people who have lost their way and do not know it. What are we to do? We do not know what is the meaning of our lives. We cannot realise it. Today we are doing one thing, tomorrow another. We are like little bits of straw rocking to and fro in water, like feathers blown about in a hurricane.

But, in the history of mankind, you will find that there come these Messengers, and that from their very birth their mission is found and formed. The whole plan is there, laid down; and you see them swerving not one inch from that. Because they come with a mission, they come with a message, they do not want to reason. Did you ever hear or read of these great Teachers, or Prophets, reasoning out what they taught? No, not one of them did so. They speak direct. Why should they reason? They see the Truth. And not only do they see it but they show it! If you ask me, "Is there any God?" and I say "Yes", you immediately ask my grounds for saying so, and poor me has to exercise all his powers to provide you with some reason. If you had come to Christ and said, "Is there any God? " he would have said, "Yes"; and if you had asked, "Is there any proof?" he would have replied, "Behold the Lord! " And thus, you see, it is a direct perception, and not at all the ratiocination of reason. There is no groping in the dark, but there is the strength of direct vision. I see this table; no amount of reason can take that faith from me. It is a direct perception. Such is their faith — faith in their ideals, faith in their mission, faith in themselves, above all else. The great shining Ones believe in themselves as nobody else ever does. The people say, "Do you believe in God? Do you believe in a future life? Do you believe in this doctrine or that dogma?" But here the base is wanting: this belief in oneself. Ay, the man who cannot believe in himself, how can they expect him to believe in anything else? I am not sure of my own existence. One moment I think that I am existing and nothing can destroy me; the next moment I am quaking in fear of death. One minute I think I am immortal; the next minute, a spook appears, and then I don't know what I am, nor where I am. I don't know whether I am living or dead. One moment I think that I am spiritual, that I am moral; and the next moment, a blow comes, and I am thrown flat on my back. And why? — I have lost faith in myself, my moral backbone is broken.

But in these great Teachers you will always find this sign: that they have intense faith in themselves. Such intense faith is unique, and we cannot understand it. That is why we try to explain away in various ways what these Teachers speak of themselves; and people invent twenty thousand theories to explain what they say about their realisation. We do not think of ourselves in the same way, and, naturally, we cannot understand them.

Then again, when they speak, the world is bound to listen. When they speak, each word is direct; it bursts like a bomb-shell. What is in the word, unless it has the Power behind? What matters it what language you speak, and how you arrange your language? What matters it whether you speak correct grammar or with fine rhetoric? What matters it whether your language is ornamental or not? The question is whether or not you have anything to give. It is a question of giving and taking, and not listening. Have you anything to give? — that is the first question. If you have, then give. Words but convey the gift: it is but one of the many modes. Sometimes we do not speak at all. There is an old Sanskrit verse which says, "I saw the Teacher sitting under a tree. He was a young man of sixteen, and the disciple was an old man of eighty. The preaching of the Teacher was silence, and the doubts of the disciple departed."

Sometimes they do not speak at all, but yet they convey the Truth from mind to mind. They come to give. They command, they are the Messengers; you have to receive the Command. Do you not remember in your own scriptures the authority with which Jesus speaks? "Go ye, therefore, and teach all nations . . . teaching them to observe all things whatsoever I have commanded you." It runs through all his utterances, that tremendous faith in his own message. That you find in the life of all these great giants whom the world worships as its Prophets.

These great Teachers are the living Gods on this earth. Whom else should we worship? I try to get an idea of God in my mind, and I find what a false little thing I conceive; it would be a sin to worship that God. I open my eyes and look at the actual life of these great ones of the earth. They are higher than any conception of God that I could ever form. For, what conception of mercy could a man like me form who would go after a man if he steals anything from me and send him to jail? And what can be my highest idea of forgiveness? Nothing beyond myself. Which of you can jump out of your own bodies? Which of you can jump out of your own minds? Not one of you. What idea of divine love can you form except what you actually live? What we have never experienced we can form no idea of. So, all my best attempts at forming an idea of God would fail in every case. And here are plain facts, and not idealism — actual facts of love, of mercy, of purity, of which I can have no conception even. What wonder that I should fall at the feet of these men and worship them as God? And what else can anyone do? I should like to see the man who can do anything else, however much he may talk. Talking is not actuality. Talking about God and the Impersonal, and this and that is all very good; but these man-Gods are the real Gods of all nations and all races. These divine men have been worshipped and will be worshipped so long as man is man. Therein is our faith, therein is our hope, of a reality. Of what avail is a mere mystical principle!

The purpose and intent of what I have to say to you is this, that I have found it possible in my life to worship all of them, and to be ready for all that are yet to come. A mother recognises her son in any dress in which he may appear before her; and if one does not do so, I am sure she is not the mother of that man. Now, as regards those of you that think that you understand Truth and Divinity and God in only one Prophet in the world, and not in any other, naturally, the conclusion which I draw is that you do not understand Divinity in anybody; you have simply swallowed words and identified yourself with one sect, just as you would in party politics, as a matter of opinion; but that is no religion at all. There are some fools in this world who use brackish water although there is excellent sweet water near by, because, they say, the brackish-water well was dug by their father. Now, in my little experience I have collected this knowledge — that for all the devilry that religion is, blamed with, religion is not at all in fault: no religion ever persecuted men, no religion ever burnt witches, no religion ever did any of these things. What then incited people to do these things? Politics, but never religion; and if such politics takes the name of religion whose fault is that?

So, when each man stands and says "My Prophet is the only true Prophet," he is not correct — he knows not the alpha of religion. Religion is neither talk, nor theory, nor intellectual consent. It is realisation in the heart of our hearts; it is touching God; it is feeling, realising that I am a spirit in relation with the Universal Spirit and all Its great manifestations. If you have really entered the house of the Father, how can you have seen His children and not known them? And if you do not recognise them, you have not entered the house of the Father. The mother recognises her child in any dress and knows him however disguised. Recognise all the great, spiritual men and women in every age and country, and see that they are not really at variance with one another. Wherever there has been actual religion — this touch of the Divine, the soul coming in direct sense-contact with the Divine — there has always been a broadening of the mind which enables it to see the light everywhere. Now, some Mohammedans are the crudest in this respect, and the most sectarian. Their watchword is: "There is one God, and Mohammed is His Prophet." Everything beyond that not only is bad, but must be destroyed forthwith; at a moment's notice, every man or woman who does not exactly believe in that must be killed; everything that does not belong to this worship must be immediately broken; every book that teaches any thing else must be burnt. From the Pacific to the Atlantic, for five hundred years blood ran all over the world. That is Mohammedanism! Nevertheless, among these Mohammedans, wherever there has a philosophic man, he was sure to protest against these cruelties. In that he showed the touch of the Divine and realised a fragment of the truth; he was not playing with his religion; for it was not his father's religion he was talking, but spoke the truth direct like a man.

Side by side with tie modern theory of evolution, there is another thing: atavism. There is a tendency in us to revert to old ideas in religion. Let us think something new, even if it be wrong. It is better to do that. Why should you not try to hit the mark? We become wiser through failures. Time is infinite. Look at the wall. Did the wall ever tell a lie? It is always the wall. Man tells a lie — and becomes a god too. It is better to do something; never mind even if it proves to be wrong it is better than doing nothing. The cow never tells a lie, but she remains a cow, all the time. Do something! Think some thought; it doesn't matter whether you are right or wrong. But think something! Because my forefathers did not think this way, shall I sit down quietly and gradually lose my sense of feeling and my own thinking faculties? I may as well be dead! And what is life worth if we have no living ideas, no convictions of our own about religion? There is some hope for the atheists, because though they differ from others, they think for themselves. The people who never think anything for themselves are not yet born into the world of religion; they have a mere jelly-fish existence. They will not think; they do not care for religion. But the disbeliever, the atheist, cares, and he is struggling. So think something! Struggle Godward! Never mind if you fail, never mind if you get hold of a queer theory. If you are afraid to be called queer, keep it in your own mind — you need not go and preach it to others. But do something! Struggle Godward! Light must come. If a man feeds me every day of my life, in the long run I shall lose the use of my hands. Spiritual death is the result of following each other like a flock of sheep. Death is the result of inaction. Be active; and wherever there is activity, there must be difference. Difference is the sauce of life; it is the beauty, it is the art of everything. Difference makes all beautiful here. It is variety that is the source of life, the sign of life. Why should we be afraid of it?

Now, we are coming into a position to understand about the Prophets. Now, we see that the historical evidence is — apart from the jelly-fish existence in religion — that where there has been any real thinking, any real love for God, the soul has grown Godwards and has got as it were, a glimpse now and then, has come into direct perception, even for a second, even once in its life. Immediately, "All doubts vanish for ever, and all the crookedness of the heart is made straight, and all bondages vanish, and the results of action and Karma fly when He is seen who is the nearest of the near and the farthest of the far." That is religion, that is all of religion; the rest is mere theory, dogma, so many ways of going to that state of direct perception. Now we are fighting over the basket and the fruits have fallen into the ditch.

If two men quarrel about religion, just ask them the question: "Have you seen God? Have you seen these things?" One man says that Christ is the only Prophet: well, has he seen Christ? "Has your father seen Him?" "No, Sir." "Has your grandfather seen Him?" "No, Sir." "Have you seen Him?" "No, Sir." "Then what are you quarrelling for? The fruits have fallen into the ditch, and you are quarrelling over the basket!" Sensible men and women should be ashamed to go on quarrelling in that way!

These great Messengers and Prophets are great and true. Why? Because, each one has come to preach a great idea. Take the Prophets of India, for instance. They are the oldest of the founders of religion. We takes first, Krishna. You who have read the Gitâ see all through the book that the one idea is non-attachment. Remain unattached. The heart's love is due to only One. To whom? To Him who never changeth. Who is that One? It is God. Do not make the mistake of giving the heart to anything that is changing, because that is misery. You may give it to a man; but if he dies, misery is the result. You may give it to a friend, but he may tomorrow become your enemy. If you give it to your husband, he may one day quarrel with you. You may give it to your wife, and she may die the day after tomorrow. Now, this is the way the world is going on. So says Krishna in the Gita: The Lord is the only One who never changes. His love never fails. Wherever we are and whatever we do, He is ever and ever the same merciful, the same loving heart. He never changes, He is never angry, whatever we do. How can God be angry with us? Your babe does many mischievous things: are you angry with that babe? Does not God know what we are going to be? He knows we are all going to be perfect, sooner or later. He has patience, infinite patience. We must love Him, and everyone that lives — only in and through Him. This is the keynote. You must love the wife, but not for the wife's sake. "Never, O Beloved, is the husband loved on account of the husband, but because the Lord is in the husband." The Vedanta philosophy says that even in the love of the husband and wife, although the wife is thinking that she is loving the husband, the real attraction is the Lord, who is present there. He is the only attraction, there is no other; but the wife in most cases does not know that it is so, but ignorantly she is doing the right thing, which is, loving the Lord. Only, when one does it ignorantly, it may bring pain. If one does it knowingly, that is salvation. This is what our scriptures say. Wherever there is love, wherever there is a spark of joy, know that to be a spark of His presence because He is joy, blessedness, and love itself. Without that there cannot be any love.

This is the trend of Krishna's instruction all the time. He has implanted that upon his race, so that when a Hindu does anything, even if he drinks water, he says "If there is virtue in it, let it go to the Lord." The Buddhist says, if he does any good deed, "Let the merit of the good deed belong to the world; if there is any virtue in what I do, let it go to the world, and let the evils of the world come to me." The Hindu says he is a great believer in God; the Hindu says that God is omnipotent and that He is the Soul of every soul everywhere; the Hindu says, If I give all my virtues unto Him, that is the greatest sacrifice, and they will go to the whole universe."

Now, this is one phase; and what is the other message of Krishna? "Whosoever lives in the midst of the world, and works, and gives up all the fruit of his action unto the Lord, he is never touched with the evils of the world. Just as the lotus, born under the water, rises up and blossoms above the water, even so is the man who is engaged in the activities of the world, giving up all the fruit of his activities unto the Lord" (Gita, V. 10).

Krishna strikes another note as a teacher of intense activity. Work, work, work day and night, says the Gita. You may ask, "Then, where is peace? If all through life I am to work like a cart-horse and die in harness, what am I here for?" Krishna says, "Yes, you will find peace. Flying from work is never the way to find peace." Throw off your duties if you can, and go to the top of a mountain; even there the mind is going — whirling, whirling, whirling. Someone asked a Sannyasin, "Sir, have you found a nice place? How many years have you been travelling in the Himalayas?" "For forty years," replied the Sannyasin. "There are many beautiful spots to select from, and to settle down in: why did you not do so?" "Because for these forty years my mind would not allow me to do so." We all say, "Let us find peace"; but the mind will not allow us to do so.

You know the story of the man who caught a Tartar. A soldier was outside the town, and he cried out when be came near the barracks, "I have caught a Tartar." A voice called out, "Bring him in." "He won't come in, sir." "Then you come in." "He won't let me come in, sir." So, in this mind of ours, we have "caught a Tartar": neither can we tone it down, nor will it let us be toned down. We have all "caught Tartars". We all say, be quiet, and peaceful, and so forth. But every baby can say that and thinks he can do it. However, that is very difficult. I have tried. I threw overboard all my duties and fled to the tops of mountains; I lived in caves and deep forests — but all the same, I "caught a Tartar" because I had my world with me all the time. The "Tartar" is what I have in my own mind, so we must not blame poor people outside. "These circumstances are good, and these are bad," so we say, while the "Tartar" is here, within; if we can quiet him down, we shall be all right.

Therefore Krishna teaches us not to shirk our duties, but to take them up manfully, and not think of the result. The servant has no right to question. The soldier has no right to reason. Go forward, and do not pay too much attention to the nature of the work you have to do. Ask your mind if you are unselfish. If you are, never mind anything, nothing can resist you! Plunge in! Do the duty at hand. And when you have done this, by degrees you will realise the Truth: "Whosoever in the midst of intense activity finds intense peace, whosoever in the midst of the greatest peace finds the greatest activity, he is a Yogi, he is a great soul, he has arrived at perfection."

Now, you see that the result of this teaching is that all the duties of the world are sanctified. There is no duty in this world which we have any right to call menial: and each man's work is quite as good as that of the emperor on his throne.

Listen to Buddha's message — a tremendous message. It has a place in our heart. Says Buddha, "Root out selfishness, and everything that makes you selfish. Have neither wife, child, nor family. Be not of the world; become perfectly unselfish." A worldly man thinks he will be unselfish, but when he looks at the face of his wife it makes him selfish. The mother thinks she will be perfectly unselfish, but she looks at her baby, and immediately selfishness comes. So with everything in this world. As soon as selfish desires arise, as soon as some selfish pursuit is followed, immediately the whole man, the real man, is gone: he is like a brute, he is a slave' he forgets his fellow men. No more does he say, "You first and I afterwards," but it is "I first and let everyone else look out for himself."

We find that Krishna's message has also a place for us. Without that message, we cannot move at all. We cannot conscientiously and with peace, joy, and happiness, take up any duty of our lives without listening to the message of Krishna: "Be not afraid even if there is evil in your work, for there is no work which has no evil." "Leave it unto the Lord, and do not look for the results."

On the other hand, there is a corner in the heart for the other message: Time flies; this world is finite and all misery. With your good food, nice clothes, and your comfortable home, O sleeping man and woman, do you ever think of the millions that are starving and dying? Think of the great fact that it is all misery, misery, misery! Note the first utterance of the child: when it enters into the world, it weeps. That is the fact — the child-weeps. This is a place for weeping! If we listen to the Messenger, we should not be selfish.

Behold another Messenger, He of Nazareth. He teaches, "Be ready, for the Kingdom of Heaven is at hand." I have pondered over the message of Krishna, and am trying to work without attachment, but sometimes I forget. Then, suddenly, comes to me the message of Buddha: "Take care, for everything in the world as evanescent, and there is always misery in this life." I listen to that, and I am uncertain which to accept. Then again comes, like a thunderbolt, the message: "Be ready, for the Kingdom of Heaven is at hand." Do not delay a moment. Leave nothing for tomorrow. Get ready for the final event, which may overtake you immediately, even now. That message, also, has a place, and we acknowledge it. We salute the Messenger, we salute the Lord.

And then comes Mohammed, the Messenger of equality. You ask, "What good can there be in his religion?" If there were no good, how could it live? The good alone lives, that alone survives; because the good alone is strong, therefore it survives. How long is the life of an impure man, even in this life? Is not the life of the pure man much longer? Without doubt, for purity is strength, goodness is strength. How could Mohammedanism have lived, had there been nothing good in its teaching? There is much good. Mohammed was the Prophet of equality, of the brotherhood of man, the brotherhood of all Mussulmans

So we see that each Prophet, each Messenger, has a particular message. When you first listen to that message, and then look at his life, you see his whole life stands explained, radiant.

Now, ignorant fools start twenty thousand theories, and put forward, according to their own mental development, explanations to suit their own ideas, and ascribe them to these great Teachers. They take their teachings and put their misconstruction upon them. With every great Prophet his life is the only commentary. Look at his life: what he did will bear out the texts. Read the Gita, and you will find that it is exactly borne out by the life of the Teacher.

Mohammed by his life showed that amongst Mohammedans there should be perfect equality and brotherhood. There was no question of race, caste, creed, colour, or sex. The Sultan of Turkey may buy a Negro from the mart of Africa, and bring him in chains to Turkey; but should he become a Mohammedan and have sufficient merit and abilities, he might even marry the daughter of the Sultan. Compare this with the way in which the Negroes and the American Indians are treated in this country! And what do Hindus do? If one of your missionaries chance to touch the food of an orthodox person, he would throw it away. Notwithstanding our grand philosophy, you note our weakness in practice; but there You see the greatness of the Mohammedan beyond other races, showing itself in equality, perfect equality regardless of race or colour.

Will other and greater Prophets come? Certainly they will come in this world. But do not look forward to that. I should better like that each one of you became a Prophet of this real New Testament, which is made up of all the Old Testaments. Take all the old messages, supplement them with your own realisations, and become a Prophet unto others. Each one of these Teachers has been great; each has left something for us; they have been our Gods. We salute them, we are their servants; and, all the same, we salute ourselves; for if they have been Prophets and children of God, we also are the same. They reached their perfection, and we are going to attain ours now. Remember the words of Jesus: "The Kingdom of Heaven is at hand!" This very moment let everyone of us make a staunch resolution: "I will become a Prophet, I will become a messenger of Light, I will become a child of God, nay, I will become a God!"

ON LORD BUDDHA

Delivered in Detroit

In every religion we find one type of self-devotion particularly developed. The type of working without a motive is most highly developed in Buddhism.

Do not mistake Buddhism and Brâhminism. In this country you are very apt to do so. Buddhism is one of our sects. It was founded by a great man called Gautama, who became disgusted at the eternal metaphysical discussions of his day, and the cumbrous rituals, and more especially with the caste system. Some people say that we are born to a certain state, and therefore we are superior to others who are not thus born. He was also against the tremendous priestcraft. He preached a religion in which there was no motive power, and was perfectly agnostic about metaphysics or theories about God. He was often asked if there was a God, and he answered, he did not know. When asked about right conduct, he would reply, "Do good and be good." There came five Brâhmins, who asked him to settle their discussion. One said, "Sir, my book says that God is such and such, and that this is the way to come to God." Another said, "That is wrong, for my book says such and such, and this is the way to come to God"; and so the others. He listened calmly to all of them, and then asked them one by one, "Does any one of your books say that God becomes angry, that He ever injures anyone, that He is impure?" "No, Sir, they all teach that God is pure and good." "Then, my friends, why do you not become pure and good first, that you may know what God is?"

Of course I do not endorse all his philosophy. I want a good deal of metaphysics, for myself. I entirely differ in many respects, but, because I differ, is that any reason why I should not see the beauty of the man? He was the only man who was bereft of all motive power. There were other great men who all said they were the Incarnations of God Himself, and that those who would believe in them would go to heaven. But what did Buddha say with his dying breath? "None can help you; help yourself; work out your own salvation." He said about himself, "Buddha is the name of infinite knowledge, infinite as the sky; I, Gautama, have reached that state; you will all reach that too if you struggle for it." Bereft of all motive power, he did not want to go to heaven, did not want money; he gave up his throne and everything else and went about begging his bread through the streets of India, preaching for the good of men and animals with a heart as wide as the ocean.

He was the only man who was ever ready to give up his life for animals to stop a sacrifice. He once said to a king, "If the sacrifice of a lamb helps you to go to heaven, sacrificing a man will help you better; so sacrifice me." The king was astonished. And yet this man was without any motive power. He stands as the perfection of the active type, and the very height to which he attained shows that through the power of work we can also attain to the highest spirituality.

To many the path becomes easier if they believe in God. But the life of Buddha shows that even a man who does not believe in God, has no metaphysics, belongs to no sect, and does not go to any church, or temple, and is a confessed materialist, even he can attain to the highest. We have no right to judge him. I wish I had one infinitesimal part of Buddha's heart. Buddha may or may not have believed in God; that does not matter to me. He reached the same state of perfection to which others come by Bhakti — love of God — Yoga, or Jnâna. Perfection does not come from belief or faith. Talk does not count for anything. Parrots can do that. Perfection comes through the disinterested performance of action.

CHRIST, THE MESSENGER

Delivered at Los Angeles, California, 1900

The wave rises on the ocean, and there is a hollow. Again another wave rises, perhaps bigger than the former, to fall down again, similarly, again to rise — driving onward. In the march of events, we notice the rise and fall, and we generally look towards the rise, forgetting the fall. But both are necessary, and both are great. This is the nature of the universe. Whether in the world of our thoughts, the world of our relations in society, or in our spiritual affairs, the same movement of succession, of rises and falls, is going on. Hence great predominances in the march of events, the liberal ideals, are marshalled ahead, to sink down, to digest, as it were, to ruminate over the past — to adjust, to conserve, to gather strength once more for a rise and a bigger rise.

The history of nations also has ever been like that. The great soul, the Messenger we are to study this afternoon, came at a period of the history of his race which we may well designate as a great fall. We catch only little glimpses here and there of the stray records that have been kept of his sayings and doings; for verily it has been well said, that the doings and sayings of that great soul would fill the world if they had all been written down. And the three years of his ministry were like one compressed, concentrated age, which it has taken nineteen hundred years to unfold, and who knows how much longer it will yet take! Little men like you and me are simply the recipients of just a little energy. A few minutes, a few hours, a few years at best, are enough to spend it all, to stretch it out, as it were, to its fullest strength, and then we are gone for ever. But mark this giant that came; centuries and ages pass, yet the energy that he left upon the world is not yet stretched, nor yet expended to its full. It goes on adding new vigour as the ages roll on.

Now what you see in the life of Christ is the life of all the past. The life of every man is, in a manner, the life of the past. It comes to him through heredity, through surroundings, through education, through his own reincarnation — the past of the race. In a manner, the past of the earth, the past of the whole world is there, upon every soul. What are we, in the present, but a result, an effect, in the hands of that infinite past? What are we but floating waveless in the eternal current of events, irresistibly moved forward and onward and incapable of rest? But you and I are only little things, bubbles. There are always some giant waves in the ocean of affairs, and in you and me the life of the past race has been embodied only a little; but there are giants who embody, as it were, almost the whole of the past and who stretch out their hands for the future. These are the sign-posts here and there which point to the march of humanity; these are verily gigantic, their shadows covering the earth — they stand undying, eternal! As it has been said by the same Messenger, "No man hath seen God at any time, but through the Son." And that is true. And where shall we see God but in the Son? It is true that you and I, and the poorest of us, the meanest even, embody that God, even reflect that God. The vibration of light is everywhere, omnipresent; but we have to strike the light of the lamp before we can see the light. The Omnipresent God of the universe cannot be seen until He is reflected by these giant lamps of the earth — The Prophets, the man-Gods, the Incarnations, the embodiments of God.

We all know that God exists, and yet we do not see Him, we do not understand Him. Take one of these great Messengers of light, compare his character with the highest ideal of God that you ever formed, and you will find that your God falls short of the ideal, and that the character of the Prophet exceeds your conceptions. You cannot even form a higher ideal of God than what the actually embodied have practically realised and set before us as an example. Is it wrong, therefore, to worship these as God? Is it a sin to fall at the feet of these man-Gods and worship them as the only divine beings in the world? If they are really, actually, higher than all our conceptions of God, what harm is there in worshipping them? Not only is there no harm, but it is the only possible and positive way of worship. However much you may try by struggle, by abstraction, by whatsoever method you like, still so long as you are a man in the world of men, your world is human, your religion is human, and your God is human. And that must be so. Who is not practical enough to take up an actually existing thing and give up an idea which is only an abstraction, which he cannot grasp, and is difficult of approach except through a concrete medium? Therefore, these Incarnations of God have been worshipped in all ages and in all countries.

We are now going to study a little of the life of Christ, the Incarnation of the Jews. When Christ was born, the Jews were in that state which I call a state of fall between two waves; a state of conservatism; a state where the human mind is, as it were, tired for the time being of moving forward and is taking care only of what it has already; a state when the attention is more bent upon particulars, upon details, than upon the great, general, and bigger problems of life; a state of stagnation, rather than a towing ahead; a state of suffering more than of doing. Mark you, I do not blame this state of things. We have no right to criticise it — because had it not been for this fall, the next rise, which was embodied in Jesus of Nazareth would have been impossible. The Pharisees and Sadducees might have been insincere, they might have been doing things which they ought not to have done; they might have been even hypocrites; but whatever they were, these factors were the very cause, of which the Messenger was the effect. The Pharisees and Sadducees at one end were the very impetus which came out at the other end as the gigantic brain of Jesus of Nazareth.

The attention to forms, to formulas, to the everyday details of religion, and to rituals, may sometimes be laughed at; but nevertheless, within them is strength. Many times in the rushing forward we lose much strength. As a fact, the fanatic is stronger than the liberal man. Even the fanatic, therefore, has one great virtue, he conserves energy, a tremendous amount of it. As with the individual so with the race, energy is gathered to be conserved. Hemmed in all around by external enemies, driven to focus in a centre by the Romans, by the Hellenic tendencies in the world of intellect, by waves from Persia, India, and Alexandria — hemmed in physically, mentally, and morally — there stood the race with an inherent, conservative, tremendous strength, which their descendants have not lost even today. And the race was forced to concentrate and focus all its energies upon Jerusalem and Judaism. But all power when once gathered cannot remain collected; it must expend and expand itself. There is no power on earth which can be kept long confined within a narrow limit. It cannot be kept compressed too long to allow of expansion at a subsequent period.

This concentrated energy amongst the Jewish race found its expression at the next period in the rise of Christianity. The gathered streams collected into a body. Gradually, all the little streams joined together, and became a surging wave on the top of which we find standing out the character of Jesus of Nazareth. Thus, every Prophet is a creation of his own times, the creation of the past of his race; he himself is the creator of the future. The cause of today is the effect of the past and the cause for the future. In this position stands the Messenger. In him is embodied all that is the best and greatest in his own race, the meaning, the life, for which that race has struggled for ages; and he himself is the impetus for the future, not only to his own race but to unnumbered other races of the world.

We must bear another fact in mind: that my view of the great Prophet of Nazareth would be from the standpoint of the Orient. Many times you forget, also, that the Nazarene himself was an Oriental of Orientals. With all your attempts to paint him with blue eyes and yellow hair, the Nazarene was still an Oriental. All the similes, the imageries, in which the Bible is written — the scenes, the locations, the attitudes, the groups, the poetry, and symbol, — speak to you of the Orient: of the bright sky, of the heat, of the sun, of the desert, of the thirsty men and animals; of men and women coming with pitchers on their heads to fill them at the wells; of the flocks, of the ploughmen, of the cultivation that is going on around; of the water-mill and wheel, of the mill-pond, of the millstones. All these are to be seen today in Asia.

The voice of Asia has been the voice of religion. The voice of Europe is the voice of politics. Each is great in its own sphere. The voice of Europe is the voice of ancient Greece. To the Greek mind, his immediate society was all in all: beyond that, it is Barbarian. None but the Greek has the right to live. Whatever the Greeks do is right and correct; whatever else there exists in the world is neither right nor correct, nor should be allowed to live. It is intensely human in its sympathies, intensely natural, intensely artistic, therefore. The Greek lives entirely in this world. He does not care to dream. Even his poetry is practical. His gods and goddesses are not only human beings, but intensely human, with all human passions and feelings almost the same as with any of us. He loves what is beautiful, but mind you, it is always external nature: the beauty of the hills, of the snows, of the flowers, the beauty of forms and of figures, the beauty in the human face, and, more often, in the human form — that is what the Greeks liked. And the Greeks being the teachers of all subsequent Europeanism, the voice of Europe is Greek.

There is another type in Asia. Think of that vast, huge continent, whose mountain-tops go beyond the clouds, almost touching the canopy of heaven's blue; a rolling desert of miles upon miles where a drop of water cannot be found, neither will a blade of grass grow; interminable forests and gigantic rivers rushing down into the sea. In the midst of all these surroundings, the oriental love of the beautiful and of the sublime developed itself in another direction. It looked inside, and not outside. There is also the thirst for nature, and there is also the same thirst for power; there is also the same thirst for excellence, the same idea of the Greek and Barbarian, but it has extended over a larger circle. In Asia, even today, birth or colour or language never makes a race. That which makes a race is its religion. We are all Christians; we are all Mohammedans; we are all Hindus, or all Buddhists. No matter if a Buddhist is a Chinaman, or is a man from Persia, they think that they are brothers, because of their professing the same religion. Religion is the tie, unity of humanity. And then again, the Oriental, for the same reason, is a visionary, is a born dreamer. The ripples of the waterfalls, the songs of the birds, the beauties of the sun and moon and the stars and the whole earth are pleasant enough; but they are not sufficient for the oriental mind; He wants to dream a dream beyond. He wants to go beyond the present. The present, as it were, is nothing to him. The Orient has been the cradle of the human race for ages, and all the vicissitudes of fortune are there — kingdoms succeeding kingdoms, empires succeeding empires, human power, glory, and wealth, all rolling down there: a Golgotha of power and learning. That is the Orient: a Golgotha of power, of kingdoms, of learning. No wonder, the oriental mind looks with contempt upon the things of this world and naturally wants to see something that changeth not, something which dieth not, something which in the midst of this world of misery and death is eternal, blissful, undying. An oriental Prophet never tires of insisting upon these ideals; and, as for Prophets, you may also remember that without one exception, all the Messengers were Orientals.

We see, therefore, in the life of this area: Messenger of life, the first watchword: "Not this life, but something higher"; and, like the true son of the Orient, he is practical in that. You people of the West are practical in your own department, in military affairs, and in managing political circles and other things. Perhaps the Oriental is not practical in those ways, but he is practical in his own field; he is practical in religion. If one preaches a philosophy, tomorrow there are hundreds who will struggle their best to make it practical in their lives. If a man preaches that standing on one foot would lead one to salvation, he will immediately get five hundred to stand on one foot. You may call it ludicrous; but, mark you, beneath that is their philosophy — that intense practicality. In the West, plans of salvation mean intellectual gymnastics — plans which are never worked out, never brought into practical life. In the West, the preacher who talks the best is the greatest preacher.

So, we find Jesus of Nazareth, in the first place, the true son of the Orient, intensely practical. He has no faith in this evanescent world and all its belongings. No need of text-torturing, as is the fashion in the West in modern times, no need of stretching out texts until the, will not stretch any more. Texts are not India rubber, and even that has its limits. Now, no making of religion to pander to the sense vanity of the present day! Mark you, let us all be honest. If we cannot follow the ideal, let us confess our weakness, but not degrade it; let not any try to pull it down. One gets sick at heart at the different accounts of the life of the Christ that Western people give. I do not know what he was or what he was not! One would make him a great politician; another, perhaps, would make of him a great military general; another, a great patriotic Jew; and so on. Is there any warrant in the books for all such assumptions? The best commentary on the life of a great teacher is his own life. "The foxes have holes, the birds of the air have nests, but the Son of man hath not where to lay his head." That is what Christ says as they only way to salvation; he lays down no other way. Let us confess in sackcloth and ashes that we cannot do that. We still have fondness for "me and mine". We want property, money, wealth. Woe unto us! Let us confess and not put to shame that great Teacher of Humanity! He had no family ties. But do you think that, that Man had any physical ideas in him? Do you think that, this mass of light, this God and not-man, came down to earth, to be the brother of animals? And yet, people make him preach all sorts of things. He had no sex ideas! He was a soul! Nothing but a soul — just working a body for the good of humanity; and that was all his relation to the body. In the soul there is no sex. The disembodied soul has no relationship to the animal, no relationship to the body. The ideal may be far away beyond us. But never mind, keep to the ideal. Let us confess that it is our ideal, but we cannot approach it yet.

He had no other occupation in life, no other thought except that one, that he was a spirit. He was a disembodied, unfettered, unbound spirit. And not only so, but he, with his marvellous vision, had found that every man and woman, whether Jew or Gentile, whether rich or poor, whether saint or sinner, was the embodiment of the same undying spirit as himself. Therefore, the one work his whole life showed was to call upon them to realise their own spiritual nature. Give up, he says, these superstitious dreams that you are low and that you are poor. Think not that you are trampled upon and tyrannised over as if you were slaves, for within you is something that can never be tyrannised over, never be trampled upon, never be troubled, never be killed. You are all Sons of God, immortal spirit. "Know", he declared, "the Kingdom of Heaven is within you." "I and my Father are one." Dare you stand up and say, not only that "I am the Son of God", but I shall also find in my heart of hearts that "I and my Father are one"? That was what Jesus of Nazareth said. He never talks of this world and of this life. He has nothing to do with it, except that he wants to get hold of the world as it is, give it a push and drive it forward and onward until the whole world has reached to the effulgent Light of God, until everyone has realised his spiritual nature, until death is vanished and misery banished.

We have read the different stories that have been written about him; we know the scholars and their writings, and the higher criticism; and we know all that has been done by study. We are not here to discuss how much of the New Testament is true, we are not here to discuss how much of that life is historical. It does not matter at all whether the New Testament was written within five hundred years of his birth, nor does it matter even, how much of that life is true. But there is something behind it, something we want to imitate. To tell a lie, you have to imitate a truth, and that truth is a fact. You cannot imitate that which never existed. You cannot imitate that which you never perceived. But there must have been a nucleus, a tremendous power that came down, a marvellous manifestation of spiritual power — and of that we are speaking. It stands there. Therefore, we are not afraid of all the criticisms of the scholars. If I, as an Oriental, have to worship Jesus of Nazareth, there is only one way left to me, that is, to worship him as God and nothing else. Have we no right to worship him in that way, do you mean to say? If we bring him down to our own level and simply pay him a little respect as a great man, why should we worship at all? Our scriptures say, "These great children of Light, who manifest the Light themselves, who are Light themselves, they, being worshipped, become, as it were, one with us and we become one with them."

For, you see, in three ways man perceives God. At first the undeveloped intellect of the uneducated man sees God as far away, up in the heavens somewhere, sitting on a throne as a great Judge. He looks upon Him as a fire, as a terror. Now, that is good, for there is nothing bad in it. You must remember that humanity travels not from error to truth, but from truth to truth; it may be, if you like it better, from lower truth to higher truth, but never from error to truth. Suppose you start from here and travel towards the sun in a straight line. From here the sun looks only small in size. Suppose you go forward a million miles, the sun will be much bigger. At every stage the sun will become bigger and bigger. Suppose twenty thousand photographs had been taken of the same sun, from different standpoints; these twenty thousand photographs will all certainly differ from one another. But can you deny that each is a photograph of the same sun? So all forms of religion, high or low, are just different stages toward that eternal state of Light, which is God Himself. Some embody a lower view, some a higher, and that is all the difference. Therefore, the religions of the unthinking masses all over the world must be, and have always been, of a God who is outside of the universe, who lives in heaven, who governs from that place, who is a punisher of the bad and a rewarder of the good, and so on. As man advanced spiritually, he began to feel that God was omnipresent, that He must be in him, that He must be everywhere, that He was not a distant God, but dearly the Soul of all souls. As my soul moves my body, even so is God the mover of my soul. Soul within soul. And a few individuals who had developed enough and were pure enough, went still further, and at last found God. As the New Testament says, "Blessed are the pure in heart, for they shall see God." And they found at last that they and the Father were one.

You find that all these three stages are taught by the Great Teacher in the New Testament. Note the Common Prayer he taught: "Our Father which art in Heaven, hallowed be Thy name," and so on — a simple prayer, a child's prayer. Mark you, it is the "Common Prayer" because it is intended for the uneducated masses. To a higher circle, to those who had advanced a little more, he gave a more elevated teaching: "I am in my Father, and ye in me, and I in you." Do you remember that? And then, when the Jews asked him who he was, he declared that he and his Father were one, and the Jews thought that that was blasphemy. What did he mean by that? This has been also told by your old Prophets, "Ye are gods and all of you are children of the Most High." Mark the same three stages. You will find that it is easier for you to begin with the first and end with the last.

The Messenger came to show the path: that the

spirit is not in forms, that it is not through all sorts of vexations and knotty problems of philosophy that you know the spirit. Better that you had no learning, better that you never read a book in your life. These are not at all necessary for salvation — neither wealth, nor position nor power, not even learning; but what is necessary is that one thing, purity. "Blessed are the pure in heart," for the spirit in its own nature is pure. How can it be otherwise? It is of God, it has come from God. In the language of the Bible, "It is the breath of God." In the language of the Koran, "It is the soul of God." Do you mean to say that the Spirit of God can ever be impure? But, alas, it has been, as it were, covered over with the dust and dirt of ages, through our own actions, good and evil. Various works which were not correct, which were not true, have covered the same spirit with the dust and dirt of the ignorance of ages. It is only necessary to clear away the dust and dirt, and then the spirit shines immediately. "Blessed are the pure in heart, for they shall see God." "The Kingdom of Heaven is within you." Where goest thou to seek for the Kingdom of God, asks Jesus of Nazareth, when it is there, within you? Cleanse the spirit, and it is there. It is already yours. How can you get what is not yours? It is yours by right. You are the heirs of immortality, sons of the Eternal Father.

This is the great lesson of the Messenger, and another which is the basis of all religions, is renunciation. How can you make the spirit pure? By renunciation. A rich young man asked Jesus, "Good Master, what shall I do that I may inherit eternal life?" And Jesus said unto him, "One thing thou lackest; go thy way, sell whatsoever thou hast, and give to the poor, and thou shalt have treasures in heaven: and come, take up thy cross, and follow Me." And he was sad at that saying and went away grieved; for he had great possessions. We are all more or less like that. The voice is ringing in our ears day and night. In the midst of our pleasures and joys, in the midst of worldly things, we think that we have forgotten everything else. Then comes a moment's pause and the voice rings in our ears "Give up all that thou hast and follow Me." "Whosoever will save his life shall lose it; and whosoever shall lose his life for My sake shall find it." For whoever gives up this life for His sake, finds the life immortal. In the midst of all our weakness there is a moment of pause and the voice rings: "Give up all that thou hast; give it to the poor and follow me." This is the one ideal he preaches, and this has been the ideal preached by all the great Prophets of the world: renunciation. What is meant by renunciation? That there is only one ideal in morality: unselfishness. Be selfless. The ideal is perfect unselfishness. When a man is struck on the right cheek, he turns the left also. When a man's coat is carried off, he gives away his cloak also.

We should work in the best way we can, without dragging the ideal down. Here is the ideal. When a man has no more self in him, no possession, nothing to call "me" or "mine", has given himself up entirely, destroyed himself as it were — in that man is God Himself; for in him self-will is gone, crushed out, annihilated. That is the ideal man. We cannot reach that state yet; yet, let us worship the ideal, and slowly struggle to reach the ideal, though, maybe, with faltering steps. It may be tomorrow, or it may be a thousand years hence; but that ideal has to be reached. For it is not only the end, but also the means. To be unselfish, perfectly selfless, is salvation itself; for the man within dies, and God alone remains.

One more point. All the teachers of humanity are unselfish. Suppose Jesus of Nazareth was teaching; and a man came and told him, "What you teach is beautiful. I believe that it is the way to perfection, and I am ready to follow it; but I do not care to worship you as the only begotten Son of God." What would be the answer of Jesus of Nazareth? "Very well, brother, follow the ideal and advance in your own way. I do not care whether you give me the credit for the teaching or not. I am not a shopkeeper. I do not trade in religion. I only teach truth, and truth is nobody's property. Nobody can patent truth. Truth is God Himself. Go forward." But what the disciples say nowadays is: "No matter whether you practise the teachings or not, do you give credit to the Man? If you credit the Master, you will be saved; if not, there is no salvation for you." And thus the whole teaching of the Master is degenerated, and all the struggle and fight is for the personality of the Man. They do not know that in imposing that difference, they are, in a manner, bringing shame to the very Man they want to honour — the very Man that would have shrunk with shame from such an idea. What did he care if there was one man in the world that remembered him or not? He had to deliver his message, and he gave it. And if he had twenty thousand lives, he would give them all up for the poorest man in the world. If he had to be tortured millions of times for a million despised Samaritans, and if for each one of them the sacrifice of his own life would be the only condition of salvation, he would have given his life. And all this without wishing to have his name known even to a single person. Quiet, unknown, silent, would he world, just as the Lord works. Now, what would the disciple say? He will tell you that you may be a perfect man, perfectly unselfish; but unless you give the credit to our teacher, to our saint, it is of no avail. Why? What is the origin of this superstition, this ignorance? The disciple thinks that the Lord can manifest Himself only once. There lies the whole mistake. God manifests Himself to you in man. But throughout nature, what happens once must have happened before, and must happen in future. There is nothing in nature which is not bound by law; and that means that whatever happens once must go on and must have been going on.

In India they have the same idea of the Incarnations of God. One of their great Incarnations, Krishna, whose grand sermon, the Bhagavad-Gitâ, some of you might have read, says, "Though I am unborn, of changeless nature, and Lord of beings, yet subjugating My Prakriti, I come into being by My own Mâyâ. Whenever virtue subsides and immorality prevails, then I body Myself forth. For the protection of the good, for the destruction of the wicked, and for the establishment of Dharma, I come into being, in every age." Whenever the world goes down, the Lord comes to help it forward; and so He does from time to time and place to place. In another passage He speaks to this effect: Wherever thou findest a great soul of immense power and purity struggling to raise humanity, know that he is born of My splendour, that I am there working through him.

Let us, therefore, find God not only in Jesus of Nazareth, but in all the great Ones that have preceded him, in all that came after him, and all that are yet to come. Our worship is unbounded and free. They are all manifestations of the same Infinite God. They are all pure and unselfish; they struggled and gave up their lives for us, poor human beings. They each and all suffer vicarious atonement for every one of us, and also for all that are to come hereafter.

In a sense you are all Prophets; every one of you is a Prophet, bearing the burden of the world on your own shoulders. Have you ever seen a man, have you ever seen a woman, who is not quietly, patiently, bearing his or her little burden of life? The great Prophets were giants — they bore a gigantic world on their shoulders. Compared with them we are pigmies, no doubt, yet we are doing the same task; in our little circles, in our little homes, we are bearing our little crosses. There is no one so evil, no one so worthless, but he has to bear his own cross. But with all our mistakes, with all our evil thoughts and evil deeds, there is a bright spot somewhere, there is still somewhere the golden thread through which we are always in touch with the divine. For, know for certain, that the moment the touch of the divine is lost there would be annihilation. And because none can be annihilated, there is always somewhere in our heart of hearts, however low and degraded we may be, a little circle of light which is in constant touch with the divine.

Our salutations go to all the past Prophets whose teachings and lives we have inherited, whatever might have been their race, clime, or creed! Our salutations go to all those Godlike men and women who are working to help humanity, whatever be their birth, colour, or race! Our salutations to those who are coming in the future — living Gods — to work unselfishly for our descendants.

MY MASTER[1]

"Whenever virtue subsides and vice prevails, I come down to help mankind," declares Krishna, in the Bhagavad-Gitâ. Whenever this world of ours, on account of growth, on account of added circumstances, requires a new adjustment, a wave of power comes; and as a man is acting on two planes, the spiritual and the material, waves of adjustment come on both planes. On the one side, of the adjustment on the material plane, Europe has mainly been the basis during modern times; and of the adjustment on the other, the spiritual plane, Asia has been the basis throughout the history of the world. Today, man requires one more adjustment on the spiritual plane; today when material ideas are at the height of their glory and power, today when man is likely to forget his divine nature, through his growing dependence on matter, and is likely to be reduced to a mere money-making machine, an adjustment is necessary; the voice has spoken, and the power is coming to drive away the clouds of gathering materialism. The power has been set in motion which, at no distant date, will bring unto mankind once more the memory of its real nature; and again the place from which this power will start will be Asia.

This world of ours is on the plan of the division of labour. It is vain to say that one man shall possess everything. Yet how childish we are! The baby in its ignorance thinks that its doll is the only possession that is to be coveted in this whole universe. So a nation which is great in the possession of material power thinks that that is all that is to be coveted, that that is all that is meant by progress, that that is all that is meant by civilisation, and if there are other nations which do not care for possession and do not possess that power, they are not fit to live, their whole existence is useless! On the other hand, another nation may think that mere material civilisation is utterly useless. From the Orient came the voice which once told the world that if a man possesses everything that is under the sun and does not possess spirituality, what avails it? This is the oriental type; the other is the occidental type.

Each of these types has its grandeur, each has its glory. The present adjustment will be the harmonising, the mingling of these two ideals. To the Oriental, the world of spirit is as real as to the Occidental is the world of senses. In the spiritual, the Oriental finds everything he wants or hopes for; in it he finds all that makes life real to him. To the Occidental he is a dreamer; to the Oriental the Occidental is a dreamer playing with ephemeral toys, and he laughs to think that grown-up men and women should make so much of a handful of matter which they will have to leave sooner or later. Each calls the other a dreamer. But the oriental ideal is as necessary for the progress of the human race as is the occidental, and I think it is more necessary. Machines never made mankind happy and never will make. He who is trying to make us believe this will claim that happiness is in the machine; but it is always in the mind. That man alone who is the lord of his mind can become happy, and none else. And what, after all, is this power of machinery? Why should a man who can send a current of electricity through a wire be called a very great man and a very intelligent man? Does not nature do a million times more than that every moment? Why not then fall down and worship nature? What avails it if you have power over the whole of the world, if you have mastered every atom in the universe? That will not make you happy unless you have the power of happiness in yourself, until you have conquered yourself. Man is born to conquer nature, it is true, but the Occidental means by "nature" only physical or external nature. It is true that external nature is majestic, with its mountains, and oceans, and rivers, and with its infinite powers and varieties. Yet there is a more majestic internal nature of man, higher than the sun, moon, and stars, higher than this earth of ours, higher than the physical universe, transcending these little lives of ours; and it affords another field of study. There the Orientals excel, just as the Occidentals excel in the other. Therefore it is fitting that, whenever there is a spiritual adjustment, it should come from the Orient. It is also fitting that when the Oriental wants to learn about machine-making, he should

---
1. Two lectures delivered in New York and England in 1896 were combined subsequently under the present heading.

sit at the feet of the Occidental and learn from him. When the Occident wants to learn about the spirit, about God, about the soul, about the meaning and the mystery of this universe, he must sit at the feet of the Orient to learn.

I am going to present before you the life of one man who has put in motion such a wave in India. But before going into the life of this man, I will try to present before you the secret of India, what India means. If those whose eyes have been blinded by the glamour of material things, whose whole dedication of life is to eating and drinking and enjoying, whose ideal of possession is lands and gold, whose ideal of pleasure is that of the senses, whose God is money, and whose goal is a life of ease and comfort in this world and death after that, whose minds never look forward, and who rarely think of anything higher than the sense-objects in the midst of which they live — if such as these go to India, what do they see? Poverty, squalor, superstition, darkness, hideousness everywhere. Why? Because in their minds enlightenment means dress, education, social politeness. Whereas occidental nations have used every effort to improve their material position, India has done differently. There live the only men in the world who, in the whole history of humanity, never went beyond their frontiers to conquer anyone, who never coveted that which belonged to anyone else, whose only fault was that their lands were so fertile, and they accumulated wealth by the hard labour of their hands, and so tempted other nations to come and despoil them. They are contented to be despoiled, and to be called barbarians; and in return they want to send to this world visions of the Supreme, to lay bare for the world the secrets of human nature, to rend the veil that conceals the real man, because they know the dream, because they know that behind this materialism lives the real, divine nature of man which no sin can tarnish, no crime can spoil, no lust can taint, which fire cannot burn, nor water wet, which heat cannot dry nor death kill. And to them this true nature of man is as real as is any material object to the senses of an Occidental.

Just as you are brave to jump at the mouth of a cannon with a hurrah, just as you are brave in the name of patriotism to stand up and give up your lives for your country, so are they brave in the name of God. There it is that when a man declares that this is a world of ideas, that it is all a dream, he casts off clothes and property to demonstrate that what he believes and thinks is true. There it is that a man sits on the bank of a river, when he has known that life is eternal, and wants to give up his body just as nothing, just as you can give up a bit of straw. Therein lies their heroism, that they are ready to face death as a brother, because they are convinced that there is no death for them. Therein lies the strength that has made them invincible through hundreds of years of oppression and foreign invasion and tyranny. The nation lives today, and in that nation even in the days of the direst disaster, spiritual giants have, never failed to arise. Asia produces giants in spirituality, just as the Occident produces giants in politics, giants in science. In the beginning of the present century, when Western influence began to pour into India, when Western conquerors, sword in hand, came to demonstrate to the children of the sages that they were mere barbarians, a race of dreamers, that their religion was but mythology, and god and soul and everything they had been struggling for were mere words without meaning, that the thousands of years of struggle, the thousands of years of endless renunciation, had all been in vain, the question began to be agitated among young men at the universities whether the whole national existence up to then had been a failure, whether they must begin anew on the occidental plan, tear up their old books, burn their philosophies, drive away their preachers, and break down their temples. Did not the occidental conqueror, the man who demonstrated his religion with sword and gun, say that all the old ways were mere superstition and idolatry? Children brought up and educated in the new schools started on the occidental plan, drank in these ideas, from their childhood; and it is not to be wondered at that doubts arose. But instead of throwing away superstition and making a real search after truth, the test of truth became, "What does the West say?" The priests must go, the Vedas must be burned, because the West has said so. Out of the feeling of unrest thus produced, there arose a wave of so-called reform in India.

If you wish to be a true reformer, three things are necessary. The first is to feel. Do you really feel for your brothers? Do you really feel that there is so much misery in the world, so much ignorance and superstition? Do you really feel that men are your brothers? Does this idea come into your whole being? Does it run with your blood? Does it tingle in your veins? Does it course through every nerve and filament of your body? Are you full of that idea of sympathy? If you are, that is only the first step. You must think next if you have found any remedy. The old ideas may be all superstition, but in and round these masses of superstition are nuggets of gold and truth. Have you discovered means by which to keep that gold alone, without any of the dross? If you have done that, that is only the second step; one more thing is necessary. What is your motive? Are you sure that you are not actuated by greed of gold, by thirst for fame or power? Are you really sure that you can stand to your ideals and work on, even if the whole world wants to crush you down? Are you sure you know what you want and will perform your duty, and that alone, even if your life is at stake? Are you sure that you will persevere so long as life endures, so long as there is one pulsation left in the heart? Then you are a real reformer, you are a teacher, a Master, a blessing to mankind. But man is so impatient, so short-sighted! He has not the patience to wait, he has not the power to see. He wants to rule, he wants results immediately. Why? He wants to reap the fruits himself, and does not really care for others. Duty for duty's sake is not what he wants. "To work you have the right, but not to the fruits thereof," says Krishna. Why cling to results? Ours are the duties. Let the fruits take care of themselves. But man has no patience. He takes up any scheme. The larger number of would-be reformers all over the world can be classed under this heading.

As I have said, the idea of reform came to India when it seemed as if the wave of materialism that had invaded her shores would sweep away the teachings of the sages. But the nation had borne the shocks of a thousand such waves of change. This one was mild in comparison. Wave after wave had flooded the land, breaking and crushing everything for hundreds of years. The sword had flashed, and "Victory unto Allah" had rent the skies of India; but these floods subsided, leaving the national ideals unchanged.

The Indian nation cannot be killed. Deathless it stands, and it will stand so long as that spirit shall remain as the background, so long as her people do not give up their spirituality. Beggars they may remain, poor and poverty-stricken, dirt and squalor may surround them perhaps throughout all time, but let them not give up their God, let them not forget that they are the children of the sages. Just as in the West, even the man in the street wants to trace his descent from some robber-baron of the Middle Ages, so in India, even an Emperor on the throne wants to trace his descent from some beggar-sage in the forest, from a man who wore the bark of a tree, lived upon the fruits of the forest and communed with God. That is the type of descent we want; and so long as holiness is thus supremely venerated, India cannot die.

Many of you perhaps have read the article by Prof. Max Müller in a recent issue of the Nineteenth Century, headed "A Real Mahâtman". The life of Shri Ramakrishna is interesting, as it was a living illustration of the ideas that he preached. Perhaps it will be a little romantic for you who live in the West in an atmosphere entirely different from that of India. For the methods and manners in the busy rush of life in the West vary entirely from those of India. Yet perhaps it will be of all the more interest for that, because it will bring into a newer light, things about which many have already heard.

It was while reforms of various kinds were being inaugurated in India that a child was born of poor Brâhmin parents on the eighteenth of February, 1836, in one of the remote villages of Bengal. The father and mother were very orthodox people. The life of a really orthodox Brahmin is one of continuous renunciation. Very few things can he do; and over and beyond them the orthodox Brahmin must not occupy himself with any secular business. At the same time he must not receive gifts from everybody. You may imagine how rigorous that life becomes. You have heard of the Brahmins and their priestcraft many times, but very few of you have ever stopped to ask what makes this wonderful band of men the rulers of their fellows. They are the poorest of all the classes in the country; and the secret of their power lies in their renunciation. They never covet wealth. Theirs is the poorest priesthood in the world, and therefore the most powerful. Even in this poverty, a Brahmin's wife will never allow a poor man to pass through the village without giving him something to eat. That is considered the highest duty of the mother in India; and because she is the mother it is her duty to be served last; she must see that everyone is served before her turn comes. That is why the mother is regarded as God in India. This particular woman, the mother of our subject, was the very type of a Hindu mother. The higher the caste, the greater the restrictions. The lowest caste people can eat and drink anything they like. But as men rise in the social scale, more and more restrictions come; and when they reach the highest caste, the Brahmin, the hereditary priesthood of India, their lives, as I have said, are very much circumscribed. Compared to Western manners, their lives are of continuous asceticism. The Hindus are perhaps the most exclusive nation in the world. They have the same great steadiness as the English, but much more amplified. When they get hold of an idea they carry it out to its very conclusion, and they, keep hold of it generation after generation until they make something out of it. Once give them an idea, and it is not easy to take it back; but it is hard to make them grasp a new idea.

The orthodox Hindus, therefore, are very exclusive, living entirely within their own horizon of thought and feeling. Their lives are laid down in our old books in every little detail, and the least detail is grasped with almost adamantine firmness by them. They would starve rather than eat a meal cooked by the hands of a man not belonging to their own small section of caste. But withal, they have intensity and tremendous earnestness. That force of intense faith and religious life occurs often among the orthodox Hindus, because their very orthodoxy comes from a tremendous conviction that it is right. We may not all think that what they hold on to with such perseverance is right; but to them it is. Now, it is written in our books that a man should always be charitable even to the extreme. If a man starves himself to death to help another man, to save that man's life, it is all right; it is even held that a man ought to do that. And it is expected of a Brahmin to carry this idea out to the very extreme. Those who are acquainted with the literature of India will remember a beautiful old story about this extreme charity, how a whole family, as related in the Mahâbhârata, starved themselves to death and gave their last meal to a beggar. This is not an exaggeration, for such things still happen. The character of the father and the mother of my Master was very much like that. Very poor they were, and yet many a time the mother would starve herself a whole day to help a poor man. Of them this child was born; and he was a peculiar child from very boyhood. He remembered his past from his birth and was conscious for what purpose he came into the world, and every power was devoted to the fulfilment of that purpose.

While he was quite young, his father died; and the boy was sent to school. A Brahmin's boy must go to school; the caste restricts him to a learned profession only. The old system of education in India, still prevalent in many parts of the country, especially in connection with Sannyasins, is very different from the modern system. The students had not to pay. It was thought that knowledge is so sacred that no man ought to sell it. Knowledge must be given freely and without any price. The teachers used to take students without charge, and not only so, most of them gave their students food and clothes. To support these teachers the wealthy families on certain occasions, such as a marriage festival, or at the ceremonies for the dead, made gifts to them. They were considered the first and foremost claimants to certain gifts; and they in their turn had to maintain their students. So whenever there is a marriage, especially in a rich family, these professors are invited, and they attend and discuss various subjects. This boy went to one of these gatherings of professors, and the professors were discussing various topics, such as logic or astronomy, subjects much beyond his age. The boy was peculiar, as I have said, and he gathered this moral out of it: "This is the outcome of all their knowledge. Why are they fighting so hard? It is simply for money; the man who can show the highest learning here will get the best pair of cloth, and that is all these people are struggling for. I will not go to school any more." And he did not; that was the end of his going to school. But this boy had an elder brother, a learned professor, who took him to Calcutta, however, to study with him. After a short time the boy became fully convinced that the aim of all secular learning was mere material advancement, and nothing more, and he resolved to give up study and devote himself solely to the pursuit of spiritual knowledge. The father being dead, the family was very poor; and this boy had to make his own living. He went to a place near Calcutta and became a temple priest. To become a temple priest is thought very degrading to a Brahmin. Our temples are not churches in your sense of the word, they are not places for public worship; for, properly speaking, there is no such thing as public worship in India. Temples are erected mostly by rich persons as a meritorious religious act.

If a man has much property, he wants to build a temple. In that he puts a symbol or an image of an Incarnation of God, and dedicates it to worship in the name of God. The worship is akin to that which is conducted in Roman Catholic churches, very much like the mass, reading certain sentences from the sacred books, waving a light before the image, and treating the image in every respect as we treat a great man. This is all that is done in the temple. The man who goes to a temple is not considered thereby a better man than he who never goes. More properly, the latter is considered the more religious man, for religion in India is to each man his own private affair. In the house of every man there is either a little chapel, or a room set apart, and there he goes morning and evening, sits down in a corner, and there does his worship. And this worship is entirely mental, for another man does not hear or know what he is doing. He sees him only sitting there, and perhaps moving his fingers in a peculiar fashion, or closing his nostrils and breathing in a peculiar manner. Beyond that, he does not know what his brother is doing; even his wife, perhaps, will not know. Thus, all worship is conducted in the privacy of his own home. Those who cannot afford to have a chapel go to the banks of a river, or a lake, or the sea if they live at the seaside, but people sometimes go to worship in a temple by making salutation to the image. There their duty to the temple ends. Therefore, you see, it has been held from the most ancient times in our country, legislated upon by Manu, that it is a degenerating occupation to become a temple priest. Some of the books say it is so degrading as to make a Brahmin worthy of reproach. Just as with education, but in a far more intense sense with religion, there is the other idea behind it that the temple priests who take fees for their work are making merchandise of sacred things. So you may imagine the feelings of that boy when he was forced through poverty to take up the only occupation open to him, that of a temple priest.

There have been various poets in Bengal whose songs have passed down to the people; they are sung in the streets of Calcutta and in every village. Most of these are religious songs, and their one central idea, which is perhaps peculiar to the religions of India, is the idea of realisation. There is not a book in India on religion which does not breathe this idea. Man must realise God, feel God, see God, talk to God. That is religion. The Indian atmosphere is full of stories of saintly persons having visions of God. Such doctrines form the basis of their religion; and all these ancient books and scriptures are the writings of persons who came into direct contact with spiritual facts. These books were not written for the intellect, nor can any reasoning understand them, because they were written by men who saw the things of which they wrote, and they can be understood only by men who have raised themselves to the same height. They say there is such a thing as realisation even in this life, and it is open to everyone, and religion begins with the opening of this faculty, if I may call it so. This is the central idea in all religions, and this is why we may find one man with the most finished oratorical powers, or the most convincing logic, preaching the highest doctrines and yet unable to get people to listen to him, while we may find another, a poor man, who scarcely can speak the language of his own motherland, yet half the nation worships him in his own lifetime as God. When in India the idea somehow or other gets abroad that a man has raised himself to that state of realisation, that religion is no more a matter of conjecture to him, that he is no more groping in the dark in such momentous questions as religion, the immortality of the soul, and God, people come from all quarters to see him and gradually they begin to worship him.

In the temple was an image of the "Blissful Mother". This boy had to conduct the worship morning and evening, and by degrees this one idea filled his mind: "Is there anything behind this images? Is it true that there is a Mother of Bliss in the universe? Is it true that She lives and guides the universe, or is it all a dream? Is there any reality in religion?"

This scepticism comes to the Hindu child. It is the scepticism of our country: Is this that we are doing real? And theories will not satisfy us, although there are ready at hand almost all the theories that have ever been made with regard to God and soul. Neither books nor theories can satisfy us, the one idea that gets hold of thousands of our people is this idea of realisation. Is it true that there is a God? If it be true, can I see Him? Can I realise the truth? The Western mind may think all this very impracticable, but to us it is intensely practical. For this their lives. You have just heard how from the earliest times there have been persons who have given up all comforts and luxuries to live in caves, and hundreds have given up their homes to weep bitter tears of misery, on the banks of sacred rivers, in order to realise this idea — not to know in the ordinary sense of the word, not intellectual understanding, not a mere rationalistic comprehension of the real thing, not mere groping in the dark, but intense realisation, much more real than this world is to our senses. That is the idea. I do not advance any proposition as to that just now, but that is the one fact that is impressed upon them. Thousands will be killed, other thousands will be ready. So upon this one idea the whole nation for thousands of years have been denying and sacrificing themselves. For this idea thousands of Hindus every year give up their homes, and many of them die through the hardships they have to undergo. To the Western mind this must seem most visionary, and I can see the reason for this point of view. But though I have resided in the West, I still think this idea the most practical thing in life.

Every moment I think of anything else is so much loss to me — even the marvels of earthly sciences; everything is vain if it takes me away from that thought. Life is but momentary, whether you have the knowledge of an angel or the ignorance of an animal. Life is but momentary, whether you have the poverty of the poorest man in rags or the wealth of the richest living person. Life is but momentary, whether you are a downtrodden man living in one of the big streets of the big cities of the West or a crowned Emperor ruling over millions. Life is but momentary, whether you have the best of health or the worst. Life is but momentary, whether you have the most poetical temperament or the most cruel. There is but one solution of life, says the Hindu, and that solution is what they call God and religion. If these be true, life becomes explained, life becomes bearable, becomes enjoyable. Otherwise, life is but a useless burden. That is our idea, but no amount of reasoning can demonstrate it; it can only make it probable, and there it rests. The highest demonstration of reasoning that we have in any branch of knowledge can only make a fact probable, and nothing further. The most demonstrable facts of physical science are only probabilities, not facts yet. Facts are only in the senses. Facts have to be perceived, and we have to perceive religion to demonstrate it to ourselves. We have to sense God to be convinced that there is a God. We must sense the facts of religion to know that they are facts. Nothing else, and no amount of reasoning, but our own perception can make these things real to us, can make my belief firm as a rock. That is my idea, and that is the Indian idea.

This idea took possession of the boy and his whole

life became concentrated upon that. Day after day he would weep and say, "Mother, is it true that Thou existest, or is it all poetry? Is the Blissful Mother an imagination of poets and misguided people, or is there such a Reality?" We have seen that of books, of education in our sense of the word, he had none, and so much the more natural, so much the more healthy, was his mind, so much the purer his thoughts, undiluted by drinking in the thoughts of others. Because he did not go to the university, therefore he thought for himself. Because we have spent half our lives in the university we are filled with a collection of other people's thoughts. Well has Prof. Max Müller said in the article I have just referred to that this was a clean, original man; and the secret of that originality was that he was not brought up within the precincts of a university. However, this thought — whether God can be seen — which was uppermost in his mind gained in strength every day until he could think of nothing else. He could no more conduct the worship properly, could no more attend to the various details in all their minuteness. Often he would forget to place the food-offering before the image, sometimes he would forget to wave the light; at other times he would wave it for hours, and forget everything else.

And that one idea was in his mind every day: "Is it true that Thou existest, O Mother? Why cost Thou not speak? Art Thou dead?" Perhaps some of us here will remember that there are moments in our lives when, tired of all these ratiocinations of dull and dead logic, tired of plodding through books — which after all teach us nothing, become nothing but a sort of intellectual opium-eating — we must have it at stated times or we die — tired with all this, the heart of our hearts sends out a wail: "Is there no one in this universe who can show me the light? If Thou art, show the light unto me. Why dost Thou not speak? Why dost Thou make Thyself so scarce, why send so many Messengers and not Thyself come to me? In this world of fights and factions whom am I to follow and believe? If Thou art the God of every man and woman alike, why comest Thou not to speak to Thy child and see if he is not ready?" Well, to us all come such thoughts in moments of great depression; but such are the temptations surrounding us, that the next moment we forget. For the moment it seemed that the doors of the heavens were going to be opened, for the moment it seemed as if we were going to plunge into the light effulgent; but the animal man again shakes off all these angelic visions. Down we go, animal man once more eating and drinking and dying, and dying and drinking and eating again and again. But there are exceptional minds which are not turned away so easily, which once attracted can never be turned back, whatever may be the temptation in the way, which want to see the Truth knowing that life must go. They say, let it go in a noble conquest, and what conquest is nobler than the conquest of the lower man, than this solution of the problem of life and death, of good and evil?

At last it became impossible for him to serve in the temple. He left it and entered into a little wood that was near and lived there. About this part of his life, he told me many times that he could not tell when the sun rose or set, or how he lived. He lost all thought of himself and forgot to eat. During this period he was lovingly watched over by a relative who put into his mouth food which he mechanically swallowed.

Days and nights thus passed with the boy. When a whole day would pass, towards the evening when the peal of bells in the temples, and the voices singing, would reach the wood, it would make the boy very sad, and he would cry, "Another day is gone in vain, Mother, and Thou hast not come. Another day of this short life has gone, and I have not known the Truth." In the agony of his soul, sometimes he would rub his face against the ground and weep, and this one prayer burst forth: "Do Thou manifest Thyself in me, Thou Mother of the universe! See that I need Thee and nothing else!" Verily, he wanted to be true to his own ideal. He had heard that the Mother never came until everything had been given up for Her. He had heard that the Mother wanted to come to everyone, but they Could not have Her, that people wanted all sorts of foolish little idols to pray to, that they wanted their own enjoyments, and not the Mother, and that the moment they really wanted Her with their whole soul, and nothing else, that moment She would come. So he began to break himself into that idea; he wanted to be exact, even on the plane of matter. He threw away all the little property he had, and took a vow that he would never touch money, and this one idea, "I will not touch money", became a part of him. It may appear to be something occult, but even in after-life when he was sleeping, if I touched him with a piece of money his hand would become bent, and his whole body would become, as it were, paralysed. The other idea that came into his mind was that lust was the other enemy. Man is a soul, and soul is sexless, neither man nor woman. The idea of sex and the idea of money were the two things, he thought, that prevented him from seeing the Mother. This whole universe is the manifestation of the Mother, and She lives in every woman's body. "Every woman represents the Mother; how can I think of woman in mere sex relation?" That was the idea: Every woman was his Mother, he must bring himself to the state when he would see nothing but Mother in every woman. And he carried it out in his life.

This is the tremendous thirst that seizes the human heart. Later on, this very man said to me, "My child, suppose there is a bag of gold in one room, and a robber in the next room; do you think that the robber can sleep? He cannot. His mind will be always thinking how to get into that room and obtain possession of that gold. Do you think then that a man, firmly persuaded that there is a Reality behind all these appearances, that there is a God, that there is One who never dies, One who is infinite bliss, a bliss compared with which these pleasures of the senses are simply playthings, can rest contented without struggling to attain It? Can he cease his efforts for a moment? No. He will become mad with longing." This divine madness seized the boy. At that time he had no teacher, nobody to tell him anything, and everyone thought that he was out of his mind. This is the ordinary condition of things. If a man throws aside the vanities of the world, we hear him called mad. But such men are the salt of the earth. Out of such madness have come the powers that have moved this world of ours, and out of such madness alone will come the powers of the future that are going to move the world.

So days, weeks, months passed in continuous struggle of the soul to arrive at truth. The boy began to see visions, to see wonderful things; the secrets of his nature were beginning to open to him. Veil after veil was, as it were, being taken off. Mother Herself became the teacher and initiated the boy into the truths he sought. At this time there came to this place a woman of beautiful appearance, learned beyond compare. Later on, this saint used to say about her that she was not learned, but was the embodiment of learning; she was learning itself, in human form. There, too, you find the peculiarity of the Indian nation. In the midst of the ignorance in which the average Hindu woman lives, in the midst of what is called in Western countries her lack of freedom, there could arise a woman of supreme spirituality. She was a Sannyâsini; for women also give up the world, throw away their property, do not marry, and devote themselves to the worship of the Lord. She came; and when she heard of this boy in the grove, she offered to go and see him; and hers was the first help he received. At once she recognised what his trouble was, and she said to him. "My son blessed is the man upon whom such madness comes. The whole of this universe is mad — some for wealth, some for pleasure, some for fame, some for a hundred other things. They are mad for gold, or husbands, or wives, for little trifles, mad to tyrannise over somebody, mad to become rich, mad for every foolish thing except God. And they can understand only their own madness. When another man is mad after gold, they have fellow-feeling and sympathy for him, and they say he is the right man, as lunatics think that lunatics alone are sane. But if a man is mad after the Beloved, after the Lord, how can they understand? They think he has gone crazy; and they say, 'Have nothing to do with him.' That is why they call you mad; but yours is the right kind of madness. Blessed is the man who is mad after God. Such men are very few." This woman remained near the boy for years, taught him the forms of the religions of India, initiated him into the different practices of Yoga, and, as it were, guided and brought into harmony this tremendous river of spirituality.

Later, there came to the same grove a Sannyasin, one of the begging friars of India, a learned man, a philosopher. He was a peculiar man, he was an idealist. He did not believe that this world existed in reality; and to demonstrate that, he would never go under a roof, he would always live out of doors, in storm and sunshine alike. This man began to teach the boy the philosophy of the Vedas; and he found very soon, to his astonishment, that the pupil was in some respects wiser than the master. He spent several months with the boy, after which he initiated him into the order of Sannyasins, and took his departure.

When as a temple priest his extraordinary worship made people think him deranged in his head, his relatives took him home and married him to a little girl, thinking that that would turn his thoughts and restore the balance of his mind. But he came back and, as we have seen, merged deeper in his madness. Sometimes, in our country, boys are married as children and have no voice in the matter; their parents marry them. Of course such a marriage is little more than a betrothal. When they are married they still continue to live with their parents, and the real marriage takes place when the wife grows older, Then it is customary for the husband to go and bring his bride to his own home. In this case, however, the husband had entirely forgotten that he had a wife. In her far off home the girl had heard that her husband had become a religious enthusiast, and that he was even considered insane by many. She resolved to learn the truth for herself, so she set out and walked to the place where her husband was. When at last she stood in her husband's presence, he at once admitted her right to his life, although in India any person, man or woman, who embraces a religious life, is thereby freed from all other obligations. The young man fell at the feet of his wife and said, "As for me, the Mother has shown me that She resides in every woman, and so I have learnt to look upon every woman as Mother. That is the one idea I can have about you; but if you wish to drag me into the world, as I have been married to you, I am at your service."

The maiden was a pure and noble soul and was able to understand her husband's aspirations and sympathise with them. She quickly told him that she had no wish to drag him down to a life of worldliness; but that all she desired was to remain near him, to serve him, and to learn of him. She became one of his most devoted disciples, always revering him as a divine being. Thus through his wife's consent the last barrier was removed, and he was free to lead the life he had chosen.

The next desire that seized upon the soul of this man as to know the truth about the various religions. Up to that time he had not known any religion but his own. He wanted to understand what other religions were like. So he sought teachers of other religions. By teachers you must always remember what we mean in India, not a bookworm, but a man of realisation, one who knows truth a; first hand and not through an intermediary. He found a Mohammedan saint and placed himself under him; he underwent the disciplines prescribed by him, and to his astonishment found that when faithfully carried out, these devotional methods led him to the same goal he had already attained. He gathered similar experience from following the true religion of Jesus the Christ. He went to all the sects he could find, and whatever he took up he went into with his whole heart. He did exactly as he was told, and in every instance he arrived at the same result. Thus from actual experience, he came to know that the goal of every religion is the same, that each is trying to teach the same thing, the difference being largely in method and still more in language. At the core, all sects and all religions have the same aim; and they were only quarrelling for their own selfish purposes — they were not anxious about the truth, but about "my name" and "your name". Two of them preached the same truth, but one of them said, "That cannot be true, because I have not put upon it the seal of my name. Therefore do not listen to him." And the other man said, "Do not hear him, although he is preaching very much the same thing, yet it is not true because he does not preach it in my name."

That is what my Master found, and he then set

about to learn humility, because he had found that the one idea in all religions is, "not me, but Thou", and he who says, "not me", the Lord fills his heart. The less of this little "I" the more of God there is in him. That he found to be the truth in every religion in the world, and he set himself to accomplish this. As I have told you, whenever he wanted to do anything he never confined himself to fine theories, but would enter into the practice immediately; We see many persons talking the most wonderfully fine things about charity and about equality and the rights of other people and all that, but it is only in theory. I was so fortunate as to find one who was able to carry theory into practice. He had the most wonderful faculty of carrying everything into practice which he thought was right.

Now, there was a family of Pariahs living near the place. The Pariahs number several millions in the whole of India and are a sect of people so low that some of our books say that if a Brahmin coming out from his house sees the face of a Pariah, he has to fast that day and recite certain prayers before he becomes holy again. In some Hindu cities when a Pariah enters, he has to put a crow's feather on his head as a sign that he is a Pariah, and he has to cry aloud, "Save yourselves, the Pariah is passing through the street", and you will find people flying off from him as if by magic, because if they touch him by chance, they will have to change their clothes, bathe, and do other things. And the Pariah for thousands of years has believed that it is perfectly right; that his touch will make everybody unholy. Now my Master would go to a Pariah and ask to be allowed to clean his house. The business of the Pariah is to clean the streets of the cities and to keep houses clean. He cannot enter the house by the front door; by the back door he enters; and as soon as he has gone, the whole place over which he has passed is sprinkled with and made holy by a little Gangâ water. By birth the Brahmin stands for holiness, and the Pariah for the very reverse. And this Brahmin asked to be allowed to do the menial services in the house of the Pariah. The Pariah of course could not allow that, for they all think that if they allow a Brahmin to do such menial work it will be an awful sin, and they will become extinct. The Pariah would not permit it; so in the dead of night, when all were sleeping, Ramakrishna would enter the house. He had long hair, and with his hair he would wipe the place, saying, "Oh, my Mother, make me the servant of the Pariah, make me feel that I am even lower than the Pariah." "They worship Me best who worship My worshippers. These are all My children and your privilege is to serve them" — is the teaching of Hindu scriptures.

There were various other preparations which would take a long time to relate, and I want to give you just a sketch of his life. For years he thus educated himself. One of the Sâdhanâs was to root out the sex idea. Soul has no sex, it is neither male nor female. It is only in the body that sex exists, and the man who desires to reach the spirit cannot at the same time hold to sex distinctions. Having been born in a masculine body, this man wanted to bring the feminine idea into everything. He began to think that he was a woman, he dressed like a woman, spoke like a woman, gave up the occupations of men, and lived in the household among the women of a good family, until, after years of this discipline, his mind became changed, and he entirely forgot the idea of sex; thus the whole view of life became changed to him.

We hear in the West about worshipping woman, but this is usually for her youth and beauty. This man meant by worshipping woman, that to him every woman's face was that of the Blissful Mother, and nothing but that. I myself have seen this man standing before those women whom society would not touch, and falling at their feet bathed in tears, saying, "Mother, in one form Thou art in the street, and in another form Thou art the universe. I salute Thee, Mother, I salute Thee." Think of the blessedness of that life from which all carnality has vanished, which can look upon every woman with that love and reverence when every woman's face becomes transfigured, and only the face of the Divine Mother, the Blissful One, the Protectress of the human race, shines upon it! That is what we want. Do you mean to say that the divinity back of a woman can ever be cheated? It never was and never will be,

It always asserts itself. Unfailingly it detects fraud, it detects hypocrisy, unerringly it feels the warmth of truth, the light of spirituality, the holiness of purity. Such purity is absolutely necessary if real spirituality is to be attained.

This rigorous, unsullied purity came into the life of that man. All the struggles which we have in our lives were past for him. His hard-earned jewels of spirituality, for which he had given three-quarters of his life, were now ready to be given to humanity, and then began his mission. His teaching and preaching were peculiar. In our country a teacher is a most highly venerated person, he is regarded as God Himself. We have not even the same respect for our father and mother. Father and mother give us our body, but the teacher shows us the way to salvation. We are his children, we are born in the spiritual line of the teacher. All Hindus come to pay respect to an extraordinary teacher, they crowd around him. And here was such a teacher, but the teacher had no thought whether he was to be respected or not, he had not the least idea that he was a great teacher, he thought that it was Mother who was doing everything and not he. He always said, "If any good comes from my lips, it is the Mother who speaks; what have I to do with it?" That was his one idea about his work, and to the day of his death he never gave it up. This man sought no one. His principle was, first form character, first earn spirituality and results will come of themselves. His favourite illustration was, "When the lotus opens, the bees come of their own accord to seek the honey; so let the lotus of your character be full-blown, and the results will follow." This is a great lesson to learn.

My Master taught me this lesson hundreds of times, yet I often forget it. Few understand the power of thought. If a man goes into a cave, shuts himself in, and thinks one really great thought and dies, that thought will penetrate the walls of that cave, vibrate through space, and at last permeate the whole human race. Such is the power of thought; be in no hurry therefore to give your thoughts to others. First have something to give. He alone teaches who has something to give, for teaching is not talking, teaching is not imparting doctrines, it is communicating. Spirituality can be communicated just as really as I can give you a flower. This is true in the most literal sense. This idea is very old in India and finds illustration in the West in the "theory, in the belief, of apostolic succession. Therefore first make character — that is the highest duty you can perform. Know Truth for yourself, and there will be many to whom you can teach it after wards; they will all come. This was the attitude of nay Master. He criticised no one. For years I lived with that man, but never did I hear those lips utter one word of condemnation for any sect. He had the same sympathy for all sects; he had found the harmony between them. A man may be intellectual, or devotional, or mystic, or active; the various religions represent one or the other of these types. Yet it is possible to combine all the four in one man, and this is what future humanity is going to do. That was his idea. He condemned no one, but saw the good in all.

People came by thousands to see and hear this wonderful man who spoke in a patois every word of which was forceful and instinct with light. For it is not what is spoken, much less the language in which it is spoken, but it is the personality of the speaker which dwells in everything he says that carries weight. Every one of us feels this at times. We hear most splendid orations, most wonderfully reasoned-out discourses, and we go home and forget them all. At other times we hear a few words in the simplest language, and they enter into our lives, become part and parcel of ourselves and produce lasting results. The words of a man who can put his personality into them take effect, but he must have tremendous personality. All teaching implies giving and taking, the teacher gives and the taught receives, but the one must have something to give, and the other must be open to receive.

This man came to live near Calcutta, the capital of India, the most important university town in our country which was sending out sceptics and materialists by the hundreds every year. Yet many of these university men — sceptics and agnostics — used to come and listen to him. I heard of this man, and I went to hear him. He looked just like an ordinary man, with nothing remarkable about him. He used the most simple language, and I thought "Can this man be a great teacher?"— crept near to him and asked him the question which I had been asking others all my life: "Do you believe in God, Sir?" "Yes," he replied. "Can you prove it, Sir?" "Yes." "How?" "Because I see Him just as I see you here, only in a much intenser sense." That impressed me at once. For the first time I found a man who dared to say that he saw God that religion was a reality to be felt, to be sensed in an infinitely more intense way than we can sense the world. I began to go to that man, day after day, and I actually saw that religion could be given. One touch, one glance, can change a whole life. I have read about Buddha and Christ and Mohammed, about all those different luminaries of ancient times, how they would stand up and say, "Be thou whole", and the man became whole. I now found it to be true, and when I myself saw this man, all scepticism was brushed aside. It could be done; and my Master used to say, "Religion can be given and taken more tangibly, more really than anything else in the world." Be therefore spiritual first; have something to give and then stand before the world and give it. Religion is not talk, or doctrines, or theories; nor is it sectarianism. Religion cannot live in sects and societies. It is the relation between the soul and God; how can it be made into a society? It would then degenerate into business, and wherever there are business and business principles in religion, spirituality dies. Religion does not consist in erecting temples, or building churches, or attending public worship. It is not to be found in books, or in words, or in lectures, or in organisations. Religion consists in realisation. As a fact, we all know that nothing will satisfy us until we know the truth for ourselves. However we may argue, however much we may hear, but one thing will satisfy us, and that is our own realisation; and such an experience is possible for every one of us if we will only try. The first ideal of this attempt to realise religion is that of renunciation. As far as we can, we must give up. Darkness and light, enjoyment of the world and enjoyment of God will never go together. "Ye cannot serve God and Mammon." Let people try it if they will, and I have seen millions in every country who have tried; but after all, it comes to nothing. If one word remains true in the saying, it is, give up every thing for the sake of the Lord. This is a hard and long task, but you can begin it here and now. Bit by bit we must go towards it.

The second idea that I learnt from my Master, and which is perhaps the most vital, is the wonderful truth that the religions of the world are not contradictory or antagonistic. They are but various phases of one eternal religion. That one eternal religion is applied to different planes of existence, is applied to the opinions of various minds and various races. There never was my religion or yours, my national religion or your national religion; there never existed many religions, there is only the one. One infinite religion existed all through eternity and will ever exist, and this religion is expressing itself in various countries in various ways. Therefore we must respect all religions and we must try to accept them all as far as we can. Religions manifest themselves not only according to race and geographical position, but according to individual powers. In one man religion is manifesting itself as intense activity, as work. In another it is manifesting itself as intense devotion, in yet another, as mysticism, in others as philosophy, and so forth. It is wrong when we say to others, "Your methods are not right." Perhaps a man, whose nature is that of love, thinks that the man who does good to others is not on the right road to religion, because it is not his own way, and is therefore wrong. If the philosopher thinks, "Oh, the poor ignorant people, what do they know about a God of Love, and loving Him? They do not know what they mean," he is wrong, because they may be right and he also.

To learn this central secret that the truth may be one and yet many at the same time, that we may have different visions of the same truth from different standpoints, is exactly what must be done. Then, instead of antagonism to anyone, we shall have infinite sympathy with all. Knowing that as long as there are different natures born in this world, the same religious truth will require different adaptations, we shall understand that we are bound to have forbearance with each other. Just as nature is unity in variety — an infinite variation in the phenomenal — as in and through all these variations of the phenomenal runs the Infinite, the Unchangeable, the Absolute Unity, so it is with every man; the microcosm is but a miniature repetition of the macrocosm; in spite of all these variations, in and through them all runs this eternal harmony, and we have to recognise this. This idea, above all other ideas, I find to be the crying necessity of the day. Coming from a country which is a hotbed of religious sects — and to which, through its good fortune or ill fortune, everyone who has a religious idea wants to send an advance-guard — I have been acquainted from my childhood with the various sects of the world. Even the Mormons come to preach in India. Welcome them all! That is the soil on which to preach religion. There it takes root more than in any other country. If you come and teach politics to the Hindus, they do not understand; but if you come to preach religion, however curious it may be, you will have hundreds and thousands of followers in no time, and you have every chance of becoming a living God in your lifetime. I am glad it is so, it is the one thing we want in India.

The sects among the Hindus are various, a great many in number, and some of them apparently hopelessly contradictory. Yet they all tell you they are but different manifestations of religion. "As different rivers, taking their start from different mountains, running crooked or straight, all come and mingle their waters in the ocean, so the different sects, with their different points of vied, at last all come unto Thee." This is not a theory, it has to be recognised, but not in that patronising way which we see with some people: "Oh yes, there are some very good things in it. These are what we call the ethnical religions. These ethnical religions have some good in them." Some even have the most wonderfully liberal idea that other religions are all little bits of a prehistoric evolution, but "ours is the fulfilment of things". One man says, because his is the oldest religion, it is the best: another makes the same claim, because his is the latest.

We have to recognise that each one of them has the same saving power as the other. What you have heard about their difference, whether in the temple or in the church, is a mass of superstition. The same God answers all; and it is not you, or I, or any body of men that is responsible for the safety and salvation of the least little bit of the soul; the same Almighty God is responsible for all. I do not understand how people declare themselves to be believers in God, and at the same time think that God has handed over to a little body of men all truth, and that they are the guardians of the rest of humanity. How can you call that religion? Religion is realisation; but mere talk — mere trying to believe, mere groping in darkness, mere parroting the words of ancestors and thinking it is religion, mere making a political something out of the truths of religion — is not religion at all. In every sect — even among the Mohammedans whom we always regard as the most exclusive — even among them we find that wherever there was a man trying to realise religion, from his lips have come the fiery words: "Thou art the Lord of all, Thou art in the heart of all, Thou art the guide of all, Thou art the Teacher of all, and Thou caress infinitely more for the land of Thy children than we can ever do." Do not try to disturb the faith of any man. If you can, give him something better; if you can, get hold of a man where he stands and give him a push upwards; do so, but do not destroy what he has. The only true teacher is he who can convert himself, as it were, into a thousand persons at a moment's notice. The only true teacher is he who can immediately come down to the level of the student, and transfer his soul to the student's soul and see through the student's eyes and hear through his ears and understand through his mind. Such a teacher can really teach and none else. All these negative, breaking-down, destructive teachers that are in the world can never do any good.

In the presence of my Master I found out that man could be perfect, even in this body. Those lips never cursed anyone, never even criticised anyone. Those eyes were beyond the possibility of seeing evil, that mind had lost the power of thinking evil. He saw nothing but good. That tremendous purity, that tremendous renunciation is the one secret of spirituality. "Neither through wealth, nor through progeny, but through renunciation alone, is immortality to be reached", say the Vedas. "Sell all that thou hast and give to the poor, and follow me", says the Christ. So all great saints and Prophets have expressed it, and have carried it out in their lives. How can great spirituality come without that renunciation? Renunciation is the background of all religious thought wherever it be, and you will always find that as this idea of renunciation lessens, the more will the senses creep into the field of religion, and spirituality will decrease in the same ratio.

That man was the embodiment of renunciation. In our country it is necessary for a man who becomes a Sannyasin to give up all worldly wealth and position, and this my Master carried out literally. There were many who would have felt themselves blest if he would only have accepted a present from their hands, who would gladly have given him thousands of rupees if he would have taken them, but these were the only men from whom he would turn away. He was a triumphant example, a living realisation of the complete conquest of lust and of desire for money. He was beyond all ideas of either, and such men are necessary for this century. Such renunciation is necessary in these days when men have begun to think that they cannot live a month without what they call their "necessities", and which they are increasing out of all proportion. It is necessary in a time like this that a man should arise to demonstrate to the sceptics of the world that there yet breathes a man who does not care a straw for all the gold or all the fame that is in the universe. Yet there are such men.

The other idea of his life was intense love for others. The first part of my Master's life was spent in acquiring spirituality, and the remaining years in distributing it. People in our country have not the same customs as you have in visiting a religious teacher or a Sannyasin. Somebody would come to ask him about something, some perhaps would come hundreds of miles, walking all the way, just to ask one question, to hear one word from him, "Tell me one word for my salvation." That is the way they come. They come in numbers, unceremoniously, to the place where he is mostly to be found; they may find him under a tree and question him; and before one set of people has gone, others have arrived. So if a man is greatly revered, he will sometimes have no rest day or night. He will have to talk constantly. For hours people will come pouring in, and this man will be teaching them.

So men came in crowds to hear him, and he would talk twenty hours in the twenty-four, and that not for one day, but for months and months until at last the body broke down under the pressure of this tremendous strain. His intense love for mankind would not let him refuse to help even the humblest of the thousands who sought his aid. Gradually, there developed a vital throat disorder and yet he could not be persuaded to refrain from these exertions. As soon as he heard that people were asking to see him, he would insist upon having them admitted and would answer all their questions. When expostulated with, he replied, "I do not care. I will give up twenty thousand such bodies to help one man. It is glorious to help even one man." There was no rest for him. Once a man asked him, "Sir, you are a great Yogi. Why do you not put your mind a little on your body and cure your disease? "At first he did not answer, but when the question had been repeated, he gently said, "My friend, I thought you were a sage, but you talk like other men of the world. This mind has been given to the Lord. Do you mean to say that I should take it back and put it upon the body which is but a mere cage of the soul?"

So he went on preaching to the people, and the news spread that his body was about to pass away, and the people began to flock to him in greater crowds than ever. You cannot imagine the way they come to these great religious teachers in India, how they crowd round them and make gods of them while they are yet living. Thousands wait simply to touch the hem of their garments. It is through this appreciation of spirituality in others that spirituality is produced. Whatever man wants and appreciates, he will get; and it is the same with nations. If you go to India and deliver a political lecture, however grand it may be, you will scarcely find people to listen to you but just go and teach religion, live it, not merely talk it, and hundreds will crowd just to look at you, to touch your feet. When the people heard that this holy man was likely to go from them soon, they began to come round him more than ever, and my Master went on teaching them without the least regard for his health. We could not prevent this. Many of the people came from long distances, and he would not rest until he had answered their questions. "While I can speak, I must teach them," he would say, and he was as good as his word. One day, he told us that he would lay down the body that day, and repeating the most sacred word of the Vedas he entered into Samâdhi and passed away.

His thoughts and his message were known to very few capable of giving them out. Among others, he left a few young boys who had renounced the world, and were ready to carry on his work. Attempts were made to crush them. But they stood firm, having the inspiration of that great life before them. Having had the contact of that blessed life for years, they stood their ground. These young men, living as Sannyasins, begged through the streets of the city where they were born, although some of them came from high families. At first they met with great antagonism, but they persevered and went on from day to day spreading all over India the message of that great man, until the whole country was filled with the ideas he had preached. This man, from a remote village of Bengal, without education, by the sheer force of his own determination, realised the truth and gave it to others, leaving only a few young boys to keep it alive.

Today the name of Shri Ramakrishna Paramahamsa is known all over India to its millions of people. Nay, the power of that man has spread beyond India; and if there has ever been a word of truth, a word of spirituality, that I have spoken anywhere in the world, I owe it to my Master; only the mistakes are mine.

This is the message of Shri Ramakrishna to the modern world: "Do not care for doctrines, do not care for dogmas, or sects, or churches, or temples; they count for little compared with the essence of existence in each man which is spirituality; and the more this is developed in a man, the more powerful is he for good. Earn that first, acquire that, and criticise no one, for all doctrines and creeds have some good in them. Show by your lives that religion does not mean words, or names, or sects, but that it means spiritual realisation. Only those can understand who have felt. Only those who have attained to spirituality can communicate it to others, can be great teachers of mankind. They alone are the powers of light."

The more such men are produced in a country, the more that country will be raised; and that country where such men absolutely do not exist is simply doomed nothing can save it. Therefore my Master's message to mankind is: "Be spiritual and realise truth for Yourself." He would have you give up for the sake of your fellow-beings. He would have you cease talking about love for your brother, and set to work to prove your words. The time has come for renunciation, for realisation, and then you will see the harmony in all the religions of the world. You will know that there is no need of any quarrel. And then only will you be ready to help humanity. To proclaim and make clear the fundamental unity underlying all religions was the mission of my Master. Other teachers have taught special religions which bear their names, but this great teacher of the nineteenth century made no claim for himself. He left every religion undisturbed because he had realised that in reality they are all part and parcel of the one eternal religion.

INDIAN RELIGIOUS THOUGHT

Delivered under the auspices of tile Brooklyn Ethical Society, in the Art Gallery of tile Pouch Mansion, Clinton Avenue, Brooklyn, U.S.A.

India, although only half the size of the United States, contains a population of over two hundred and ninety millions, and there are three religions which hold sway over them — the Mohammedan, the Buddhist [1], and the Hindu. The adherents of the first mentioned number about sixty millions, of the second about nine millions, while the last embrace nearly two hundred and six millions. The cardinal features of the Hindu religion are founded on the meditative and speculative philosophy and on the ethical teachings contained in the various books of the Vedas, which assert that the universe is infinite in space and eternal in duration. It never had a beginning, and it never will have an end. Innumerable have been the manifestations of the power of the spirit in the realm of matter, of the force of the Infinite in the domain of the finite; but the Infinite Spirit Itself is self-existent, eternal, and unchangeable. The passage of time makes no mark whatever on the dial of eternity. In its supersensuous region which cannot be comprehended at all by the human understanding, there is no past, and there is no future. The Vedas teach that the soul of man is immortal. The body is subject to the law of growth and decay, what grows must of necessity decay. But the in dwelling spirit is related to the infinite and eternal life; it never had a beginning and it never will have an end, One of the chief distinctions between the Hindu and the (Christian religions is that the Christian religion teaches that each human soul had its beginning at its birth into this world, whereas the Hindu religion asserts that the spirit of man is an emanation of the Eternal Being, and had no more a beginning than God Himself. Innumerable have been and will be its manifestations in its passage from one personality to another, subject to the great law of spiritual evolution, until it reaches perfection, when there is no more change.

It has been often asked: If this be so, why is it we do not remember anything of our past lives? This is our explanation: Consciousness is the name of the surface only of the mental ocean, but within its depths are stored up all our experiences, both pleasant and painful. The desire of the human soul is to find out something that is stable. The mind and the body, in fact all the various phenomena of nature, are in a condition of incessant change. But the highest aspiration of our spirit is to find out something that does not change, that has reached a state of permanent perfection. And this is the aspiration of the human soul after the Infinite! The finer our moral and intellectual development, the stronger will become this aspiration after the Eternal that changes not.

The modern Buddhists teach that everything that cannot be known by the five senses is non-existent, and that it is a delusion to suppose that man is an independent entity. The idealists, on the contrary, claim that each individual is an independent entity, and the external world does not exist outside of his mental conception. But the sure solution of this problem is that nature is a mixture of independence and dependence, of reality and idealism. Our mind and bodies are dependent on the external world, and this dependence varies according to the nature of their relation to it; but the indwelling spirit is free, as God is free, and is able to direct in a greater or lesser degree, according to the state of their development, the movements of our minds and bodies.

Death is but a change of condition. We remain in the same universe, and are subject to the same laws as before. Those who have passed beyond and have attained high planes of development in beauty and wisdom are but the advance-guard of a universal army who are following after them. The spirit of the highest is related to the spirit of the lowest, and the germ of infinite perfection exists in all. We should cultivate the optimistic temperament, and endeavour to see the good that dwells in everything. If we sit down and lament over the imperfection of our bodies and minds, we profit nothing; it is the heroic endeavour to subdue adverse circumstances that carries our spirit upwards. The object of life is to learn the laws of spiritual progress. Christians can learn from Hindus, and Hindus can learn from Christians. Each has made a contribution of value to the wisdom of the world.

Impress upon your children that true religion is positive and not negative, that it does not consist in merely refraining from evil, but in a persistent performance of noble decals. True religion comes not front the teaching of men or the reading of books; it is the awakening of the spirit within us, consequent upon pure and heroic action. Every child born into the world brings with it a certain accumulated experience from previous incarnations; and the impress of this experience is seen in the structure of its mind and body. But the feeling of independence which possesses us all shows there is something in us besides mind and body. The soul that reigns within is independent stud creates the desire for freedom. If we are not free, how can we hope to make the world better? We hold that human progress is the result of the action of the human spirit. What the world is, and what we ourselves are, are the fruits of the freedom of the spirit.

We believe in one God, the Father of us all, who is omnipresent and omnipotent, and who guides and preserves His children with infinite love. We believe in a Personal God as the Christians do, but we go further: we below that we are He! That His personality is manifested in us, that God is in us, and that we are in God We believe there is a germ of truth in all religions, and the Hindu bows down to them all; for in this world, truth is to be found not in subtraction but in addition. We would offer God a bouquet of the most beautiful flowers of all the diverse faiths. We must love God for love's sake, not for the hope of reward. We must do our duty for duty's sake not for the hope of reward. We must worship the beautiful for beauty's sake, not for the hope of reward. Thus in the purity of our hearts shall we see God. Sacrifices genuflexions, mumblings, and mutterings are not religion. They are only good if they stimulate us to the brave performance of beautiful and heroic deeds and lift our thoughts to the apprehension of the divine perfection

What good is it, if we acknowledge in our prayers that God is the Father of us all, and in our daily lives do not treat every man as our brother? Books are only made so that they may point the way to a higher life; but no good results unless the path is trodden with unflinching steps! Every human personality may be compared to a glass globe. There is the same pure white light — an emission of the divine Being — in the centre of each, but the glass being of different colours and thickness, the rays assume diverse aspects in the transmission. The equality and beauty of each central flame is the same, and the apparent inequality is only in the imperfection of the temporal instrument of its expression. As we rise higher and higher in the scale of being, the medium becomes more and more translucent.

THE BASIS FOR PSYCHIC OR SPIRITUAL RESEARCH

It was not often that Swami Vivekananda, while in the West, took part in debates. One such occasion in London when he did so was during the discussion of a lecture on, "Can Psychic Phenomena be proved from a Scientific Basis?" Referring first to a remark which he had heard in the course of this debate, not for the first time in the West, he said:

One point I want to remark upon. It is a mistaken statement that has been made to us that the Mohammedans do not believe that women have souls. I am very sorry to say it is an old mistake among Christian people, and they seem to like the mistake. That is a peculiarity in human nature, that people want to say something very bad about others whom they do not like. By the by, you know I am not a Mohammedan, but yet I have had opportunity for studying this religion, and there is not one word in the Koran which says that women have no souls, but in fact it says they have.

About the psychical things that have been the subject of discussion, I have very little to say here, for in the first place, the question is whether psychical subjects are capable of scientific demonstration. What do you mean by this demonstration? First of all, there will be the subjective and the objective side necessary. Taking chemistry and physics, with which we are so familiar, and of which we have read so much, is it true that everyone in this world is able to understand the demonstration even of the commonest subjects? Take any boor and show him one of your experiments. What will he understand of it? Nothing. It requires a good deal of previous training to be brought up to the point of understanding an experiment. Before that he cannot understand it at all. That is a area difficulty in the way. If scientific demonstration mean bringing down certain facts to a plane which is universe for all human beings, where all beings can understand it I deny that there can be any such scientific demonstration for any subject in the world. If it were so, all our universities and education would be in vain. Why are we educated if by birth we can understand everything scientific? Why so much study? It is of no use whatsoever. So, on the face of it, it is absurd if this be the meaning of scientific demonstration, the bringing down of intricate facts to the plane on which we are now. The next meaning should be the correct one, perhaps, that certain facts should be adduced as proving certain more intricate facts. There are certain more complicated intricate phenomena, which we explain by less intricate ones, and thus get, perhaps, nearer to them; in this way they are gradually brought down to the plane of our present ordinary consciousness. But even this is very complicated and very difficult, and means a training also, a tremendous amount of education. So an I have to say is that in order to have scientific explanation of psychical phenomena, we require not only perfect evidence on the side of the phenomena themselves, but a good deal of training on the part of those who want to see. All this being granted, we shall be in a position to say yea or nay, about the proof or disproof of any phenomena which are presented before us. But, before that, the most remarkable phenomena or the most oft-recorded phenomena that have happened in human society, in my opinion, would be very hard indeed to prove even in an offhand manner.

Next, as to those hasty explanations that religions are the outcome of dreams, those who have made a particular study of them would think of them but as mere guesses. We no reason to suppose that religions were the outcome of dreams as has been so easily explained. Then it would be very easy indeed to take even the agnostic's position, but unfortunately the matter cannot be explained so easily. There are many other wonderful phenomena happening, even at the present time, and these have all to be investigated, and not only have to be, but have been investigated all along. The blind man says there is no sun. That does not prove that there is no sun. These phenomena have been investigated years before. Whole races of mankind have trained themselves for centuries to become fit instruments for discovering the fine workings of the nerves; their records have been published ages ago, colleges have been created to study these subjects, and men and women there are still who are living demonstrations of these phenomena. Of course I admit that there is a good deal of hoax in the whole thing, a good deal of what is wrong and untrue in these things; but with what is this not the case? Take any common scientific phenomenon; there are two or three facts which either scientists or ordinary men may regard as absolute truths, and the rest as mere frothy suppositions. Now let the agnostic apply the same test to his own science which he would apply to what he does not want to believe. Half of it would be shaken to its foundation at once. We are bound to live on suppositions. We cannot live satisfied where we are; that is the natural growth of the human soul. We cannot become agnostics on this side and at the same time go about seeking for anything here; we have to pick. And, for this reason, we have to get beyond our limits, struggle to know what seems to be unknowable; and this struggle must continue.

In my opinion, therefore, I go really one step further than the lecturer, and advance the opinion that most of the psychical phenomena — not only little things like spirit-rappings or table-rappings which are mere child's play, not merely little things like telepathy which I have seen boys do even — most of the psychical phenomenal which the last speaker calls the higher clairvoyance, but which I would rather beg to call the experiences of the superconscious state of the mind, are the very stepping-stones to real psychological investigation. The first thing to be; seen is whether the mind can attain to that state or not. My explanation would, of course, be a little different from his, but we should probably agree when we explain terms. Not much depends on the question whether this present consciousness continues after death or not, seeing that this universe, as it is now, is not bound to this state of consciousness. Consciousness is not co-existent with existence. In my own body, and in all of our bodies, we must all admit that we are conscious of very little of the body, and of the greater part of it we are unconscious. Yet it exists. Nobody is ever conscious of his brain, for example. I never saw my brain, and I am never conscious of it. Yet I know that it exists. Therefore we may say that it is not consciousness that we want, but the existence of something which is not this gross matter; and that that knowledge can be gained even in this life, and that that knowledge has been gained and demonstrated, as far as any science has been demonstrated, is a fact. We have to look into these things, and I would insist on reminding those who are here present on one other point. It is well to remember that very many times we are deluded on this. Certain people place before us the demonstration of a fact which is not ordinary to the spiritual nature, and we reject that fact because we say we cannot find it to be true. In many cases the fact may not be correct. But in many cases also we forget to consider whether we are fit to receive the demonstration or not, whether we have permitted our bodies and our minds to become fit subjects for their discovery.

ON ART IN INDIA

"Arts and Sciences in India" was the topic under which the Swami Vivekananda was introduced to the audience at Wendte Hall, San Francisco. The Swami held the attention of his hearers throughout as was demonstrated by the many questions which were put to him after his address.

The Swami said in part:

In the history of nations, the government at the beginning has always been in the hands of the priests. All the learning also has proceeded from the priests. Then, after the priests, the government changes hands, and the Kshatriya or the kingly power prevails, and the military rule is triumphant. This has always been true. And last comes the grasp of luxury, and the people sink down under it to be dominated by stronger and more barbarous races.

Amongst all races of the world, from the earliest time in history, India has been called the land of wisdom. For ages India itself has never gone out to conquer other nations. Its people have never been fighters. Unlike your Western people, they do not eat meat, for meat makes fighters; the blood of animals makes you restless, and you desire to do something.

Compare India and England in the Elizabethan period. What a dark age it was for your people, and how enlightened we were even then. The Anglo-Saxon people have always been badly fitted for art. They have good poetry — for instance, how wonderful is the blank verse of Shakespeare! Merely the rhyming of words is not good. It is not the most civilised thing in the world.

In India, music was developed to the full seven notes, even to half and quarter notes, ages ago. India led in music, also in drama and sculpture. Whatever is done now is merely an attempt at imitation. Everything now in India hinges on the question of how little a man requires to live upon.

IS INDIA A BENIGHTED COUNTRY?

The following is a report of a lecture at Detroit, United States, America, with the editorial comments of the Boston Evening Transcript, 5th April, 1894:

Swami Vivekananda has been in Detroit recently and made a proofed impression there. All classes flocked to hear him, and professional men in particular were greatly interested in his logic and his soundness of thought. The opera-house alone was large enough for his audience. He speaks English extremely well, and he is as handsome as he is good. The Detroit newspapers have devoted much space to the reports of his lectures. An editorial in the Detroit Evening News says: Most people will be inclined to think that Swami Vivekananda did better last night in his opera-house lecture than he did in any of his former lectures in this city. The merit of the Hindu's utterances last night lay in their clearness. He drew a very sharp line of distinction between Christianity and Christianity, and told his audience plainly wherein he himself is a Christian in one sense and not a Christian in another sense. He also drew a sharp line between Hinduism and Hinduism, carrying the implication that he desired to be classed as a Hindu only in its better sense. Swami Vivekananda stands superior to all criticism when he says, "We want missionaries of Christ. Let such come to India by the hundreds and thousands. Bring Christ's life to us and let it permeate the very core of society. Let him be preached in every village and corner of India."

When a man is as sound as that on the main question, all else that he may say must refer to the subordinate details. There is infinite humiliation in this spectacle of a pagan priest reading lessons of conduct and of life to the men who have assumed the spiritual supervision of Greenland's icy mountains and India's coral strand; but the sense of humiliation is the sine qua non of most reforms in this world. Having said what he did of the glorious life of the author of the Christian faith, Vivekananda has the right to lecture the way he has the men who profess to represent that life among the nations abroad. And after all, how like the Nazarene that sounds: "Provide neither gold nor silver, nor brass in your purses, nor scrip for your journey, neither two coats, neither shoes, nor yet staves; for the workman is worthy of his meat." Those who have become at all familiar with the religious, literature of India before the advent of Vivekananda are best prepared to understand the utter abhorrence of the Orientals of our Western commercial spirit — or what Vivekananda calls, "the shopkeeper's spirit" — in all that we do even in our very religion.

Here is a point for the missionaries which they cannot afford to ignore. They who would convert the Eastern world of paganism must live up to what they preach, in contempt for the kingdoms of this world and all the glory of them.

Brother Vivekananda considers India the most moral nation in the world. Though in bondage, its spirituality still endures. Here are extracts from the notices of some of his recent Detroit addresses: At this point the lecturer struck the great moral keynote of his discourse stating that with his people it was the belief that all non-self is good and all self is bad. This point was emphasised throughout the evening and might be termed the text of the address. "To build a home is selfish, argues the Hindu, so he builds it for the worship of God and for the entertainment of guests. To cook food is selfish, so he cooks it for the poor; he will serve himself last if any hungry stranger applies; and this feeling extends throughout the length and breadth of the land. Any man can ask for food and shelter and any house will be opened to him.

"The caste system has nothing to do with religion. A man's occupation is hereditary — a carpenter is born a carpenter: a goldsmith, a goldsmith; a workman, a workman: and a priest, a priest.

"Two gifts are especially appreciated, the gift of learning and the gift of life. But the gift of learning takes precedence. One may save a man's life, and that is excellent; one may impart to another knowledge, and that is better. To instruct for money is an evil, and to do this would bring opprobrium upon the head of the man who barters learning for gold as though it were an article of trade. The Government makes gifts from time to time to the instructors, and the moral effect is better than it would be if the conditions were the same as exist in certain alleged civilised countries." The speaker had asked throughout the length and breadth of the land what was the definition of "civilization", and he had asked the question in many countries. Sometimes the reply has been, "What we are, that is civilization." He begged to differ in the definition of the word. A nation may conquer the waves, control the elements, develop the utilitarian problems of life seemingly to the utmost limits, and yet not realise that in the individual, the highest type of civilization is found in him who has learned to conquer self. This condition is found more in India than in any other country on earth, for there the material conditions are subservient to the spiritual, and the individual looks to the soul manifestations in everything that has life, studying nature to this end. Hence that gentle disposition to endure with indomitable patience the flings of what appears unkind fortune, the while there is a full consciousness of a spiritual strength and knowledge greater than that possessed by any other people. Therefore the existence of a country and people from which flows an unending stream that attracts the attention of thinkers far and near to approach and throw from their shoulders an oppressive earthly burden.

This lecture was prefaced with the statement that the speaker had been asked many questions. A number of these he preferred to answer privately, but three he had selected for reasons, which would appear, to answer from the pulpit. They were: "Do the people of India throw their children into the jaws of the crocodiles?" "Do they kill themselves beneath the wheels of Jagannâtha?" "Do they burn widows with their husbands?" The first question the lecturer treated in the same vein as an American abroad would in answering inquiries about Indians running round in the streets of New York and similar myths which are even today entertained by many persons on the Continent. The statement was too ludicrous to give a serious response to it. When asked by certain well-meaning but ignorant people why they gave only female children to the crocodiles, he could only ironically reply that probably it was because they were softer and more tender and could be more easily masticated by the inhabitants of the river in that benighted country. Regarding the Jagannatha legend, the lecturer explained the old practice of the Car-festival in the sacred city, and remarked that possibly a few pilgrims in their zeal to grasp the rope and participate in the drawing of the Car slipped and fell and were so destroyed. Some such mishaps had been exaggerated into the distorted versions from which the good people of other countries shrank with horror. Vivekananda denied that people burned widows. It was true, however, that widows had burned themselves. In the few cases where this had happened, they had been urged not to do so by holy men, Who were always opposed to suicide. Where the devoted widows insisted, stating that they desired to accompany their husbands in the transformation that had taken place, they were obliged to submit themselves to the fiery tests. That is, they thrust Her hands within the flames, and if they permitted them to be consumed, no further opposition was placed in the way of the fulfilment of their desires. But India is not the only country where women, who have loved, have followed immediately the beloved one to the realms of immortality; suicides in such cases have occurred in every land. It is an uncommon bit of fanaticism in any country — as unusual in India as elsewhere. "No," the speaker repeated, "the people do not burn women in India; nor have they ever burned witches."

This latter touch is decidedly acute by way of reflection. No analysis of the philosophy of the Hindu monk need be attempted here, except to say that it is based in general on the struggle of the soul to individually attain Infinity. One learned Hindu opened the Lowell Institute Course this year. What Mr. Mozoomdar began, might worthily be ended by Brother Vivekananda. This new visitor has by far the most interesting personality, although in the Hindu philosophy, of course, personality is not to be taken into consideration. At the Parliament of Religions they used to keep Vivekananda until the end of the programme to make people stay until the end of the session. On a warm day, when a prosy speaker talked too long and people began going home by hundreds, the Chairman would get up and announce that Swami Vivekananda would make a short address just before the benediction. Then he would have the peaceable hundreds perfectly in tether. The four thousand fanning people in the Hall of Columbus would sit smiling and expectant, waiting for an hour or two of other men's speeches, to listen to Vivekananda for fifteen minutes. The Chairman knew the old rule of keeping the best until the last.

THE CLAIMS OF RELIGION[1]

Sunday, 5th January

Many of you remember the thrill of joy with which in your childhood you saw the glorious rising sun; all of you, sometimes in your life, stand and gaze upon the glorious setting sun, and at least in imagination, try to pierce through the beyond. This, in fact, is at the bottom of the whole universe — this rising from and this setting into the beyond, this whole universe coming up out of the unknown, and going back again into the unknown, crawling in as a child out of darkness, and crawling out again as an old man into darkness.

This universe of ours, the universe of the senses, the rational, the intellectual, is bounded on both sides by the illimitable, the unknowable, the ever unknown. Herein is the search, herein art the inquiries, here are the facts; from this comes the light which is known to the world as religion. Essentially, however, religion belongs to the supersensuous and not to the sense plane. It is beyond all reasoning, and not on the plane of intellect. It is a vision, an inspiration, a plunge into the unknown and unknowable making the unknowable more than known, for it can never be "known". This search has been in the human mind, as I believe from the very beginning of humanity. There cannot have been human reasoning and intellect in any period of the world's history without this struggle, this search beyond. In our little universe this human mind, we see a thought arise. Whence it rises we do not know, and when it disappears, where it goes, we know not either. The macrocosm and the microcosm are, as it were in the same groove, passing through the same stages, vibrating in the same key.

I shall try to bring before you the Hindu theory that religions do not come from without, but from within. It is my belief that religious thought is in man's very constitution, so much so that it is impossible for him to give up religion until he can give up his mind and body, until he can stop thought and life. As long as a man thinks, this struggle must go on, and so long man must have some form of religion. Thus we see various forms of religion in the world. It is a bewildering study; but it is not, as many of us think, a vain speculation. Amidst this chaos there is harmony, throughout these discordant sounds there is a note of concord; and he who is prepared to listen to it, will catch the tone.

The great question of all questions at the present time is this: Taking for granted that the knowable and the known are bounded on both sides by the unknowable and the infinitely unknown, why struggle for that unknown? Why shall we not be content with the known? Why shall we not rest satisfied with eating, drinking, and doing a little good to society? This idea is in the air. From the most learned professor to the prattling baby, we are told, "Do good to the world, that is all of religion, and don't bother your head about questions of the beyond." So much so is this the case that it has become a truism.

But fortunately we must inquire into the beyond. This present, this expressed, is only one part of that unexpressed. The sense universe is, as it were, only one portion, one bit of that infinite spiritual universe projected into the plane of sense consciousness. How can this little bit of projection be explained, be understood, without knowing that which is beyond? It is said of Socrates that one day while lecturing at Athens, he met a Brâhmana who had travelled into Greece, and Socrates told the Brahmana that the greatest study for mankind is man. And the Brahmana sharply retorted, "How can you know man until you know God?" This God, this eternally Unknowable, or Absolute, or Infinite, or without name — you may call Him by what name you like — is the rationale, the only explanation, the raison d'etre of that which is known and knowable, this present life. Take anything before you, the most material thing — take any one of these most materialistic sciences, such as chemistry or physics, astronomy or biology — study it, push the study forward and forward, and the gross forms will begin to melt and

---
[1]. Portions of this lecture were published in Vol. III, The published portions are reproduced here in small type. The year of the lecture is not known.

become finer and finer, until they come to a point where you are bound to make a tremendous leap from these material things into the immaterial. The gross melts into the fine, physics into metaphysics in every department of knowledge.

So with everything we have — our society, our relations With each other, our religion, and what you call ethics. There are attempts at producing a system of ethics from mere grounds of utility. I challenge any man to produce such a rational system of ethics. Do good to others. Why? Because it is the highest utility. Suppose a man says, "I do not care for utility; I want to cut the throats of others and make myself rich." What will you answer? It is out-Heroding Herod! But where is the utility of my doing good to the world? Am I a fool to work my life out that others may be happy? Why shall I myself not be happy, if there is no other sentiency beyond society, no other power in the universe beyond the five senses? What prevents me from cutting the throats of my brothers so long as I can make myself safe from the police, and make myself happy. What will you answer? You are bound to show some utility. When you are pushed from your ground you answer, "My friend, it is good to be good." What is the power in the human mind which says, "It is good to do good", which unfolds before us in glorious view the grandeur of the soul, the beauty of goodness, the all attractive power of goodness, the infinite power of goodness? That is what we call God. Is it not?

Secondly, I want to tread on a little more delicate ground. I want your attention, and ask you not to make any hasty conclusions from what I say. We cannot do much good to this world. Doing good to the world is very good. But can we do much good to the world? Have we done much good these hundreds of years that we have been struggling — have we increased the sum total of the happiness in the world? Thousands of means have been created every day to conduce to the happiness of the world, and this has been going on for hundreds and thousands of years. I ask you: Is the sum total of the happiness in the world today more than what it divas a century ago? It cannot be. Each wave that rises in the ocean must be at the expense of a hollow somewhere. If one nation becomes rich and powerful, it must be at the expense of another nation somewhere. Each piece of machinery that is invented will make twenty people rich and a twenty thousand people poor. It is the law of competition throughout. The sum total of the energy displayed remains the same throughout. It is, too, a foolhardy task. It is unreasonable to state that we can have happiness without misery. With the increase of all these means, you are increasing the want of the world, and increased wants mean insatiable thirst which will never be quenched. What can fill this want, this thirst? And so long as there is this thirst, misery is inevitable. It is the very nature of life to be happy and miserable by turns. Then again is this world left to you to do good to it? Is there no other power working in this universe? Is God dead and gone, leaving His universe to you and me — the Eternal, the Omnipotent the All-merciful, the Ever-awakened, the One who never sleeps when the universe is sleeping, whose eyes never blink? This infinite sky is, as it were, His ever-open eye. Is He dead and gone? Is He not acting in this universe? It is going on; you need not be in a hurry; you need not make yourself miserable.

[The Swami here told the story of the man who wanted a ghost to work for him, but who, when he had the ghost, could not keep him employed, until he gave him a curly dog's tail to straighten.]

Such is the case with us, with this doing good to the universe. So, my brothers, we are trying to straighten out the tail of the dog these hundreds and thousands of years. It is like rheumatism. You drive it out from the feet, and it goes to the head; you drive it from the head, and it goes somewhere else.

This will seem to many of you to be a terrible, pessimistic view of the world, but it is not. Both pessimism and optimism are wrong. Both are taking up the extremes. So long as a man has plenty to eat and drink, and good clothes to wear, he becomes a great optimist; but that very man, when he loses everything, becomes a great pessimist. When a man loses all his money and is very poor, then and then alone, with the greatest force come to him the ideas of brotherhood of humanity. This is the world, and the more I go to different countries and see of this world, and the older I get, the more I am trying to avoid both these extremes of optimism and pessimism. This world is neither good nor evil. It is the Lord's world. It is beyond both good and evil, perfect in itself. His will is going on, showing all these different pictures; and it will go on without beginning and without end. It is a great gymnasium in which you and I, and millions of souls must come and get exercises, and make ourselves strong and perfect. This is what it is for. Not that God could not make a perfect universe; not that He could not help the misery of the world. You remember the story of the young lady and the clergyman, who were both looking at the moon through the telescope, and found the moon spots. And the clergyman said, "I am sure they are the spires of some churches." "Nonsense," said the young lady, "I am sure they are the young lovers kissing each other." So we are doing with this world. When we are inside, we think we are seeing the inside. According to the plane of existence in which we are, we see the universe. Fire in the kitchen is neither good nor bad. When it cooks a meal for you, you bless the fire, and say, "How good it is!" And when it burns your finger, you say, "What a nuisance it is!" It would be equally correct and logical to say: This universe is neither good nor evil. The world is the world, and will be always so. If we open ourselves to it in such a manner that the action of the world is beneficial to us, we call it good. If we put ourselves in the position in which it is painful, we call it evil. So you will always find children, who are innocent and joyful and do not want to injure anyone, are very optimistic. They are dreaming golden dreams. Old men who have all the desires in their hearts and not the means to fulfil them, and especially those who have been thumped and bumped by the world a good deal, are very pessimistic. Religion wants to know the truth. And the first thing it has discovered is that without a knowledge of this truth there will be no life worth living.

Life will be a desert, human life will be vain, it we cannot know the beyond. It is very good to say: Be contented with the things of the present moment. The cows and the dogs are, and so are all animals, and that is what makes them animals. So if man rests content with the present and gives up all search into the beyond, mankind will all have to go back to the animal plane again. It is religion, this inquiry into the beyond, that makes the difference between man and an animal. Well has it been said that man is the only animal that naturally looks upwards; every other animal naturally looks down. That looking upward and going upward and seeking perfection are what is called salvation, and the sooner a man begins to go higher, the sooner he raises himself towards this idea of truth as salvation. It does not consist in the amount of money in your pocket, or the dress you wear, or the house You live in, but in the wealth of spiritual thought in your brain. That is what makes for human progress; that is the source of all material and intellectual progress, the motive power behind, the enthusiasm that pushes mankind forward.

What again is the goal of mankind? Is it happiness, sensuous pleasure? They used to say in the olden time that in heaven they will play on trumpets and live round a throne; in modern time I find that they think this ideal is very weak, and they have improved upon it and say that they will have marriages and all these things there. If there is any improvement in these two things, the second is an improvement for the worse. All these various theories of heaven that are being put forward show weakness in the mind. And that weakness is here: First, they think that sense happiness is the goal of life. Secondly they cannot conceive of anything that is beyond the five senses. They are as irrational as the Utilitarians. Still they are much better than the modern Atheistic Utilitarians, at any rate. Lastly, this Utilitarian position is simply childish. What right have you to say, "Here is my standard, and the whole universe must be governed by my standard?" What right have you to say that every truth shall be judged by this standard of yours — the standard that preaches mere bread, and money, and clothes as God?

Religion does not live in bread, does not dwell in a house. Again and again you hear this objection advanced: "What good can religion do? Can it take away the poverty of the poor and give them more clothes?" Supposing it cannot, would that prove the untruth of religion? Suppose a baby stands up among you, when you are trying to demonstrate an astronomical theory, and says, "Does it bring gingerbread?" "No, it does not," you answer. "Then," says the baby, "it is useless." Babies judge the whole universe from their own standpoint, that of producing gingerbread, and so do the babies of the world.

Sad to say at the later end of this nineteenth century that these are passing for the learned, the most rational, the most logical, the most intelligent crowd ever seen on this earth.

We must not judge of higher things from this low standpoint of ours. Everything must be judged by its own standard, and the infinite must be judged by the standard of infinity. Religion permeates the whole of man's life, not only the present, but the past, present, and future. It is therefore the eternal relation between the eternal Soul, and the eternal God. Is it logical to measure its value by its action upon five minutes of human life? Certainly not. But these are all negative arguments.

Now comes the question: Can religion really do anything? It can.

Can religion really bring bread and clothes? It does. It is always doing so, and it does infinitely more than that; it brings to man eternal life. It has made man what he is, and will make of this human animal a God. That is what religion can do. Take off religion from human society, what will remain? Nothing but a forest of brutes. As I have just tried to show you that it is absurd to suppose that sense happiness is the goal of humanity, we find as a conclusion that knowledge is the goal of all life. I have tried to show to you that in these thousands of years of struggle for the search of truth and the benefit of mankind, we have scarcely made the least appreciable advance. But mankind has made gigantic advance in knowledge. The highest utility of this progress lies not in the creature comforts that it brings, but in manufacturing a god out of this animal man. Then, with knowledge, naturally comes bliss. Babies think that the happiness of the senses is the highest thing they can have. Most of you know that there is a keener enjoyment in man in the intellect than in the senses. No one of you can feel the same pleasure in eating as a dog does. You can mark that. Where does the pleasure come from in man? Not that whole-souled enjoyment of eating that the pig or the dog has. See how the pig eats. It is unconscious of the universe while it is eating; its whole soul is bound up in the food. It may be killed but it does not care when it has food. Think of the intense enjoyment that the pig has! No man has that. Where is it gone? Man has changed it into intellectual enjoyment. The pig cannot enjoy religious lectures. That is one step higher and keener yet than intellectual pleasures, and that is the spiritual plane, spiritual enjoyment of things divine, soaring beyond reason and intellect. To procure that we shall have to lose all these sense-enjoyments. This is the highest utility. Utility is what I enjoy, and what everyone enjoys, and we run for that.

We find that man enjoys his intellect much more than an animal enjoys his senses, and we see that man enjoys his spiritual nature even more than his rational nature. So the highest wisdom must be this spiritual knowledge. With this knowledge will come bliss. All these things of this world are but the shadows, the manifestations in the third or fourth degree of the real Knowledge and Bliss.

It is this Bliss that comes to you through the love of humanity; the shadow of this spiritual Bliss is this human love, but do not confound it with that human bliss. There is that great error: We are always mistaking the: love that we have — this carnal, human love, this attachment for particles, this electrical attraction for human beings in society — for this spiritual Bliss. We are apt to mistake this for that eternal state, which it is not. For want of any other name in English, I would call it Bliss, which is the same as eternal knowledge — and that is our goal. Throughout the world, wherever there has been a religion, and wherever there will be a religion, they have all sprung and will all spring out of one source, called by various names in various countries; and that is what in the Western countries you call "inspiration". What is this inspiration? Inspiration is the only source of religious knowledge. We have seen that religion essentially belongs to the plane beyond the senses. It is "where the eyes cannot go, or the ears, where the mind cannot reach, or what words cannot express". That is the field and goal of religion, and from this comes that which we call inspiration. It naturally follows, therefore, that there must be some way to go beyond the senses. It is perfectly true that our reason cannot go beyond the senses; all reasoning is within the senses, and reason is based upon the facts which the senses reach. But can a man go beyond the senses? Can a man know the unknowable? Upon this the whole question of religion is to be and has been decided. From time immemorial there was that adamantine wall, the barrier to the senses; from time immemorial hundreds and thousands of men and women haven't dashed themselves against this wall to penetrate beyond. Millions have failed, and millions have succeeded. This is the history of the world. Millions more do not believe that anyone ever succeeded; and these are the sceptics of the present day. Man succeeds in going beyond this wall if he only tries. Man has not only reason, he has not only senses, but there is much in him which is beyond the senses. We shall try to explain it a little. I hope you will feel that it is within you also.

I move my hand, and I feel and I know that I am moving my hand. I call it consciousness. I am conscious that I am moving my hand. But my heart is moving. I am not conscious of that; and yet who is moving the heart? It must be the same being. So we see that this being who moves the hands and speaks, that is to say, acts consciously, also acts unconsciously. We find, therefore, that this being can act upon two planes — one, the plane of consciousness, and the other, the plane below that. The impulsions from the plane of unconsciousness are what we call instinct, and when the same impulsions come from the plane of consciousness, we call it reason. But there is a still higher plane, superconsciousness in man. This is apparently the same as unconsciousness, because it is beyond the plane of consciousness, but it is above consciousness and not below it.

It is not instinct, it is inspiration. There is proof of it. Think of all these great prophets and sages that the world has produced, and it is well known how there will be times in their lives, moments in their existence, when they will be apparently unconscious of the external world; and all the knowledge that subsequently comes out of them, they claim, was gained during this state of existence. It is said of Socrates that while marching with the army, there was a beautiful sunrise, and that set in motion in his mind a train of thought; he stood there for two days in the sun quite unconscious. It was such moments that gave the Socratic knowledge to the world. So with all the great preachers and prophets, there are moments in their lives when they, as it were, rise from the conscious and go above it. And when they come back to the plane of consciousness, they come radiant with light; they have brought news from the beyond, and they are the inspired seers of the world.

But there is a great danger. Any man may say he is inspired; many times they say that. Where is the test? During sleep we are unconscious; a fool goes to sleep; he sleeps soundly for three hours; and when he comes back from that state, he is the same fool if not worse. Jesus of Nazareth goes into his transfiguration, and when he comes out, he has become Jesus the Christ. That is all the difference. One is inspiration, and the other is instinct. The one is a child, and the other is the old experienced man. This inspiration is possible for everyone of us. It is the source of all religions, and will ever be the source of all higher knowledge. Yet there are great dangers in the way. Sometimes fraudulent people try to impose themselves upon mankind. In these days it is becoming all too prevalent. A friend of mine had a very fine picture. Another gentleman who was rather religiously inclined, and a rich man, had his eyes upon this picture; but my friend would not sell it. This other gentleman one day comes and says to my friend, I have an inspiration and I have a message from God. "What is your message?" my friend asked. "The message is that you must deliver that picture to me." My friend was up to his mark; he immediately added, "Exactly so; how beautiful! I had exactly the same inspiration, that I should have to deliver to you the picture. Have you brought your cheque?" "Cheque? What cheque?' "Then", said my friend, "I don't think your inspiration was right. My inspiration was that I must give the picture to the man who brought a cheque for $100,000. You must bring the cheque first." The other man found he was caught, and gave up the inspiration theory. These are the dangers. A man came to me in Boston and said he had visions in which he had been talked to in the Hindu language. I said, "If I can see what he says I will believe it." But he wrote down a lot of nonsense. I tried my best to understand it, but I could not. I told him that so far as my knowledge went, such language never was and never will be in India. They had not become civilised enough to have such a language as that. He thought of course that I was a rogue and sceptic, and went away; and I would not be surprised next to hear that he was in a lunatic asylum. These are the two dangers always in this world — the danger from frauds, and the danger from fools. But that need not deter us, for all great things in this world are fraught with danger. At the same time we must take a little precaution. Sometimes I find persons perfectly wanting in logical analysis of anything. A man comes and says, "I have a message from such and such a god", and asks, "Can you deny it? Is it not possible that there will be such and such a god, and that he will give such a message? And 90 per cent of fools will swallow it. They think that that is reason enough. But one thing you ought to know, that it is possible for anything to happen - quite possible that the earth may come into contact with the Dog star in the next year and go to pieces. But if I advance this proposition, you have the right to stand up and ask me to prove it to you. What the lawyers call the onus probandi is on the man who made the proposition. It is not your duty to prove that I got my inspiration from a certain god, but mine, because I produced the proposition to you. If I cannot prove it, I should better hold my tongue. Avoid both these dangers, and you can get anywhere you please. Many of us get many messages in our lives, or think we get them, and as long as the message is regarding our own selves, go on doing what you please; but when it is in regard to our contact with and behaviour to others, think a hundred times before you act upon it; and then you will be safe.

We find that this inspiration is the only source of religion; yet it has always been fraught with many dangers; and the last and worst of all dangers is excessive claims. Certain men stand up and say they have a communication from God, and they are the mouthpiece of God Almighty, and no one else has the right to have that communication. This, on the face of it, is unreasonable. If there is anything in the universe, it must be universal; there is not one movement here that is not universal, because the whole universe is governed by laws. It is systematic and harmonious all through. Therefore what is anywhere must be everywhere. Each atom in the universe is built on the same plan as the biggest sun and the stars. If one man was ever inspired, it is possible for each and every one of us to be inspired, and that is religion. Avoid all these dangers, illusions and delusions, and fraud and making excessive claims, but come face to face with religious facts, and come into direct contact with the science of religion. Religion does not consist in believing any number of doctrines or dogmas, in going to churches or temples, in reading certain books. Have you seen God? Have you seen the soul? If not, are you struggling for it? It is here and now, and you have not to wait for the future. What is the future but the present illimitable? What is the whole amount of time but one second repeated again and again? Religion is here and now, in this present life.

One question more: What is the goal? Nowadays it is asserted that man is progressing infinitely, forward and forward, and there is no goal of perfection to attain to. Ever approaching, never attaining, whatever that may mean, and however wonderful it may be, it is absurd on the face of it. Is there any motion in a straight line? A straight line infinitely projected becomes a circle, it returns back to the starting point. You must end where you begin; and as you began in God, you must go back to God. What remains? Detail work. Through eternity you have to do the detail work.

Yet another question: Are we to discover new

truths of religion as we go on? Yea and nay. In the first place, we cannot know anything more of religion; it has been all known. In all the religions of the world you will find it claimed that there is a unity within us. Being one with the Divinity, there cannot be any further progress in that sense. Knowledge means Ending this unity in variety. I see you as men and women, and this is variety. It becomes scientific knowledge when I group you together and call you hyenas beings. Take the science of chemistry, for instance. Chemists are seeking to resolve all known substances into their original elements, and if possible, to find the one element from which all these are derived. The time may come when they will find the one element. That is the source of all other elements. Reaching that, they can go no further; the science of chemistry will have become perfect. So it is with the science of religion. If we can discover this perfect unity, then there cannot be any further progress.

When it was discovered that "I and my Father are one", the last word was said of religion. Then there only remained detail work. In true religion there is no faith or belief in the sense of blind faith. No great preacher ever preached that. That only comes with degeneracy. Fools pretend to be followers of this or that spiritual giant, and although they may be without power, endeavour to teach humanity to believe blindly. Believe what? To believe blindly is to degenerate the human soul. Be an atheist if you want, but do not believe in anything unquestioningly. Why degrade the soul to the level of animals? You not only hurt yourselves thereby, but you injure society, and make danger for those that come after you. Stand up and reason out, having no blind faith. Religion is a question of being and becoming, not of believing. This is religion, and when you have attained to that you have religion. Before that you are no better than the animals. "Do not believe in what you have heard," says the great Buddha, "do not believe in doctrines because they have been handed down to you through generations; do not believe in anything because it is followed blindly by many; do not believe because some old sage makes a statement; do not believe in truths to which you have become attached by habit; do not believe merely on the authority of your teachers and elders. Have deliberation and analyse, and when the result agrees with reason and conduces to the good of one and all, accept it and live up to it."

CONCENTRATION

Delivered at the Washington Hall, San Francisco, on March 16, 1900

[This and the following two lectures (Meditation and The Practice of Religion) are reproduced here from the Vedanta and the West with the kind permission of the Vedanta Society of Southern California, by whom is reserved the copyright for America. The lectures were recorded by Ida Ansell under circumstances which she herself relates thus:

"Swami Vivekananda's second trip to the West occurred in 1899-1900. During the first half of 1900 he worked in and around San Francisco, California. I was a resident of that city, twenty-two years old at the time. ... I heard him lecture perhaps a score of times from March to May of 1900, and recorded seventeen of his talks. ...

"The lectures were given in San Francisco, Oakland, and Alameda, in churches, in the Alameda and San Francisco Homes of Truth, and in rented halls. ... Altogether Swamiji gave, besides nearly daily interviews and informal classes, at least thirty or forty major addresses in March, April, and May. ...

"I was long hesitant about transcribing and releasing these lectures because of the imperfectness of my notes. I was just an amateur stenographer, at the time I took them. ... One would have needed a speed of at least three hundred words per minute to capture all of Swamiji's torrents of eloquence. I possessed less than half the required speed, and at the time I had no idea that the material would have value to anyone but myself. In addition to his fast speaking pace, Swamiji was a superb actor. His stories and imitations absolutely forced one to stop writing, to enjoy watching him. ... Even though my notes were somewhat fragmentary, I have yielded to the opinion that their contents are precious and must be given for publication.

Swamiji's speaking style was colloquial, fresh, and forceful. No alterations have been made in it; no adjusting or smoothing out of his spontaneous flow for purposes of publication has been done. Where omissions were made because of some obscurity in the meaning, they have been indicated by three dots. Anything inserted for purposes of clarification has been placed in square brackets. With these qualifications, the words are exactly as Swamiji spoke them.

Everything Swamiji said had tremendous power. These lectures have slept in my old stenographer's notebook for more than fifty years. Now as they emerge, one feels that the power is still there."]

All knowledge that we have, either of the external or internal world, is obtained through only one method — by the concentration of the mind. No knowledge can be had of any science unless we can concentrate our minds upon the subject. The astronomer concentrates his mind through the telescope... and so on. If you want to study your own mind, it will be the same process. You will have to concentrate your mind and turn it back upon itself. The difference in this world between mind and mind is simply the fact of concentration. One, more concentrated than the other, gets more knowledge.

In the lives of all great men, past and present, we find this tremendous power of concentration. Those are men of genius, you say. The science of Yoga tells us that we are all geniuses if we try hard to be. Some will come into this life better fitted and will do it quicker perhaps. We can all do the same. The same power is in everyone. The subject of the present lecture is how to concentrate the mind in order to study the mind itself. Yogis have laid down certain rules and this night I am going to give you a sketch of some of these rules.

Concentration, of course, comes from various sources. Through the senses you can get concentration. Some get it when they hear beautiful music, others when they see beautiful scenery. ... Some get concentrated by lying upon beds of spikes, sharp iron spikes, others by sitting upon sharp pebbles. These are extraordinary cases [using] most unscientific procedure. Scientific procedure is gradually training the mind.

One gets concentrated by holding his arm up. Torture gives him the concentration he wants. But all these are extraordinary.

Universal methods have been organised according to different philosophers. Some say the state we want to attain is superconsciousness of the mind — going beyond the limitations the body has made for us. The value of ethics to the Yogi lies in that it makes the mind pure. The purer the mind, the easier it is to control it. The mind takes every thought that rises and works it out. The grosser the mind, the more difficult [it is] to control [it]. The immoral man will never be able to concentrate his mind to study psychology. He may get a little control as he begins, get a little power of hearing. ... and even those powers will go from him. The difficulty is that if you study closely, you see how [the] extraordinary power arrived at was not attained by regular scientific training. The men who, by the power of magic, control serpents will be killed by serpents. ... The man who attains any extraordinary powers will in the long run succumb to those powers. There are millions [who] receive power through all sorts of ways in India. The vast majority of them die raving lunatics. Quite a number commit suicide, the mind [being] unbalanced.

The study must be put on the safe side: scientific, slow, peaceful. The first requisite is to be moral. Such a man wants the gods to come down, and they will come down and manifest themselves to him. That is our psychology and philosophy in essence, [to be] perfectly moral. Just think what that means! No injury, perfect purity, perfect austerity! These are absolutely necessary. Just think, if a man can attain all these in perfection! What more do you want? If he is free from all enmity towards any being, ... all animals will give up their enmity [in his presence]. The Yogis lay down very strict laws... so that one cannot pass off for a charitable man without; being charitable. ...

If you believe me, I have seen a man who used to live[1] in a hole and there were cobras and frogs living with him. ... Sometimes he would fast for [days and months] and then come out. He was always silent. One day there came a robber. ...

My old master used to say, "When the lotus of the heart has bloomed, the bees will come by themselves." Men like that are there yet. They need not talk. ... When the man is perfect from his heart, without a thought of hatred, all animals will give up their hatred [before him]. So with purity. These are necessary for our dealings with our fellow beings. We must love all. ... We have no business to look at the faults of others: it does no good We must not even think of them. Our business is with the good. We are not here to deal with faults. Our business is to be good.

Here comes Miss So-and-so. She says, "I am going to be a Yogi." She tells the news twenty times, meditates fifty days, then she says, "There is nothing in this religion. I have tried it. There is nothing in it."

The very basis [of spiritual life] is not there. The foundation [must be] this perfect morality. That is the great difficulty. ...

In our country there are vegetarian sects. They will take in the early morning pounds of sugar and place it on the ground for ants, and the story is, when one of them was putting sugar on the ground for ants, a man placed his foot upon the ants. The former said, "Wretch, you have killed the animals!" And he gave him such a blow, that it killed the man.

External purity is very easy and all the world rushes towards [it]. If a certain kind of dress is the kind of morality [to be observed], any fool can do that. When it is grappling with the mind itself, it is hard work.

The people who do external, superficial things are so self-righteous! I remember, when I was a boy I had great regard for the character of Jesus Christ. [Then I read about the wedding feast in the Bible.]

---

1. The reference is evidently to Pavhari Baba (see *Sketch of the Life of Pavhari Baba* in this volume)

I closed the book and said, "He ate meat and drank wine! He cannot be a good man."

We are always losing sight of the real meaning of things. The little eating and dress! Every fool can see that. Who sees that which is beyond? It is culture of the heart that we want. ... One mass of people in India we see bathing twenty times a day sometimes, making themselves very pure. And they do not touch anyone. ... The coarse facts, the external things! [If by bathing one could be pure,] fish are the purest beings.

Bathing, and dress, and food regulation — all these have their proper value when they are complementary to the spiritual. .... That first, and these all help. But without it, no amount of eating grass... is any good at all. They are helps if properly understood. But improperly understood, they are derogatory. ...

This is the reason why I am explaining these things: First, because in all religions everything degenerates upon being practiced by [the ignorant]. The camphor in the bottle evaporated, and they are fighting over the bottle.

Another thing: ... [Spirituality] evaporates when they say, "This is right, and that is wrong." All quarrels are [with forms and creeds] never in the spirit. The Buddhist offered for years glorious preaching; gradually, this spirituality evaporated. ... [Similarly with Christianity.] And then began the quarrel whether it is three gods in one or one in three, when nobody wants to go to God Himself and know what He is. We have to go to God Himself to know whether He is three in one or one in three.

Now, with this explanation, the posture. Trying to control the mind, a certain posture is necessary. Any posture in which the person can sit easily — that is the posture for that person. As a rule, you will find that the spinal column must be left free. It is not intended to bear the weight of the body. ... The only thing to remember in the sitting posture: [use] any posture in which the spine is perfectly free of the weight of the body.

Next [Prânâyâma] ... the breathing exercises. A great deal of stress is laid upon breathing. ... What I am telling you is not something gleaned from some sect in India. It is universally true. Just as in this country you teach your children certain prayers, [in India] they get the children and give them certain facts etc.

Children are not taught any religion in India except one or two prayers. Then they begin to seek for somebody with whom they can get en rapport. They go to different persons and find that "This man is the man for me", and get initiation. If I am married, my wife may possibly get another man teacher and my son will get somebody else, and that is always my secret between me and my teacher. The wife's religion the husband need not know, and he would not dare ask her what her religion is. It is well known that they would never say. It is only known to that person and the teacher. ... Sometimes you will find that what would be quite ludicrous to one will be just teaching for another. ... Each is carrying his own burden and is to be helped according to his particular mind. It is the business of every individual, between him, his teacher, and God. But there are certain general methods which all these teachers preach. Breathing [and] meditating are universal. That is the worship in India.

On the banks of the Gangâ, we will see men, women, and children all [practicing] breathing and then meditating. Of course, they have other things to do. They cannot devote much time to this. But those who have taken this as the study of life, they practice various methods. There are eighty-four different Âsanas (postures). Those that take it up under some person, they always feel the breath and the movements in all the different parts of the body. ...

Next comes Dhâranâ [concentration]. ... Dharana is holding the mind in certain spots.

The Hindu boy or girl ... gets initiation. He gets from his Guru a word. This is called the root word. This word is given to the Guru [by his Guru], and he gives it to his disciple. One such word is OM. All these symbols have a great deal of meaning, and they hold it secret, never write it. They must receive it through the ear — not through writing — from the teacher, and then hold it as God himself. Then they meditate on the word. ...

I used to pray like that at one time, all through the rainy season, four months. I used to get up and take a plunge in the river, and with all my wet clothes on repeat [the Mantra] till the sun set. Then I ate something — a little rice or something. Four months in the rainy season!

The Indian mind believes that there is nothing in the world that cannot be obtained. If a man wants money in this country, he goes to work and earns money. There, he gets a formula and sits under a tree and believes that money must come. Everything must come by the power of his [thought]. You make money here. It is the same thing. You put forth your whole energy upon money making.

There are some sects called Hatha-Yogis. ... They say the greatest good is to keep the body from dying. ... Their whole process is clinging to the body. Twelve years training! And they begin with little children, others wise it is impossible. ... One thing [is] very curious about the Hatha-Yogi: When he first becomes a disciple, he goes into the wilderness and lives alone forty days exactly. All they have they learn within those forty days. ...

A man in Calcutta claims to have lived five hundred years. The people all tell me that their grandfathers saw him. ... He takes a constitutional twenty miles, never walks, he runs. Goes into the water, covers himself [from] top to toe with mud. After that he plunges again into the water, again sticks himself with mud. ... I do not see any good in that. (Snakes, they say, live two hundred years.) He must be very old, because I have travelled fourteen years in India and wherever I went everybody knew him. He has been travelling all his life. ... [The Hatha-Yogi] will swallow a piece of rubber eighty inches long and take it out again. Four times a day he has to wash every part of his body, internal and external parts. ...

The walls can keep their bodies thousands of years. ... What of that? I would not want to live so long. "Sufficient unto the day is the evil thereof." One little body, with all its delusions and limitations, is enough.

There are other sects. ... They give you a drop of

the elixir of life and you remain young. ... It will take me months to enumerate [all the sects]. All their activity is on this side [in the material world]. Every day a new sect. ...

The power of all those sects is in the mind. Their idea is to hold the mind. First concentrate it and hold it at a certain place. They generally say, at certain parts of the body along the spinal column or upon the nerve centres. By holding the mind at the nerve centres, [the Yogi] gets power over the body. The body is the great cause of disturbance to his peace, is opposite of his highest ideal, so he wants control: [to] keep the body as servant.

Then comes meditation. That is the highest state. ... When [the mind] is doubtful that is not its great state. Its great state is meditation. It looks upon things and sees things, not identifying itself with anything else. As long as I feel pain, I have identified myself with the body. When I feel joy or pleasure, I have identified myself with the body. But the high state will look with the same pleasure or blissfulness upon pleasure or upon pain. ... Every meditation is direct superconsciousness. In perfect concentration the soul becomes actually free from the bonds of the gross body and knows itself as it is. Whatever one wants, that comes to him. Power and knowledge are already there. The soul identifies itself with that which is powerless matter and thus weeps. It identifies itself with mortal shapes. ... But if that free soul wants to exercise any power, it will have it. If it does not, it does not come. He who has known God has become God. There is nothing impossible to such a free soul. No more birth and death for him. He is free for ever.

MEDITATION

Delivered at the Washington Hall, San Francisco, April 3, 1900

Meditation has been laid stress upon by all religions. The meditative state of mind is declared by the Yogis to be the highest state in which the mind exists. When the mind is studying the external object, it gets identified with it, loses itself. To use the simile of the old Indian philosopher: the soul of man is like a piece of crystal, but it takes the colour of whatever is near it. Whatever the soul touches ... it has to take its colour. That is the difficulty. That constitutes the bondage. The colour is so strong, the crystal forgets itself and identifies itself with the colour. Suppose a red flower is near the crystal and the crystal takes the colour and forgets itself, thinks it is red. We have taken the colour of the body and have forgotten what we are. All the difficulties that follow come from that one dead body. All our fears, all worries, anxieties, troubles, mistakes, weakness, evil, are front that one great blunder — that we are bodies. This is the ordinary person. It is the person taking the colour of the flower near to it. We are no more bodies than the crystal is the red flower.

The practice of meditation is pursued. The crystal knows what it is, takes its own colour. It is meditation that brings us nearer to truth than anything else. ...

In India two persons meet. In English they say, "How do you do?" The Indian greeting is, "Are you upon yourself?" The moment you stand upon something else, you run the risk of being miserable. This is what I mean by meditation — the soul trying to stand upon itself. That state must surely be the healthiest state of the soul, when it is thinking of itself, residing in its own glory. No, all the other methods that we have — by exciting emotions, prayers, and all that — really have that one end in view. In deep emotional excitement the soul tries to stand upon itself. Although the emotion may arise from anything external, there is concentration of mind.

There are three stages in meditation. The first is what is called [Dhâranâ], concentrating the mind upon an object. I try to concentrate my mind upon this glass, excluding every other object from my mind except this glass. But the mind is wavering . . . When it has become strong and does not waver so much, it is called [Dhyâna], meditation. And then there is a still higher state when the differentiation between the glass and myself is lost — [Samâdhi or absorption]. The mind and the glass are identical. I do not see any difference. All the senses stop and all powers that have been working through other channels of other senses [are focused in the mind]. Then this glass is under the power of the mind entirely. This is to be realised. It is a tremendous play played by the Yogis. ... Take for granted, the external object exists. Then that which is really outside of us is not what we see. The glass that I see is not the external object certainly. That external something which is the glass I do not know and will never know.

Something produces an impression upon me. Immediately I send the reaction towards that, and the glass is the result of the combination of these two. Action from outside — X. Action from inside — Y. The glass is XY. When you look at X, call it external world — at Y, internal world ... If you try to distinguish which is your mind and which is the world — there is no such distinction. The world is the combination of you and something else. ...

let us take another example. You are dropping stones upon the smooth surface of a lake. Every stone you drop is followed by a reaction. The stone is covered by the little waves in the lake. Similarly, external things are like the stones dropping into the lake of the mind. So we do not really see the external ...; we see the wave only. ...

These waves that rise in the mind have caused many things outside. We are not discussing the [merits of] idealism and realism. We take for granted that things exist outside, but what we see is different from things that exist outside, as we see what exists outside plus ourselves.

Suppose I take my contribution out of the glass. What remains? Almost nothing. The glass will disappear. If I take my contribution from the table, what would remain of the table? Certainly not this table, because it was a mixture of the outside plus my contribution. The poor lake has got to throw the wave towards the stone whenever [the stone] is thrown in it. The mind must create the wave towards any sensation. Suppose ... we can withhold the mind. At once we are masters. We refuse to contribute our share to all these phenomena.... If I do not contribute my share, it has got to stop.

You are creating this bondage all the time. How? By putting in your share. We are all making our own beds, forging our own chains.... When the identifying ceases between this external object and myself, then I will be able to take my contribution off, and this thing will disappear. Then I will say, "Here is the glass", and then take my mind off, and it disappears.... If you can take away your share, you can walk upon water. Why should it drown you any more? What of poison? No more difficulties. In every phenomenon in nature you contribute at least half, and nature brings half. If your half is taken off, the thing must stop.

... To every action there is equal reaction.... If a man strikes me and wounds me it is that man's actions and my body's reaction. ... Suppose I have so much power over the body that I can resist even that automatic action. Can such power be attained? The books say it can. ... If you stumble on [it], it is a miracle. If you learn it scientifically, it is Yoga.

I have seen people healed by the power of mind. There is the miracle worker. We say he prays and the man is healed. Another man says, "Not at all. It is just the power of the mind. The man is scientific. He knows what he is about."

The power of meditation gets us everything. If you want to get power over nature, [you can have it through meditation]. It is through the power of meditation all scientific facts are discovered today. They study the subject and forget everything, their own identity and everything, and then the great fact comes like a flash. Some people think that is inspiration. There is no more inspiration than there is expiration; and never was anything got for nothing.

The highest so-called inspiration was the work of Jesus. He worked hard for ages in previous births. That was the result of his previous work — hard work. ... It is all nonsense to talk about inspiration. Had it been, it would have fallen like rain. Inspired people in any line of thought only come among nations who have general education and [culture]. There is no inspiration.... Whatever passes for inspiration is the result that comes from causes already in the mind. One day, flash comes the result! Their past work was the [cause].

Therein also you see the power of meditation — intensity of thought. These men churn up their own souls. Great truths come to the surface and become manifest. Therefore the practice of meditation is the great scientific method of knowledge. There is no knowledge without the power of meditation. From ignorance, superstition, etc. we can get cured by meditation for the time being and no more. [Suppose] a man has told me that if you drink such a poison you will be killed, and another man comes in the night and says, "Go drink the poison!" and I am not killed, [what happens is this:] my mind cut out from the meditation the identity between the poison and myself just for the time being. In another case of [drinking] the poison, I will be killed.

If I know the reason and scientifically raise myself up to that [state of meditation], I can save anyone. That is what the books say; but how far it is correct you must appraise.

I am asked, "Why do you Indian people not conquer these things? You claim all the time to be superior to all other people. You practice Yoga and do it quicker than anybody else. You are fitter. Carry it out! If you are a great people, you ought to have a great system. You will have to say good-bye to all the gods. Let them go to sleep as you take up the great philosophers. You are mere babies, as superstitious as the rest of the world. And all your claims are failures. If you have the claims, stand up and be bold, and all the heaven that ever existed is yours. There is the musk deer with fragrance inside, and he does not know where the fragrance [comes from]. Then after days and days he finds it in himself. All these gods and demons are within them. Find out, by the powers of reason, education, and culture that it is all in yourself. No more gods and superstitions. You want to be rational, to be Yogis, really spiritual."

[My reply is: With you too] everything is material What is more material than God sitting on a throne? You look down upon the poor man who is worshipping the image. You are no better. And you, gold worshippers, what are you? The image worshipper worships his god, something that he can see. But you do not even do that. You do not worship the spirit nor something that you can understand. ... Word worshippers! "God is spirit!" God is spirit and should be worshipped in spirit and faith. Where does the spirit reside? On a tree? On a cloud? What do you mean by God being ours? You are the spirit. That is the first fundamental belief you must never give up. I am the spiritual being. It is there. All this skill of Yoga and this system of meditation and everything is just to find Him there.

Why am I saying all this just now? Until you fix the location, you cannot talk. You fix it up in heaven and all the world ever except in the right place. I am spirit, and therefore the spirit of all spirits must be in my soul. Those who think it anywhere else are ignorant. Therefore it is to be sought here in this heaven; all the heaven that ever existed [is within myself]. There are some sages who, knowing this, turn their eyes inward and find the spirit of all spirits in their own spirit. That is the scope of meditation. Find out the truth about God and about your own soul and thus attain to liberation. ...

You are all running after life, and we find that is foolishness. There is something much higher than life even. This life is inferior, material. Why should I live at all? I am something higher than life. Living is always slavery. We always get mixed up. ... Everything is a continuous chain of slavery.

You get something, and no man can teach another. It is through experience [we learn]. ... That young man cannot be persuaded that there are any difficulties in life. You cannot persuade the old man that life is all smooth. He has had many experiences. That is the difference.

By the power of meditation we have got to control, step by step, all these things. We have seen philosophically that all these differentiations — spirit, mind, matter, etc. — [have no real existences. ... Whatever exists is one. There cannot be many. That is what is meant by science and knowledge. Ignorance sees manifold. Knowledge realises one. ... Reducing the many into one is science. ... The whole of the universe has been demonstrated into one. That science is called the science of Vedanta. The whole universe is one. The one runs through all this seeming variety. ...

We have all these variations now and we see them — what we call the five elements: solid, liquid, gaseous, luminous, ethereal. After that the state of existence is mental and beyond that spiritual. Not that spirit is one and mind is another, ether another, and so on. It is the one existence appearing in all these variations. To go back, the solid must become liquid. The way [the elements evolved] they must go back. The solids will become liquid, etherised. This is the idea of the macrocosm — and universal. There is the external universe and universal spirit, mind, ether, gas, luminosity, liquid, solid.

The same with the mind. I am just exactly the same in the microcosm. I am the spirit; I am mind; I am the ether, solid, liquid, gas. What I want to do is to go back to my spiritual state. It is for the individual to live the life of the universe in one short life. Thus man can be free in this life. He in his own short lifetime shall have the power to live the whole extent of life....

We all struggle. . . . If we cannot reach the Absolute, we will get somewhere, and it will be better than we are now.

Meditation consists in this practice [of dissolving every thing into the ultimate Reality — spirit]. The solid melts into liquid, that into gas, gas into ether, then mind, and mind will melt away. All is spirit.

Some of the Yogis claim that this body will become liquid etc. You will be able to do any thing with it — make it little, or gas pass through this wall — they claim. I do not know. I have never seen anybody do it. But it is in the books. We have no reason to disbelieve the books.

Possibly, some of us will be able to do it in this life. Like a flash it comes, as the result of our past work. Who knows but some here are old Yogis with just a little to do to finish the whole work. Practice!

Meditation, you know, comes by a process imagination. You go through all these processes purification of the elements — making the one melt the other, that into the next higher, that into mind, that into spirit, and then you are spirit[1].

Spirit is always free, omnipotent, omniscient. Of course, under God. There cannot be many Gods. These liberated souls are wonderfully powerful, almost omnipotent. [But] none can be as powerful as God. If one [liberated soul] said, "I will make this planet go this way", and another said, "I will make it go that way", [there would be confusion].

Don't you make this mistake! When I say in English, "I am God!" it is because I have no better word. In Sanskrit, God means absolute existence, knowledge, and wisdom, infinite self-luminous consciousness. No person. It is impersonal. ...

I am never Râma [never one with Ishvara, the personal aspect of God], but I am [one with Brahman, the impersonal, all-pervading existence]. Here is a huge mass of clay. Out of that clay I made a little [mouse] and you made a little [elephant]. Both are clay. Melt both down They are essentially one. "I and my Father are one." [But the clay mouse can never be one with the clay elephant.]

I stop somewhere; I have a little knowledge. You a little more; you stop somewhere. There is one soul which is the greatest of all. This is Ishvara, Lord of Yoga [God as Creator, with attributes]. He is the individual. He is omnipotent. He resides in every heart. There is no body. He does not need a body. All you get by the practice of meditation etc., you can get by meditation upon Ishvara, Lord of Yogis. ...

The same can be attained by meditating upon a great soul; or upon the harmony of life. These are called objective meditations. So you begin to meditate upon certain external things, objective things, either outside or inside. If you take a long sentence, that is no meditation at all. That is simply trying

---

1. This purification of the elements, known as Bhuta-shuddhi, is part of the ritualistic worship. The worshipper tries to feel that he is dissolving earth, water, fire, air, and ether with their subtle essences, and the sense-organs into mind. Mind, intellect, and sense of individual ego are merged into Mahat, the cosmic ego; Mahat is dissolved into Prakriti, the power of Brahman, and Prakriti merges into Brahman, the ultimate Reality. The Kundalini, the coiled-up power at the base of the spine, in his thoughts is led to the highest centre of consciousness in the brain, where he meditates on his oneness with the supreme Spirit.

to get the mind collected by repetition. Meditation means the mind is turned back upon itself. The mind stops all the [thought-waves] and the world stops. Your consciousness expands. Every time you meditate you will keep your growth. ... Work a little harder, more and more, and meditation comes. You do not feel the body or anything else. When you come out of it after the hour, you have had the most beautiful rest you ever had in your life. That is the only way you ever give rest to your system. Not even the deepest sleep will give you such rest as that. The mind goes on jumping even in deepest sleep. Just those few minutes [in meditation] your brain has almost stopped. Just a little vitality is kept up. You forget the body. You may be cut to pieces and not feel it at all. You feel such pleasure in it. You become so light. This perfect rest we will get in meditation.

Then, meditation upon different objects. There are meditations upon different centres of the spine. [According to the Yogis, there are two nerves in the spinal column, called Idâ and Pingalâ. They are the main channels through which the afferent and efferent currents travel.] The hollow [canal called Sushumnâ] runs through the middle of the spinal column. The Yogis claim this cord is closed, but by the power of meditation it has to be opened. The energy has to be sent down to [the base of the spine], and the Kundalini rises. The world will be changed[1]. ...

Thousands of divine beings are standing about you. You do not see them because our world is determined by our senses. We can only see this outside. Let us call it X. We see that X according to our mental state. Let us take the tree standing outside. A thief came and what did he see in the stump? A policeman. The child saw a huge ghost. The young man was waiting for his sweetheart, and what did he see? His sweetheart. But the stump of the tree had not changed. It remained the same. This is God Himself, and with our foolishness we see Him to be man, to be dust, to be dumb, miserable.

Those who are similarly constituted will group together naturally and live in the same world. Otherwise stated, you live in the same place. All the heavens and all the hells are right here. For example: [take planes in the form of] big circles cutting each other at certain points. . . . On this plane in one circle we can be in touch with a certain point in another [circle]. If the mind gets to the centre, you begin to be conscious on all planes. In meditation sometimes you touch another plane, and you see other beings, disembodied spirits, and so on. You get there by the power of meditation. This power is changing our senses, you see, refining our senses. If you begin to practise meditation five days, you will feel the pain from within these centres [of consciousness] and hearing [becomes finer][2]. ...That is why all the Indian gods have three eyes. That is the psychic eye that opens out and shows you spiritual things.

As this power of Kundalini rises from one centre to the other in the spine, it changes the senses and you begin to see this world another. It is heaven. You cannot talk. Then the Kundalini goes down to the lower centres. You are again man until the Kundalini reaches the brain, all the centres have been passed, and the whole vision vanishes and you [perceive] . . . nothing but the one existence. You are God. All heavens you make out of Him, all worlds out of Him. He is the one existence. Nothing else exists.

THE PRACTICE OF RELIGION

Delivered at Alameda, California, on April 18, 1900

We read many books, many scriptures. We get various ideas from our childhood, and change them every now and then. We understand what is meant by theoretical religion. We think we understand what is meant by practical religion. Now I am going to present to you my idea of practical religion.

We hear all around us about practical religion, and analysing all that, we find that it can be brought

---

1. See Complete Works, Vol. I.

2. See Complete Works, Vol. I.

down to one conception — charity to our fellow beings. Is that all of religion? Every day we hear in this country about practical Christianity — that a man has done some good to his fellow beings. Is that all?

What is the goal of life? Is this world the goal of life? Nothing more? Are we to be just what we are, nothing more? Is man to be a machine which runs smoothly without a hitch anywhere? Are all the sufferings he experiences today all he can have, and doesn't he want anything more?

The highest dream of many religions is the world. ... The vast majority of people are dreaming of the time when there will be no more disease, sickness, poverty, or misery of any kind. They will have a good time all around. Practical religion, therefore, simply means. "Clean the streets! Make it nice!" We see how all enjoy it.

Is enjoyment the goal of life? Were it so, it would be a tremendous mistake to become a man at all. What man can enjoy a meal with more gusto than the dog or the cat? Go to a menagerie and see the [wild animals] tearing the flesh from the bone. Go back and become a bird! ... What a mistake then to become a man! Vain have been my years — hundreds of years — of struggle only to become the man of sense-enjoyments.

Mark, therefore, the ordinary theory of practical religion, what it leads to. Charity is great, but the moment you say it is all, you run the risk of running into materialism. It is not religion. It is no better than atheism - a little less. ... You Christians, have you found nothing else in the Bible than working for fellow creatures, building ... hospitals? ... Here stands a shopkeeper and says how Jesus would have kept the shop! Jesus would neither have kept a saloon, nor a shop, nor have edited a newspaper. That sort of practical religion is good, not bad; but it is just kindergarten religion. It leads nowhere. ... If you believe in God, if you are Christians and repeat everyday, "Thy will be done", just think what it means! You say every moment, "Thy will be done", really meaning, "My will be done by Thee, O God." The Infinite is working His own plans out. Even He has made mistakes, and you and I are going to remedy that! The Architect of the universe is going to be taught by the carpenters! He has left the world a dirty hole, and you are going to make it a beautiful place!

What is the goal of it all? Can senses ever be the goal? Can enjoyment of pleasure ever be the goal? Can this life ever be the goal of the soul? If it is, better die this moment; do not want this life! If that is the fate of man, that he is going to be only the perfected machine, it would just mean that we go back to being trees and stones and things like that. Did you ever hear a cow tell a lie or see a tree steal? They are perfect machines. They do not make mistakes. They live in a world where everything is finished. ...

What is the ideal of religion, then, if this cannot be practical [religion]? And it certainly cannot be. What are we here for? We are here for freedom, for knowledge. We want to know in order to make ourselves free. That is our life: one universal cry for freedom. What is the reason the . . . plant grows from the seed, overturning the ground and raising itself up to the skies? What is the offering for the earth from the sun? What is your life? The same struggle for freedom. Nature is trying all around to suppress us, and the soul wants to express itself. The struggle with nature is going on. Many things will be crushed and broken in this struggle for freedom. That is your real misery. Large masses of dust and dirt must be raised on the battlefield. Nature says, "I will conquer." The soul says, "I must be the conqueror." Nature says, "Wait! I will give you a little enjoyment to keep you quiet." The soul enjoys a little, becomes deluded a moment, but the next moment it [cries for freedom again]. Have you marked the eternal cry going on through the ages in every breast? We are deceived by poverty. We become wealthy and are deceived with wealth. We are ignorant. We read and learn and are deceived with knowledge. No man is ever satisfied. That is the cause of misery, but it is also the cause of all blessing. That is the sure sign. How can you be satisfied with this world? . . . If tomorrow this world becomes heaven, we will say, "Take this away. Give us something else."

The infinite human soul can never be satisfied but

by the Infinite itself .... Infinite desire can only be satisfied by infinite knowledge — nothing short of that. Worlds will come and go. What of that? The soul lives and for ever expands. Worlds must come into the soul. Worlds must disappear in the soul like drops in the ocean. And this world to become the goal of the soul! If we have common sense, we cannot he satisfied, though this has been the theme of the poets in all the ages, always telling us to be satisfied. And nobody has been satisfied yet! Millions of prophets have told us, "Be satisfied with your lot"; poets sing. We have told ourselves to be quiet and satisfied, yet we are not. It is the design of the Eternal that there is nothing in this world to satisfy my soul, nothing in the heavens above, and nothing beneath. Before the desire of my soul, the stars and the worlds, upper and lower, the whole universe, is but a hateful disease, nothing but that. That is the meaning. Everything is an evil unless that is the meaning. Every desire is evil unless that is the meaning, unless you understand its true importance, its goal. All nature is crying through all the atoms for one thing — its perfect freedom.

What is practical religion, then? To get to that state — freedom, the attainment of freedom. And this world, if it helps us on to that goal, [is] all right; if not — if it begins to bind one more layer on the thousands already there, it becomes an evil. Possessions, learning, beauty, everything else — as long as they help us to that goal, they are of practical value. When they have ceased helping us on to that goal of freedom, they are a positive danger. What is practical religion, then? Utilise the things of this world and the next just for one goal — the attainment of freedom. Every enjoyment, every ounce of pleasure is to be bought by the expenditure of the infinite heart and mind combined.

Look at the sum total of good and evil in this world. Has it changed? Ages have passed, and practical religion has worked for ages. The world thought that each time the problem would be solved. It is always the same problem. At best it changes its form. ... It trades consumption and nerve disease for twenty thousand shops. . . . It is like old rheumatism: Drive it from one place, it goes to another.

A hundred years ago man walked on foot or bought horses. Now he is happy because he rides the railroad; but he is unhappy because he has to work more and earn more. Every machine that saves labour puts more stress upon labour.

This universe, nature, or whatever you call it, must be limited; it can never be unlimited. The Absolute, to become nature, must be limited by time, space, and causation. The energy [at our disposal] is limited. You can spend it in one place, losing it in another. The sum total is always the same. Wherever there is a wave in one place, there is a hollow in another. If one nation becomes rich, others become poor. Good balances evil. The person for the moment on top of the wave thinks all is good; the person at the bottom says the world is [all evil]. But the man who stands aside sees the divine play going on. Some weep and others laugh. The latter will weep in their turn and the others laugh. What can we do? We know we cannot do anything. ...

Which of us do anything because we want to do good? How few! They can be counted on the fingers. The rest of us also do good, but because we are forced to do so. ... We cannot stop. Onward we go, knocked about from place to place. What can we do? The world will be the same world, the earth the same. It will be changed from blue to brown and from brown to blue. One language translated into another, one set of evils changed into another set of evils — that is what is going on. ... Six of one, half a dozen of the other. The American Indian in the forest cannot attend a lecture on metaphysics as you can, but he can digest his meal. You cut him to pieces, and the next moment he is all right. You and I, if we get scratched, we have to go to the hospital for six months. ...

The lower the organism, the greater is its pleasure in the senses. Think of the lowest animals and the power of touch. Everything is touch. ... When you come to man, you will see that the lower the civilization of the man, the greater is the power of the senses. ... The higher the organism, the lesser is the pleasure of the senses. A dog can eat a meal, but cannot understand the exquisite pleasure of thinking about metaphysics. He is deprived of the wonderful pleasure which you get through the intellect. The pleasures of the senses are great. Greater than those is the pleasure of the intellect. When you attend the fine fifty-course dinner in Paris, that is pleasure indeed. But in the observatory, looking at the stars, seeing . . . worlds coming and developing — think of that! It must be greater, for I know you forget all about eating. That pleasure must be greater than what you get from worldly things. You forget all about wives, children, husbands, and everything; you forget all about the sense-plane. That is intellectual pleasure. It is common sense that it must be greater than sense pleasure. It is always for greater joy that you give up the lesser. This is practical religion — the attainment of freedom, renunciation. Renounce!

Renounce the lower so that you may get the higher. What is the foundation of society? Morality, ethics, laws. Renounce. Renounce all temptation to take your neighbour's property, to put hands upon your neighbour, all the pleasure of tyrannising over the weak, all the pleasure of cheating others by telling lies. Is not morality the foundation of society? What is marriage but the renunciation of unchastity? The savage does not marry. Man marries because he renounces. So on and on. Renounce! Renounce! Sacrifice! Give up! Not for zero. Not for nothing. But to get the higher. But who can do this? You cannot, until you have got the higher. You may talk. You may struggle. You may try to do many things. But renunciation comes by itself when you have got the higher. Then the lesser falls away by itself.

This is practical religion. What else? Cleaning streets and building hospitals? Their value consists only in this renunciation. And there is no end to renunciation. The difficulty is they try to put a limit to it — thus far and no farther. But there is no limit to this renunciation.

Where God is, there is no other. Where the world is, there is no God. These two will never unite. [Like] light and darkness. That is what I have understood from Christianity and the life of the Teacher. Is not that Buddhism? Is not that Hinduism? Is not that Mohammedanism? Is not that the teaching of all the great sages and teachers? What is the world that is to be given up? It is here. I am carrying it all with me. My own body. It is all for this body that I put my hand voluntarily upon my fellow man, just to keep it nice and give it a little pleasure; [all for this body] that I injure others and make mistakes. ...

Great men have died. Weak men have died. Gods have died. Death — death everywhere. This world is a graveyard of the infinite past, yet we cling to this [body]: "I am never going to die". Knowing for sure [that the body must die] and yet clinging to it. There is meaning in that too [because in a sense we do not die]. The mistake is that we cling to the body when it is the spirit that is really immortal.

You are all materialists, because you believe that you are the body. If a man gives me a hard punch, I would say I am punched. If he strikes me, I would say I am struck. If I am not the body, why should I say so? It makes no difference if I say I am the spirit. I am the body just now. I have converted myself into matter. That is why I am to renounce the body, to go back to what I really am. I am the spirit — the soul no instrument can pierce, no sword can cut asunder, no fire can burn, no air can dry. Unborn and uncreated, without beginning and without end, deathless, birthless and omnipresent — that is what I am; and all misery comes just because I think this little lump of clay is myself. I am identifying myself with matter and taking all the consequences.

Practical religion is identifying myself with my Self. Stop this wrong identification! How far are you advanced in that? You may have built two thousand hospitals, built fifty thousand roads, and yet what of that, if you, have not realised that you are the spirit? You die a dog's; death, with the same feelings that the dog does. The dog howls and weeps because he knows that he is only matter and he is going to be dissolved.

There is death, you know, inevitable death, in water, in air, in the palace, in the prison - death everywhere. What makes you fearless? When you have realised what you are — that infinite spirit, deathless, birthless. Him no fire can burn, no instrument kill, no poison hurt. Not theory, mind you. Not reading books. . . . [Not parroting.] My old Master used to say, "It is all very good to teach the parrot to say, 'Lord, Lord, Lord' all the time; but let the cat come and take hold of its neck, it forgets all about it" [You may] pray all the time, read all the scriptures in the world, and worship all the gods there are, [but] unless you realise the soul there is no freedom. Not talking, theorising, argumentation, but realisation. That I call practical religion.

This truth about the soul is first to be heard. If you have heard it, think about it. Once you have done that, meditate upon it. No more vain arguments! Satisfy yourself once that you are the infinite spirit. If that is true, it must be nonsense that you are the body. You are the Self, and that must be realised. Spirit must see itself as spirit. Now the spirit is seeing itself as body. That must stop. The moment you begin to realise that, you are released.

You see this glass, and you know it is simply an illusion. Some scientists tell you it is light and vibration. ... Seeing the spirit must be infinitely more real: than that, must be the only true state, the only true sensation, the only true vision. All these [objects you see], are but dreams. You know that now. Not the old idealists alone, but modern physicists also tell you that light is there. A little more vibration makes all the difference. ...

You must see God. The spirit must be realised, and that is practical religion. It is not what Christ preached that you call practical religion: "Blessed are the poor in spirit for theirs is the Kingdom of Heaven." Was it a joke? What is the practical religion you are thinking, of? Lord help us! "Blessed are the pure in heart, for they shall see God." That means street-cleaning, hospital-building, and all that? Good works, when you do them with a pure mind. Don't give the man twenty dollars and buy all the papers in San Francisco to see your name! Don't you read in your own books how no man will help you? Serve as worship of the Lord Himself in the poor, the miserable, the weak. That done, the result is secondary. That sort of work, done without any thought of gain, benefits the soul. And even of such is the Kingdom of Heaven.

The Kingdom of Heaven is within us. He is there.

He is the soul of all souls. See Him in your own soul. That is practical religion. That is freedom. Let us ask each other how much we are advanced in that: how much we are worshippers of the body, or real believers in God, the spirit; how much we believe ourselves to be spirit. That is selfless. That is freedom. That is real worship. Realise yourself. That is all there is to do. Know yourself as you are — infinite spirit. That is practical religion. Everything else is impractical, for everything else will vanish. That alone will never vanish. It Is eternal. Hospitals will tumble down. Railroad givers will all die. This earth will be blown to pieces, suns wiped out. The soul endureth for ever.

Which is higher, running after these things which perish or. . . . worshipping that which never changes? Which is more practical, spending all the energies of life in getting things, and before you have got them death comes and you have to leave them all? — like the great [ruler] who conquered all, [who when] death came, said, "Spread out all the jars of things before me." He said "Bring me that big diamond." And he placed it on his breast and wept. Thus weeping, he died the same as the dog dies.

Man says, "I live." He knows not that it is [the fear of] death that makes him cling slavishly to life. He says "I enjoy." He never dreams that nature has enslaved him.

Nature grinds all of us. Keep count of the ounce of pleasure you get. In the long run, nature did her work through you, and when you die your body will make other plants grow. Yet we think all the time that we are getting pleasure ourselves. Thus the wheel goes round.

Therefore to realise the spirit as spirit is practical religion. Everything else is good so far as it leads to this one grand idea. That [realization] is to be attained by renunciation, by meditation — renunciation of all the senses, cutting the knots, the chains that bind us down to matter. "I do not want to get material life, do not want the sense-life, but something higher." That is renunciation. Then, by the power of meditation, undo the mischief that has been done.

We are at the beck and call of nature. If there is sound outside, I have to hear it. If something is going on, I have to see it. Like monkeys. We are two thousand monkeys concentrated, each one of us. Monkeys are very curious. So we cannot help ourselves, and call this "enjoying". Wonderful this language! We are enjoying the world! We cannot help enjoying it. Nature wants us to do it. A beautiful sound: I am hearing it. As if I could choose to hear it or not! Nature says, "Go down to the depths of misery." I become miserable in a moment. ... We talk about pleasures [of the senses] and possessions. One man thinks me very learned. Another thinks, "He is a fool." This degradation, this slavery, without knowing anything! In the dark room we are knocking our heads against each other.

What is meditation? Meditation is the power which enables us to resist all this. Nature may call us, "Look there is a beautiful thing!" I do not look. Now she says, "There is a beautiful smell; smell it! " I say to my nose, "Do not smell it", and the nose doesn't. "Eyes, do not see!" Nature does such an awful thing - kills one of my children, and says, "Now, rascal, sit down and weep! Go to the depths!" I say, "I don't have to." I jump up. I must be free. Try it sometimes. ... [In meditation], for a moment, you can change this nature. Now, if you had that power in yourself, would not that be heaven, freedom? That is the power of meditation.

How is it to be attained? In a dozen different ways. Each temperament has its own way. But this is the general principle: get hold of the mind. The mind is like a lake, and every stone that drops into it raises waves. These waves do not let us see what we are. The full moon is reflected in the water of the lake, but the surface is so disturbed that we do not see the reflection clearly. Let it be calm. Do not let nature raise the wave. Keep quiet, and then after a little while she will give you up. Then we know what we are. God is there already, but the mind is so agitated, always running after the senses. You close the senses and [yet] you whirl and whirl about. Just this moment I think I am all right and I will meditate upon God, and then my mind goes to London in one minute. And if I pull it away from there, it goes to New York to think about the things I have done there in the past. These [waves] are to be stopped by the power of meditation.

Slowly and gradually we are to train ourselves. It is no joke — not a question of a day, or years, or maybe of births. Never mind! The pull must go on. Knowingly, voluntarily, the pull must go on. Inch by inch we will gain ground. We will begin to feel and get real possessions, which no one can take away from us — the wealth that no man can take, the wealth that nobody can destroy, the joy that no misery can hurt any more. ...

All these years we have depended upon others. If I have a little pleasure and that person goes away, my pleasure is gone. ... See the folly of man: he depends for happiness upon men! All separations are misery. Naturally. Depending upon wealth for happiness? There is fluctuation of wealth. Depending upon health or upon anything except the unchangeable spirit must bring misery today or tomorrow.

Excepting the infinite spirit, everything else is changing. There is the whirl of change. Permanence is nowhere except in yourself. There is the infinite joy, unchanging. Meditation is the gate that opens that to us. Prayers, ceremonials, and all the other forms of worship are simply kindergartens of meditation. You pray, you offer something. A certain theory existed that everything raised one's spiritual power. The use of certain words, flowers, images, temples, ceremonials like the waving of lights brings the mind to that attitude, but that attitude is always in the human soul, nowhere else. [People] are all doing it; but what they do without knowing it, do knowingly. That is the power of meditation. All knowledge you have — how did it come? From the power of meditation. The soul churned the knowledge out of its own depths. What knowledge was there ever outside of it? In the long run this power of meditation separates ourselves from the body, and then the soul knows itself as it is — the unborn, the deathless, and birthless being. No more is there any misery, no more births upon this earth, no more evolution. [The soul knows itself as having] ever been perfect and free.

WRITINGS: PROSE

IS THE SOUL IMMORTAL?[1]

"None has power to destroy the unchangeable."

— Bhagavad-Gitâ.

In the great Sanskrit epic, the Mahâbhârata, the story is told how the hero, Yudhishthira, when asked by Dharma to tell what was the most wonderful thing in the world, replied, that it was the persistent belief of man kind in their own deathlessness in spite of their witnessing death everywhere around them almost every moment of their lives. And, in fact, this is the most stupendous wonder in human life. In spite of all arguments to the contrary urged in different times by different schools, in spite of the inability of reason to penetrate the veil of mystery which will ever hang between the sensuous and the supersensuous worlds, man is thoroughly persuaded that he cannot die.

We may study all our lives, and in the end fail to bring the problem of life and death to the plane of rational demonstration, affirmative or negative. We may talk or write, preach or teach, for or against the permanency or impermanency of human existence as much as we like; we may become violent partisans of this side or that; we may invent names by the hundred, each more intricate than its predecessor, and lull ourselves into a momentary rest under the delusion of our having solved the problem once for all; we may cling with all our powers to any one of the curious religious superstitions or the far more objectionable scientific superstitions — but in the end, we find ourselves playing an external game in the bowling alley of reason and raising intellectual pin after pin, only to be knocked over again and again.

But behind all this mental strain and torture, not infrequently productive of more dangerous results than mere games, stands a fact unchallenged and unchallengeable — the fact, the wonder, which the Mahabharata points out as the inability of our mind to conceive our own annihilation. Even to imagine my own annihilation I shall have to stand by and look on as a witness.

Now, before trying to understand what this curious phenomenon means, we want to note that upon this one fact the whole world stands. The permanence of the external world is inevitably joined to the permanence of the internal; and, however plausible any theory of the universe may seem which asserts the permanence of the one and denies that of the other, the theorist himself will find that in his own mechanism not one conscious action is possible, without the permanence of both the internal and the external worlds being one of the factors in the motive cause. Although it is perfectly true that when the human mind transcends its own limitations, it finds the duality reduced to an indivisible unity, on this side of the unconditioned, the whole objective world — that is to say, the world we know — is and can be alone known to us as existing for the subject, and therefore, before we would be able to conceive the annihilation of the subject we are bound to conceive the annihilation of the object.

So far it is plain enough. But now comes the difficulty. I cannot think of myself ordinarily as anything else but a body. My idea of my own permanence includes my idea of myself as a body. But the body is obviously impermanent, as is the whole of nature — a constantly vanishing quantity.

Where, then, is this permanence?

There is one more wonderful phenomenon connected with our lives, without which "who will be able to live, who will be able to enjoy life a moment?" — the idea of freedom.

This is the idea that guides each footstep of ours, makes our movements possible, determines our relations to each other — nay, is the very warp and woof in the fabric of human life. Intellectual knowledge tries to drive it inch by inch from its territory, post after post is snatched away from its domains, and each step is made fast and ironbound with the railroadings of cause and effect. But it laughs at all our attempts, and, lo, it keeps itself above all this

---

[1]. The Swamiji's contribution to the discussion of this question, carried on in the pages of *The New York Morning Advertiser*.

massive pile of law and causation with which we tried to smother it to death! How can it be otherwise? The limited always requires a higher generalization of the unlimited to explain itself. The bound can only be explained by the free, the caused by the uncaused. But again, the same difficulty is also here. What is free? The body or even the mind? It is apparent to all that they are as much bound by law as anything else in the universe.

Now the problem resolves itself into this dilemma: either the whole universe is a mass of never-ceasing change and nothing more, irrevocably bound by the law of causation, not one particle having a unity of itself, yet is curiously producing an ineradicable delusion of permanence and freedom, or there is in us and in the universe something which is permanent and free, showing that the basal constitutional belief of the human mind is not a delusion. It is the duty of science to explain facts by bringing them to a higher generalization. Any explanation, therefore that first wants to destroy a part of the fact given to be explained, in order to fit itself to the remainder, is not scientific, whatever else it may be.

So any explanation that wants to overlook the fact of this persistent and all-necessary idea of freedom commits the above-mentioned mistake of denying a portion of the fact in order to explain the rest, and is, therefore, wrong. The only other alternative possible, then, is to acknowledge, in harmony with our nature, that there is something in us which is free and permanent.

But it is not the body; neither is it the mind. The body is dying every minute. The mind is constantly changing. The body is a combination, and so is the mind, and as such can never reach to a state beyond all change. But beyond this momentary sheathing of gross matter, beyond even the finer covering of the mind is the Âtman, the true Self of man, the permanent, the ever free. It is his freedom that is percolating through layers of thought and matter, and, in spite of the colourings of name and form, is ever asserting its unshackled existence. It is his deathlessness, his bliss, his peace, his divinity that shines out and makes itself felt in spite of the thickest layers of ignorance. He is the real man, the fearless one, the deathless one, the free.

Now freedom is only possible when no external power can exert any influence, produce any change. Freedom is only possible to the being who is beyond all conditions, all laws, all bondages of cause and effect. In other words, the unchangeable alone can be free and, therefore, immortal. This Being, this Atman, this real Self of man, the free, the unchangeable is beyond all conditions, and as such, it has neither birth nor death.

"Without birth or death, eternal, ever-existing is this soul of man."

REINCARNATION[1]

"Both you and I have passed through many births; you know them not, I know them all."

— Bhagavad-Gitâ

Of the many riddles that have perplexed the intellect of man in all climes and times, the most intricate is himself. Of the myriad mysteries that have called forth his energies to struggle for solution from the very dawn of history, the most mysterious is his own nature. It is at once the most insoluble enigma and the problem of all problems. As the starting-point and the repository of all we know and feel and do, there never has been, nor will be, a time when man's own nature will cease to demand his best and foremost attention.

Though through hunger after that truth, which of all others has the most intimate connection with his very existence, though through an all-absorbing desire for an inward standard by which to measure the outward universe though through the absolute and inherent necessity of finding a fixed point in a universe of change, man has sometimes clutched at handfuls of dust for gold, and even when urged on by a voice higher than reason or intellect, he has many times failed rightly to interpret the real

---

[1]. Contributed to the *Metaphysical Magazine*, New York, March, 1895

meaning of the divinity within — still there never was a time since the search began, when some race, or some individuals, did not hold aloft the lamp of truth.

Taking a one-sided, cursory and prejudiced view of the surroundings and the unessential details, sometimes disgusted also with the vagueness of many schools and sects, and often, alas, driven to the opposite extreme by the violent superstitions of organised priestcraft — men have not been wanting, especially among advanced intellects, in either ancient or modern times, who not only gave up the search in despair, but declared it fruitless and useless. Philosophers might fret and sneer, and priests ply their trade even at the point of the sword, but truth comes to those alone who worship at her shrine for her sake only, without fear and without shopkeeping.

Light comes to individuals through the conscious efforts of their intellect; it comes, slowly though, to the whole race through unconscious percolations. The philosophers show the volitional struggles of great minds; history reveals the silent process of permeation through which truth is absorbed by the masses.

Of all the theories that have been held by man about himself, that of a soul entity, separate from the body and immortal, has been the most widespread; and among those that held the belief in such a soul, the majority of the thoughtful had always believed also in its pre-existence.

At present the greater portion of the human race, having organised religion, believe in it; and many of the best thinkers in the most favoured lands, though nurtured in religions avowedly hostile to every idea of the preexistence of the soul, have endorsed it. Hinduism and Buddhism have it for their foundation; the educated classes among the ancient Egyptians believed in it; the ancient Persians arrived at it; the Greek philosophers made it the corner-stone of their philosophy; the Pharisees among the Hebrews accepted it; and the Sufis among the Mohammedans almost universally acknowledged its truth.

There must be peculiar surroundings which generate and foster certain forms of belief among nations. It required ages for the ancient races to arrive at any idea about a part, even of the body, surviving after death; it took ages more to come to any rational idea about this something which persists and lives apart from the body. It was only when the idea was reached of an entity whose connection with the body was only for a time, and only among those nations who arrived at such a conclusion, that the unavoidable question arose: Whither? Whence?

The ancient Hebrews never disturbed their equanimity by questioning themselves about the soul. With them death ended all. Karl Heckel justly says, "Though it is true that in the Old Testament, preceding the exile, the Hebrews distinguish a life-principle, different from the body, which is sometimes called 'Nephesh', or 'Ruakh', or 'Neshama', yet all these words correspond rather to the idea of breath than to that of spirit or soul. Also in the writings of the Palestinean Jews, after the exile, there is never made mention of an individual immortal soul, but always only of a life-breath emanating from God, which, after the body is dissolved, is reabsorbed into the Divine 'Ruakh'."

The ancient Egyptians and the Chaldeans had peculiar beliefs of their own about the soul; but their ideas about this living part after death must not be confused with those of the ancient Hindu, the Persian, the Greek, or any other Aryan race. There was, from the earliest times, a broad distinction between the Âryas and the non-Sanskrit speaking Mlechchhas in the conception of the soul. Externally it was typified by their disposal of the dead — the Mlechchhas mostly trying their best to preserve the dead bodies either by careful burial or by the more elaborate processes of mummifying, and the Aryas generally burning their dead.

Herein lies the key to a great secret — the fact that no Mlechchha race, whether Egyptian, Assyrian, or Babylonian, ever attained to the idea of the soul as a separate entity which can live independent of the body, without he help of the Aryas, especially of the Hindus.

Although Herodotus states that the Egyptians

were the first to conceive the idea of the immortality of the soul, and states as a doctrine of the Egyptians "that the soul after the dissolution of the body enters again and again into a creature that comes to life; then, that the soul wanders through all the animals of the land and the sea and through all the birds, and finally after three thousand years returns to a human body," yet, modern researches into Egyptology have hitherto found no trace of metempsychosis in the popular Egyptian religion. On the other hand, the most recent researches of Maspero, A. Erman, and other eminent Egyptologists tend to confirm the supposition that the doctrine of palingenesis was not at home with the Egyptians.

With the ancient Egyptians the soul was only a double, having no individuality of its own, and never able to break its connection with the body. It persists only so long as the body lasts; and if by chance the corpse is destroyed, the departed soul must suffer a second death and annihilation. The soul after death was allowed to roam freely all over the world, but always returning at night to where the corpse was, always miserable, always hungry and thirsty, always extremely desirous to enjoy life once more, and never being able to fulfil the desire. If any part of its old body was injured, the soul was also invariably injured in its corresponding part. And this idea explains the solicitude of the ancient Egyptians to preserve their dead. At first the deserts were chosen as the burial-place, because the dryness of the air did not allow the body to perish soon, thus granting to the departed soul a long lease of existence. In course of time one of the gods discovered the process of making mummies, through which the devout hoped to preserve the dead bodies of their ancestors for almost an infinite length of time, thus securing immortality to the departed ghost, however miserable it might be.

The perpetual regret for the world, in which the soul can take no further interest, never ceased to torture the deceased. "O. my brother," exclaims the departed "withhold not thyself from drinking and eating, from drunkenness, from love, from all enjoyment, from following thy desire by night and by day; put not sorrow within thy heart, for, what are the years of man upon earth? The West is a land of sleep and of heavy shadows, a place wherein the inhabitants, when once installed, slumber on in their mummy forms, never more waking to see their brethren; never more to recognise their fathers and mothers, with hearts forgetful of their wives and children The living water, which earth giveth to all who dwell upon it, is for me stagnant and dead; that water floweth to all who are on earth, while for me it is but liquid putrefaction, this water that is mine. Since I came into this funeral valley I know not where nor what I am. Give me to drink of running water . . . let me be placed by the edge of the water with my face to the North, that the breeze may caress me and my heart be refreshed from its sorrow."[1]

Among the Chaldeans also, although they did not speculate so much as the Egyptians as to the condition of the soul after death, the soul is still a double and is bound to its sepulchre. They also could not conceive of a state without this physical body, and expected a resurrection of the corpse again to life; and though the goddess Ishtar, after great perils and adventures, procured the resurrection of her shepherd, husband, Dumuzi, the son of Ea and Damkina, "The most pious votaries pleaded in rain from temple to temple, for the resurrection of their dead friends."

Thus we find, that the ancient Egyptians or Chaldeans never could entirely dissociate the idea of the soul from the corpse of the departed or the sepulchre. The state of earthly existence was best after all; and the departed are always longing to have a chance once more to renew it; and the living are fervently hoping to help them in prolonging the existence of the miserable double and striving the best they can to help them.

This is not the soil out of which any higher knowledge of the soul could spring. In the first place it is grossly materialistic, and even then it is one of terror and agony. Frightened by the almost innumerable powers of evil, and with hopeless, agonised efforts to avoid them, the souls of the living, like

---

1. This text has been translated into German by Brugsch, *Die Egyptische Gräberwelt*, pp. 39, 40, and into French by Maspero, *Études Égyptiennes*, vol. I., pp. 181-90.

their ideas of the souls of the departed — wander all over the world though they might — could never get beyond the sepulchre and the crumbling corpse.

We must turn now for the source of the higher ideas of the soul to another race, whose God was an all-merciful, all-pervading Being manifesting Himself through various bright, benign, and helpful Devas, the first of all the human race who addressed their God as Father "Oh, take me by the hands even as a father takes his dear son"; with whom life was a hope and not a despair; whose religion was not the intermittent groans escaping from the lips of an agonised man during the intervals of a life of mad excitement; but whose ideas come to us redolent with the aroma of the field and forest; whose songs of praise — spontaneous, free, joyful, like the songs which burst forth from the throats of the birds when they hail this beautiful world illuminated by the first rays of the lord of the day — come down to us even now through the vista of eighty centuries as fresh calls from heaven; we turn to the ancient Aryas.

"Place me in that deathless, undecaying world where is the light of heaven, and everlasting lustre shines"; "Make me immortal in that realm where dwells the King Vivasvân's son, where is the secret shrine of heaven"; "Make me immortal in that realm where they move even as they list"; "In the third sphere of inmost heaven, where worlds are full of light, make me immortal in that realm of bliss"— These are the prayers of the Aryas in their oldest record, the Rig-Veda Samhitâ.

We find at once a whole world of difference between the Mlechchha and the Aryan ideals. To the one, this body and this world are all that are real, and all that are desirable. A little life-fluid which flies off from the body at death, to feel torture and agony at the loss of the enjoyments of the senses, can, they fondly hope, be brought back if the body is carefully preserved; and thus a corpse became more an object of care than the living man. The other found out that, that which left the body was the real man; and when separated from the body, it enjoyed a state of bliss higher than it ever enjoyed when in the body. And they hastened to annihilate the corrupted corpse by burning it.

Here we find the germ out of which a true idea of the soul could come. Here it was — where the real man was not the body, but the soul, where all ideas of an inseparable connection between the real man and the body were utterly absent — that a noble idea of the freedom of the soul could rise. And it was when the Aryas penetrated even beyond the shining cloth of the body with which the departed soul was enveloped, and found its real nature of a formless, individual, unit principle, that the question inevitably arose: Whence?

It was in India and among the Aryas that the doctrine of the pre-existence, the immortality, and the individuality of the soul first arose. Recent researches in Egypt have failed to show any trace of the doctrines of an independent and individual soul existing before and after the earthly phase of existence. Some of the mysteries were no doubt in possession of this idea, but in those it has been traced to India.

"I am convinced", says Karl Heckel, "that the deeper we enter into the study of the Egyptian religion, the clearer it is shown that the doctrine of metempsychosis was entirely foreign to the popular Egyptian religion; and that even that which single mysteries possessed of it was not inherent to the Osiris teachings, but derived from Hindu sources."

Later on, we find the Alexandrian Jews imbued with the doctrine of an individual soul, and the Pharisees of the time of Jesus, as already stated, not only had faith in an individual soul, but believed in its wandering through various bodies; and thus it is easy to find how Christ was recognised as the incarnation of an older Prophet, and Jesus himself directly asserted that John the Baptist was the Prophet Elias come back again. "If ye will receive it, this is Elias, which was for to come." — Matt. XI. 14.

The ideas of a soul and of its individuality among the Hebrews, evidently came through the higher mystical teachings of the Egyptians, who in their turn derived it from India. And that it should come through Alexandria is significant, as the Buddhistic records clearly show Buddhistic missionary activity in Alexandria and Asia Minor.

Pythagoras is said to have been the first Greek who taught the doctrine of palingenesis among the Hellenes. As an Aryan race, already burning their dead and believing in the doctrine of an individual soul, it was easy for the Greeks to accept the doctrine of reincarnation through the Pythagorean teachings. According to Apuleius, Pythagoras had come to India, where he had been instructed by the Brâhmins.

So far we have learnt that wherever the soul was held to be an individual, the real man, and not a vivifying part of the body only, the doctrine of its pre-existence had inevitably come, and that externally those nations that believed in the independent individuality of the soul had almost always signified it by burning the bodies of the departed. Though one of the ancient Aryan races, the Persian, developed at an early period and without any; Semitic influence a peculiar method of disposing of the bodies of the dead, the very name by which they call their "Towers of silence", comes from the root Dah, to burn.

In short, the races who did not pay much attention to the analysis of their own nature, never went beyond the material body as their all in all, and even when driven by higher light to penetrate beyond, they only came to the conclusion that somehow or other, at some distant period of time, this body will become incorruptible.

On the other hand, that race which spent the best part of its energies in the inquiry into the nature of man as a thinking being — the Indo-Aryan — soon found out that beyond this body, beyond even the shining body which their forefathers longed after, is the real man, the principle, the individual who clothes himself with this body, and then throws it off when worn out. Was such a principle created? If creation means something coming out of nothing, their answer is a decisive "No". This soul is without birth and without death; it is not a compound or combination but an independent individual, and as such it cannot be created or destroyed. It is only travelling through various states.

Naturally, the question arises: Where was it all this time? The Hindu philosophers say, "It was passing through different bodies in the physical sense, or, really and metaphysically speaking, passing through different mental planes."

Are there any proofs apart from the teachings of the Vedas upon which the doctrine of reincarnation has been founded by the Hindu philosophers? There are, and we hope to show later on that there are grounds as valid for it as for any other universally accepted doctrine. But first we will see what some of the greatest of modern European thinkers have thought about reincarnation.

I. H. Fichte, speaking about the immortality of the soul, says:

"It is true there is one analogy in nature which might be brought forth in refutation of the continuance. It is the well-known argument that everything that has a beginning in time must also perish at some period of time; hence, that the claimed past existence of the soul necessarily implies its pre-existence. This is a fair conclusion, but instead of being an objection to, it is rather an additional argument for its continuance. Indeed, one needs only to understand the full meaning of the metaphysico-physiological axiom that in reality nothing can be created or annihilated, to recognise that the soul must have existed prior to its becoming visible in a physical body."

Schopenhauer, in his book, *Die Welt als Wille und Vorstellung*, speaking about palingenesis, says:

"What sleep is for the individual, death is for the 'will'. It would not endure to continue the same actions and sufferings throughout an eternity without true gain, if memory and individuality remained to it. It flings them off, and this is Lethe, and through this sleep of death it reappears fitted out with another intellect as a new being; a new day tempts to new shores. These constant new births, then, constitute the succession of the life-dreams of a will which in itself is indestructible, until instructed and improved by so much and such various successive knowledge in a constantly new form, it abolishes and abrogates itself.... It must not be neglected that even empirical grounds support a palingenesis of this kind. As a matter of fact, there does exist a connection between the birth of the newly appearing beings and the death of those that are worn out. It shows itself in the great fruitfulness of the human race which appears as a consequence of devastating diseases. When in the fourteenth century the Black Death had for the most part depopulated the Old World, a quite abnormal fruitfulness appeared among the human race, and twin-births were very frequent. The circumstance was also remarkable that none of the children born at this time obtained their full number of teeth; thus nature, exerting itself to the utmost, was niggardly in details. This is related by F. Schnurrer in his Chronik der Seuchen, 1825. Casper, also, in his Ueber die Wahrscheinliche Lebensdauer des Menschen, 1835, confirms the principle that the number of births in a given population has the most decided influence upon the length of life and mortality in it, as this always keeps pace with mortality; so that always and everywhere the deaths and the births increase and decrease in like proportion, which he places beyond doubt by an accumulation of evidence collected from many lands and their various provinces. And yet it is impossible that there can be physical, causal connection between my early death and the fruitfulness of a marriage with which I have nothing to do, or conversely. Thus here the metaphysical appears undeniable, and in a stupendous manner, as the immediate ground of explanation of the physical. Every new-born being comes fresh and blithe into the new existence, and enjoys it as a free gift; but there is and can be nothing freely given. Its fresh existence is paid for by the old age and death of a worn-out existence which has perished, but which contained the indestructible seed out of which the new existence has arisen; they are one being."

The great English philosopher Hume, nihilistic though he was, says in the sceptical essay on immortality, "The metempsychosis is therefore the only system of this kind that philosophy can listen to." The philosopher Lessing, with a deep poetical insight, asks, "Is this hypothesis so laughable merely because it is the oldest, because the human understanding, before the sophistries of the schools had dissipated and debilitated it, lighted upon it at once? . . . Why should not I come back as often as I am capable of acquiring fresh knowledge, fresh experience? Do I bring away so much from once that there is nothing to repay the trouble of coming back?"

The arguments for and against the doctrine of a preexisting soul reincarnating through many lives have been many, and some of the greatest thinkers of all ages have taken up the gauntlet to defend it; and so far as we can see, if there is an individual soul, that it existed before seems inevitable. If the soul is not an individual but a combination of "Skandhas" (notions), as the Mâdhyamikas among the Buddhists insist, still they find pre-existence absolutely necessary to explain their position.

The argument showing the impossibility of an infinite existence beginning in time is unanswerable, though attempts have been made to ward it off by appealing to the omnipotence of God to do anything, however contrary to reason it may be. We are sorry to find this most fallacious argument proceeding from some of the most thoughtful persons.

In the first place, God being the universal and common cause of all phenomena, the question was to find the natural causes of certain phenomena in the human soul, and the Deus ex machina theory is, therefore, quite irrelevant. It amounts to nothing less than confession of ignorance. We can give that answer to every question asked in every branch of human knowledge and stop all inquiry and, therefore, knowledge altogether.

Secondly, this constant appeal to the omnipotence of God is only a word-puzzle. The cause, as cause, is and can only be known to us as sufficient for the effect, and nothing more. As such we have no more idea of an infinite effect than of an omnipotent cause. Moreover, all our ideas of God are only limited; even the idea of cause limits our idea of God. Thirdly, even taking the position for granted, we are not bound to allow any such absurd theories as "Something coming out of nothing", or "Infinity beginning in time", so long as we can give a better explanation.

A so-called great argument is made against the idea of pre-existence by asserting that the majority of mankind are not conscious of it. To prove the validity of this argument, the party who offers it must prove that the whole of the soul of man is bound up in the faculty of memory. If memory be the test of existence, then all that part of our lives which is not now in it must be non-existent, and every, person who in a state of coma or otherwise loses his memory must be non-existent also.

The premises from which the inference is drawn of a previous existence, and that too on the plane of conscious' action, as adduced by the Hindu philosophers, are chiefly these:

First, how else to explain this world of inequalities? Here is one child born in the province of a just and merciful God, with every circumstance conducing to his becoming a good and useful member of the human race, and perhaps at the same instant and in the same city another child is born under circumstances every one of which is against his becoming good. We see children born to suffer, perhaps all their lives, and that owing to no fault of theirs. Why should it be so? What is the cause? Of whose ignorance is it the result? If not the child's, why should it suffer for its parents' actions?

It is much better to confess ignorance than to try to evade the question by the allurements of future enjoyments in proportion to the evil here, or by posing "mysteries". Not only undeserved suffering forced upon us by any agent is immoral — not to say unjust — but even the future-makingup theory has no legs to stand upon.

How many of the miserably born struggle towards a higher life, and how many more succumb to the circumstances they are placed under? Should those who grow worse and more wicked by being forced to be born under evil circumstances be rewarded in the future for the wickedness of their lives? In that case the more wicked the man is here, the better will be his deserts hereafter.

There is no other way to vindicate the glory and the liberty of the human soul and reconcile the inequalities and the horrors of this world than by placing the whole burden upon the legitimate cause — our own independent actions or Karma. Not only so, but every theory of the creation of the soul from nothing inevitably leads to fatalism and preordination, and instead of a Merciful Father, places before us a hideous, cruel, and an ever-angry God to worship. And so far as the power of religion for good or evil is concerned, this theory of a created soul, leading to its corollaries of fatalism and predestination, is responsible for the horrible idea prevailing among some Christians and Mohammedans that the heathens are the lawful victims of their swords, and all the horrors that have followed and are following it still.

But an argument which the philosophers of the Nyâya school have always advanced in favour of reincarnations and which to us seems conclusive, is this: Our experiences cannot be annihilated. Our actions (Karma) though apparently disappearing, remain still unperceived (Adrishta), and reappear again in their effect as tendencies (Pravrittis). Even little babies come with certain tendencies — fear of death, for example.

Now if a tendency is the result of repeated actions, the tendencies with which we are born must be explained on that ground too. Evidently we could not have got them in this life; therefore we must have to seek for their genesis in the past. Now it is also evident that some of our tendencies are the effects of the self-conscious efforts peculiar to man; and if it is true that we are born with such tendencies, it rigorously follows that their causes were conscious efforts in the past — that is, we must have been on the same mental plane which we call the human plane, before this present life.

So far as explaining the tendencies of the present life by past conscious efforts goes, the reincarnationists of India and the latest school of evolutionists are at once; the only difference is that the Hindus, as spiritualists, explain it by the conscious efforts of individual souls, and the materialistic school of evolutionists, by a hereditary physical transmission. The schools which hold to the theory of creation out of nothing are entirely out of court.

The issue has to be fought out between the reincarnationists who hold that all experiences are stored up as; tendencies in the subject of those experiences, the individual soul, and are transmitted by reincarnation of that unbroken individuality — and the materialists who hold that the brain is the subject of all actions and the theory of the transmission through cells.

It is thus that the doctrine of reincarnation assumes an infinite importance to our mind, for the fight between reincarnation and mere cellular transmission is, in reality, the fight between spiritualism and materialism. If cellular transmission is the all-sufficient explanation, materialism is inevitable, and there is no necessity for the theory of a soul. If it is not a sufficient explanation, the theory of an individual soul bringing into this life the experiences of the past is as absolutely true. There is no escape from the alternative, reincarnation or materialism. Which shall we accept?

ON DR. PAUL DEUSSEN[1]

More than a decade has passed since a young German student, one of eight children of a not very well-to-do clergyman, heard on a certain day Professor Lassen lecturing on a language and literature new — very new even at that time — to European scholars, namely, Sanskrit. The lectures were of course free; for even now it is impossible for any one in any European University to make a living by teaching Sanskrit, unless indeed the University backs him.

Lassen was almost the last of that heroic band of German scholars, the pioneers of Sanskrit scholarship in Germany. Heroic certainly they were — what interest except their pure and unselfish love of knowledge could German scholars have had at that time in Indian literature? The veteran Professor was expounding a chapter of Shakuntalâ; and on that day there was no one present more eagerly and attentively listening to Lassen's exposition than our

1. Written for the *Brahmavâdin*, 1896.

young student. The subject-matter of the exposition was of course interesting and wonderful, but more wonderful was the strange language, the strange sounds of which, although uttered with all those difficult peculiarities that Sanskrit consonants are subjected to in the mouths of unaccustomed Europeans, had strange fascination for him. He returned to his lodgings, but that night sleep could not make him oblivious of what he had heard. A glimpse of a hitherto unknown land had been given to him, a land far more gorgeous in its colours than any he had yet seen, and having a power of fascination never yet experienced by his young and ardent soul.

Naturally his friends were anxiously looking forward to the ripening of his brilliant parts, and expected that he would soon enter a learned profession which might bring him respect, fame, and, above all, a good salary and a high position. But then there was this Sanskrit! The vast majority of European scholars had not even heard of it then; as for making it pay — I have already said that such a thing is impossible even now. Yet his desire to learn it was strong.

It has unfortunately become hard for us modern Indians to understand how it could be like that; nevertheless, there are to be met with in Varanasi and Nadia and other places even now, some old as well as young persons among our Pandits, and mostly among the Sannyasins, who are mad with this kind of thirst for knowledge for its own sake. Students, not placed in the midst of the luxurious surroundings and materials of the modern Europeanised Hindu, and with a thousand times less facilities for study, poring over manuscripts in the flickering light of an oil lamp, night after night, which alone would have been enough to completely destroy the eye-sight of the students of any other nation; travelling on foot hundreds of miles, begging their way all along, in search of a rare manuscript or a noted teacher; and wonderfully concentrating all the energy of their body and mind upon their one object of study, year in and year out, till the hair turns grey and the infirmity of age overtakes them — such students have not, through God's mercy, as yet disappeared altogether from our country.

Whatever India now holds as a proud possession, has been undeniably the result of such labour on the part of her worthy sons in days gone by; and the truth of this remark will become at once evident on comparing the depth and solidity as well as the unselfishness and the earnestness of purpose of India's ancient scholarship with the results attained by our modern Indian Universities. Unselfish and genuine zeal for real scholarship and honest earnest thought must again become dominant in the life of our countrymen if they are ever to rise to occupy among nations a rank worthy of their own historic past. It is this kind of desire for knowledge which has made Germany what she is now — one of the foremost, if not the foremost, among the nations of the world.

Yes, the desire to learn Sanskrit was strong in the heart of this German student. It was long, uphill work — this learning of Sanskrit; with him too it was the same world-old story of successful scholars and their hard work, their privations and their indomitable energy — and also the same glorious conclusion of a really heroic achievement. He thus achieved success; and now — not only Europe, but all India knows this man, Paul Deussen, who is the Professor of Philosophy in the University of Kiel. I have seen professors of Sanskrit in America and in Europe. Some of them are very sympathetic towards Vedantic thought. I admire their intellectual acumen and their lives of unselfish labour. But Paul Deussen — or as he prefers to be called in Sanskrit, Deva-Sena — and the veteran Max Müller have impressed me as being the truest friends of India and Indian thought. It will always be among the most pleasing episodes in my life — my first visit to this ardent Vedantist at Kiel, his gentle wife who travelled with him in India, and his little daughter, the darling of his heart — and our travelling together through Germany and Holland to London, and the pleasant meetings we had in and about London.

The earliest school of Sanskritists in Europe entered into the study of Sanskrit with more imagination than critical ability. They knew a little, expected much from that little, and often tried to make too much of what little they knew. Then, in those days even, such vagaries as the estimation of Shakuntala as forming the high watermark of Indian philosophy were not altogether unknown! These were naturally followed by a reactionary band of superficial critics, more than real scholars of any kind, who knew little or nothing of Sanskrit, expected nothing from Sanskrit studies, and ridiculed everything from the East. While criticising the unsound imaginativeness of the early school to whom everything in Indian literature was rose and musk, these, in their turn, went into speculations which, to say the least, were equally highly unsound and indeed very venturesome. And their boldness was very naturally helped by the fact that these over-hasty and unsympathetic scholars and critics were addressing an audience whose entire qualification for pronouncing any judgment in the matter was their absolute ignorance of Sanskrit. What a medley of results from such critical scholarship! Suddenly, on one fine morning, the poor Hindu woke up to find that everything that was his was gone; one strange race had snatched away from him his arts, another his architecture, and a third, whatever there was of his ancient sciences; why, even his religion was not his own! Yes — that too had migrated into India in the wake of a Pehlevi cross of stone! After a feverish period of such treading-on-each-other's-toes of original research, a better state of things has dawned. It has now been found out that mere adventure without some amount of the capital of real and ripe scholarship produces nothing but ridiculous failure even in the business of Oriental research, and that the traditions in India are not to be rejected with supercilious contempt, as there is really more in them than most people ever dream of.

There is now happily coming into existence in Europe a new type of Sanskrit scholars, reverential, sympathetic, and learned — reverential because they are a better stamp of men, and sympathetic because they are learned. And the link which connects the new portion of the chain with the old one is, of course, our Max Müller. We Hindus certainly owe more to him than to any other Sanskrit scholar in the West, and I am simply astonished when I think of the gigantic task which he, in his enthusiasm, undertook as a young man and brought to a successful conclusion in his old age. Think of this man without any help, poring over old manuscripts, hardly legible to the Hindus themselves, and in a language to acquire which takes a lifetime even in India — without even the help of any needy Pandit whose "brains could be picked", as the Americans say, for ten shillings a month, and a mere mention of his name in the introduction to some book of "very new researches" — think of this man, spending days and sometimes months in elucidating the correct reading and meaning of a word or a sentence in the commentary of Sâyana (as he has himself told me), and in the end succeeding in making an easy road through the forest of Vedic literature for all others to go along; think of him and his work, and then say what he really is to us! Of course we need not all agree with him in all that he says in his many writings; certainly such an agreement is impossible. But agreement or no agreement, the fact remains that this one man has done a thousand times more for the preservation, spreading, and appreciation of the literature of our forefathers than any of us can ever hope to do, and he has done it all with a heart which is full of the sweet balm of love and veneration.

If Max Müller is thus the old pioneer of the new movement, Deussen is certainly one of its younger advance-guard. Philological interest had hidden long from view the gems of thought and spirituality to be found in the mine of our ancient scriptures. Max Müller brought out a few of them and exhibited them to the public gaze, compelling attention to them by means of his authority as the foremost philologist. Deussen, unhampered by any philological leanings and possessing the training of a philosopher singularly well versed in the speculations of ancient Greece and modern Germany, took up the cue and plunged boldly into the metaphysical depths of the Upanishads, found them to be fully safe and satisfying, and then — equally boldly declared that fact before the whole world. Deussen is certainly the freest among scholars in the expression of his opinion about the Vedanta. He never stops to think about the "What they would say" of the vast majority of scholars. We indeed require bold men in this world to tell us bold words about truth; and nowhere, is this more true now than in Europe where, through the fear of social opinion and such other causes, there has been enough in all conscience of the whitewashing and apologising attitude among scholars towards creeds and customs which, in all probability, not many among them really believe in. The greater is the glory, therefore, to Max Müller and to Deussen for their bold and open advocacy of truth! May they be as bold in showing to us our defects, the later corruptions in our thought-systems in India, especially in their application to our social needs! Just now we very much require the help of such genuine friends as these to check the growing virulence of the disease, very prevalent in India, of running either to the one extreme of slavish panegyrists who cling to every village superstition as the innermost essence of the Shâstras, or to the other extreme of demoniacal denouncers who see no good in us and in our history, and will, if they can, at once dynamite all the social and spiritual organizations of our ancient land of religion and philosophy.

ON PROFESSOR MAX MÜLLER[1]

Though the ideal of work of our Brahmavâdin should always be "कर्मण्येवाधिकारस्ते मा फलेषु कदाचन — To work thou hast the right, but never to the fruits thereof", yet no sincere worker passes out of the field of activity without making himself known and catching at least a few rays of light.

The beginning of our work has been splendid, and the steady earnestness shown by our friends is beyond all praise. Sincerity of conviction and purity of motive will surely gain the day; and even a small minority, armed with these, is surely destined to prevail against all odds.

Keep away from all insincere claimants to super-

---
1. Written for the *Brahmâvadin*, from London, June 6, 1896.

natural illumination; not that such illumination is impossible, but, my friends, in this world of ours "lust, or gold, or fame" is the hidden motive behind ninety per cent of all such claims, and of the remaining ten per cent, nine per cent are cases which require the tender care of physicians more than the attention of metaphysicians.

The first great thing to accomplish is to establish a character, to obtain, as we say, the प्रतिष्ठिता प्रज्ञा (established Wisdom). This applies equally to individuals and to organised bodies of individuals. Do not fret because the world looks with suspicion at every new attempt, even though it be in the path of spirituality. The poor world, how often has it been cheated! The more the संसार that is, the worldly aspect of life, looks at any growing movement with eyes of suspicion, or, even better still, presents to it a semi-hostile front, so much the better is it for the movement. If there is any truth this movement has to disseminate, any need it is born to supply, soon will condemnation be changed into praise, and contempt converted into love. People in these days are apt to take up religion as a means to some social or political end. Beware of this. Religion is its own end. That religion which is only a means to worldly well-being is not religion, whatever else it may be; and it is sheer blasphemy against God and man to hold that man has no other end than the free and full enjoyment of all the pleasure of his senses.

Truth, purity, and unselfishness — wherever these are present, there is no power below or above the sun to crush the possessor thereof. Equipped with these, one individual is able to face the whole universe in opposition.

Above all, beware of compromises. I do not mean that you are to get into antagonism with anybody, but you have to hold on to your own principles in weal or woe and never adjust them to others' "fads" through the greed of getting supporters. Your Âtman is the support of the universe — whose support do you stand in need of? Wait with patience and love and strength; if helpers are not ready now, they will come in time. Why should we be in a hurry? The real working force of all great work is in its almost unperceived beginnings.

Whoever could have thought that the life and teachings of a boy born of poor Brâhmin parents in a wayside Bengal village would, in a few years, reach such distant lands as our ancestors never even dreamed of? I refer to Bhagavan Ramâkrishna. Do you know that Prof. Max Müller has already written an article on Shri Ramakrishna for the Nineteenth Century, and will be very glad to write a larger and fuller account of his life and teachings if sufficient materials are forthcoming? What an extraordinary man is Prof. Max Müller! I paid a visit to him a few days ago. I should say, that I went to pay my respects to him, for whosoever loves Shri Ramakrishna, whatever be his or her sect, or creed, or nationality, my visit to that person I hold as a pilgrimage. "मद्भक्तानां च ये भक्तास्ते मे भक्ततमा मताः — They who are devoted to those who love Me — they are My best devotees." Is that not true?

The Professor was first induced to inquire about the power behind, which led to sudden and momentous changes in the life of the late Keshab Chandra Sen, the great Brâhmo leader; and since then, he has been an earnest student and admirer of the life and teachings of Shri Ramakrishna. "Ramakrishna is worshipped by thousands today, Professor", I said. "To whom else shall worship be accorded, if not to such", was the answer. The Professor was kindness itself, and asked Mr. Sturdy and myself to lunch with him. He showed us several colleges in Oxford and the Bodleian library. He also accompanied us to the railway station; and all this he did because, as he said, "It is not every day one meets a disciple of Ramakrishna Paramahamsa."

The visit was really a revelation to me. That nice little house in its setting of a beautiful garden, the silverheaded sage, with a face calm and benign, and forehead smooth as a child's in spite of seventy winters, and every line in that face speaking of a deep-seated mine of spirituality somewhere behind; that noble wife, the helpmate of his life through his long and arduous task of exciting interest, overriding opposition and contempt, and at last creating a respect for the thoughts of the sages of ancient India — the trees, the flowers, the calmness, and the clear sky — all these sent me back in imagination to the glorious days of Ancient India, the days of our Brahmarshis and Râjarshis, the days of the great Vânaprasthas, the days of Arundhatis and Vasishthas.

It was neither the philologist nor the scholar that I saw, but a soul that is every day realising its oneness with the Brahman, a heart that is every moment expanding to reach oneness with the Universal. Where others lose themselves in the desert of dry details, he has struck the well-spring of life. Indeed his heartbeats have caught the rhythm of the Upanishads "तमेवैकं जानथ जात्मानमन्या वाचो वमुञ्चथ — Know the Atman alone, and leave off all other talk."

Although a world-moving scholar and philosopher, his learning and philosophy have only led him higher and higher to the realisation of the Spirit, his अपरा विद्या (lower knowledge) has indeed helped him to reach the परा विद्या (higher knowledge). This is real learning. विद्या ददाति विनयम् — "Knowledge gives humility." Of what use is knowledge if it does not show us the way to the Highest?

And what love he bears towards India! I wish I had a hundredth part of that love for my own motherland! Endued with an extraordinary, and at the same time intensely active mind, he has lived and moved in the world of Indian thought for fifty years or more, and watched the sharp interchange of light and shade in the interminable forest of Sanskrit literature with deep interest and heartfelt love, till they have all sunk into his very soul and coloured his whole being.

Max Müller is a Vedantist of Vedantists. He has, indeed, caught the real soul of the melody of the Vedanta, in the midst of all its settings of harmonies and discords — the one light that lightens the sects and creeds of the world, the Vedanta, the one principle of which all religions are only applications. And what was Ramakrishna Paramahamsa? The practical demonstration of this ancient principle, the embodiment of India that is past, and a foreshadowing of the India that is to be, the bearer of spiritual light unto nations. The jeweller alone can understand the worth of jewels; this is an old proverb. Is it a wonder that this Western sage does study and appreciate every new star in the firmament of Indian thought, before even the Indians themselves realise its magnitude?

"When are you coming to India? Every heart there would welcome one who has done so much to place the thoughts of their ancestors in the true light", I said. The face of the aged sage brightened up — there was almost a tear in his eyes, a gentle nodding of the head, and slowly the words came out: "I would not return then; you would have to cremate me there." Further questions seemed an unwarrantable intrusion into realms wherein are stored the holy secrets of man's heart. Who knows but that it was what the poet has said—

तच्चेतसा समरति नूनमबोधपूर्वं ।
भावस्थिराणि जननान्तरसौहृदानि ॥

—"He remembers with his mind the friendships of former births, firmly rooted in his heart."

His life has been a blessing to the world; and may it be many, many years more, before he changes the present plane of his existence!

SKETCH OF THE LIFE OF PAVHARI BABA

To help the suffering world was the gigantic task to which the Buddha gave prominence, brushing aside for the time being almost all other phases of religion; yet he had to spend years in self-searching to realise the great truth of the utter hollowness of clinging to a selfish individuality. A more unselfish and untiring worker is beyond our most sanguine imagination: yet who had harder struggles to realise the meaning of things than he? It holds good in all times that the greater the work, the more must have been the power of realisation behind. Working out the details of an already laid out masterly plan may not require much concentrated thought to back it, but the great impulses are only transformed great concentrations. The theory alone perhaps is sufficient for small exertions, but the push that creates the ripple is very different from the impulse that raises the wave, and yet the ripple is only the embodiment of a bit of the power that generates the wave.

Facts, naked facts, gaunt and terrible may be; truth, bare truth, though its vibrations may snap every chord of the heart; motive selfless and sincere, though to reach it, limb after limb has to be lopped off — such are to be arrived at, found, and gained, before the mind on the lower plane of activity can raise huge work-waves. The fine accumulates round itself the gross as it rolls on through time and becomes manifest, the unseen crystallises into the seen, the possible becomes the practical, the cause the effect, and thought, muscular work.

The cause, held back by a thousand circumstances, will manifest itself, sooner or later, as the effect; and potent thought, however powerless at present, will have its glorious day on the plane of material activity. Nor is the standard correct which judges of everything by its power to contribute to our sense-enjoyment.

The lower the animal, the more is its enjoyment in the senses, the more it lives in the senses. Civilisation, true civilization, should mean the power of taking the animal-man out of his sense-life — by giving him visions and tastes of planes much higher — and not external comforts.

Man knows this instinctively. He may not formulate it to himself under all circumstances. He may form very divergent opinions about the life of thought. But it is there, pressing itself to the front in spite of everything, making him pay reverence to the hoodoo-worker, the medicine-man, the magician, the priest, or the professor of science. The growth of man can only be gauged by his power of living in the higher atmosphere where the senses are left behind, the amount of the pure thought-oxygen his lungs can breathe in, and the amount of time he can spend on that height.

As it is, it is an obvious fact that, with the exception of what is taken up by the necessities of life, the man of culture is loth to spend his time on so-called comforts, and even necessary actions are performed with lessened zeal, as the process moves forward.

Even luxuries are arranged according to ideas and ideals, to make them reflect as much of thought-life as possible — and this is Art.

"As the one fire coming into the universe is manifesting itself in every form, and yet is more besides" — yes, infinitely more besides! A bit, only a small bit, of infinite thought can be made to descend to the plane of matter to minister to our comfort — the rest will not allow itself to be rudely handled. The superfine always eludes our view and laughs at our attempts to bring it down. In this case, Mohammed must go to the mountain, and no "nay". Man must raise himself to that higher plane if he wants to enjoy its beauties, to bathe in its light, to feel his life pulsating in unison with the Cause-Life of the universe.

It is knowledge that opens the door to regions of wonder, knowledge that makes a god of an animal: and that knowledge which brings us to That, "knowing which everything else is known" (the heart of all knowledge — whose pulsation brings life to all sciences — the science of religion) is certainly the highest, as it alone can make man live a complete and perfect life in thought. Blessed be the land which has styled it "supreme science"!

The principle is seldom found perfectly expressed in the practical, yet the ideal is never lost. On the one hand, it is our duty never to lose sight of the ideal, whether we can approach it with sensible steps, or crawl towards it with imperceptible motion: on the other hand, the truth is, it is always loosening in front of us — though we try our best to cover its light with our hands before our eyes.

The life of the practical is in the ideal. It is the ideal that has penetrated the whole of our lives, whether we philosophise, or perform the hard, everyday duties of life. The rays of the ideal, reflected and refracted in various straight or tortuous lines, are pouring in through every aperture and windhole, and consciously or unconsciously, every function has to be performed in its light, every object has to be seen transformed, heightened, or deformed by it.

It is the ideal that has made us what we are, and will make us what we are going to be. It is the power of the ideal that has enshrouded us, and is felt in our joys or sorrows, in our great acts or mean doings, in our virtues and vices.

If such is the power of the ideal over the practical, the practical is no less potent in forming the ideal. The truth of the ideal is in the practical. The fruition of the ideal has been through the sensing of the practical. That the ideal is there is a proof of the existence of the practical somehow, somewhere. The ideal may be vaster, yet it is the multiplication of little bits of the practical. The ideal mostly is the summed-up, generalized, practical units.

The power of the ideal is in the practical. Its work on us is in and through the practical. Through the practical, the ideal is brought down to our sense-perception, changed into a form fit for our assimilation. Of the practical we make the steps to rise to the ideal. On that we build our hopes; it gives us courage to work.

One man who manifests the ideal in his life is more powerful than legions whose words can paint it in the most beautiful colours and spin out the finest principles.

Systems of philosophy mean nothing to mankind, or at best only intellectual gymnastics, unless they are joined to religion and can get a body of men struggling to bring them down to practical life with more or less success. Even systems having not one positive hope, when taken up by groups and made somewhat practical, had always a multitude; and the most elaborate positive systems of thought withered away without it.

Most of us cannot keep our activities on a par with our thought-lives. Some blessed ones can. Most of us seem to lose the power of work as we think deeper, and the power of deep thought if we work more. That is why most great thinkers have to leave to time the practical realisation of their great ideals. Their thoughts must wait for more active brains to work them out and spread them. Yet, as we write, comes before us a vision of him, the charioteer of Arjuna, standing in his chariot between the contending hosts, his left hand curbing the fiery steeds — a mail-clad warrior, whose eagle-glance sweeps over the vast army, and as if by instinct weighs every detail of the battle array of both parties — at the same time that we hear, as it were, falling from his lips and thrilling the awestruck Arjuna, that most marvellous secret of work: "He who finds rest in the midst of activity, and activity in rest, he is the wise amidst men, he the Yogi, he is the doer of all work" (Gita, IV. 18).

This is the ideal complete. But few ever reach it. We must take things as they are, therefore, and be contented to piece together different aspects of human perfection, developed in different individuals.

In religion we have the man of intense thought, of great activity in bringing help to others, the man of boldness and daring self-realisation, and the man of meekness and humility.

The subject of this sketch was a man of wonderful humility and intense self-realisation.

Born of Brâhmin parents in a village near Guzi, Varanasi, Pavhâri Bâbâ, as he was called in after life, came to study and live with his uncle in Ghazipur, when a mere boy. At present, Hindu ascetics are split up into the main divisions of Sannyâsins, Yogis, Vairâgis, and Panthis. The Sannyasins are the followers of Advaitism after Shankarâchârya; the Yogis, though following the Advaita system, are specialists in practicing the different systems of Yoga; the Vairagis are the dualistic disciples of Râmânujâchârya and others; the Panthis, professing either philosophy, are orders founded during the Mohammedan rule. The uncle of Pavhari Baba belonged to the Ramanuja or Shri sect, and was a Naishthika Brahmachârin, i.e. one who takes the vow of lifelong celibacy. He had a piece of land on the banks of the Ganga, about two miles to the north of Ghazipur, and had established himself there. Having several nephews, he took Pavhari Baba into his home and adopted him, intending him to succeed to his property and position.

Not much is known of the life of Pavhari Baba at this period. Neither does there seem to have been any indication of those peculiarities which made him so well known in after years. He is remembered merely as a diligent student of Vyâkarana and Nyâya, and the theology of his sect, and as an active lively boy whose jollity at times found vent in hard practical jokes at the expense of his fellow-students.

Thus the future saint passed his young days, going through the routine duties of Indian students of the old school; and except that he showed more than ordinary application to his studies, and a remarkable aptitude for learning languages, there was scarcely anything in that open, cheerful, playful student life to foreshadow the tremendous seriousness which was to culminate in a most curious and awful sacrifice.

Then something happened which made the young scholar feel, perhaps for the first time, the serious import of life, and made him raise his eyes, so long riveted on books, to scan his mental horizon critically and crave for something in religion which was a fact, and not mere book-lore. His uncle passed away. One face on which all the love of that young heart was concentrated had gone, and the ardent boy, struck to the core with grief, determined to supply the gap with a vision that can never change.

In India, for everything, we want a Guru. Books, we Hindus are persuaded, are only outlines. The living secrets must be handed down from Guru to disciple, in every art, in every science, much more so in religion. From time immemorial earnest souls in India have always retired to secluded spots, to carry on uninterrupted their study of the mysteries of the inner life, and even today there is scarcely a forest, a hill, or a sacred spot which rumour does not consecrate as the abode of a great sage. The saying is well known:

"The water is pure that flows.

The monk is pure that goes."

As a rule, those who take to the celibate religious life in India spend a good deal of their life in journeying through various countries of the Indian continent, visiting different shrines — thus keeping themselves from rust, as it were, and at the same time bringing religion to the door of everyone. A visit to the four great sacred places, situated in the four corners of India, is considered almost necessary to all who renounce the world.

All these considerations may have had weight with our young Brahmacharin, but we are sure that the chief among them was the thirst for knowledge. Of his travels we know but little, except that, from his knowledge of Dravidian languages, in which a good deal of the literature of his sect is written, and his thorough acquaintance with the old Bengali of the Vaishnavas of Shri Chaitanya's order, we infer that his stay in Southern India and Bengal could not have been very short.

But on his visit to one place, the friends of his youth lay great stress. It was on the top of mount Girnâr in Kathiawar, they say, that he was first initiated into the mysteries of practical Yoga.

It was this mountain which was so holy to the Buddhists. At its foot is the huge rock on which is inscribed the first-deciphered edict of the "divinest of monarchs", Asoka. Beneath it, through centuries of oblivion, lay the conclave of gigantic Stupas, forest covered, and long taken for hillocks of the Girnar range. No less sacred is it still held by the sect of which Buddhism is now thought to be a revised edition, and which strangely enough did not venture into the field of architectural triumphs till its world-conquering descendant had melted away into modern Hinduism. Girnar is celebrated amongst Hindus as having been sanctified by the stay of the great Avadhuta Guru Dattâtreya, and rumour has it that great and perfected Yogis are still to be met with by the fortunate on its top.

The next turning-point in the career of our youthful Brahmacharin we trace to the banks of the Ganga some where near Varanasi, as the disciple of a Sannyasin who practiced Yoga and lived in a hole dug in the high bank of the river. To this yogi can be traced the after-practice of our saint, of living inside a deep tunnel, dug out of the ground on the bank of the Ganga near Ghazipur. Yogis have always inculcated the advisability of living in caves or other spots where the temperature is even, and where sounds do not disturb the mind. We also learn that he was about the same time studying the Advaita system under a Sannyasin in Varanasi.

After years of travel, study, and discipline, the young Brahmacharin came back to the place where he had been brought up. Perhaps his uncle, if alive, would have found in the face of the boy the same light which of yore a greater sage saw in that of his disciple and exclaimed, "Child, thy face today shines with the glory of Brahman!" But those that welcomed him to his home were only the companions of his boyhood — most of them gone into, and claimed for ever by, the world of small thought and eternal toil.

Yet there was a change, a mysterious — to them an awe-inspiring — change, in the whole character and demeanour of that school-day friend and playmate whom they had been wont to understand. But it did not arouse in them emulation, or the same research. It was the mystery of a man who had gone beyond this world of trouble and materialism, and this was enough. They instinctively respected it and asked no questions.

Meanwhile, the peculiarities of the saint began to grow more and more pronounced. He had a cave dug in the ground, like his friend near Varanasi, and began to go into it and remain there for hours. Then began a process of the most awful dietary discipline. The whole day he worked in his little Âshrama, conducted the worship of his beloved Râmachandra, cooked good dinners — in which art he is said to have been extraordinarily proficient — distributed the whole of the offered food amongst his friends and the poor, looked after their comforts till night came, and when they were in their beds, the young man stole out, crossed the Ganga by swimming, and reached the other shore. There he would spend the whole night in the midst of his practices and prayers, come back before daybreak and wake up his friends, and then begin once more the routine business of "worshipping others", as we say in India.

His own diet, in the meanwhile, was being attenuated every day, till it came down, we are told, to a handful of bitter Nimba leaves, or a few pods of red pepper, daily. Then he gave up going nightly to the woods on the other bank of the river and took more and more to his cave. For days and months, we are told, he would be in the hole, absorbed in meditation, and then come out. Nobody knows what he subsisted on during these long intervals, so the people called him Pav-âhâri (or air-eater) Bâbâ (or father).

He would never during his life leave this place. Once, however, he was so long inside the cave that people gave him up as dead, but after a long time, the Baba emerged and gave a Bhândârâ (feast) to a large number of Sâdhus.

When not absorbed in his meditations, he would be living in a room above the mouth of his cave, and during this time he would receive visitors. His fame began to spread, and to Rai Gagan Chandra Bahadur of the Opium Department, Ghazipur — a gentleman whose innate nobility and spirituality have endeared him to all — we owe our introduction to the saint.

Like many others in India, there was no striking or stirring external activity in this life. It was one more example of that Indian ideal of teaching through life and not through words, and that truth bears fruit in those lives only which have become ready to receive. Persons of this type are entirely averse to preaching what they know, for they are for ever convinced that it is internal discipline alone that leads to truth, and not words. Religion to them is no motive to social conduct, but an intense search after and realisation of truth in this life. They deny the greater potentiality of one moment over another, and every moment in eternity being equal to every other, they insist on seeing the truths of religion face to face now and here, not waiting for death.

The present writer had occasion to ask the saint the reason of his not coming out of his cave to help the world. At first, with his native humility and humour, he gave the following strong reply:

"A certain wicked person was caught in some criminal act and had his nose cut off as a punishment. Ashamed to show his noseless features to the world and disgusted with himself, he fled into a forest; and there, spreading a tiger-skin on the ground, he would feign deep meditation whenever he thought anybody was about. This conduct, instead of keeping people off, drew them in crowds to pay their respects to this wonderful saint; and he found that his forest-life had brought him once again an easy living. Thus years went by. At last the people around became very eager to listen to some instruction from the lips of the silent meditative saint; and one young man was specially anxious to be initiated into the order. It came to such a pass that any more delay in that line would undermine the reputation of the saint. So one day he broke his silence and asked the enthusiastic young man to bring on the morrow a sharp razor with him. The young man, glad at the prospect of the great desire of his life being speedily fulfilled, came early the next morning with the razor. The noseless saint led him to a very retired spot in the forest, took the razor in his hand, opened it, and with one stroke cut off his nose, repeating in a solemn voice, 'Young man, this has been my initiation into the order. The same I give to you. Do you transmit it diligently to others when the opportunity comes!' The young man could not divulge the secret of this wonderful initiation for shame, and carried out to the best of his ability the injunctions of his master. Thus a whole sect of nose-cut saints spread over the country. Do you want me to be the founder of another such?"

Later on, in a more serious mood, another query brought the answer: "Do you think that physical help is the only help possible? Is it not possible that one mind can help other minds even without the activity of the body?"

When asked on another occasion why he, a great Yogi, should perform Karma, such as pouring oblations into the sacrificial fire, and worshipping the image of Shri Raghunâthji, which are practices only meant for beginners, the reply came: "Why do you take for granted that everybody makes Karma for his own good? Cannot one perform Karma for others?"

Then again, everyone has heard of the thief who had come to steal from his Ashrama, and who at the sight of the saint got frightened and ran away, leaving the goods he had stolen in a bundle behind; how the saint took the bundle up, ran after the thief, and came up to him after miles of hard running; how the saint laid the bundle at the feet of the thief, and with folded hands and tears in his eyes asked his pardon for his own intrusion, and begged hard for his acceptance of the goods, since they belonged to him, and not to himself.

We are also told, on reliable authority, how once he was bitten by a cobra; and though he was given up for hours as dead, he revived; and when his friends asked him about it, he only replied that the cobra "was a messenger from the Beloved".

And well may we believe this, knowing as we do the extreme gentleness, humility, and love of his nature. All sorts of physical illness were to him only "messengers from the Beloved", and he could not even bear to hear them called by any other name, even while he himself suffered tortures from them. This silent love and gentleness had conveyed themselves to the people around, and those who have travelled through the surrounding villages can testify to the unspoken influence of this wonderful man. Of late, he did not show himself to anyone. When out of his underground retiring-place, he would speak to people with a closed door between. His presence above, ground was always indicated by the rising smoke of oblations in the sacrificial fire, or the noise of getting things ready for worship.

One of his great peculiarities was his entire absorption at the time in the task in hand, however trivial. The same amount of care and attention was bestowed in cleaning a copper pot as in the worship of Shri Raghunathji, he himself being the best example of the secret he once told us of work: "The means should be loved and cared for as if it were the end itself."

Neither was his humility kindred to that which means pain and anguish or self-abasement. It sprang naturally from the realization of that which he once so beautifully explained to us, "O King, the Lord is the wealth of those who have nothing — yes, of those", he continued, "who have thrown away all desires of possession, even that of one's own soul."

He would never directly teach, as that would be assuming the role of a teacher and placing himself in a higher position than another. But once the spring was touched, the fountain welled up with infinite wisdom; yet always the replies were indirect.

In appearance he was tall and rather fleshy, had but one eye, and looked much younger than his real age. His voice was the sweetest we have ever heard. For the last ten years or more of his life, he had withdrawn himself entirely from the gaze of mankind. A few potatoes and a little butter were placed behind the door of his room, and sometimes during the night this was taken in when he was not in Samâdhi and was living above ground. When inside his cave, he did not require even these. Thus, this silent life went on, witnessing to the science of Yoga, and a living example of purity, humility, and love.

The smoke, which, as we have said already, indicated his coming out of Samadhi, one clay smelled of burning flesh. The people around could not guess what was happening; but when the smell became overpowering, and the smoke was seen to rise up in volumes, they broke open the door, and found that the great Yogi had offered himself as the last oblation to his sacrificial fire, and very soon a heap of ashes was all that remained of his body.

Let us remember the words of Kâlidâsa: "Fools blame the actions of the great, because they are extraordinary and their reasons past the finding-out of ordinary mortals."

Yet, knowing him as we do, we can only venture to suggest that the saint saw that his last moments had come, and not wishing to cause trouble to any, even after death, performed this last sacrifice of an Ârya, in full possession of body and mind.

The present writer owes a deep debt of gratitude to the departed saint and dedicates these lines, however unworthy, to the memory of one of the greatest Masters he has loved and served.

ARYANS AND TAMILIANS

A veritable ethnological museum! Possibly, the half-ape skeleton of the recently discovered Sumatra link will be found on search here, too. The Dolmens are not wanting. Flint implements can be dug out almost anywhere. The lake-dwellers — at least the river-dwellers — must have been abundant at one time. The cave-men and leaf-wearers still persist. The primitive hunters living in forests are in evidence in various parts of the country. Then there are the more historical varieties — the Negrito-Kolarian, the Dravidian, and the Aryan. To these have been added from time to time dashes of nearly all the known races, and a great many yet unknown — various breeds of Mongoloids, Mongols, Tartars, and the so-called Aryans of the philologists. Well, here are the Persian, the Greek, the Yunchi, the Hun, the Chin, the Scythian, and many more, melted and fused, the Jews, Parsees, Arabs, Mongols, down to the descendants of the Vikings and the lords of the German forests, yet undigested — an ocean of humanity, composed of these race-waves seething, boiling, struggling, constantly changing form, rising to the surface, and spreading, and swallowing little ones, again subsiding — this is the history of India.

In the midst of this madness of nature, one of the contending factions discovered a method and, through the force of its superior culture, succeeded in bringing the largest number of Indian humanity under its sway.

The superior race styled themselves the Âryas or nobles, and their method was the Varnâshramâchâra — the so-called caste.

Of course the men of the Aryan race reserved for themselves, consciously or unconsciously a good many privileges; yet the institution of caste has always been very flexible, sometimes too flexible to ensure a healthy uprise of the races very low in the scale of culture.

It put, theoretically at least, the whole of India under the guidance — not of wealth, nor of the sword — but of intellect — intellect chastened and controlled by spirituality. The leading caste in India is the highest of the Aryans — the Brahmins.

Though apparently different from the social methods of other nations, on close inspection, the Aryan method of caste will not be found so very different except on two points:

The first is, in every other country the highest honour belongs to the Kshatriya — the man of the sword. The Pope of Rome will be glad to trace his descent to some robber baron on the banks of the Rhine. In India, the highest honour belongs to the man of peace — the Sharman the Brahmin, the man of God.

The greatest Indian king would be gratified to trace his descent to some ancient sage who lived in the forest, probably a recluse, possessing nothing, dependent upon the villagers for his daily necessities, and all his life trying to solve the problems of this life and the life hereafter.

The second point is, the difference of unit. The law of caste in every other country takes the individual man or woman as the sufficient unit. Wealth, power, intellect, or beauty suffices for the individual to leave the status of birth and scramble up to anywhere he can.

Here, the unit is all the members of a caste community.

Here, too, one has every chance of rising from a low caste to a higher or the highest: only, in this birth-land of altruism, one is compelled to take his whole caste along with him.

In India, you cannot, on account of your wealth, power, or any other merit, leave your fellows behind and make common cause with your superiors; you cannot deprive those who helped in your acquiring the excellence of any benefit therefrom and give them in return only contempt. If you want to rise to a higher caste in India, you have to elevate all your caste first, and then there is nothing in your onward path to hold you back.

This is the Indian method of fusion, and this has been going on from time immemorial. For in India, more there elsewhere. Such words as Aryans and Dravidians are only of philological import, the so-called craniological differentiation finding no solid ground to work upon.

Even so are the names Brahmin, Kshatriya, etc. They simply represent the status of a community in itself continuously fluctuating, even when it has reached the summit and all further endeavours are towards fixity of the type by non-marriage, by being forced to admit fresh groups, from lower castes or foreign lands, within its pale.

Whatever caste has the power of the sword, becomes Kshatriya; whatever learning, Brahmin; whatever wealth, Vaishya.

The groups that have already reached the coveted goal, indeed, try to keep themselves aloof from the newcomers, by making sub-divisions in the same caste, but the fact remains that they coalesce in the long run. This is going on before our own eyes, all over India.

Naturally, a group having raised itself would try to preserve the privileges to itself. Hence, whenever it was possible to get the help of a king, the higher castes, especially the Brahmins, have tried to put down similar aspirations in lower castes, by the sword if practicable. But the question is: Did they succeed? Look closely into your Purânas and Upa-puranas, look especially into the local Khandas of the big Puranas, look round and see what is happening before your eyes, and you will find the answer.

We are, in spite of our various castes, and in spite of the modern custom of marriage restricted within the sub-divisions of a caste (though this is not universal), a mixed race in every sense of the word.

Whatever may be the import of the philological terms "Aryan" and "Tamilian", even taking for granted that both these grand sub-divisions of Indian humanity came from outside the Western frontier, the dividing line had been, from the most ancient times, one of language and not of blood. Not one of the epithets expressive of contempt for the ugly physical features of the Dasyus of the Vedas would apply to the great Tamilian race; in fact if there be a toss for good looks between the Aryans and Tamilians, no sensible man would dare prognosticate the result.

The super-arrogated excellence of birth of any caste in India is only pure myth, and in no part of India has it, we are sorry to say, found such congenial soil, owing to linguistic differences, as in the South.

We purposely refrain from going into the details of this social tyranny in the South, just as we have stopped ourselves from scrutinising the genesis of the various modern Brahmins and other castes. Sufficient for us to note the extreme tension of feeling that is evident between the Brahmins and non-Brahmins of the Madras Presidency.

We believe in Indian caste as one of the greatest social institutions that the Lord gave to man. We also believe that though the unavoidable defects, foreign persecutions, and, above all, the monumental ignorance and pride of many Brahmins who do not deserve the name, have thwarted, in many ways, the legitimate fructification of this most glorious Indian institution, it has already worked wonders for the land of Bharata and is destined to lead Indian humanity to its goal.

We earnestly entreat the Brahmins of the South not to forget the ideal of India — the production of a universe of Brahmins, pure as purity, good as God Himself: this was at the beginning, says the Mahâbhârata, and so will it be in the end.

Then anyone who claims to be a Brahmin should prove his pretensions, first by manifesting that spirituality, and next by raising others to the same status. On the face of this, it seems that most of them are only nursing a false pride of birth; and any schemer, native or foreign, who can pander to this vanity and inherent laziness by fulsome sophistry, appears to satisfy most.

Beware, Brahmins, this is the sign of death! Arise and show your manhood, your Brahminhood, by raising the non-Brahmins around you — not in the spirit of a master — not with the rotten canker of egotism crawling with superstitions and the charlatanry of East and West — but in the spirit of a servant. For verily he who knows how to serve knows how to rule.

The non-Brahmins also have been spending their energy in kindling the fire of caste hatred — vain and useless to solve the problem — to which every non-Hindu is only too glad to throw on a load of fuel.

Not a step forward can be made by these inter-caste quarrels, not one difficulty removed; only the beneficent onward march of events would be thrown back, possibly for centuries, if the fire bursts out into flames

It would be a repetition of Buddhistic political blunders.

In the midst of this ignorant clamour and hatred, we are delighted to find Pandit D. Savariroyan pursuing the only legitimate and the only sensible course. Instead of wasting precious vitality in foolish and meaningless quarrels, Pandit Savariroyan has undertaken in his articles on the "Admixture of the Aryan with Tamilian" in the Siddhânta Deepikâ, to clear away not only a lot of haze, created by a too adventurous Western philology, but to pave the way to a better understanding of the caste problem in the South.

Nobody ever got anything by begging. We get only what we deserve. The first step to deserve is to desire: and we desire with success what we feel ourselves worthy to get.

A gentle yet clear brushing off of the cobwebs of the so-called Aryan theory and all its vicious corollaries is therefore absolutely necessary, especially for the South, and a proper self-respect created by a knowledge of the past grandeur of one of the great ancestors of the Aryan race — the great Tamilians.

We stick, in spite of Western theories, to that definition of the word "Arya" which we find in our sacred books, and which includes only the multitude we now call Hindus. This Aryan race, itself a mixture of two great races, Sanskrit-speaking and Tamil-speaking, applies to all Hindus alike. That the Shudras have in some Smritis been excluded from this epithet means nothing, for the Shudras were and still are only the waiting Aryas — Aryas in novitiate.

Though we know Pandit Savariroyan is walking

over rather insecure ground, though we differ from many of his sweeping explanations of Vedic names and races, yet we are glad that he has undertaken the task of beginning a proper investigation into the culture of the great mother of Indian civilisation — if the Sanskrit-speaking race was the father.

We are glad also that he boldly pushes forward the Accado-Sumerian racial identity of the ancient Tamilians. And this makes us proud of the blood of the great civilisation which flowered before all others — compared to whose antiquity the Aryans and Semites are babies.

We would suggest, also, that the land of Punt of the Egyptians was not only Malabar, but that the Egyptians as a race bodily migrated from Malabar across the ocean and entered the delta along the course of the Nile from north to south, to which Punt they have been always fondly looking back as the home of the blessed.

This is a move in the right direction. Detailed and more careful work is sure to follow with a better study of the Tamilian tongues and the Tamilian elements found in the Sanskrit literature, philosophy, and religion. And who are more competent to do this work than those who learn the Tamilian idioms as their mother-tongue?

As for us Vedântins and Sannyâsins, ore are proud of our Sanskrit-speaking ancestors of the Vedas; proud of our Tamil-speaking ancestors whose civilization is the oldest yet known; we are proud of our Kolarian ancestors older than either of the above — who lived and hunted in forests; we are proud of our ancestors with flint implements — the first of the human race; and if evolution is true, we are proud of our animal ancestors, for they antedated man himself. We are proud that we are descendants of the whole universe, sentient or insentient. Proud that we are born, and work, and suffer — prouder still that we die when the task is finished and enter forever the realm where there is no more delusion.

THE SOCIAL CONFERENCE ADDRESS

"God created the native, God created the European, but somebody else created the mixed breed" — we heard a horribly blasphemous Englishman say.

Before us lies the inaugural address of Mr. Justice Ranade, voicing the reformatory zeal of tie Indian Social Conference. In it there is a huge array of instances of inter-caste marriages of yore, a good leaf about the liberal spirit of the ancient Kshatriyas, good sober advice to students, all expressed with an earnestness of goodwill and gentleness of language that is truly admirable.

The last part, however, which offers advice as to the creation of a body of teachers for the new movement strong in the Punjab, which we take for granted is the Ârya Samâj, founded by a Sannyâsin, leaves us wondering and asking ourselves the question:

It seems God created the Brâhmin, God created the Kshatriya, but who created the Sannyasin?

There have been and are Sannyasins or monks in every known religion. There are Hindu monks, Buddhist monks, Christian monks, and even Islam had to yield its rigorous denial and take in whole orders of mendicant monks.

There are the wholly shaved, the partly shaved, the long hair, short hair, matted hair, and various other hirsute types.

There are the sky-clad, the rag-clad, the ochre-clad, the yellow-clad (monks), the black-clad Christian and the blue-clad Mussulman. Then there have been those that tortured their flesh in various ways, and others who believed in keeping their bodies well and healthy. There was also, in odd days in every country, the monk militant. The same spirit and similar manifestations haste run in parallel lines with the women, too — the nuns. Mr. Ranade is not only the President of the Indian Social Conference but a chivalrous gentleman also: the nuns of the Shrutis and Smritis seem to have been to his entire satisfaction. The ancient celibate Brahmavâdinis, who travelled from court to court challenging great philosophers, do not seem to him to thwart the central plan of the Creator — the propagation of species; nor did they seem to have lacked in the variety and completeness of human experience, in Mr. Ranade's opinion, as the stronger sex following the same line of conduct seem to have done.

We therefore dismiss the ancient nuns and their modern spiritual descendants as having passed muster.

The arch-offender, man alone, has to bear the brunt of Mr. Ranade's criticism, and let us see whether he survives it or not.

It seems to be the consensus of opinion amongst savants that this world-wide monastic institution had its first inception in this curious land of ours, which appears to stand so much in need of "social reform".

The married teacher and the celibate are both as old as the Vedas. Whether the Soma-sipping married Rishi with his "all-rounded" experience was the first in order of appearance, or the lack-human-experience celibate Rishi was the primeval form, is hard to decide just now. Possibly Mr. Ranade will solve the problem for us independently of the hearsay of the so-called Western Sanskrit scholars; till then the question stands a riddle like the hen and egg problem of yore.

But whatever be the order of genesis, the celibate teachers of the Shrutis and Smritis stand on an entirely different platform from the married ones, which is perfect chastity, Brahmacharya.

If the performance of Yajnas is the corner-stone of the work-portion of the Vedas, as surely is Brahmacharya the foundation of the knowledge-portion.

Why could not the blood-shedding sacrificers be the exponents of the Upanishads — why?

On the one side was the married Rishi, with his meaningless, bizarre, nay, terrible ceremonials, his misty sense of ethics, to say the least; on the other hand, the celibate monks tapping, in spite of their want of human experience, springs of spirituality and ethics at which the monastic Jinas, the Buddhas, down to Shankara, Ramanuja, Kabir, and Chaitanya, drank deep and acquired energy to propagate their marvellous spiritual and social reforms, and which, reflected third-hand, fourth-hand from the West, is giving our social reformers the power even to criticise the Sannyasins.

At the present day, what support, what pay, do the mendicants receive in India, compared to the pay and privilege of our social reformers? And what work does the social reformer do, compared to the Sannyasin's silent selfless labour of love?

But they have not learnt the modern method of self-advertisement!!

The Hindu drank in with his mother's milk that this life is as nothing — a dream! In this he is at one with the Westerners; but the Westerner sees no further and his conclusion is that of the Chârvâka — to "make hay while the sun shines". "This world being a miserable hole, let us enjoy to the utmost what morsels of pleasure are left to us." To the Hindu, on the other hand, God and soul are the only realities, infinitely more real than this world, and he is therefore ever ready to let this go for the other.

So long as this attitude of the national mind continues, and we pray it will continue for ever, what hope is there in our anglicised compatriots to check the impulse in Indian men and women to renounce all "for the good of the universe and for one's own freedom"?

And that rotten corpse of an argument against the monk — used first by the Protestants in Europe, borrowed by the Bengali reformers, and now embraced by our Bombay brethren — the monk on account of his celibacy must lack the realisation of life "in all its fullness and in all its varied experience!" We hope this time the corpse will go for good into the Arabian Sea, especially in these days of plague, and notwithstanding the filial love one may suppose the foremost clan of Brahmins there may have for ancestors of great perfume, if the Paurânika accounts are of any value in tracing their ancestry.

By the bye, in Europe, between the monks and nuns, they have brought up and educated most of the children, whose parents, though married people, were utterly unwilling to taste of the "varied experiences of life".

Then, of course, every faculty has been given to us by God for some use. Therefore the monk is wrong in not propagating the race — a sinner! Well, so also have been given us the faculties of anger, lust, cruelty, theft, robbery, cheating, etc., every one of these being absolutely necessary for the maintenance of social life, reformed or unreformed. What about these? Ought they also to be maintained at full steam, following the varied-experience theory or not? Of course the social reformers, being in intimate acquaintance with God Almighty and His purposes, must answer the query in the positive. Are we to follow Vishvâmitra, Atri, and others in their ferocity and the Vasishtha family in particular in their "full and varied experience" with womankind? For the majority of married Rishis are as celebrated for their liberality in begetting children wherever and whenever they could, as for their hymn-singing and Soma-bibbing; or are we to follow the celibate Rishis who upheld Brahmacharya as the sine qua non of spirituality?

Then there are the usual backsliders, who ought to come in for a load of abuse — monks who could not keep up to their ideal — weak, wicked.

But if the ideal is straight and sound, a backsliding monk is head and shoulders above any householder in the land, on the principle, "It is better to have loved and lost."

Compared to the coward that never made the attempt, he is a hero.

If the searchlight of scrutiny were turned on the inner workings of our social reform conclave, angels would have to take note of the percentage of backsliders as between the monk and the householder; and the recording angel is in our own heart.

But then, what about this marvellous experience of standing alone, discarding all help, breasting the storms of life, of working without any sense of recompense, without any sense of putrid duty? Working a whole life, joyful, free — not goaded on to work like slaves by false human love or ambition?

This the monk alone can have. What about religion? Has it to remain or vanish? If it remains, it requires its experts, its soldiers. The monk is the religious expert, having made religion his one métier of life. He is the soldier of God. What religion dies so long as it has a band of devoted monks?

Why are Protestant England and America shaking before the onrush of the Catholic monk?

Vive Ranade and the Social Reformers! — but, O India! Anglicised India! Do not forget, child, that there are in this society problems that neither you nor your Western Guru can yet grasp the meaning of — much less solve!

INDIA'S MESSAGE TO THE WORLD

The following notes were discovered among Swami Vivekananda's papers. He intended to write a book and jotted down forty-two points as a syllabus for the work, but only a few points were dealt with as an introduction by him and the work was left unfinished. We give the manuscript as found.

Syllabus

1. Bold has been my message to the people of the West. Bolder to those at home.

2. Four years of residence in the marvellous West has made India only the better understood. The shades are deeper and the lights brighter.

3. The survey — it is not true that the Indians have degenerated.

4. The problem here has been as it has been everywhere else — the assimilation of various races, but nowhere has it been so vast as here.

5. Community of language, government and, above all, religion has been the power of fusion.

6. In other lands this has been attempted by "force", that is, the enforcement of the culture of one race only over the rest. The result being

the production of a short-lived vigorous national life; then, dissolution.

7. In India, on the other hand, the attempts have been as gentle as the problem vast, and from the earliest times, the customs, and especially the religions, of the different elements tolerated.
8. Where it was a small problem and force was sufficient to form a unity, the effect really was the nipping in the bud of various healthy types in the germ of all the elements except the dominant one. It was only one set of brains using the vast majority for its own good, thus losing the major portion of the possible amount of development, and thus when the dominant type had spent itself, the apparently impregnable building tottered to its ruins, e.g., Greece, Rome, the Norman.
9. A common language would be a great desideratum; but the same criticism applies to it, the destruction of the vitality of the various existing ones.
10. The only solution to be reached was the finding of a great sacred language of which all the others would be considered as manifestations, and that was found in the Sanskrit.
11. The Dravidian languages may or may not have been originally Sanskritic, but for practical purposes they are so now, and every day we see them approaching the ideal more and more, yet keeping their distinctive vital peculiarities.
12. A racial background was found — the Âryas.
13. The speculation whether there was a distinct, separate race called the Aryas living in Central Asia to the Baltic.
14. The so-called types. Races were always mixed.
15. The "blonde" and the "brunette".
16. Coming to practical common sense from so-called historical imagination. The Aryas in their oldest records were in the land between Turkistan and the Punjab and N. W. Tibet.
17. This leads to the attempt at fusion between races and tribes of various degrees of culture.
18. Just as Sanskrit has been the linguistic solution, so the Arya the racial solution. So the Brâhminhood is the solution of the varying degrees of progress and culture as well as that of all social and political problems.
19. The great ideal of India — Brahminhood.
20. Property-less, selfless, subject to no laws, no king except the moral.
21. Brahminhood by descent — various races have claimed and acquired the right in the past as well as in the present.
22. No claim is made by the doer of great deeds, only by lazy worthless fools.
23. Degradation of Brahminhood and Kshatriyahood. The Puranas said there will be only non-Brahmins in the Kali Yuga, and that is true, becoming truer every day. Yet a few Brahmins remain, and in India alone.
24. Kshatriyahood — we must pass through that to become a Brahmin. Some may have passed through in the past, but the present must show that.
25. But the disclosure of the whole plan is to be found in religion.
26. The different tribes of the same race worship similar gods, under a generic name as the Baals of the Babylonians, the Molochs of the Hebrews.
27. The attempt in Babylonia of making all the Baals merge in Baal-Merodach — the attempt of the Israelites to merge all the Molochs in the Moloch Yavah or Yahu.
28. The Babylonians destroyed by the Persians; and the Hebrews who took the Babylonian mythology and adapted it to their own needs, succeeded in producing a strict monotheistic religion.
29. Monotheism like absolute monarchy is quick in executing orders, and a great centralization of force, but it grows no farther, and its worst feature is its cruelty and persecution. All nations coming within its influence perish very soon after a flaring up of a few years.

30. In India the same problem presented itself - the solution found — एकं सद्विप्रा बहुधा वदन्ति।

    This is the keynote to everything which has succeeded, and the keystone of the arch.

31. The result is that wonderful toleration of the Vedantist.

32. The great problem therefore is to harmonise and unify without destroying the individuality of these various elements.

33. No form of religion which depends Upon persons, either of this earth or even of heaven, is able to do that.

34. Here is the glory of the Advaita system preaching a principle, not a person, yet allowing persons, both human and divine, to have their full play.

35. This has been going on all the time; in this sense we have been always progressing. The Prophets during the Mohammedan rule.

36. It was fully conscious and vigorous in old days, and less so of late; in this sense alone we have degenerated.

37. This is going to be in the future. If the manifestation of the power of one tribe utilising the labours of the rest produced wonderful results at least for a certain length of time, here is going to be the accumulation and the concentration of all the races that have been slowly and inevitably getting mixed up in blood and ideas, and in my mind's eye, I see the future giant slowly maturing. The future of India, the youngest and the most glorious of the nations of earth as well as the oldest.

38. The way — we will have to work. Social customs as barriers, some as founded upon the Smritis. But none from the Shrutis. The Smritis must change with time. This is the admitted law.

39. The principles of the Vedanta not only should be preached everywhere in India, but also outside. Our thought must enter into the make-up of the minds of every nation, not through writings, but through persons.

40. Gift is the only Karma in Kali Yuga. None attaining knowledge until purified by Karma.

41. Gift of spiritual and secular knowledge.

42. Renunciation — Renouncers — the national call.

Introduction

Bold has been my message to the people of the West, bolder is my message to you, my beloved countrymen. The message of ancient India to new Western nations I have tried my best to voice — ill done or well done the future is sure to show; but the mighty voice of the same future is already sending forward soft but distinct murmurs, gaining strength as the days go by, the message of India that is to be to India as she is at present.

Many wonderful institutions and customs, and many wonderful manifestations of strength and power it has been my good fortune to study in the midst of the various races I have seen, but the most wonderful of all was to find that beneath all these apparent variations of manners and customs, of culture and power, beats the same mighty human heart under the impulsion of the same joys and sorrows, of the same weakness and strength

Good and evil are everywhere and the balance is wondrously even; but, above all, is the glorious soul of man everywhere which never fails to understand any one who knows how to speak its own language. Men and women are to be found in every race whose lives are blessings to humanity, verifying the words of the divine Emperor Asoka: "In every land dwell Brâhmins and Shramanas."

I am grateful to the lands of the West for the many warm hearts that received me with all the love that pure and disinterested souls alone could give; but my life's allegiance is to this my motherland; and if I had a thousand lives, every moment of the whole series would be consecrated to your service, my countrymen, my friends.

For to this land I owe whatever I possess, physical, mental, and spiritual; and if I have been successful in anything, the glory is yours, not mine. Mine alone are my weaknesses and failures, as they come through my inability of profiting by the mighty lessons with which this land surrounds one, even from his very birth.

And what a land! Whosoever stands on this sacred land, whether alien or a child of the soil, feels himself surrounded — unless his soul is degraded to the level of brute animals — by the living thoughts of the earth's best and purest sons, who have been working to raise the animal to the divine through centuries, whose beginning history fails to trace. The very air is full of the pulsations of spirituality. This land is sacred to philosophy, to ethics and spirituality, to all that tends to give a respite to man in his incessant struggle for the preservation of the animal to all training that makes man throw off the garment of brutality and stand revealed as the spirit immortal, the birthless, the deathless, the ever-blessed — the land where the cup of pleasure was full, and fuller has been the cup of misery, until here, first of all, man found out that it was all vanity; here, first of all in the prime of youth, in the lap of luxury, in the height of glory and plenitude of power, he broke through the fetters of delusion. Here, in this ocean of humanity, amidst the sharp interaction of strong currents of pleasure and pain, of strength and weakness, of wealth and poverty, of joy and sorrow, of smile and tear, of life and death, in the melting rhythm of eternal peace and calmness, arose the throne of renunciation! Here in this land, the great problems of life and death, of the thirst for life, and the vain mad struggles to preserve it only resulting in the accumulation of woes were first grappled with and solved — solved as they never were before and never will be hereafter; for here and here alone was discovered that even life itself is an evil, the shadow only of something which alone is real. This is the land where alone religion was practical and real, and here alone men and women plunged boldly in to realise the goal, just as in other lands they madly plunge in to realise the pleasures of life by robbing their weaker brethren. Here and here alone the human heart expanded till it included not only the human, but birds, beasts, and plants; from the highest gods to grains of sand, the highest and the lowest, all find a place in the heart of man, grown great, infinite. And here alone, the human soul studied the universe as one unbroken unity whose every pulse was his own pulse.

We all hear so much about the degradation of India. There was a time when I also believed in it. But today standing on the vantage-ground of experience, with eyes cleared of obstructive predispositions and above all, of the highly-coloured pictures of other countries toned down to their proper shade and light by actual contact, I confess in all humility that I was wrong. Thou blessed land of the Aryas, thou wast never degraded. Sceptres have been broken and thrown away, the ball of power has passed from hand to hand, but in India, courts and kings always touched only a few; the vast mass of the people, from the highest to the lowest, has been left to pursue its own inevitable course, the current of national life flowing at times slow and half-conscious, at others, strong and awakened. I stand in awe before the unbroken procession of scores of shining centuries, with here and there a dim link in the chain, only to flare up with added brilliance in the next, and there she is walking with her own majestic steps — my motherland — to fulfil her glorious destiny, which no power on earth or in heaven can check — the regeneration of man the brute into man the God.

Ay, a glorious destiny, my brethren, for as far back as the days of the Upanishads we have thrown the challenge to the world: न प्रजया धनेन त्यागेनैके अमृतत्वमानशुः— "Not by progeny, not by wealth, but by renunciation alone immortality is reached." Race after race has taken the challenge up and tried their utmost to solve the world-riddle on the plane of desires. They have all failed in the past — the old ones have become extinct under the weight of wickedness and misery, which lust for power and gold brings in its train, and the new ones are tottering to their fall. The question has yet to be decided whether peace will survive or war; whether patience will survive or non-forbearance, whether goodness will survive or wickedness; whether muscle will survive or brain; whether worldliness will survive or spirituality. We have solved our problem ages ago, and held on to it through good or evil fortune, and mean to hold on to it till the end of time. Our solution is unworldliness — renunciation.

This is the theme of Indian life-work, the burden of her eternal songs, the backbone of her existence, the foundation of her being, the raison d'être of her very existence — the spiritualisation of the human race. In this her life-course she has never deviated, whether the Tartar ruled or the Turk, whether the Mogul ruled or the English.

And I challenge anybody to show one single period of her national life when India was lacking in spiritual giants capable of moving the world. But her work is spiritual, and that cannot be done with blasts of war-trumpets or the march of cohorts. Her influence has always fallen upon the world like that of the gentle dew, unheard and scarcely marked, yet bringing into bloom the fairest flowers of the earth. This influence, being in its nature gentle, would have to wait for a fortunate combination of circumstances, to go out of the country into other lands, though it never ceased to work within the limits of its native land. As such, every educated person knows that whenever the empire-building Tartar or Persian or Greek or Arab brought this land in contact with the outside world, a mass of spiritual influence immediately flooded the world from here. The very same circumstances have presented themselves once more before us. The English high roads over land and sea and the wonderful power manifested by the inhabitants of that little island have once more brought India in contact with the rest of the world, and the same work has already begun. Mark my words, this is but the small beginning, big things are to follow; what the result of the present work outside India will be I cannot exactly state, but this I know for certain that millions, I say deliberately, millions in every civilised land are waiting for the message that will save them from the hideous abyss of materialism into which modern money-worship is driving them headlong, and many of the leaders of the new social movements have already discovered that Vedanta in its highest form can alone spiritualise their social aspirations. I shall have to return to this towards the end I take up therefore the other great subject, the work within the country.

The problem assumes a twofold aspect, not only spiritualisation but assimilation of the various elements of which the nation is composed. The assimilation of different races into one has been the common task in the life of every nation.

STRAY REMARKS ON THEOSOPHY[1]

The Theosophists are having a jubilee time of it this year, and several press-notices are before us of their goings and doings for the last twenty-five years.

Nobody has a right now to say that the Hindus are not liberal to a fault. A coterie of young Hindus has been found to welcome even this graft of American Spiritualism, with its panoply of taps and raps and hitting back and forth with Mahâtmic pellets.

The Theosophists claim to possess the original divine knowledge of the universe. We are glad to learn of it, and gladder still that they mean to keep it rigorously a secret. Woe unto us, poor mortals, and Hindus at that, if all this is at once let out on us! Modern Theosophy is Mrs. Besant. Blavatskism and Olcottism seem to have taken a back seat. Mrs. Besant means well at least — and nobody can deny her perseverance and zeal.

There are, of course, carping critics. We on our part see nothing but good in Theosophy — good in what is directly beneficial, good in what is pernicious, as they say, indirectly good as we say — the intimate geographical knowledge of various heavens, and other places, and the denizens thereof; and the dexterous finger work on the visible plane accompanying ghostly communications to live Theosophists — all told. For Theosophy is the best serum we know of, whose injection never fails to develop the queer moths finding lodgment in some brains

---
1. Found among Swami Vivekananda's papers.

attempting to pass muster as sound.

We have no wish to disparage the good work of the Theosophical or any other society. Yet exaggeration has been in the past the bane of our race and if the several articles on the work of the Theosophical Society that appeared in the Advocate of Lucknow be taken as the temperamental gauge of Lucknow, we are sorry for those it represents, to say the least; foolish depreciation is surely vicious, but fulsome praise is equally loathsome.

This Indian grafting of American Spiritualism — with only a few Sanskrit words taking the place of spiritualistic jargon — Mahâtmâ missiles taking the place of ghostly raps and taps, and Mahatmic inspiration that of obsession by ghosts.

We cannot attribute a knowledge of all this to the writer of the articles in the Advocate, but he must not confound himself and his Theosophists with the great Hindu nation, the majority of whom have clearly seen through the Theosophical phenomena from the start and, following the great Swami Dayânanda Sarasvati who took away his patronage from Blavatskism the moment he found it out, have held themselves aloof.

Again, whatever be the predilection of the writer in question, the Hindus have enough of religious teaching and teachers amidst themselves even in this Kali Yuga, and they do not stand in need of dead ghosts of Russians and Americans.

The articles in question are libels on the Hindus and their religion. We Hindus — let the writer, like that of the articles referred to, know once for all — have no need nor desire to import religion from the West. Sufficient has been the degradation of importing almost everything else.

The importation in the case of religion should be mostly on the side of the West, we are sure, and our work has been all along in that line. The only help the religion of the Hindus got from the Theosophists in the West was not a ready field, but years of uphill work, necessitated by Theosophical sleight-of-hand methods. The writer ought to have known that the Theosophists wanted to crawl into the heart of Western Society, catching on to the skirts of scholars like Max Müller and poets like Edwin Arnold, all the same denouncing these very men and posing as the only receptacles of universal wisdom. And one heaves a sigh of relief that this wonderful wisdom is kept a secret. Indian thought, charlatanry, and mango-growing fakirism had all become identified in the minds of educated people in the West, and this was all the help rendered to Hindu religion by the Theosophists.

The great immediate visible good effect of Theosophy in every country, so far as we can see, is to separate, like Prof. Koch's injections into the lungs of consumptives, the healthy, spiritual, active, and patriotic from the charlatans, the morbids, and the degenerates posing as spiritual beings.

REPLY TO THE ADDRESS OF THE MAHARAJA OF KHETRI

INDIA — THE LAND OF RELIGION

During the residence of the Swamiji in America, the following Address from the Maharaja of Khetri (Rajputana), dated March 4th, 1895, was received by him:

My dear Swamiji,

As the head of this Durbar (a formal stately assemblage) held today for this special purpose, I have much pleasure in conveying to you, in my own name and that of my subjects, the heartfelt thanks of this State for your worthy representation of Hinduism at the Parliament of Religions, held at Chicago, in America.

I do not think the general principles of Hinduism could be expressed more accurately and clearly in English than what you have done, with all the restrictions imposed by the very natural shortcomings of language itself.

The influence of your speech and behaviour in foreign lands has not only spread admiration among men of different countries and different religions, but has also served to familiarise you with them, to help in the furtherance of your unselfish cause. This is very highly and inexpressibly appreciated by us all, and we should feel to be failing in our duty, were I not to write to you formally at least these few lines, expressing our sincere gratitude for all the trouble you have taken in going to foreign countries, and to expound in the American Parliament of Religions the truths of our ancient religion which we ever hold so dear. It is certainly applicable to the pride of India that it has been fortunate in possessing the privilege of having secured so able a representative as yourself.

Thanks are also due to those noble souls whose efforts succeeded in organising the Parliament of Religions, and who accorded to you a very enthusiastic reception. As you were quite a foreigner in that continent, their kind treatment of you is due to their love of the several qualifications you possess, and this speaks highly of their noble nature.

I herewith enclose twenty printed copies of this letter and have to request that, keeping this one with yourself you will kindly distribute the other copies among your friends.

With best regards,
I remain,
Yours very sincerely,
Raja Ajit Singh Bahadur of Khetri .

The Swamiji sent the following reply:

"Whenever virtue subsides, and wickedness raises its head, I manifest Myself to restore the glory of religion" — are the words, O noble Prince, of the Eternal One in the holy Gitâ, striking the keynote of the pulsating ebb and flow of the spiritual energy in the universe.

These changes are manifesting themselves again and again in rhythms peculiar to themselves, and like every other tremendous change, though affecting, more or less, every particle within their sphere of action, they show their effects more intensely upon those particles which are naturally susceptible to their power.

As in a universal sense, the primal state is a state of sameness of the qualitative forces — a disturbance of this equilibrium and all succeeding struggles to regain it, composing what we call the manifestation of nature, this universe, which state of things remains as long as the primitive sameness is not reached — so, in a restricted sense on our own earth, differentiation and its inevitable counterpart, this struggle towards homogeneity, must remain as long as the human race shall remain as such, creating strongly marked peculiarities between ethnic divisions, sub-races and even down to individuals in all parts of the world.

In this world of impartial division and balance, therefore, each nation represents, as it were, a wonderful dynamo for the storage and distribution of a particular species of energy, and amidst all other possessions that particular property shines forth as the special characteristic of that race. And as any upheaval in any particular part of human nature, though affecting others more or less, stirs to its very depth that nation of which it is a special characteristic, and from which as a centre it generally starts, so any commotion in the religious world is sure to produce momentous changes in India, that land which again and again has had to furnish the centre of the wide-spread religious upheavals; for, above all, India is the land of religion.

Each man calls that alone real which helps him to realise his ideal. To the worldly-minded, everything that can be converted into money is real, that which cannot be so converted is unreal. To the man of a domineering spirit, anything that will conduce to his ambition of ruling over his fellow men is real — the rest is naught; and man finds nothing in that which does not echo back the heartbeats of his special love in life.

Those whose only aim is to barter the energies

of life for gold, or name, or any other enjoyment; those to whom the tramp of embattled cohorts is the only manifestation of power; those to whom the enjoyments of the senses are the only bliss that life can give — to these, India will ever appear as an immense desert whose every blast is deadly to the development of life, as it is known by them.

But to those whose thirst for life has been quenched for ever by drinking from the stream of immortality that flows from far away beyond the world of the senses, whose souls have cast away — as a serpent its slough — the threefold bandages of lust, gold, and fame, who, from their height of calmness, look with love and compassion upon the petty quarrels and jealousies and fights for little gilded puff-balls, filled with dust, called "enjoyment" by those under a sense-bondage; to those whose accumulated force of past good deeds has caused the scales of ignorance to fall off from their eyes, making them see through the vanity of name and form — to such wheresoever they be, India, the motherland and eternal mine of spirituality, stands transfigured, a beacon of hope to everyone in search of Him who is the only real Existence in a universe of vanishing shadows.

The majority of mankind can only understand power when it is presented to them in a concrete form, fitted to their perceptions. To them, the rush and excitement of war, with its power and spell, is something very tangible, and any manifestation of life that does not come like a whirlwind, bearing down everything before it, is to them as death. And India, for centuries at the feet of foreign conquerors, without any idea or hope of resistance, without the least solidarity among its masses, without the least idea of patriotism, must needs appear to such, as a land of rotten bones, a lifeless putrescent mass.

It is said — the fittest alone survive. How is it, then, that this most unfitted of all races, according to commonly accepted ideas, could bear the most awful misfortunes that ever befall a race, and yet not show the least signs of decay? How is it that, while the multiplying powers of the so-called vigorous and active races are dwindling every day, the immoral (?) Hindu shows a power of increase beyond them all? Great laurels are due, no doubt, to those who can deluge the world with blood at a moment's notice; great indeed is the glory of those who, to keep up a population of a few millions in plenty, have to starve half the population of the earth, but is no credit due to those who can keep hundreds of millions in peace and plenty, without snatching the bread from the mouth of anyone else? Is there no power displayed in bringing up and guiding the destinies of countless millions of human beings, through hundreds of centuries, without the least violence to others?

The mythologists of all ancient races supply us with fables of heroes whose life was concentrated in a certain small portion of their bodies, and until that was touched they remained invulnerable. It seems as if each nation also has such a peculiar centre of life, and so long as that remains untouched, no amount of misery and misfortune can destroy it.

In religion lies the vitality of India, and so long as the Hindu race do not forget the great inheritance of their forefathers, there is no power on earth to destroy them.

Nowadays everybody blames those who constantly look back to their past. It is said that so much looking back to the past is the cause of all India's woes. To me, on the contrary, it seems that the opposite is true. So long as they forgot the past, the Hindu nation remained in a state of stupor; and as soon as they have begun to look into their past, there is on every side a fresh manifestation of life. It is out of this past that the future has to be moulded; this past will become the future.

The more, therefore, the Hindus study the past, the more glorious will be their future, and whoever tries to bring the past to the door of everyone, is a great benefactor to his nation. The degeneration of India came not because the laws and customs of the ancients were bad, but because they were not allowed to be carried to their legitimate conclusions.

Every critical student knows that the social laws of India have always been subject to great periodic changes. At their inception, these laws were the embodiment of a gigantic plan, which was to unfold itself slowly through time. The great seers of ancient India saw so far ahead of their time that the world has to wait centuries yet to appreciate their wisdom, and it is this very inability on the part of their own descendants to appreciate the full scope of this wonderful plan that is the one and only cause of the degeneration of India.

Ancient India had for centuries been the battlefield for the ambitious projects of two of her foremost classes — the Brâhmins and the Kshatriyas.

On the one hand, the priesthood stood between the lawless social tyranny of the princes over the masses whom the Kshatriyas declared to be their legal food. On the other hand, the Kshatriya power was the one potent force which struggled with any success against the spiritual tyranny of the priesthood and the ever-increasing chain of ceremonials which they were forging to bind down the people with.

The tug of war began in the earliest periods of the history of our race, and throughout the Shrutis it can be distinctly traced. A momentary lull came when Shri Krishna, leading the faction of Kshatriya power and of Jnâna, showed the way to reconciliation. The result was the teachings of the Gita — the essence of philosophy, of liberality, of religion. Yet the causes were there, and the effect must follow.

The ambition of these two classes to be the masters of the poor and ignorant was there, and the strife once more became fierce. The meagre literature that has come down to us from that period brings to us but faint echoes of that mighty past strife, but at last it broke out as a victory for the Kshatriyas, a victory for Jnana, for liberty — and ceremonial had to go down, much of it for ever. This upheaval was what is known as the Buddhistic reformation. On the religious side, it represented freedom from ceremonial; on the political side, overthrow of the priesthood by the Kshatriyas.

It is a significant fact that the two greatest men ancient India produced, were both Kshatriyas — Krishna and Buddha — and still more significant is the fact that both of these God-men threw open the door of knowledge to everyone, irrespective of birth or sex.

In spite of its wonderful moral strength, Buddhism was extremely iconoclastic; and much of its force being spent in merely negative attempts, it had to die out in the land of its birth, and what remained of it became full of superstitions and ceremonials, a hundred times cruder than those it was intended to suppress. Although it partially succeeded in putting down the animal sacrifices of the Vedas, it filled the land with temples, images, symbols, and bones of saints.

Above all, in the medley of Aryans, Mongols, and aborigines which it created, it unconsciously led the way to some of the hideous Vâmâchâras. This was especially the reason why this travesty of the teaching of the great Master had to be driven out of India by Shri Shankara and his band of Sannyâsins.

Thus even the current of life, set in motion by the greatest soul that ever wore a human form, the Bhagavân Buddha himself, became a miasmatic pool, and India had to wait for centuries until Shankara arose, followed in quick succession by Râmânuja and Madhva.

By this time, an entirely new chapter had opened in the history of India. The ancient Kshatriyas and the Brahmins had disappeared. The land between the Himalayas and the Vindhyas, the home of the Âryas, the land which gave birth to Krishna and Buddha, the cradle of great Râjarshis and Brahmarshis, became silent, and from the very farther end of the Indian Peninsula, from races alien in speech and form, from families claiming descent from the ancient Brahmins, came the reaction against the corrupted Buddhism.

What had become of the Brahmins and Kshatriyas of Âryâvarta? They had entirely disappeared, except here and there a few mongrel clans claiming to be Brahmins and Kshatriyas, and in spite of their inflated, self-laudatory assertions that the whole world ought to learn from एतद्देशप्रसूतस्य सकाशादग्रजन्मनः, they had to sit in sackcloth and ashes, in all humility, to learn at the feet of the Southerners. The result was the bringing back of the Vedas to India — a revival of Vedânta, such as India never before had seen; even the householders began to study the Âranyakas.

In the Buddhistic movement, the Kshatriyas were the real leaders, and whole masses of them became Buddhists. In the zeal of reform and conversion, the popular dialects had been almost exclusively cultivated to the neglect of Sanskrit, and the larger portion of Kshatriyas had become disjointed from the Vedic literature and Sanskrit learning. Thus this wave of reform, which came from the South, benefited to a certain extent the priesthood, and the priests only. For the rest of India's millions, it forged more chains than they had ever known before.

The Kshatriyas had always been the backbone of India, so also they had been the supporters of science and liberty, and their voices had rung out again and again to clear the land from superstitions; and throughout the history of India they ever formed the invulnerable barrier to aggressive priestly tyranny.

When the greater part of their number sank into ignorance, and another portion mixed their blood with savages from Central Asia and lent their swords to establish the rules of priests in India, her cup became full to the brim, and down sank the land of Bharata, not to rise again, until the Kshatriya rouses himself, and making himself free, strikes the chains from the feet of the rest. Priestcraft is the bane of India. Can man degrade his brother, and himself escape degradation?

Know, Rajaji, the greatest of all truths, discovered by your ancestors, is that the universe is one. Can one injure anyone without injuring himself? The mass of Brahmin and Kshatriya tyranny has recoiled upon their own heads with compound interest; and a thousand years of slavery and degradation is what the inexorable law of Karma is visiting upon them.

This is what one of your ancestors said: "Even in this life, they have conquered relativity whose mind is fixed in sameness" — one who is believed to be God incarnate. We all believe it. Are his words then vain and without meaning? If not, and we know they are not, any attempt against this perfect equality of all creation, irrespective of birth, sex, or even qualification, is a terrible mistake, and no one can be saved until he has attained to this idea of sameness.

Follow, therefore, noble Prince, the teachings of the Vedanta, not as explained by this or that commentator, but as the Lord within you understands them. Above all, follow this great doctrine of sameness in all things, through all beings, seeing the same God in all.

This is the way to freedom; inequality, the way to bondage. No man and no nation can attempt to gain physical freedom without physical equality, nor mental freedom without mental equality.

Ignorance, inequality, and desire are the three causes of human misery, and each follows the other in inevitable union. Why should a man think himself above any other man, or even an animal? It is the same throughout:

त्वं स्त्री त्वं पुमानसि त्वं कुमार उत वा कुमारी।

—"Thou art the man, Thou the woman, Thou art the young man, Thou the young woman."

Many will say, "That is all right for the Sannyasins, but we are householders." No doubt, a householder having many other duties to perform, cannot as fully attain to this sameness; yet this should be also their ideal, for it is the ideal of all societies, of all mankind, all animals, and all nature, to attain to this sameness. But alas! they think inequality is the way to attain equality as if they could come to right by doing wrong!

This is the bane of human nature, the curse upon mankind, the root of all misery — this inequality. This is the source of all bondage, physical, mental, and spiritual.

समं पश्यन् हि सर्वत्र समवस्थितमीश्वरम् ।
न हिनस्त्यात्मनात्मानं ततो याति परां गतिम् ॥

— "Since seeing the Lord equally existent everywhere he injures not Self by self, and so goes to the Highest Goal" (Gita, XIII. 28).

This one saying contains, in a few words, the universal way to salvation.

You, Rajputs, have been the glories of ancient India. With your degradation came national decay, and India can only be raised if the descendants of the Kshatriyas co-operate with the descendants of the Brahmins, not to share the spoils of pelf and power, but to help the weak to enlighten the ignorant, and to restore the lost glory of the holy land of their forefathers.

And who can say but that the time is propitious? Once more the wheel is turning up, once more vibrations have been set in motion from India, which are destined at no distant day to reach the farthest limits of the earth. One voice has spoken, whose echoes are rolling on and gathering strength every day, a voice even mightier than those which have preceded it, for it is the summation of them all. Once more the voice that spoke to the sages on the banks of the Sarasvati, the voice whose echoes reverberated from peak to peak of the "Father of Mountains", and descended upon the plains through Krishna Buddha, and Chaitanya in all-carrying floods, has spoken again. Once more the doors have opened. Enter ye into the realms of light, the gates have been opened wide once more.

And you, my beloved Prince — you the scion of a race who are the living pillars upon which rests the religion eternal, its sworn defenders and helpers, the descendants of Râma and Krishna, will you remain outside? I know, this cannot be. Yours, I am sure, will be the first hand that will be stretched forth to help religion once more. And when I think of you, Raja Ajit Singh, one in whom the well-known scientific attainments of your house have been joined to a purity of character of which a saint ought to be proud, to an unbounded love for humanity, I cannot help believing in the glorious renaissance of the religion eternal, when such hands are willing to rebuild it again.

May the blessings of Ramakrishna be on you and yours for ever and ever, and that you may live long for the good of many, and for the spread of truth is the constant prayer of —

VIVEKANANDA.

REPLY TO THE MADRAS ADDRESS[1]

Friends, Fellow-Countrymen and Co-Religionists of Madras,

It is most gratifying to me to find that my insignificant service to the cause of our religion has been accept able to you, not because it is as a personal appreciation of me and my work in a foreign and distant land, but as a sure sign that, though whirlwind after whirlwind of foreign invasion has passed over the devoted head of India, though centuries of neglect on our part and contempt on the part of our conquerors have visibly dimmed the glories of ancient Âryâvarta, though many a stately column on which it rested, many a beautiful arch, and many a marvellous corner have been washed away by the inundations that deluged the land for centuries — the centre is all sound, the keystone is unimpaired. The spiritual foundation upon which the marvellous monument of glory to God and charity to all beings has been reared stands unshaken, strong as ever. Your generous appreciation of Him whose message to India and to the whole world, I, the most unworthy of His servants, had the privilege to bear shows your innate spiritual instinct which saw in Him and His message the first murmurs of that tidal wave of spirituality which is destined at no distant future to break upon India in all its irresistible powers, carrying away in its omnipotent flood all that is weak and defective, and raising the Hindu race to the platform it is destined to occupy in the providence of God, crowned with more glory than it ever had even in the past, the reward of centuries of silent suffering, and fulfilling its mission amongst the races of the world — the evolution of spiritual humanity.

The people of Northern India are especially grateful to you of the South, as the great source to which most of the impulses that are working in India today can be traced. The great Bhâshyakâras,

---

1. When the success of the Swami in America became well known in India, several meetings were held and addresses of thanks and congratulations were forwarded to him. The first reply which he wrote was that to the Address of the Hindus of Madras.

epoch-making Âchâryas, Shankara, Râmânuja, and Madhva were born in Southern India. Great Shankara to whom every Advâitavâdin in the world owes allegiance; great Ramanuja whose heavenly touch converted the downtrodden pariahs into Âlwârs; great Madhva whose leadership was recognised even by the followers of the only Northern Prophet whose power has been felt all over the length and breadth of India — Shri Krishna Chaitanya. Even at the present day it is the South that carries the palm in the glories of Varanasi — your renunciation controls the sacred shrines on the farthest peaks of the Himalayas, and what wonder that with the blood of Prophets running in your veins, with your lives blessed by such Acharyas, you are the first and foremost to appreciate and hold on to the message of Bhagavân Shri Ramakrishna.

The South had been the repository of Vedic learning, and you will understand me when I state that, in spite of the reiterated assertions of aggressive ignorance, it is the Shruti still that is the backbone of all the different divisions of the Hindu religion.

However great may be the merits of the Samhitâ and the Brâhmana portions of the Vedas to the ethnologists or the philologists, however desirable may be the results that the अग्निमीले[1] or इषेत्वोर्जेत्वा[2] or शन्नो देवीरभीष्टये[3] in conjunction with the different Vedis (altars) and sacrifices and libations produce — it was all in the way of Bhoga; and no one ever contended that it could produce Moksha. As such, the Jnâna-Kânda, the Āranyakas, the Shrutis par excellence which teach the way to spirituality, the Moksha-Mârga, have always ruled and will always rule in India.

Lost in the mazes and divisions of the "Religion Eternal", by prepossession and prejudice unable to grasp the meaning of the only religion whose universal adaptation is the exact shadow of the अणोरणीयान् महतो महीयान्[4] God it preaches, groping in the dark with a standard of spiritual truth borrowed second-hand from nations who never knew anything but rank materialism, the modern young Hindu struggles in vain to understand the religion of his forefathers, and gives up the quest altogether, and becomes a hopeless wreck of an agnostic, or else, unable to vegetate on account of the promptings of his innate religious nature, drinks carelessly of some of those different decoctions of Western materialism with an Eastern flavour, and thus fulfils the prophecy of the Shruti:

परियन्ति मूढा अन्धेनैव नीयमाना यथान्धाः।

— "Fools go staggering to and fro, like blind men led by the blind."

They alone escape whose spiritual nature has been touched and vivified by the life-giving touch of the "Sad-Guru"[5].

Well has it been said by Bhagavan Bhashyakara:

दुर्लभं त्रयमेवैतत् देवानुग्रहहेतुकम्।

मनुष्यत्वं मुमुक्षुत्वं महापुरुषसंश्रयः॥

— "These three are difficult to obtain in this world, and depend on the mercy of the gods — the human birth, the desire for salvation, and the company of the great-souled ones."

Either in the sharp analysis of the Vaisheshikas, resulting in the wonderful theories about the Paramânus, Dvyanus, and Trasarenus[6], or the still more wonderful analysis displayed in the discussions of the Jâti, Dravya, Guna, Samavâya[7], and to the various categories of the Naiyâyikas, rising to the solemn march of the thought of the Sânkhyas, the fathers of the theories of evolution, ending with the ripe fruit, the result of all these researches, the Sutras of Vyâsa — the one background to all these

---

1. ॐ अग्निमीले पुरोहितं यज्ञस्य देवमृत्विजम्। होतारं रत्नधातमम्॥ ऋग्वेदः।१।१।१।

2. ॐ इषेत्वोर्जेत्वा वायवः स्थोपायवः सथ देवो वः सविता प्रापयतु श्रेष्ठतमाय कर्मणे। यजुर्वेदः।१।१।१।

3. ॐ शन्नो देवीरभीष्टये आपो भवन्तु पीतये शंयोरभिस्रवन्तु नः॥ अथर्ववेदः।१।१।१।

4. Smaller than the smallest, greater than the greatest (Katha, II. 20).

5. The good teacher.

6. Atoms, Entities composed of two atoms, Entities composed of three atoms.

7. Genus, Substance, Quality, Inhesion or Inseparability.

different analyses and syntheses of the human mind is still the Shrutis. Even in the philosophical writings of the Buddhists or Jains, the help of Shrutis is never rejected, and at least in some of the Buddhistic schools and in the majority of the Jain writings, the authority of the Shrutis is fully admitted, excepting what they call the Himsaka Shrutis, which they hold to be interpolations of the Brahmins. In recent times, such a view has been held by the late great Swami Dayânanda Saraswati.

If one be asked to point out the system of thought towards which as a centre all the ancient and modern Indian thoughts have converged, if one wants to see the real backbone of Hinduism in all its various manifestations, the Sutras of Vyasa will unquestionably be pointed out as constituting all that.

Either one hears the Advaita-Keshari roaring in peals of thunder — the Asti, Bhâti, and Priya[1] — amidst the heart-stopping solemnities of the Himalayan forests, mixing with the solemn cadence of the river of heaven, or listens to the cooing of the Piyâ, Pitam in the beautiful bowers of the grove of Vrindâ: whether one mingles with the sedate meditations of the monasteries of Varanasi or the ecstatic dances of the followers of the Prophet of Nadia; whether one sits at the feet of the teacher of the Vishishtâdvaita system with its Vadakale, Tenkale[2], and all the other subdivisions, or listens with reverence to the Acharyas of the Mâdhva school; whether one hears the martial "Wâ Guruki Fateh"[3] of the secular Sikhs or the sermons on the Grantha Sâhib of the Udâsis and Nirmalâs; whether he salutes the Sannyâsin disciples of Kabir with "Sat Sâhib" and listens with joy to the Sâkhis (Bhajans); whether he pores upon the wonderful lore of that reformer of Rajputana, Dâdu, or the works of his royal disciple, Sundaradâsa, down to the great Nishchaladâsa, the celebrated author of Vichâra sâgara, which book has more influence in India than any that has been written in any language within the last three centuries; if even one asks the Bhangi Mehtar of Northern India to sit down and give an account of the teachings of his Lâlguru — one will find that all these various teachers and schools have as their basis that system whose authority is the Shruti, Gitâ its divine commentary, the Shâriraka-Sutras its organised system, and all the different sects in India, from the Paramahamsa Parivrâjakâchâryas to the poor despised Mehtar disciples of Lâlguru, are different manifestations.

The three Prasthânas[4], then, in their different explanations as Dvaita, Vishishtadvaita, or Advaita, with a few minor recensions, form the "authorities" of the Hindu religion. The Purânas, the modern representations of the ancient Nârâsamsi (anecdote portion of the Vedas), supply the mythology, and the Tantras, the modern representations of the Brâhmanas (ritual and explanatory portion of the Vedas), supply the ritual. Thus the three Prasthanas, as authorities, are common to all the sects; but as to the Puranas and Tantras, each sect has its own.

The Tantras, as we have said, represent the Vedic rituals in a modified form; and before any one jumps into the most absurd conclusions about them, I will advise him to read the Tantras in conjunction with the Brahmanas, especially the Adhvaryu portion. And most of the Mantras, used in the Tantras, will be found taken verbatim from their Brahmanas. As to their influence, apart from the Shrauta and Smârta rituals, all the forms of the rituals in vogue from the Himalayas to the Comorin have been taken from the Tantras, and they direct the worship of the Shâkta, or Shaiva, or Vaishnava, and all the others alike.

Of course, I do not pretend that all the Hindus are thoroughly acquainted with these sources of their religion. Many, especially in lower Bengal, have not heard of the names of these sects and these great systems; but consciously or unconsciously, it is the plan laid down in the three Prasthanas that they are all working out.

Wherever, on the other hand, the Hindi language is spoken, even the lowest classes have more knowledge of the Vedantic religion than many of the

---

1. Exists (Sat), Shines (Chit), Is beloved (Ânanda) — the three indicatives of Brahman.
2. The two divisions of the Ramanuja sect.
3. Victory to the Guru
4. "Courses", viz, the Upanishad (Shruti), the Gita, and the *Shariraka-Sutras*.

highest in lower Bengal.

And why so?

Transported from the soil of Mithilâ to Navadvipa, nurtured and developed by the fostering genius of Shiromani, Gadâdhara, Jagadisha, and a host of other great names, an analysis of the laws of reasoning, in some points superior to every other system in the whole world, expressed in a wonderful and precise mosaic of language, stands the Nyâya of Bengal, respected and studied throughout the length and breadth of Hindusthân. But, alas, the Vedic study was sadly neglected, and until within the last few years, scarcely anyone could be found in Bengal to teach the Mahâbhâshya of Patanjali. Once only a mighty genius rose above the never-ending Avachchhinnas and Avachchhedakas[1] — Bhagavân Shri Krishna Chaitanya. For once the religious lethargy of Bengal was shaken, and for a time it entered into a communion with the religious life of other parts of India.

It is curious to note that though Shri Chaitanya obtained his Sannyâsa from a Bhârati, and as such was a Bharati himself, it was through Mâdhavendra Puri that his religious genius was first awakened.

The Puris seem to have a peculiar mission in rousing the spirituality of Bengal. Bhagavan Shri Ramakrishna got his Sannyâsâshrama from Totâ Puri.

The commentary that Shri Chaitanya wrote on the Vyâsa-Sutras has either been lost or not found yet. His disciples joined themselves to the Madhvas of the South, and gradually the mantles of such giants as Rupa and Sanâtana and Jiva Goswâmi fell on the shoulders of Bâbâjis, and the great movement of Shri Chaitanya was decaying fast, till of late years there is a sign of revival. Hope that it will regain its lost splendour.

The influence of Shri Chaitanya is all over India. Wherever the Bhakti-Mârga is known, there he is appreciated, studied, and worshipped. I have every reason to believe that the whole of the Vallabhâchârya recension is only a branch of the sect founded by Shri Chaitanya. But most of his so-called disciples in Bengal do not know how his power is still working all over India; and how can they? The disciples have become Gadiâns (Heads of monasteries), while he was preaching barefooted from door to door in India, begging Âchandâlas (all down to the lowest) to love God.

The curious and unorthodox custom of hereditary Gurus that prevails in Bengal, and for the most part in Bengal alone, is another cause of its being cut off from the religious life of the rest of India.

The greatest cause of all is that the life of Bengal never received an influx from that of the great brotherhood of Sannyasins who are the representatives and repositories of the highest Indian spiritual culture even at the present day.

Tyâga (renunciation) is never liked by the higher classes of Bengal. Their tendency is for Bhoga (enjoyment). How can they get a deep insight into spiritual things? त्यागेनेके अमृतत्वमानशुः — "By renunciation alone immortality was reached." How can it be otherwise?

On the other hand, throughout the Hindi-speaking world, a succession of brilliant Tyâgi teachers of far-reaching influence has brought the doctrines of the Vedanta to every door. Especially the impetus given to Tyaga during the reign of Ranjit Singh of the Punjab has made the highest teachings of the Vedantic philosophy available for the very lowest of the low. With true pride, the Punjabi peasant girl says that even her spinning wheel repeats: "Soham", "Soham". And I have seen Mehtar Tyagis in the forest of Hrishikesh wearing the garb of the Sannyasin, studying the Vedanta. And many a proud high-class man would be glad to sit at their feet and learn. And why not? अन्त्यादपि परं धर्मं — "Supreme knowledge (can be learnt) even from the man of low birth."

Thus it is that the North-West and the Punjab have a religious education which is far ahead of that of Bengal, Bombay, or Madras. The ever-travelling Tyagis of the various orders, Dashanâmis or Vairâgis or Panthis bring religion to everybody's door, and the cost is only a bit of bread. And how noble and disinterested most of them are! There is one Sannyasin belonging to the Kachu Panthis or

---
1. In Nyaya, 'Determined', and 'determining attribute'.

independents (who do not identify themselves with any sect), who has been instrumental in the establishing of hundreds of schools and charitable asylums all over Rajputana. He has opened hospitals in forests, and thrown iron bridges over the gorges in the Himalayas, and this man never touches a coin with his hands, has no earthly possession except a blanket, which has given him the nickname of the "Blanket Swami", and begs his bread from door to door. I have never known him taking a whole dinner from one house, lest it should be a tax on the householder. And he is only one amongst many. Do you think that so long as these Gods on earth live in India and protect the "Religion Eternal" with the impenetrable rampart of such godly characters, the old religion will die?

In this country[1], the clergymen sometimes receive as high salaries as rupees thirty thousand, forty thousand, fifty thousand, even ninety thousand a year, for preaching two hours on Sunday only, and that only six months in a year. Look at the millions upon millions they spend for the support of their religion, and Young Bengal has been taught that these Godlike, absolutely unselfish men like Kambli-Swami are idle vagabonds. मद्भक्तानाञ्च ये भक्तास्ते मे भक्ततमा मताः — "Those who are devoted to My worshippers are regarded as the best of devotees."

Take even an extreme case, that of an extremely ignorant Vairagi. Even he, when he goes into a village tries his best to impart to the villagers whatever he knows, from Tulasidâsa, or Chaitanya-Charitâmrita or the Âlwârs in Southern India. Is that not doing some good? And all this for only a bit of bread and a rag of cloth. Before unmercifully criticising them, think how much you do, my brother, for your poor fellow-countrymen, at whose expense you have got your education, and by grinding whose face you maintain your position and pay your teachers for teaching you that the Babajis are only vagabonds.

A few of your fellow-countrymen in Bengal have criticised what they call a new development of Hinduism. And well they may. For Hinduism is only just now penetrating into Bengal, where so long the whole idea of religion was a bundle of Deshâchâras (local customs) as to eating and drinking and marriage.

This short paper has not space for the discussion of such a big subject as to whether the view of Hinduism, which the disciples of Ramakrishna have been preaching all over India, was according to the "Sad-Shâstras" or not. But I will give a few hints to our critics, which may help them in understanding our position better.

In the first place, I never contended that a correct idea of Hinduism can be gathered from the writings of Kâshidâsa or Krittivâsa, though their words are "Amrita Samâna" (like nectar), and those that hear them are "Punyavâns" (virtuous). But we must go to Vedic and Dârshanika authorities, and to the great Acharyas and their disciples all over India.

If, brethren, you begin with the Sutras of Gautama, and read his theories about the Âptas (inspired) in the light of the commentaries of Vâtsyâyana, and go up to the Mimâmsakas with Shabara and other commentators, and find out what they say about the अलौकिकप्रत्यक्षम् (supersensuous realisation), and who are Aptas, and whether every being can become an Apta or not, and that the proof of the Vedas is in their being the words of such Aptas if you have time to look into the introduction of Mahidhara to the Yajur-Veda, you will find a still more lucid discussion as to the Vedas being laws of the inner life of man, and as such they are eternal.

As to the eternity of creation — this doctrine is the corner-stone not only of the Hindu religion, but of the Buddhists and Jains also.

Now all the sects in India can be grouped roughly as following the Jnana-Mârga or the Bhakti-Mârga. If you will kindly look into the introduction to the Shâriraka-Bhâshya of Shri Shankarâchârya, you will find there the Nirapekshatâ (transcendence) of Jnana is thoroughly discussed, and the conclusion is that realisation of Brahman or the attainment of Moksha do not depend upon ceremonial, creed, caste, colour, or doctrine. It will come to any being who has the four Sâdhanâs, which are the most per-

---
1. United States of America

fect moral culture.

As to the Bhaktas, even Bengali critics know very well that some of their authorities even declared that caste or nationality or sex, or, as to that, even the human birth, was never necessary to Moksha. Bhakti is the one and only thing necessary.

Both Jnana and Bhakti are everywhere preached to be unconditioned, and as such there is not one authority who lays down the conditions of caste or creed or nationality in attaining Moksha. See the discussion on the Sutra of Vyâsa — अन्तरा चापि तु तद्दृष्टेः[1] by Shankara, Ramanuja, and Madhva.

Go through all the Upanishads, and even in the Samhitas, nowhere you will find the limited ideas of Moksha which every other religion has. As to toleration, it is everywhere, even in the Samhita of the Adhvaryu Veda, in the third or fourth verse of the fortieth chapter, if my memory does not fail; it begins with न बुध्दभिदं जनयेदज्ञानां कर्मसंगिनाम्।[2]. This is running through every where. Was anybody persecuted in India for choosing his Ishta Devatâ, or becoming an atheist or agnostic even, so long as he obeyed the social regulations? Society may punish anybody by its disapprobation for breaking any of its regulations, but no man, the lowest Patita (fallen), is ever shut out from Moksha. You must not mix up the two together. As to that, in Malabar a Chandâla is not allowed to pass through the same street as a high-caste man, but let him become a Mohammedan or Christian, he will be immediately allowed to go anywhere; and this rule has prevailed in the dominion of a Hindu sovereign for centuries. It may be queer, but it shows the idea of toleration for other religions even in the most untoward circumstances.

The one idea the Hindu religions differ in from every other in the world, the one idea to express which the sages almost exhaust the vocabulary of the Sanskrit language, is that man must realise God even in this life. And the Advaita texts very logically add, "To know God is to become God."

And here comes as a necessary consequence the broadest and most glorious idea of inspiration — not only as asserted and declared by the Rishis of the Vedas, not only by Vidura and Dharmavyâdha and a number of others, but even the other day Nischaladâsa, a Tyagi of the Dâdu panthi sect, boldly declared in his Vichâra-Sâgara: "He who has known Brahman has become Brahman. His words are Vedas, and they will dispel the darkness of ignorance, either expressed in Sanskrit or any popular dialect."

Thus to realise God, the Brahman, as the Dvaitins say, or to become Brahman, as the Advaitins say — is the aim and end of the whole teaching of the Vedas; and every other teaching, therein contained, represents a stage in the course of our progress thereto. And the great glory of Bhagavan Bhashyakara Shankaracharya is that it was his genius that gave the most wonderful expression to the ideas of Vyasa.

As absolute, Brahman alone is true; as relative truth, all the different sects, standing upon different manifestations of the same Brahman, either in India or elsewhere, are true. Only some are higher than others. Suppose a man starts straight towards the sun. At every step of his journey he will see newer and newer visions of the sun — the size, the view, and light will every moment be new, until he reaches the real sun. He saw the sun at first like a big ball, and then it began to increase in size. The sun was never small like the ball he saw; nor was it ever like all the succession of suns he saw in his journey. Still is it not true that our traveller always saw the sun, and nothing but the sun? Similarly, all these various sects are true — some nearer, some farther off from the real sun which is our एकमेवाद्वितीयम् — "One without a second".

And as the Vedas are the only scriptures which teach this real absolute God, of which all other ide-

---

[1] "But also (persons standing) between (are qualified for knowledge); for that is seen (in scripture)." — III. iv. 36. A person even if he does not belong to an Ashrama (possessing not the means to entitle him to one or other of the Ashramas, stages of life) and thus stands between, as it were, is qualified for the knowledge of Brahman; for we meet scriptural passages declaring that persons of such a class possessed the knowledge of Brahman. Vide Chhând. Upa. IV. i; Bri. Upa. III. vi. & viii.

[2] "(The wise one) should not unsettle the understanding of the ignorant, attached to action." The line also occurs in the Gita (III. 26).

as of God are but minimised and limited visions; as the सर्वलोकहितैषिणी¹ Shruti takes the devotee gently by the hand, and leads him from one stage to another, through all the stages that are necessary for him to travel to reach the Absolute; and as all other religions represent one or other of these stages in an unprogressive and crystallized form, all the other religions of the world are included in the nameless, limitless, eternal Vedic religion.

Work hundreds of lives out, search every corner of your mind for ages — and still you will not find one noble religious idea that is not already imbedded in that infinite mine of spirituality.

As to the so-called Hindu idolatry — first go and learn the forms they are going through, and where it is that the worshippers are really worshipping, whether in the temple, in the image, or in the temple of their own bodies. First know for certain what they are doing — which more than ninety per cent of the revilers are thoroughly ignorant of — and then it will explain itself in the light of the Vedantic philosophy.

Still these Karmas are not compulsory. On the other hand, open your Manu and see where it orders every old man to embrace the fourth Ashrama, and whether he embraces it or not, he must give up all Karma. It is reiterated everywhere that all these Karmas ज्ञाने परिसमाप्यते। — "finally end in Jnana".

As to the matter of that, a Hindu peasant has more religious education than many a gentleman in other countries. A friend criticised the use of European terms of philosophy and religion in my addresses. I would have been very glad to use Sanskrit terms; it would have been much more easy, as being the only perfect vehicle of religious thought. But the friend forgot that I was addressing an audience of Western people; and although a certain Indian missionary declared that the Hindus had forgotten the meaning of their Sanskrit books, and that it was the missionaries who unearthed the meaning, I could not find one in that large concourse of missionaries who could understand a line in Sanskrit — and yet some of them read learned papers criticising the Vedas, and all the sacred sources of the Hindu religion!

It is not true that I am against any religion. It is equally untrue that I am hostile to the Christian missionaries in India. But I protest against certain of their methods of raising money in America. What is meant by those pictures in the school-books for children where the Hindu mother is painted as throwing her children to the crocodiles in the Ganga? The mother is black, but the baby is painted white, to arouse more sympathy, and get more money. What is meant by those pictures which paint a man burning his wife at a stake with his own hands, so that she may become a ghost and torment the husband's enemy? What is meant by the pictures of huge cars crushing over human beings? The other day a book was published for children in this country, where one of these gentlemen tells a narrative of his visit to Calcutta. He says he saw a car running over fanatics in the streets of Calcutta. I have heard one of these gentlemen preach in Memphis that in every village of India there is a pond full of the bones of little babies.

What have the Hindus done to these disciples of Christ that every Christian child is taught to call the Hindus "vile", and "wretches", and the most horrible devils on earth? Part of the Sunday School education for children here consists in teaching them to hate everybody who is not a Christian, and the Hindus especially, so that, from their very childhood they may subscribe their pennies to the missions. If not for truth's sake, for the sake of the morality of their own children, the Christian missionaries ought not to allow such things going on. Is it any wonder that such children grow up to be ruthless and cruel men and women? The greater a preacher can paint the tortures of eternal hell — the fire that is burning there, the brimstone - the higher is his position among the orthodox. A servant-girl in the employ of a friend of mine had to be sent to a lunatic asylum as a result of her attending what they call here the revivalist-preaching. The dose of hell-fire and brimstone was too much for her. Look again at the books published in Madras against the Hindu religion. If a Hindu writes one line

---

1. The well-wisher to all the world.

against the Christian religion, the missionaries will cry fire and vengeance.

My countrymen, I have been more than a year in this country. I have seen almost every corner of the society, and, after comparing notes, let me tell you that neither are we devils, as the missionaries tell the world we are, nor are they angels, as they claim to be. The less the missionaries talk of immorality, infanticide, and the evils of the Hindu marriage system, the better for them. There may be actual pictures of some countries before which all the imaginary missionary pictures of the Hindu society will fade away into light. But my mission in life is not to be a paid reviler. I will be the last man to claim perfection for the Hindu society. No man is more conscious of the defects that are therein, or the evils that have grown up under centuries of misfortunes. If, foreign friends, you come with genuine sympathy to help and not to destroy, Godspeed to you. But if by abuses, incessantly hurled against the head of a prostrate race in season and out of season, you mean only the triumphant assertion of the moral superiority of your own nation, let me tell you plainly, if such a comparison be instituted with any amount of justice, the Hindu will be found head and shoulders above all other nations in the world as a moral race.

In India religion was never shackled. No man was ever challenged in the selection of his Ishta Devatâ, or his sect, or his preceptor, and religion grew, as it grew nowhere else. On the other hand, a fixed point was necessary to allow this infinite variation to religion, and society was chosen as that point in India. As a result, society became rigid and almost immovable. For liberty is the only condition of growth.

On the other hand, in the West, the field of variation was society, and the constant point was religion. Conformity was the watchword, and even now is the watchword of European religion, and each new departure had to gain the least advantage only by wading through a river of blood. The result is a splendid social organisation, with a religion that never rose beyond the grossest materialistic conceptions.

Today the West is awakening to its wants; and the "true self of man and spirit" is the watchword of the advanced school of Western theologians. The student of Sanskrit philosophy knows where the wind is blowing from, but it matters not whence the power comes so longs as it brings new life.

In India, new circumstances at the same time are persistently demanding a new adjustment of social organisations. For the last three-quarters of a century, India has been bubbling over with reform societies and reformers. But, alas, every one of them has proved a failure. They did not know the secret. They had not learnt the great lesson to be learnt. In their haste, they laid all the evils in our society at the door of religion; and like the man in the story, wanting to kill the mosquito that sat on a friend's forehead, they were trying to deal such heavy blows as would have killed man and mosquito together. But in this case, fortunately, they only dashed themselves against immovable rocks and were crushed out of existence in the shock of recoil. Glory unto those noble and unselfish souls who have struggled and failed in their misdirected attempts. Those galvanic shocks of reformatory zeal were necessary to rouse the sleeping leviathan. But they were entirely destructive, and not constructive, and as such they were mortal, and therefore died.

Let us bless them and profit by their experience. They had not learnt the lesson that all is a growth from inside out, that all evolution is only a manifestation of a preceding involution. They did not know that the seed can only assimilate the surrounding elements, but grows a tree in its own nature. Until all the Hindu race becomes extinct, and a new race takes possession of the land, such a thing can never be — try East or West, India can never be Europe until she dies.

And will she die — this old Mother of all that is noble or moral or spiritual, the land which the sages trod, the land in which Godlike men still live and breathe? I will borrow the lantern of the Athenian sage and follow you, my brother, through the cities and villages, plains and forests, of this broad world — show me such men in other lands if you can. Truly have they said, the tree is known by its fruits. Go under every mango tree in India; pick up bushels of the worm-eaten, unripe, fallen ones from the ground, and write hundreds of the most learned volumes on each one of them — still you have not described a single mango. Pluck a luscious, full-grown, juicy one from the tree, and now you have known all that the mango is.

Similarly, these Man-Gods show what the Hindu religion is. They show the character, the power, and the possibilities of that racial tree which counts culture by centuries, and has borne the buffets of a thousand years of hurricane, and still stands with the unimpaired vigour of eternal youth.

Shall India die? Then from the world all spirituality will be extinct, all moral perfection will be extinct, all sweet-souled sympathy for religion will be extinct, all ideality will be extinct; and in its place will reign the duality of lust and luxury as the male and female deities, with money as its priest, fraud, force, and competition its ceremonies, and the human soul its sacrifice. Such a thing can never be. The power of suffering is infinitely greater than the power of doing; the power of love is infinitely of greater potency than the power of hatred. Those that think that the present revival of Hinduism is only a manifestation of patriotic impulse are deluded.

First, let us study the quaint phenomenon.

Is it not curious that, whilst under the terrific onset of modern scientific research, all the old forts of Western dogmatic religions are crumbling into dust; whilst the sledge-hammer blows of modern science are pulverising the porcelain mass of systems whose foundation is either in faith or in belief or in the majority of votes of church synods; whilst Western theology is at its wit's end to accommodate itself to the ever-rising tide of aggressive modern thought; whilst in all other sacred books the texts have been stretched to their utmost tension under the ever-increasing pressure of modern thought, and the majority of them are broken and have been stored away in lumber rooms; whilst the vast majority of thoughtful Western humanity have broken asunder all their ties with the church and are drifting about in a sea of unrest, the religions which have drunk the water of life at that fountain of light, the Vedas — Hinduism and Buddhism — alone are reviving?

The restless Western atheist or agnostic finds in the Gitâ or in the Dhammapada the only place where his soul can anchor.

The tables have been turned, and the Hindu, who saw through tears of despair his ancient homestead covered with incendiary fire, ignited by unfriendly hands, now sees, when the searchlight of modern thought has dispersed the smoke, that his home is the one that is standing in all its strength, and all the rest have either vanished or are building their houses anew after the Hindu plan. He has wiped away his tears, and has found that the axe that tried to cut down to the roots the ऊर्ध्वमूलमधःशाखमश्वत्थं प्राहुरव्ययम् (Gita, XV. 1) has proved the merciful knife of the surgeon.

He has found that he has neither to torture texts nor commit any other form of intellectual dishonesty to save his religion. Nay, he may call all that is weak in his scriptures, weak, because they were meant to be so by the ancient sages, to help the weak, under the theory of अरुन्धतीदर्शनन्याय[1]. Thanks to the ancient sages who have discovered such an all-pervading, ever-expanding system of religion that can accommodate all that has been discovered in the realm of matter, and all that is to be known; he has begun to appreciate them anew, and discover anew, that those discoveries which have proved so disastrous to every limited little scheme of religion are but rediscoveries, in the plane of intellect and sense-consciousness, of truths which his ancestors discovered ages ago in the higher plane of intuition and superconsciousness.

He has not, therefore, to give up anything, nor go about seeking for anything anywhere, but it will be

---

1. When a bride is brought to the house of her husband for the first time he shows her a very tiny star, called Arundhati. To do this, he has to direct her gaze the right way, which he does by asking her to look at something near and something big in the direction of the star, e.g., a branch of a tree. Next he draws her attention to a large bright star observed beyond this branch and so on, till by several steps, he succeeds in leading her eyes to the right thing. This method of leading to a subtle object through easy and gradual steps is called Arundhati Nyaya

enough for him if he can utilise only a little from the infinite store he has inherited and apply it to his needs. And that he has begun to do and will do more and more. Is this not the real cause of this revival?

Young men of Bengal, to you I especially appeal. Brethren, we know to our shame that most of the real evils for which the foreign races abuse the Hindu nation are only owing to us. We have been the cause of bringing many undeserved calumnies on the head of the other races in India. But glory unto God, we have been fully awakened to it, and with His blessings, we will not only cleanse ourselves, but help the whole of India to attain the ideals preached in the religion eternal.

Let us wipe off first that mark which nature always puts on the forehead of a slave — the stain of jealousy. Be jealous of none. Be ready to lend a hand to every worker of good. Send a good thought for every being in the three worlds.

Let us take our stand on the one central truth in our religion — the common heritage of the Hindus, the Buddhists, and Jains alike — the spirit of man, the Atman of man, the immortal, birthless, all-pervading, eternal soul of man whose glories the Vedas cannot themselves express, before whose majesty the universe with its galaxy upon galaxy of suns and stars and nebulae is as a drop. Every man or woman, nay, from the highest Devas to the worm that crawls under our feet, is such a spirit evoluted or involuted. The difference is not in kind, but in degree.

This infinite power of the spirit, brought to bear upon matter evolves material development, made to act upon thought evolves intellectuality, and made to act upon itself makes of man a God.

First, let us be Gods, and then help others to be Gods. "Be and make." Let this be our motto. Say not man is a sinner. Tell him that he is a God. Even if there were a devil, it would be our duty to remember God always, and not the devil.

If the room is dark, the constant feeling and repeating of darkness will not take it away, but bring in the light. Let us know that all that is negative, all that is destructive, all that is mere criticism, is bound to pass away; it is the positive, the affirmative, the constructive that is immortal, that will remain for ever. Let us say, "We are" and "God is" and "We are God", "Shivoham, Shivoham", and march on. Not matter but spirit. All that has name and form is subject to all that has none. This is the eternal truth the Shrutis preach. Bring in the light; the darkness will vanish of itself. Let the lion of Vedanta roar; the foxes will fly to their holes. Throw the ideas broadcast, and let the result take care of itself. Let us put the chemicals together; the crystallization will take its own course. Bring forth the power of the spirit, and pour it over the length and breadth of India; and all that is necessary will come by itself.

Manifest the divinity within you, and everything will be harmoniously arranged around it. Remember the illustration of Indra and Virochana in the Vedas; both were taught their divinity. But the Asura, Virochana, took his body for his God. Indra, being a Deva, understood that the Atman was meant. You are the children of India. You are the descendants of the Devas. Matter can never be your God; body can never be your God.

India will be raised, not with the power of the flesh, but with the power of the spirit; not with the flag of destruction, but with the flag of peace and love, the garb of the Sannyâsin; not by the power of wealth, but by the power of the begging bowl. Say not that you are weak. The spirit is omnipotent. Look at that handful of young men called into existence by the divine touch of Ramakrishna's feet. They have preached the message from Assam to Sindh, from the Himalayas to Cape Comorin. They have crossed the Himalayas at a height of twenty thousand feet, over snow and ice on foot, and penetrated into the mysteries of Tibet. They have begged their bread, covered themselves with rags; they have been persecuted, followed by the police, kept in prison, and at last set free when the Government was convinced of their innocence.

They are now twenty. Make them two thousand tomorrow. Young men of Bengal, your country requires it. The world requires it. Call up the divinity within you, which will enable you to bear hunger and thirst, heat and cold. Sitting in luxurious homes, surrounded with all the comforts of life, and doling out a little amateur religion may be good for other lands, but India has a truer instinct. It intuitively detects the mask. You must give up. Be great. No great work can be done without sacrifice. The Purusha Himself sacrificed Himself to create this world. Lay down your comforts, your pleasures, your names, fame or position, nay even your lives, and make a bridge of human chains over which millions will cross this ocean of life. Bring all the forces of good together. Do not care under what banner you march. Do not care what be your colour — green, blue, or red — but mix up all the colours and produce that intense glow of white, the colour of love. Ours is to work. The results will take care of themselves. If any social institution stands in your way of becoming God, it will give way before the power of Spirit. I do not see into the future; nor do I care to see. But one vision I see dear as life before me: that the ancient Mother has awakened once more, sitting on Her throne rejuvenated, more glorious than ever. Proclaim Her to all the world with the voice of peace and benediction.

Yours ever in love and labour, Vivekananda.

A MESSAGE OF SYMPATHY TO A FRIEND[1]

"Naked came I out of my mother's womb, and naked shall I return thither; the Lord gave and the Lord hath taken away; blessed be the name of the Lord." Thus said the old Jewish saint when suffering the greatest calamities that could befall man, and he erred not. Herein lies the whole secret of Existence. Waves may roll over the surface and tempest rage, but deep down there is the stratum of infinite calmness, infinite peace, and infinite bliss. "Blessed are they that mourn, for they shall be comforted." And why? Because it is during these moments of visitations when the heart is wrung by hands which never stop for the father's cries or the mother's wail, when under the load of sorrow, dejection, and despair, the world seems to be cut off from under our feet, and when the whole horizon seems to be nothing but an impenetrable sheet of misery and utter despair — that the internal eyes open, light flashes all of a sudden, the dream vanishes, and intuitively we come face to face with the grandest mystery in nature — Existence. Yes, then it is — when the load would be sufficient to sink a lot of frail vessels — that the man of genius, of strength, the hero, sees that infinite, absolute, ever-blissful Existence per se, that infinite being who is called and worshipped under different names in different climes. Then it is, the shackles that bind the soul down to this hole of misery break, as it were, for a time, and unfettered it rises and rises until it reaches the throne of the Lord, "Where the wicked cease from troubling and the weary are at rest". Cease not, brother, to send up petitions day and night, cease not to say day and night — THY WILL BE DONE.

> "Ours not to question why,
> Ours but to do and die."

Blessed be Thy name, O Lord! And Thy will be done. Lord, we know that we are to submit; Lord, we know that it is the Mother's hand that is striking, and "The spirit is willing but the flesh is weak." There is. Father of Love, an agony at the heart which is fighting against that calm resignation which Thou teaches". Give us strength, O Thou who sawest Thy whole family destroyed before Thine eyes, with Thine hands crossed on Thy breast. Come, Lord, Thou Great Teacher, who has taught us that the soldier is only to obey and speak not. Come, Lord, come Arjuna's Charioteer, and teach me as Thou once taughtest him, that resignation in Thyself is the highest end and aim of this life, so that with those great ones of old, I may also firmly and resignedly cry, Om Shri Krishnârpanamastu.

May the Lord send you peace is the prayer day and night of —

VIVEKANANDA.

---
1. Written from Bombay on 23rd May,1893 to D. R. Balaji Rao who just had a severe domestic affliction.

WHAT WE BELIEVE IN[1]

I agree with you so far that faith is a wonderful insight and that it alone can save; but there is the danger in it of breeding fanaticism and barring further progress.

Jnâna is all right; but there is the danger of its becoming dry intellectualism. Love is great and noble; but it may die away in meaningless sentimentalism.

A harmony of all these is the thing required. Ramakrishna was such a harmony. Such beings are few and far between; but keeping him and his teachings as the ideal, we can move on. And if amongst us, each one may not individually attain to that perfection, still we may get it collectively by counteracting, equipoising, adjusting, and fulfilling one another. This would be harmony by a number of persons and a decided advance on all other forms and creeds.

For a religion to be effective, enthusiasm is necessary. At the same time we must try to avoid the danger of multiplying creeds. We avoid that by being a nonsectarian sect, having all the advantages of a sect and the broadness of a universal religion.

God, though everywhere, can be known to us in and through human character. No character was ever so perfect as Ramakrishna's, and that should be the centre round which we ought to rally, at the same time allowing everybody to regard him in his own light, either as God, saviour, teacher, model, or great man, just as he pleases. We preach neither social equality nor inequality, but that every being has the same rights, and insist upon freedom of thought and action in every way.

We reject none, neither theist, nor pantheist, monist, polytheist, agnostic, nor atheist; the only condition of being a disciple is modelling a character at once the broadest and the most intense. Nor do we insist upon particular codes of morality as to conduct, or character, or eating and drinking, except so far as it injures others.

Whatever retards the onward progress or helps the downward fall is vice; whatever helps in coming up and becoming harmonised is virtue.

We leave everybody free to know, select, and follow whatever suits and helps him. Thus, for example, eating meat may help one, eating fruit another. Each is welcome to his own peculiarity, but he has no right to criticise the conduct of others, because that would, if followed by him, injure him, much less to insist that others should follow his way. A wife may help some people in this progress, to others she may be a positive injury. But the unmarried man has no right to say that the married disciple is wrong, much less to force his own ideal of morality upon his brother.

We believe that every being is divine, is God. Every soul is a sun covered over with clouds of ignorance, the difference between soul and soul is owing to the difference in density of these layers of clouds. We believe that this is the conscious or unconscious basis of all religions, and that this is the explanation of the whole history of human progress either in the material, intellectual, or spiritual plane — the same Spirit is manifesting through different planes.

We believe that this is the very essence of the Vedas.

We believe that it is the duty of every soul to treat, think of, and behave to other souls as such, i.e. as Gods, and not hate or despise, or vilify, or try to injure them by any manner or means. This is the duty not only of the Sannyasin, but of all men and women.

The soul has neither sex, nor caste, nor imperfection

We believe that nowhere throughout the Vedas, Darshanas, or Purânas, or Tantras, is it ever said that the soul has any sex, creed, or caste. Therefore we agree with those who say, "What has religion to do with social reforms?" But they must also agree with us when we tell them that religion has no business to formulate social laws and insist on the difference between beings, because its aim and end is to obliterate all such fictions and monstrosities.

If it be pleaded that through this difference we would reach the final equality and unity, we answer

---

1. Written to "Kidi" on March 3, 1894, from Chicago.

that the same religion has said over and over again that mud cannot be washed with mud. As if a man can be moral by being immoral!

Social laws were created by economic conditions under the sanction of religion. The terrible mistake of religion was to interfere in social matters. But how hypocritically it says and thereby contradicts itself, "Social reform is not the business of religion"! True, what we want is that religion should not be a social reformer, but we insist at the same time that society has no right to become a religious law-giver. Hands off! Keep yourself to your own bounds and everything would come right.

Education is the manifestation of the perfection already in man.

Religion is the manifestation of the Divinity already in man.

Therefore the only duty of the teacher in both cases is to remove all obstructions from the way. Hands off! as I always say, and everything will be right. That is, our duty is to clear the way. The Lord does the rest.

Especially, therefore, you must bear in mind that religion has to do only with the soul and has no business to interfere in social matters; you must also bear in mind that this applies completely to the mischief which has already been done. It is as if a man after forcibly taking possession of another's property cries through the nose when that man tries to regain it — and preaches the doctrine of the sanctity of human right!

What business had the priests to interfere (to the misery of millions of human beings) in every social matter?

You speak of the meat-eating Kshatriya. Meat or no meat, it is they who are the fathers of all that is noble and beautiful in Hinduism. Who wrote the Upanishads? Who was Râma? Who was Krishna? Who was Buddha? Who were the Tirthankaras of the Jains? Whenever the Kshatriyas have preached religion, they have given it to everybody; and whenever the Brahmins wrote anything, they would deny all right to others. Read the Gitâ and the Sutras of Vyâsa, or get someone to read them to you. In the Gita the way is laid open to all men and women, to all caste and colour, but Vyasa tries to put meanings upon the Vedas to cheat the poor Shudras. Is God a nervous fool like you that the flow of His river of mercy would be dammed up by a piece of meat? If such be He, His value is not a pie!

Hope nothing from me, but I am convinced as I have written to you, and spoken to you, that India is to be saved by the Indians themselves. So you, young men of the motherland, can dozens of you become almost fanatics over this new ideal? Take thought, collect materials, write a sketch of the life of Ramakrishna, studiously avoiding all miracles. The life should be written as an illustration of the doctrines he preached. Only his — do not bring me or any living persons into that. The main aim should be to give to the world what he taught, and the life as illustrating that. I, unworthy though I am, had one commission — to bring out the casket of jewels that was placed in my charge and make it over to you. Why to you? Because the hypocrites, the jealous, the slavish, and the cowardly, those who believe in matter only, can never do anything. Jealousy is the bane of our national character, natural to slaves. Even the Lord with all His power could do nothing on account of this jealousy. Think of me as one who has done all his duty and is now dead and gone. Think that the whole work is upon your shoulders. Think that you, young men of our motherland, are destined to do this. Put yourselves to the task. Lord bless you. Leave me, throw me quite out of sight. Preach the new ideal, the new doctrine, the new life. Preach against nobody, against no custom. Preach neither for nor against caste or any other social evil. Preach to let "hands off", and everything will come right.

My blessings on you all, my brave, steadfast, and loving souls.

OUR DUTY TO THE MASSES[1]

Shri Nârâyana bless you and yours. Through your Highness' kind help it has been possible for me to come to this country. Since then I have become well known here, and the hospitable people of this country have supplied all my wants. It is a wonderful country, and this is a wonderful nation in many respects. No other nation applies so much machinery in their everyday work as do the people of this country. Everything is machine. Then again, they are only one-twentieth of the whole population of the world. Yet they have fully one-sixth of all the wealth of the world. There is no limit to their wealth and luxuries. Yet everything here is so dear. The wages of labour are the highest in the world; yet the fight between labour and capital is constant.

Nowhere on earth have women so many privileges as in America. They are slowly taking everything into their hands; and, strange to say, the number of cultured women is much greater than that of cultured men. Of course, the higher geniuses are mostly from the rank of males. With all the criticism of the Westerners against our caste, they have a worse one — that of money. The almighty dollar, as the Americans say, can do anything here.

No country on earth has so many laws, and in no country are they so little regarded. On the whole our poor Hindu people are infinitely more moral than any of the Westerners. In religion they practice here either hypocrisy or fanaticism. Sober-minded men have become disgusted with their superstitious religions and are looking forward to India for new light. Your Highness cannot realise without seeing how eagerly they take in any little bit of the grand thoughts of the holy Vedas, which resist and are unharmed by the terrible onslaughts of modern science. The theories of creation out of nothing, of a created soul, and of the big tyrant of a God sitting on a throne in a place called heaven, and of the eternal hell-fires have disgusted all the educated; and the noble thoughts of the Vedas about the eternity of creation and of the soul, and about the God in our own soul, they are imbibing fast in one shape or other. Within fifty years the educated of the world will come to believe in the eternity of both soul and creation, and in God as our highest and perfect nature, as taught in our holy Vedas. Even now their learned priests are interpreting the Bible in that way. My conclusion is that they require more spiritual civilisation, and we, more material.

The one thing that is at the root of all evils in India is the condition of the poor. The poor in the West are devils; compared to them ours are angels, and it is therefore so much the easier to raise our poor. The only service to be done for our lower classes is to give them education, to develop their lost individuality. That is the great task between our people and princes. Up to now nothing has been done in that direction. Priest-power and foreign conquest have trodden them down for centuries, and at last the poor of India have forgotten that they are human beings. They are to be given ideas; their eyes are to be opened to what is going on in the world around them; and then they will work out their own salvation. Every nation, every man and every woman must work out their own salvation. Give them ideas — that is the only help they require, and then the rest must follow as the effect. Ours is to put the chemicals together, the crystallization comes in the law of nature. Our duty is to put ideas into their heads, they will do the rest. This is what is to be done in India. It is this idea that has been in my mind for a long time. I could not accomplish it in India, and that was the reason of my coming to this country. The great difficulty in the way of educating the poor is this. Supposing even your Highness opens a free school in every village, still it would do no good, for the poverty in India is such, that the poor boys would rather go to help their fathers in the fields, or otherwise try to make a living, than come to the school. Now if the mountain does not come to Mohammed, Mohammed must go to the mountain. If the poor boy cannot come to education, education must go to him. There are thousands of single-minded, self-sacrificing Sannyâsins in our

---

1. Written from Chicago to H. H. the Maharaja of Mysore on June 23, 1894.

own country, going from village to village, teaching religion. If some of them can be organised as teachers of secular things also, they will go from place to place, from door to door, not only preaching, but teaching also. Suppose two of these men go to a village in the evening with a camera, a globe, some maps, etc. They can teach a great deal of astronomy and geography to the ignorant. By telling stories about different nations, they can give the poor a hundred times more information through the ear than they can get in a lifetime through books. This requires an organization, which again means money. Men enough there are in India to work out this plan, but alas! they have no money. It is very difficult to set a wheel in motion; but when once set, it goes on with increasing velocity. After seeking help in my own country and failing to get any sympathy from the rich, I came over to this country through your Highness' aid. The Americans do not care a bit whether the poor of India die or live. And why should they, when our own people never think of anything but their own selfish ends?

My noble Prince, this life is short, the vanities of the world are transient, but they alone live who live for others, the rest are more dead than alive. One such high, noble-minded, and royal son of India as your Highness can do much towards raising India on her feet again and thus leave a name to posterity which shall be worshipped.

That the Lord may make your noble heart feel intensely for the suffering millions of India, sunk in ignorance, is the prayer of —

VIVEKANANDA.

REPLY TO THE CALCUTTA ADDRESS[1]

I am in receipt of the resolutions that were passed at the recent Town Hall meeting in Calcutta and the kind words my fellow-citizens sent over to me.

Accept, sir, my most heartfelt gratitude for your appreciation of my insignificant services.

I am thoroughly convinced that no individual or nation can live by holding itself apart from the community of others, and whenever such an attempt has been made under false ideas of greatness, policy, or holiness — the result has always been disastrous to the secluding one.

To my mind, the one great cause of the downfall and the degeneration of India was the building of a wall of custom — whose foundation was hatred of others — round the nation, and the real aim of which in ancient times was to prevent the Hindus from coming in contact with the surrounding Buddhistic nations.

Whatever cloak ancient or modern sophistry may try to throw over it, the inevitable result — the vindication of the moral law, that none can hate others without degenerating himself — is that the race that was foremost amongst the ancient races is now a byword, and a scorn among nations. We are object-lessons of the violation of that law which our ancestors were the first to discover and disseminate.

Give and take is the law; and if India wants to raise herself once more, it is absolutely necessary that she brings out her treasures and throws them broadcast among the nations of the earth, and in return be ready to receive what others have to give her. Expansion is life, contraction is death. Love is life, and hatred is death. We commenced to die the day we began to hate other races; and nothing can prevent our death unless we come back to expansion, which is life.

We must mix, therefore, with all the races of the earth. And every Hindu that goes out to travel in foreign parts renders more benefit to his country than hundreds of men who are bundles of superstitions and selfishness, and whose one aim in life seems to be like that of the dog in the manger. The wonderful structures of national life which the Western nations have raised, are supported by the strong pillars of character, and until we can pro-

---

1. Written from New York on Nov. 18, 1894, to Raja Pyari Mohan Mukherji, President of the public meeting held on Sept. 5, 1894 at the Calcutta Town Hall in appreciation of Swami Vivekananda's work in the West.

duce members of such, it is useless to fret and fume against this or that power.

Do any deserve liberty who are not ready to give it to others? Let us calmly and in a manly fashion go to work, instead of dissipating our energy in unnecessary frettings and fumings. I, for one, thoroughly believe that no power in the universe can withhold from anyone anything he really deserves. The past was great no doubt, but I sincerely believe that the future will be more glorious still.

May Shankara keep us steady in purity, patience, and perseverance!

TO MY BRAVE BOYS[1]

Push on with the organization. Nothing else is necessary but these — love, sincerity, and patience. What is life but growth, i.e. expansion, i.e. love? Therefore all love is life, it is the only law of life; all selfishness is death, and this is true here or hereafter. It is life to do good, it is death not to do good to others. Ninety per cent of human brutes you see are dead, are ghosts — for none lives, my boys, but he who loves. Feel, my children, feel; feel for the poor, the ignorant, the downtrodden; feel till the heart stops and the brain reels and you think you will go mad — then pour the soul out at the feet of the Lord, and then will come power, help, and indomitable energy. Struggle, struggle, was my motto for the last ten years. Struggle, still say I. When it was all dark, I used to say, struggle; when light is breaking in, I still say, struggle. Be not afraid, my children. Look not up in that attitude of fear towards that infinite starry vault as if it would crush you. Wait! In a few hours more, the whole of it will be under your feet. Wait, money does not pay, nor name; fame does not pay, nor learning. It is love that pays; it is character that cleaves its way through adamantine walls of difficulties.

Now the question before us is this. There cannot be any growth without liberty. Our ancestors freed religious thought, and we have a wonderful religion. But they put a heavy chain on the feet of society, and our society is, in a word, horrid, diabolical. In the West, society always had freedom, and look at them. On the other hand, look at their religion.

Liberty is the first condition of growth. Just as man must have liberty to think and speak, so he must have liberty in food, dress, and marriage, and in every other thing, so long as he does not injure others.

We talk foolishly against material civilisation. The grapes are sour. Even taking all that foolishness for granted, in all India there are, say, a hundred thousand really spiritual men and women. Now, for the spiritualisation of these, must three hundred millions be sunk in savagery and starvation? Why should any starve? How was it possible for the Hindus to have been conquered by the Mohammedans? It was due to the Hindus' ignorance of material civilization. Even the Mohammedans taught them to wear tailor-made clothes. Would the Hindus had learnt from the Mohammedans how to eat in a cleanly way without mixing their food with the dust of the streets! Material civilization, nay, even luxury, is necessary to create work for the poor. Bread! Bread! I do not believe in a God, who cannot give me bread here, giving me eternal bliss in heaven! Pooh! India is to be raised, the poor are to be fed, education is to be spread, and the evil of priestcraft is to be removed. No priestcraft, no social tyranny! More bread, more opportunity for everybody! Our young fools organise meetings to get more power from the English. They only laugh. None deserves liberty who is not ready to give liberty. Suppose the English give over to you all the power. Why, the powers that be then, will hold the people down, and let them not have it. Slaves want power to make slaves.

Now, this is to be brought about slowly, and by only insisting on our religion and giving liberty to society. Root up priestcraft from the old religion, and you get the best religion in the world. Do you understand me? Can you make a European society with India's religion? I believe it is possible, and must be.

---

1. Written to Alasinga Perumal from New York on 19th November, 1894.

The grand plan is to start a colony in Central India, where you can follow your own ideas independently, and then a little leaven will leaven all. In the meanwhile form a Central Association and go on branching off all over India. Start only on religious grounds now, and do not preach any violent social reform at present; only do not countenance foolish superstitions. Try to revive society on the old grounds of universal salvation and equality as laid down by the old Masters, such as Shankarâchârya, Râmânuja, and Chaitanya.

Have fire and spread all over. Work, work. Be the servant while leading. Be unselfish, and never listen to one friend in private accusing another. Have infinite patience, and success is yours.

Now take care of this: Do not try to "boss" others, as the Yankees say. Because I always direct my letters to you, you need not try to show your consequence over my other friends. I know you never can be such a fool, but still I think it my duty to warn you. This is what kills all organizations. Work, work, for, to work only for the good of others is life.

I want that there should be no hypocrisy, no Jesuitism, no roguery. I have depended always on the Lord, always on Truth broad as the light of day. Let me not die with stains on my conscience for having played Jesuitism to get up name or fame, or even to do good. There should not be a breath of immorality, nor a stain of policy which is bad.

No shilly-shally, no esoteric blackguardism, no secret humbug, nothing should be done in a corner. No special favouritism of the Master, no Master at that, even. Onward, my brave boys — money or no money — men or no men! Have you love? Have you God? Onward and forward to the breach, you are irresistible.

How absurd! The Theosophical magazines saying that they, the Theosophists, prepared the way to my success! Indeed! Pure nonsense! Theosophists prepared the way!

Take care! Beware of everything that is untrue; stick to truth and we shall succeed, maybe slowly, but surely. Work on as if I never existed. Work as if on each of you depended the whole work. Fifty centuries are looking on you, the future of India depends on you. Work on. I do not know when I shall be able to come. This is a great field for work. They can at best praise in India, but they will not give a cent for anything; and where shall they get it, beggars themselves? Then, they have lost the faculty of doing public good for the last two thousand years or more. They are just learning the ideas of nation, public, etc. So I need not blame them.

Blessings to you all!

A PLAN OF WORK FOR INDIA[1]

It is with a heart full of love, gratitude, and trust that I take up my pen to write to you. Let me tell you first, that you are one of the few men that I have met in my life who are thorough in their convictions. You have a whole-souled possession of a wonderful combination of feeling and knowledge, and withal a practical ability to bring ideas into realised forms. Above all, you are sincere, and as such I confide to you some of my ideas.

The work has begun well in India, and it should not only be kept up, but pushed on with the greatest vigour. Now or never is the time. After taking a far and wide view of things, my mind has now been concentrated on the following plan. First, it would be well to open a Theological College in Madras, and then gradually extend its scope, to give a thorough education to young men in the Vedas and the different Bhâshyas and philosophies, including a knowledge of the other religions of the world. At the same time a paper in English and the vernacular should be started as an organ of the College.

This is the first step to be taken, and huge things grow out of small undertakings. Madras just now is following the golden mean by appreciating both the ancient and modern phases of life.

I fully agree with the educated classes in India

---
1. Written to Justice Sir Subrahmanya Iyer from Chicago, 3rd Jan., 1895.

that a thorough overhauling of society is necessary. But how to do it? The destructive plans of reformers have failed. My plan is this. We have not done badly in the past, certainly not. Our society is not bad but good, only I want it to be better still. Not from error to truth, nor from bad to good, but from truth to higher truth, from good to better, best. I tell my countrymen that so far they have done well — now is the time to do better.

Now, take the case of caste — in Sanskrit, Jâti, i.e. species. Now, this is the first idea of creation. Variation (Vichitratâ), that is to say Jati, means creation. "I am One, I become many" (various Vedas). Unity is before creation, diversity is creation. Now if this diversity stops, creation will be destroyed. So long as any species is vigorous and active, it must throw out varieties. When it ceases or is stopped from breeding varieties, it dies. Now the original idea of Jati was this freedom of the individual to express his nature, his Prakriti, his Jati, his caste; and so it remained for thousands of years. Not even in the latest books is inter-dining prohibited; nor in any of the older books is inter-marriage forbidden. Then what was the cause of India's downfall? — the giving up of this idea of caste. As Gitâ says, with the extinction of caste the world will be destroyed. Now does it seem true that with the stoppage of these variations the world will be destroyed? The present caste is not the real Jati, but a hindrance to its progress. It really has prevented the free action of Jati, i.e. caste or variation. Any crystallized custom or privilege or hereditary class in any shape really prevents caste (Jati) from having its full sway; and whenever any nation ceases to produce this immense variety, it must die. Therefore what I have to tell you, my countrymen, is this, that India fell because you prevented and abolished caste. Every frozen aristocracy or privileged class is a blow to caste and is not-caste. Let Jati have its sway; break down every barrier in the way of caste, and we shall rise. Now look at Europe. When it succeeded in giving free scope to caste and took away most of the barriers that stood in the way of individuals, each developing his caste — Europe rose. In America, there is the best scope for caste (real Jati) to develop, and so the people are great. Every Hindu knows that astrologers try to fix the caste of every boy or girl as soon as he or she is born. That is the real caste — the individuality, and Jyotisha (astrology) recognises that. And we can only rise by giving it full sway again. This variety does not mean inequality, nor any special privilege.

This is my method — to show the Hindus that they have to give up nothing, but only to move on in the line laid down by the sages and shake off their inertia, the result of centuries of servitude. Of course, we had to stop advancing during the Mohammedan tyranny, for then it was not a question of progress but of life and death. Now that that pressure has gone, we must move forward, not on the lines of destruction directed by renegades and missionaries, but along our own line, our own road. Everything is hideous because the building is unfinished. We had to stop building during centuries of oppression. Now finish the building and everything will look beautiful in its own place. This is all my plan. I am thoroughly convinced of this. Each nation has a main current in life; in India it is religion. Make it strong and the waters on either side must move along with it. This is one phase of my line of thought. In time, I hope to bring them all out, but at present I find I have a mission in this country also. Moreover, I expect help in this country and from here alone. But up to date I could not do anything except spreading my ideas. Now I want that a similar attempt be made in India.

I do not know when I shall go over to India. I obey the leading of the Lord. I am in His hands.

"In this world in search of wealth, Thou art, O Lord, the greatest jewel I have found. I sacrifice myself unto Thee."

"In search of some one to love, Thou art the One Beloved I have found. I sacrifice myself unto Thee." (Yajurveda Samhitâ).

May the Lord bless you for ever and ever!

FUNDAMENTALS OF RELIGION[1]

My mind can best grasp the religions of the world, ancient or modern, dead or living, through this fourfold division:

1. Symbology — The employment of various external aids to preserve and develop the religious faculty of man.

2. History — The philosophy of each religion as illustrated in the lives of divine or human teachers acknowledged by each religion. This includes mythology; for what is mythology to one race, or period, is or was history to other races or periods. Even in cases of human teachers, much of their history is taken as mythology by successive generations.

3. Philosophy — The rationale of the whole scope of each religion.

4. Mysticism — The assertion of something superior to sense-knowledge and reason which particular persons, or all persons under certain circumstances, possess; runs through the other divisions also.

All the religions of the world, past or present, embrace one or more of these principles, the highly developed ones having all the four.

Of these highly developed religions again, some had no sacred book or books and they have disappeared; but those which were based on sacred books are living to the present day. As such, all the great religions of the world today are founded on sacred books.

- The Vedic on the Vedas (misnamed the Hindu or Brahminic).
- The Avestic on the Avesta.
- The Mosaic on the Old Testament.
- The Buddhistic on the Tripitaka.
- The Christian on the New Testament.
- The Mohammedan on the Koran.

[1]. This incomplete article was found in the papers of Miss S. E. Waldo. The heading is inserted by us — *Publisher*.

The Taoists and the Confucianists in China, having also books, are so inextricably mixed up with the Buddhistic form of religion as to be catalogued with Buddhism.

Again, although strictly speaking there are no absolutely racial religions, yet it may be said that, of this group, the Vedic, the Mosaic, and the Avestic religions are confined to the races to which they originally belonged; while the Buddhistic, the Christian, and the Mohammedan religions have been from their very beginning spreading religions.

The struggle will be between the Buddhists and Christians and Mohammedans to conquer the world, and the racial religions also will have unavoidably to join in the struggle. Each one of these religions, racial or spreading, has been already split into various branches and has undergone vast changes consciously or unconsciously to adapt itself to varying circumstances. This very fact shows that not one of them is fitted alone to be the religion of the entire human race. Each religion being the effect of certain peculiarities of the race it sprang from, and being in turn the cause of the intensification and preservation of those very peculiarities, not one of them can fit the universal human nature. Not only so, but there is a negative element in each. Each one helps the growth of a certain part of human nature, but represses everything else which the race from which it sprang had not. Thus one religion to become universal would be dangerous and degenerating to man.

Now the history of the world shows that these two dreams — that of a universal political Empire and that of a universal religious Empire — have been long before mankind, but that again and again the plans of the greatest conquerors had been frustrated by the splitting up of his territories before he could conquer only a little part of the earth; and similarly every religion has been split into sects before it was fairly out of its cradle.

Yet it seems to be true, that the solidarity of the human race, social as well as religious, with a scope for infinite variation, is the plan of nature; and if the line of least resistance is the true line of action, it seems to me that this splitting up of each religion into sects is the preservation of religion by frustrating the tendency to rigid sameness, as well as the dear indication to us of the line of procedure.

The end seems, therefore, to be not destruction but a multiplication of sects until each individual is a sect unto himself. Again a background of unity will come by the fusion of all the existing religions into one grand philosophy. In the mythologies or the ceremonials there never will be unity, because we differ more in the concrete than in the abstract. Even while admitting the same principle, men will differ as to the greatness of each of his ideal teacher.

So, by this fusion will be found out a union of philosophy as the basis of union, leaving each at liberty to choose his teacher or his form as illustrations of that unity. This fusion is what is naturally going on for thousands of years; only, by mutual antagonism, it has been woefully held back.

Instead of antagonising, therefore, we must help all such interchange of ideas between different races, by sending teachers to each other, so as to educate humanity in all the various religions of the world; but we must insist as the great Buddhist Emperor of India, Asoka, did, in the second century before Christ, not to abuse others, or to try to make a living out of others' faults; but to help, to sympathise, and to enlighten.

There is a great outcry going over the world against metaphysical knowledge as opposed to what is styled physical knowledge. This crusade against the metaphysical and the beyond-this-life, to establish the present life and the present world on a firmer basis, is fast becoming a fashion to which even the preachers of religion one after the other are fast succumbing. Of course, the unthinking multitude are always following things which present to them a pleasing surface; but when those who ought to know better, follow unmeaning fashions, pseudo-philosophical though they profess to be, it becomes a mournful fact.

Now, no one denies that our senses, as long as they are normal, are the most trustworthy guides we have, and the facts they gather in for us form the very foundation of the structure of human knowledge. But if they mean that all human knowledge is only sense-perception and nothing but that, we deny it. If by physical sciences are meant systems of knowledge which are entirely based and built upon sense-perception, and nothing but that, we contend that such a science never existed nor will ever exist. Nor will any system of knowledge, built upon sense-perception alone, ever be a science.

Senses no doubt cull the materials of knowledge and find similarities and dissimilarities; but there they have to stop. In the first place the physical gatherings of facts are conditioned by certain metaphysical conceptions, such as space and time. Secondly, grouping facts, or generalisation, is impossible without some abstract notion as the background. The higher the generalization, the more metaphysical is the abstract background upon which the detached facts are arranged. Now, such ideas as matter, force, mind, law, causation, time, and space are the results of very high abstractions, and nobody has ever sensed any one of them; in other words, they are entirely metaphysical. Yet without these metaphysical conceptions, no physical fact is possible to be understood. Thus a certain motion becomes understood when it is referred to a force; certain sensations, to matter; certain changes outside, to law; certain changes in thought, to mind; certain order singly, to causation — and joined to time, to law. Yet nobody has seen or even imagined matter or force, law or causation, time or space.

It may be urged that these, as abstracted concepts do not exist, and that these abstractions are nothing separate or separable from the groups of which they are, so to say, only qualities.

Apart from the question whether abstractions are possible or not, or whether there is something besides the generalized groups or not, it is plain that these notions of matter or force, time or space, causation, law, or mind, are held to be units abstracted and independent (by themselves) of the groups, and that it is only when they are thought of as such, they furnish themselves as explanations of the facts in sense-perception. That is to say, apart from the validity of these notions, we see two facts about them — first, they are metaphysical; second, that only as metaphysical do they explain the physical and not otherwise.

Whether the external conforms to the internal, or the internal to the external, whether matter conforms to mind, or mind to matter, whether the surroundings mould the mind, or the mind moulds the circumstances, is old, old question, and is still today as new and vigorous as it ever was. Apart from the question of precedence or causation — without trying to solve the problem as to whether the mind is the cause of matter or matter the cause of mind — it is evident that whether the external was formed by the internal or not, it must conform itself to the internal for us to be able to know it. Supposing that the external world is the cause of the internal, yet we shall of have to admit that the external world, as cause of ours mind, is unknown and unknowable, because the mind can only know that much or that view of the external or that view which conforms to or is a reflection of its own nature. That which is its own reflection could not have been its cause. Now that view of the whole mass of existence, which is cut off by mind and known, certainly cannot be the cause of mind, as its very existence is known in and through the mind.

Thus it is impossible to deduce a mind from matter. Nay, it is absurd. Because on the very face of it that portion of existence which is bereft of the qualities of thought and life and endowed with the quality of externality is called matter, and that portion which is bereft of externality and endowed with the qualities of thought and life is called mind. Now to prove matter from mind, or mind from matter, is to deduce from each the very qualities we have taken away from each; and, therefore, all the fight about the causality of mind or matter is merely a word puzzle and nothing more. Again, throughout all these controversies runs, as a rule, the fallacy of imparting different meanings to the words mind and matter. If sometimes the word mind is used as something opposed and external to matter, at others as something which embraces both the mind and matter, i.e. of which both the external and internal are parts on the materialistic side; the word matter is sometimes used in is the restricted sense of something external which we sense, and again it means something which is the cause of all the phenomena both external and internal. The materialist frightens the idealist by claiming to derive his mind from the elements of the laboratory, while all the time he is struggling to express something higher than all elements and atoms, something of which both the external and the internal phenomena are results, and which he terms matter. The idealist, on the other hand, wants to derive all the elements and atoms of the materialist from his own thought, even while catching glimpses of something which is the cause of both mind and matter, and which he oft-times calls God. That is to say, one party wants to explain the whole universe by a portion of it which is external, the other by another portion which is internal. Both of these attempts are impossible. Mind and matter cannot explain each other. The only explanation is to be sought for in something which will embrace both matter and mind.

It may be argued that thought cannot exist without mind, for supposing there was a time when there was no thought, matter, as we know it, certainly could not have existed. On the other hand, it may be said that knowledge being impossible without experience, and experience presupposing the external world, the existence of mind, as we know it, is impossible without the existence of matter.

Nor is it possible that either of them had a beginning. Generalisation is the essence of knowledge. Generalisation is impossible without a storage of similarities. Even the fact of comparison is impossible without previous experience. Knowledge thus is impossible without previous knowledge — and knowledge necessitating the existence of both thought and matter, both of them are without beginning.

Again generalization, the essence of sense-knowledge, is impossible without something upon which the detached facts of perception unite. The whole world of external perceptions requires something upon which to unite in order to form a concept of the world, as painting must have its canvas. If thought or mind be this canvas to the external world, it, in its turn requires another. Mind being a series of different feelings and willing — and not a unit, requires something besides itself as its background of unity. Here all analysis is bound to stop, for a real unity has been found. The analysis of a compound cannot stop until an indivisible unit has been reached. The fact that presents us with such a unity for both thought and matter must necessarily be the last indivisible basis of every phenomenon, for we cannot conceive any further analysis; nor is any further analysis necessary, as this includes an analysis of all our external and internal perceptions.

So far then, we see that a totality of mental and material phenomena, and something beyond, upon which they are both playing, are the results of our investigation.

Now this something beyond is not in sense-perception; it is a logical necessity, and a feeling of its indefinable presence runs through all our sense-perceptions. We see also that to this something we are driven by the sheer necessity of being true to our reason and generalising faculty.

It may be urged that there is no necessity whatsoever of postulating any such substance or being beyond the mass of mental and material phenomena. The totality of phenomena is all that we know or can know, and it requires nothing beyond itself to explain itself. An analysis beyond the senses is impossible, and the feeling of a substance in which everything inheres is simply an illusion.

We see, that from the most ancient times, there has been these two schools among thinkers. One party claims that the unavoidable necessity of the human mind to form concepts and abstractions is the natural guide to knowledge, and that it can stop nowhere until we have transcended all phenomena and formed a concept which is absolute in all directions, transcending time and space and causality. Now if this ultimate concept is arrived at by analysing the whole phenomena of thought and matter, step by step, taking the cruder first and resolving it into a finer, and still finer, until we arrive at something which stands as the solution of everything else, it is obvious that everything else beyond this final result is a momentary modification of itself, and as such, this final result alone is real and everything else is but its shadow. The reality, therefore, is not in the senses but beyond them.

On the other hand, the other party holds that the only reality in the universe is what our senses bring to us, and although a sense of something beyond hangs on to all our sense-perceptions, that is only a trick of the mind, and therefore unreal.

Now a changing something can never be understood, without the idea of something unchanging; and if it be said that that unchanging something, to which the changing is referred, is also a changing phenomenon only relatively unchanging, and is therefore to be referred to something else, and so on, we say that however infinitely long this series be, the very fact of our inability to understand a changeable without an unchangeable forces us to postulate one as the background of all the changeable. And no one has the right to take one part of a whole as right and reject the other at will. If one takes the obverse he must take the reverse of the same coin also, however he may dislike it.

Again, with every movement, man asserts his freedom. From the highest thinker to the most ignorant man everyone knows that he is free. Now every man at the same time finds out with a little thinking that every action of his had motives and conditions, and given those motives and conditions his particular action can be as rigorously deduced as any other fact in causation.

Here, again, the same difficulty occurs. Man's will is as rigorously bound by the law of causation as the growth of any little plant or the falling of a stone, and yet, through all this bondage runs the indestructible idea of freedom. Here also the totality side will declare that the idea of freedom is an illusion and man is wholly a creature of necessity.

Now, on one hand, this denial of freedom as an illusion is no explanation; on the other hand, why not say that the idea of necessity or bondage or causation is an illusion of the ignorant? Any theory which can fit itself to facts which it wants to explain, by first cutting as many of them as prevents its fitting itself into them, is on the face of it wrong. Therefore the only way left to us is to admit first that the body is not free, neither is the will but that there must be something beyond both the mind and body which is free and

(incomplete)

WRITINGS: POEMS

Kali the Mother

The stars are blotted out,
The clouds are covering clouds,
It is darkness vibrant, sonant.
In the roaring, whirling wind
Are the souls of a million lunatics
Just loose from the prison-house,
Wrenching trees by the roots,
Sweeping all from the path.
The sea has joined the fray,
And swirls up mountain-waves,
To reach the pitchy sky.
The flash of lurid light
Reveals on every side
A thousand, thousand shades
Of Death begrimed and black —
Scattering plagues and sorrows,
Dancing mad with joy,
Come, Mother, come!
For Terror is Thy name,
Death is in Thy breath,
And every shaking step
Destroys a world for e'er.
Thou "Time", the All-Destroyer!
Come, O Mother, come!
Who dares misery love,
And hug the form of Death,
Dance in Destruction's dance,
To him the Mother comes.

Angels Unawares[1]

I

One bending low with load of life—
That meant no joy, but suffering harsh and hard—
And wending on his way through dark and dismal paths
Without a flash of light from brain or heart
To give a moment's cheer, till the line
That marks out pain from pleasure, death from life,
And good from what is evil was well-nigh wiped from sight,
Saw, one blessed night, a faint but beautiful ray of light
Descend to him. He knew not what or where from,
But called it God and worshipped.
Hope, an utter stranger, came to him and spread
Through all his parts, and life to him meant more
Than he could ever dream and covered all he knew,
Nay, peeped beyond his world. The Sages
Winked, and smiled, and called it "superstition".
But he did feel its power and peace
And gently answered back—
"O Blessed Superstition!"

II

One drunk with wine of wealth and power
And health to enjoy them both, whirled on
His maddening course, till the earth, he thought,
Was made for him, his pleasure-garden, and man,
The crawling worm, was made to find him sport,
Till the thousand lights of joy, with pleasure fed,

---

[1]. Written on 1 September, 1898.

That flickered day and night before his eyes,
With constant change of colours, began to blur
His sight, and cloy his senses ; till selfishness,
Like a horny growth, had spread all o'er his heart ;
And pleasure meant to him no more than pain,
Bereft of feeling; and life in the sense,
So joyful, precious once, a rotting corpse between his arms,
Which he forsooth would shun, but more he tried, the more
It clung to him; and wished, with frenzied brain,
A thousand forms of death, but quailed before the charm,
Then sorrow came—and Wealth and Power went—
And made him kinship find with all the human race
In groans and tears, and though his friends would laugh,
His lips would speak in grateful accents—
"O Blessed Misery!"

III

One born with healthy frame — but not of will
That can resist emotions deep and strong,
Nor impulse throw, surcharged with potent strength —
And just the sort that pass as good and kind,
Beheld that he was safe, whilst others long
And vain did struggle 'gainst the surging waves.
Till, morbid grown, his mind could see, like flies
That seek the putrid part, but what was bad.
Then Fortune smiled on him, and his foot slipped.
That ope'd his eyes for e'er, and made him find
That stones and trees ne'er break the law,
But stones and trees remain ; that man alone
Is blest with power to fight and conquer Fate,
Transcending bounds and laws.

From him his passive nature fell, and life appeared
As broad and new, and broader, newer grew,
Till light ahead began to break, and glimpse of That
Where Peace Eternal dwells—yet one can only reach
By wading through the sea of struggles—courage-giving, came.
Then looking back on all that made him kin
To stocks and stones, and on to what the world
Had shunned him for, his fall, he blessed the fall,
And with a joyful heart, declared it —
"Blessed Sin!"

To the Awakened India[1]

Once more awake!

For sleep it was, not death, to bring thee life
Anew, and rest to lotus-eyes for visions
Daring yet. The world in need awaits, O Truth!
No death for thee!

Resume thy march,

With gentle feet that would not break the
Peaceful rest even of the roadside dust
That lies so low. Yet strong and steady,
Blissful, bold, and free. Awakener, ever
Forward! Speak thy stirring words.

Thy home is gone,

Where loving hearts had brought thee up and
Watched with joy thy growth. But Fate is strong—
This is the law—all things come back to the source
They sprung, their strength to renew.

Then start afresh

From the land of thy birth, where vast cloud-belted
Snows do bless and put their strength in thee,
For working wonders new. The heavenly
River tune thy voice to her own immortal song;
Deodar shades give thee eternal peace.

---

1. Written to Prabuddha Bharata or *Awakened India*, in August 1898, when the journal was transferred from Madras to Almora Himalayas, into the hands of the Brotherhood founded by Swami Vivekananda.

And all above,

Himala's daughter Umâ, gentle, pure,
The Mother that resides in all as Power
And Life, who works all works and
Makes of One the world, whose mercy
Opens the gate to Truth and shows
The One in All, give thee untiring
Strength, which is Infinite Love.

They bless thee all,

The seers great, whom age nor clime
Can claim their own, the fathers of the
Race, who felt the heart of Truth the same,
And bravely taught to man ill-voiced or
Well. Their servant, thou hast got
The secret—'tis but One.

Then speak, O Love!

Before thy gentle voice serene, behold how
Visions melt and fold on fold of dreams
Departs to void, till Truth and Truth alone
In all its glory shines—

And tell the world—

Awake, arise, and dream no more!
This is the land of dreams, where Karma
Weaves unthreaded garlands with our thoughts

Of flowers sweet or noxious, and none
Has root or stem, being born in naught, which
The softest breath of Truth drives back to
Primal nothingness. Be bold, and face
The Truth! Be one with it! Let visions cease,
Or, if you cannot, dream but truer dreams,
Which are Eternal Love and Service Free.

Requiescat in Pace[1]

Speed forth, O Soul! upon thy star-strewn path ;
Speed, blissful one! where thought is ever free,
Where time and space no longer mist the view,
Eternal peace and blessings be with thee!

Thy service true, complete thy sacrifice,
Thy home the heart of love transcendent find ;
Remembrance sweet, that kills all space and time,
Like altar roses fill thy place behind!

Thy bonds are broke, thy quest in bliss is found,
And one with That which comes as Death and Life ;
Thou helpful one! unselfish e'er on earth,
Ahead! still help with love this world of strife!

---

[1]. Written in memoriam to J. J. Goodwin, August, 1898.

Hold on Yet a While, Brave Heart[1]

If the sun by the cloud is hidden a bit,
If the welkin shows but gloom,
Still hold on yet a while, brave heart,
The victory is sure to come.

No winter was but summer came behind,
Each hollow crests the wave,
They push each other in light and shade;
Be steady then and brave.

The duties of life are sore indeed,
And its pleasures fleeting, vain,
The goal so shadowy seems and dim,
Yet plod on through the dark, brave heart,
With all thy might and main.

Not a work will be lost, no struggle vain,
Though hopes be blighted, powers gone;
Of thy loins shall come the heirs to all,
Then hold on yet a while, brave soul,
No good is e'er undone.

Though the good and the wise in life are few,
Yet theirs are the reins to lead,
The masses know but late the worth;
Heed none and gently guide.

With thee are those who see afar,
With thee is the Lord of might,
All blessings pour on thee, great soul,
To thee may all come right

---

1. Written to H. H. The Maharaja of Khetri, Rajputana.

Nirvanashatkam, on Six Stanzas on Nirvana[1]

I am neither the mind, nor the intellect, nor the ego, nor the mind-stuff;
I am neither the body, nor the changes of the body;
I am neither the senses of hearing, taste, smell, or sight,
Nor am I the ether, the earth, the fire, the air;
I am Existence Absolute, Knowledge Absolute, Bliss Absolute—
I am He, I am He. (Shivoham, Shivoham).

I am neither the Prâna, nor the five vital airs;
I am neither the materials of the body, nor the five sheaths;
Neither am I the organs of action, nor object of the senses;
I am Existence Absolute, Knowledge Absolute, Bliss Absolute—
I am He, I am He. (Shivoham, Shivoham).

I have neither aversion nor attachment, neither greed nor delusion;
Neither egotism nor envy, neither Dharma nor Moksha;
I am neither desire nor objects of desire;
I am Existence Absolute, Knowledge Absolute, Bliss Absolute—
I am He, I am He. (Shivoham, Shivoham).

I am neither sin nor virtue, neither pleasure nor pain;
Nor temple nor worship, nor pilgrimage nor scriptures,
Neither the act of enjoying, the enjoyable nor the enjoyer;
I am Existence Absolute, Knowledge Absolute, Bliss Absolute—
I am He, I am He. (Shivoham, Shivoham).

I have neither death nor fear of death, nor caste;
Nor was I ever born, nor had I parents, friends, and relations;
I have neither Guru, nor disciple;
I am Existence Absolute, Knowledge Absolute, Bliss Absolute—
I am He, I am He. (Shivoham, Shivoham).

---

1. Translation of a poem by Shankarâchârya.

I am untouched by the senses, I am neither Mukti nor knowable ;
I am without form, without limit, beyond space, beyond time ;
I am in everything ; I am the basis of the universe ; everywhere am I.
I am Existence Absolute, Knowledge Absolute, Bliss Absolute—
I am He, I am He. (Shivoham, Shivoham)

The Song of the Sannyâsin[1]

Wake up the note! the song that had its birth
Far off, where worldly taint could never reach,
In mountain caves and glades of forest deep,
Whose calm no sigh for lust or wealth or fame
Could ever dare to break; where rolled the stream
Of knowledge, truth, and bliss that follows both.
Sing high that note, Sannyâsin bold! Say—
"Om Tat Sat, Om!"

Strike off thy fetters! Bonds that bind thee down,
Of shining gold, or darker, baser ore ;
Love, hate—good, bad—and all the dual throng,
Know, slave is slave, caressed or whipped, not free ;
For fetters, though of gold, are not less strong to bind ;
Then off with them, Sannyâsin bold! Say—
"Om Tat Sat, Om!"

Let darkness go; the will-o'-the-wisp that leads
With blinking light to pile more gloom on gloom.
This thirst for life, for ever quench ; it drags
From birth to death, and death to birth, the soul.
He conquers all who conquers self. Know this
And never yield, Sannyâsin bold! Say—
"Om Tat Sat, Om!"

"Who sows must reap," they say, "and cause must bring
The sure effect ; good, good ; bad, bad ; and none
Escape the law. But whoso wears a form
Must wear the chain." Too true ; but far beyond
Both name and form is Âtman, ever free.
Know thou art That, Sannyâsin bold! Say—

---
[1]. Composed at the Thousand Island Park, New York, in July, 1895.

"Om Tat Sat, Om!"

They know not truth who dream such vacant dreams
As father, mother, children, wife, and friend.
The sexless Self! whose father He? whose child?
Whose friend, whose foe is He who is but One?
The Self is all in all, none else exists ;
And thou art That, Sannyâsin bold! Say—
"Om Tat Sat, Om!"

There is but One—The Free—The Knower—Self!
Without a name, without a form or stain.
In Him is Mâyâ dreaming all this dream.
The witness, He appears as nature, soul.
Know thou art That, Sannyâsin bold! Say—
"Om Tat Sat, Om!"

Where seekest thou? That freedom, friend, this world
Nor that can give. In books and temples vain
Thy search. Thine only is the hand that holds
The rope that drags thee on. Then cease lament,
Let go thy hold, Sannyâsin bold! Say —
"Om Tat Sat, Om!"

Say, "Peace to all: From me no danger be
To aught that lives. In those that dwell on high,
In those that lowly creep, I am the Self in all!
All life both here and there, do I renounce,
All heavens and earths and hells, all hopes and fears."
Thus cut thy bonds, Sannyâsin bold! Say—
"Om Tat Sat, Om!"

Heed then no more how body lives or goes,
　Its task is done. Let Karma float it down ;
　　Let one put garlands on, another kick
This frame ; say naught. No praise or blame can be
Where praiser praised, and blamer blamed are one.
　　Thus be thou calm, Sannyâsin bold! Say—
　　　"Om Tat Sat, Om!"

Truth never comes where lust and fame and greed
　Of gain reside. No man who thinks of woman
　　As his wife can ever perfect be ;
Nor he who owns the least of things, nor he
Whom anger chains, can ever pass thro' Maya's gates.
　　So, give these up, Sannyâsin bold! Say—
　　　"Om Tat Sat, Om!"

Have thou no home. What home can hold thee, friend?
　The sky thy roof, the grass thy bed; and food
What chance may bring, well cooked or ill, judge not.
　No food or drink can taint that noble Self
　　Which knows Itself. Like rolling river free
　　Thou ever be, Sannyâsin bold! Say—
　　　"Om Tat Sat, Om!"

Few only know the truth. The rest will hate
And laugh at thee, great one ; but pay no heed.
Go thou, the free, from place to place, and help
Them out of darkness, Maya's veil. Without
　The fear of pain or search for pleasure, go
　　Beyond them both, Sannyâsin bold! Say—
　　　"Om Tat Sat, Om!"

Thus, day by day, till Karma's powers spent
Release the soul for ever. No more is birth,
Nor I, nor thou, nor God, nor man. The "I"
Has All become, the All is "I" and Bliss.
Know thou art That, Sannyâsin bold! Say —
"Om Tat Sat, Om!"

Peace[1]

Behold, it comes in might,
The power that is not power,
The light that is in darkness,
The shade in dazzling light.

It is joy that never spoke,
And grief unfelt, profound,
Immortal life unlived,
Eternal death unmourned.

It is not joy nor sorrow,
But that which is between,
It is not night nor morrow,
But that which joins them in.

It is sweet rest in music;
And pause in sacred art;
The silence between speaking;
Between two fits of passion—
It is the calm of heart.

It is beauty never seen,
And love that stands alone,
It is song that lives un-sung,
And knowledge never known.

It is death between two lives,
And lull between two storms,
The void whence rose creation,
And that where it returns.

---

1. Composed at Ridgely Manor, New York, 1899.

To it the tear-drop goes,
To spread the smiling form
It is the Goal of Life,
And Peace—its only home!..!

TRANSLATION: PROSE

THE PROBLEM OF MODERN INDIA AND ITS SOLUTION[1]

The ancient history of India is full of descriptions of the gigantic energies and their multifarious workings, the boundless spirit, the combination of indomitable action and reaction of the various forces, and, above all, the profound thoughtfulness of a godly race. If the word history is understood to mean merely narratives of kings and emperors, and pictures of society — tyrannised over from time to time by the evil passions, haughtiness, avarice, etc., of the rulers of the time, portraying the acts resulting from their good or evil propensities, and how these reacted upon the society of that time — such a history India perhaps does not possess. But every line of that mass of the religious literature of India, her ocean of poetry, her philosophies and various scientific works reveal to us — a thousand times more clearly than the narratives of the life-incidents and genealogies of particular kings and emperors can ever do — the exact position and every step made in advance by that vast body of men who, even before the dawn of civilisation, impelled by hunger and thirst, lust and greed, etc., attracted by the charm of beauty, endowed with a great and indomitable mental power, and moved by various sentiments, arrived through various ways and means at that stage of eminence. Although the heaps of those triumphal flags which they gathered in their innumerable victories over nature with which they had been waging war for ages, have, of late, been torn and tattered by the violent winds of adverse circumstances and become worn out through age, yet they still proclaim the glory of Ancient India.

Whether this race slowly proceeded from Central Asia, Northern Europe, or the Arctic regions, and gradually came down and sanctified India by settling there at last, or whether the holy land of India was their original native place, we have no proper means of knowing now. Or whether a vast race living in or outside India, being displaced from its original abode, in conformity with natural laws, came in the course of time to colonise and settle over Europe and other places — and whether these people were white or black, blue-eyed or dark-eyed, golden-haired or black-haired — all these matters — there is no sufficient ground to prove now, with the one exception of the fact of the kinship of Sanskrit with a few European languages. Similarly, it is not easy to arrive at a final conclusion as to the modern Indians, whether they all are the pure descendants of that race, or how much of the blood of that race is flowing in their veins, or again, what races amongst them have any of that even in them.

However, we do not, in fact, lose much by this uncertainty.

But there is one fact to remember. Of that ancient Indian race, upon which the rays of civilisation first dawned, where deep thoughtfulness first revealed itself in full glory, there are still found hundreds of thousands of its children, born of its mind — the inheritors of its thoughts and sentiments — ready to claim them.

Crossing over mountains, rivers, arid oceans, setting at naught, as it were, the obstacles of the distance of space and time, the blood of Indian thought has flowed, and is still flowing into the veins of other nations of the globe, whether in a distinct or in some subtle unknown way. Perhaps to us belongs the major portion of the universal ancient inheritance.

In a small country lying in the eastern corner of the Mediterranean Sea, beautiful and adorned by nature, and garlanded by well-formed and beautiful-looking islands, lived a race of men who were few in number, but of a very charming aspect, perfectly formed, and strong in muscles and sinews, light of body, yet possessing steadiness and perseverance, and who were unrivalled for the creation of all earthly beauties, as well as endowed with extraordinary practicality and intellect. The other ancient nations used to call them Yavanas, but they

---

1. The above is a translation of the first Bengali article written by Swami Vivekananda as an introduction to the *Udbodhana*, when it was started on the 14th of January, 1899, as the Bengali fortnightly (afterwards monthly) journal of the Ramakrishna Order.

called themselves Greeks. This handful of a vigorous and wonderful race is a unique example in the annals of man. Wherever and in whatever nation there has been, or is, any advance made in earthly science up to the present day — such as social, martial, political, sculptural, etc. — there the shadow of ancient Greece has fallen. Let us leave apart the consideration of ancient times, for even in this modern age, we, the Bengalis, think ourselves proud and enlightened simply by following the footmarks of these Yavana Gurus for these last fifty years, illumining our homes with what light of theirs is reaching us through the European literature.

The whole of Europe nowadays is, in every respect, the disciple of ancient Greece, and her proper inheritor; so much so that a wise man of England had said, "Whatever nature has not created, that is the creation of the Greek mind."

These two gigantic rivers (Aryans and Yavanas), issuing from far-away and different mountains (India and Greece), occasionally come in contact with each other, and whenever such confluence takes place, a tremendous intellectual or spiritual tide, rising in human societies, greatly expands the range of civilisation and confirms the bond of universal brotherhood among men.

Once in far remote antiquity, the Indian philosophy, coming in contact with Greek energy, led to the rise of the Persian, the Roman, and other great nations. After the invasion of Alexander the Great, these two great waterfalls colliding with each other, deluged nearly half of the globe with spiritual tides, such as Christianity. Again, a similar commingling, resulting in the improvement and prosperity of Arabia, laid the foundation of modern European civilisation. And perhaps, in our own day, such a time for the conjunction of these two gigantic forces has presented itself again. This time their centre is India.

The air of India pre-eminently conduces to quietness, the nature of the Yavana is the constant expression of power; profound meditation characterises the one, the indomitable spirit of dexterous activity, the other; one's motto is "renunciation", the other's "enjoyment". One's whole energy is directed inwards, the other's, outwards; one's whole learning consists in the knowledge of the Self or the Subject, the other's, in the knowledge of the not-Self or the object (perishable creation); one loves Moksha (spiritual freedom), the other loves political independence; one is unmindful of gaining prosperity in this world, the other sets his whole heart on making a heaven of this world; one, aspiring after eternal bliss, is indifferent to all the ephemeral pleasures of this life, and the other, doubting the existence of eternal bliss, or knowing it to be far away, directs his whole energy to the attainment of earthly pleasures as much as possible.

In this age, both these types of mankind are extinct, only their physical and mental children, their works and thoughts are existing.

Europe and America are the advanced children of the Yavanas, a glory to their forefathers; but the modern inhabitants of the land of Bharata are not the glory of the ancient Aryas. But, as fire remains intact under cover of ashes, so the ancestral fire still remains latent in these modern Indians. Through the grace of the Almighty Power, it is sure to manifest itself in time.

What will accrue when that ancestral fire manifests itself?

Would the sky of India again appear clouded over by waving masses of smoke springing from the Vedic sacrificial fire? Or is the glory of Rantideva again going to be revived in the blood of the sacrificed animals? Are the old customs of Gomedha, Ashvamedha, or perpetuating the lineage from a husband's brother, and other usages of a like nature to come back again? Or is the deluge of a Buddhistic propaganda again going to turn the whole of India into a big monastery? Are the laws of Manu going to be rehabilitated as of yore? Or is the discrimination of food, prescribed and forbidden, varying in accordance with geographical dimensions, as it is at the present day, alone going to have its all-powerful domination over the length and breadth of the country? Is the caste system to remain, and is it going to depend eternally upon the birthright of a man, or is it going to be determined by his qualification? And again in that caste system, is the discrimination of food, its touchableness or untouchableness, dependent upon the purity or the impurity of the man who touches it, to be observed as it is in Bengal, or will it assume a form more strict as it does in Madras? Or, as in the Punjab, will all such restrictions be obliterated? Are the marriages of the different Varnas to take place from the upper to the lower Varna in the successive order, as in Manu's days, and as it is still in vogue in Nepal? Or, as in Bengal and other places, are they to be kept restricted to a very limited number of individuals constituting one of the several communities of a certain class of the Varna? To give a conclusive answer to all these questions is extremely difficult. They become the more difficult of solution, considering the difference in the customs prevailing in different parts of the country — nay, as we find even in the same part of the country such a wide divergence of customs among different castes and families.

Then what is to be?

What we should have is what we have not, perhaps what our forefathers even had not — that which the Yavanas had; that, impelled by the life-vibration of which, is issuing forth in rapid succession from the great dynamo of Europe, the electric flow of that tremendous power vivifying the whole world. We want that. We want that energy, that love of independence, that spirit of self-reliance, that immovable fortitude, that dexterity in action, that bond of unity of purpose, that thirst for improvement. Checking a little the constant looking back to the past, we want that expansive vision infinitely projected forward; and we want — that intense spirit of activity (Rajas) which will flow through our every vein, from head to foot.

What can be a greater giver of peace than renunciation? A little ephemeral worldly good is nothing in comparison with eternal good; no doubt of that. What can bring greater strength than Sattva Guna (absolute purity of mind)? It is indeed true that all other kinds of knowledge are but non-knowledge in comparison with Self-knowledge. But I ask: How many are there in the world fortunate enough to gain that Sattva Guna? How many in this land of Bharata? How many have that noble heroism which can renounce all, shaking off the idea of "I and mine"? How many are blessed enough to possess that far-sight of wisdom which makes the earthly pleasures appear to be but vanity of vanities? Where is that broad-hearted man who is apt to forget even his own body in meditating over the beauty and glory of the Divine? Those who are such are but a handful in comparison to the population of the whole of India; and in order that these men may attain to their salvation, will the millions and millions of men and women of India have to be crushed under the wheel of the present-day society and religion?

And what good can come out of such a crushing?

Do you not see — talking up this plea of Sattva, the country has been slowly and slowly drowned in the ocean of Tamas or dark ignorance? Where the most dull want to hide their stupidity by covering it with a false desire for the highest knowledge which is beyond all activities, either physical or mental; where one, born and bred in lifelong laziness, wants to throw the veil of renunciation over his own unfitness for work; where the most diabolical try to make their cruelty appear, under the cloak of austerity, as a part of religion; where no one has an eye upon his own incapacity, but everyone is ready to lay the whole blame on others; where knowledge consists only in getting some books by heart, genius consists in chewing the cud of others' thoughts, and the highest glory consists in taking the name of ancestors: do we require any other proof to show that that country is being day by day drowned in utter Tamas?

Therefore Sattva or absolute purity is now far away from us. Those amongst us who are not yet fit, but who hope to be fit, to reach to that absolutely pure Paramahamsa state — for them the acquirement of Rajas or intense activity is what is most beneficial now. Unless a man passes through Rajas, can he ever attain to that perfect Sâttvika state? How can one expect Yoga or union with God, unless one has previously finished with his thirst for Bhoga or enjoyment? How can renunciation come where there is no Vairâgya or dispassion for all the charms of enjoyment?

On the other hand, the quality of Rajas is apt to die down as soon as it comes up, like a fire of palm leaves. The presence of Sattva and the Nitya or Eternal Reality is almost in a state of juxtaposition — Sattva is nearly Nitya. Whereas the nation in which the quality of Rajas predominates is not so long-lived, but a nation with a preponderance of Sattva is, as it were, immortal. History is a witness to this fact.

In India, the quality of Rajas is almost absent: the same is the case with Sattva in the West. It is certain, therefore, that the real life of the Western world depends upon the influx, from India, of the current of Sattva or transcendentalism; and it is also certain that unless we overpower and submerge our Tamas by the opposite tide of Rajas, we shall never gain any worldly good or welfare in this life; and it is also equally certain that we shall meet many formidable obstacles in the path of realisation of those noble aspirations and ideals connected with our after-life.

The one end and aim of the Udbodhana is to help the union and intermingling of these two forces, as far as it lies in its power.

True, in so doing there is a great danger — lest by this huge wave of Western spirit are washed away all our most precious jewels, earned through ages of hard labour; true, there is fear lest falling into its strong whirlpool, even the land of Bharata forgets itself so far as to be turned into a battlefield in the struggle after earthly enjoyments; ay, there is fear, too, lest going to imitate the impossible and impracticable foreign ways, rooting out as they do our national customs and ideals, we lose all that we hold dear in this life and be undone in the next!

To avoid these calamities we must always keep the wealth of our own home before our eyes, so that every one down to the masses may always know and see what his own ancestral property is. We must exert ourselves to do that; and side by side, we should be brave to open our doors to receive all available light from outside. Let rays of light come in, in sharp-driving showers from the four quarters of the earth; let the intense flood of light flow in from the West — what of that? Whatever is weak and corrupt is liable to die — what are we to do with it? If it goes, let it go, what harm does it do to us? What is strong and invigorating is immortal. Who can destroy that?

How many gushing springs and roaring cataracts, how many icy rivulets and ever-flowing streamlets, issuing from the eternal snow-capped peaks of the Himalayas, combine and flow together to form the gigantic river of the gods, the Gangâ, and rush impetuously towards the ocean! So what a variety of thoughts and ideas, how many currents of forces, issuing from innumerable saintly hearts, and from brains of geniuses of various lands have already enveloped India, the land of Karma, the arena for the display of higher human activities! Look! how under the dominion of the English, in these days of electricity, railroad, and steamboat, various sentiments, manners, customs, and morals are spreading all over the land with lightning speed. Nectar is coming, and along with it, also poison; good is coming, as well as evil. There has been enough of angry opposition and bloodshed; the power of stemming this tide is not in Hindu society. Everything, from water filtered by machinery and drawn from hydrants, down to sugar purified with bone-ash, is being quietly and freely taken by almost every one, in spite of much show of verbal protest. Slowly and slowly, by the strong dint of law, many of our most cherished customs are falling off day by day — we have no power to withstand that. And why is there no power? Is truth really powerless? "Truth alone conquers and not falsehood." — Is this Divine Vedic saying false? Or who knows but that those very customs which are being swept away by the deluge of the power of Western sovereignty or of Western education were not real Âchâras, but were Anâchâras after all. This also is a matter for serious consideration.

बहुजनहिताय बहुजनसुखाय — "For the good of the many, as well as for the happiness of the many" — in an unselfish manner, with a heart filled with love and reverence, the Udbodhana invites all wise and large-hearted men who love their motherland to discuss these points and solve these problems; and, being devoid of the feeling of hatred or antagonism, as well as turning itself away from the infliction of abusive language directed towards any individual, or society, or any sect, it offers its whole self for the service of all classes.

To work we have the right, the result is in the hands of the Lord. We only pray: "O Thou Eternal Spirit, make us spiritual; O Thou Eternal Strength, make us strong; O Thou Mighty One, make us mighty."

RAMAKRISHNA: HIS LIFE AND SAYINGS[1]

Among the Sanskrit scholars of the West, Professor Max Müller takes the lead. The Rig-Veda Samhitâ, the whole of which no one could even get at before, is now very neatly printed and made accessible to the public, thanks to the munificent generosity of the East India Company and to the Professor's prodigious labours extending over years. The alphabetical characters of most of the manuscripts, collected from different parts of India, are of various forms, and many words in them are inaccurate. We cannot easily comprehend how difficult it is for a foreigner, however learned he may be, to find out the accuracy or inaccuracy of these Sanskrit characters, and more especially to make out clearly the meaning of an extremely condensed and complicated commentary. In the life of Professor Max Müller, the publication of the Rig-Veda is a great event. Besides this, he has been dwelling, as it were, and spending his whole lifetime amidst ancient Sanskrit literature; but notwithstanding this, it does not imply that in the Professor's imagination India is still echoing as of old with Vedic hymns, with her sky clouded with sacrificial smoke, with many a Vasishtha, Vishvâmitra, Janaka, and Yâjnavalkya, with her every home blooming with a Gârgi or a Maitreyi and herself guided by the Vedic rules or canons of Grihya-Sutra.

1. Translation of a review of *Ramakrishna: His Life and Sayings* by Prof. Max Müller, contributed to the *Udbodhana*, 14th March, 1899.

The Professor, with ever-watchful eyes, keeps himself well-informed of what new events are occurring even in the out-of-the-way corners of modern India, half-dead as she is, trodden down by the feet of the foreigner professing an alien religion, and all but bereft of her ancient manners, rites, and customs. As the Professor's feet never touched these shores, many Anglo-Indians here show an unmixed contempt for his opinions on the customs, manners, and codes of morality of the Indian people. But they ought to know that, even after their lifelong stay, or even if they were born and brought up in this country, except any particular information they may obtain about that stratum of society with which they come in direct contact, the Anglo-Indian authorities have to remain quite ignorant in respect of other classes of people; and the more so, when, of this vast society divided into so many castes, it is very hard even among themselves for one caste to properly know the manners and peculiarities of another.

Some time ago, in a book, named, Residence in India, written by a well-known Anglo-Indian officer, I came across such a chapter as "Native Zenana Secrets". Perhaps because of that strong desire in every human heart for knowledge of secrets, I read the chapter, but only to find that this big Anglo-Indian author is fully bent upon satisfying the intense curiosity of his own countrymen regarding the mystery of a native's life by describing an affaire d'amour, said to have transpired between his sweeper, the sweeper's wife, and her paramour! And from the cordial reception given to the book by the Anglo-Indian community, it seems the writer's object has been gained, and he feels himself quite satisfied with his work "God-speed to you, dear friends!" — What else shall we say? Well has the Lord said in the Gita:

ध्यायतो विषयान्पुंसः सङ्गस्तेषूपजायते ।

सङ्गात्सञ्जायते कामः कामात्क्रोधोऽभिजायते ॥

—"Thinking of objects, attachment to them is formed in a man. From attachment longing, and from longing anger grows."

Let such irrelevant things alone. To return to our

subject: After all, one wonders at Professor Max Müller's knowledge of the social customs and codes of law, as well as the contemporaneous occurrences in the various provinces of present-day India; this is borne out by our own personal experiences.

In particular, the Professor observes with a keen eye what new waves of religion are rising in different parts of India, and spares no pains in letting the Western world not remain in the dark about them. The Brâhmo Samaj guided by Debendranâth Tagore and Keshab Chandra Sen, the Ârya Samaj established by Swami Dayânanda Sarasvati, and the Theosophical movement — have all come under the praise or censure of his pen. Struck by the sayings and teachings of Shri Ramakrishna published in the two well-established journals, the Brahmavâdin and the Prabuddha Bhârata, and reading what the Brahmo preacher, Mr. Pratâp Chandra Mazumdâr, wrote about Shri Ramakrishna,[1] he was attracted by the sage's life. Some time ago, a short sketch of Shri Ramakrishna's life[2] also appeared in the well-known monthly journal of England, The Imperial and Asiatic Quarterly Review, contributed by Mr. C. H. Tawney, M.A., the distinguished librarian of the India House. Gathering a good deal of information from Madras and Calcutta, the Professor discussed Shri Ramakrishna's life and his teachings in a short article[3] in the foremost monthly English journal, The Nineteenth Century. There he expressed himself to the effect that this new sage easily won his heart by the originality of his thoughts, couched in novel language and impregnate with fresh spiritual power which he infused into India when she was merely echoing the thoughts of her ancient sages for several centuries past, or, as in recent times, those of Western scholars. He, the Professor, had read often India's religious literature and thereby well acquainted himself with the life-stories of many of her ancient sages and saints; but is it possible to expect such lives again in this age in this India of modern times? Ramakrishna's life was a reply in the affirmative to such a question. And it brought new life by sprinkling water, as it were, at the root of the creeper of hope regarding India's future greatness and progress, in the heart of this great-souled scholar whose whole life has been dedicated to her.

There are certain great souls in the West who sincerely desire the good of India, but we are not aware whether Europe can point out another well-wisher of India who feels more for India's well-being than Professor Max Müller. Not only is Max Müller a well-wisher of India, but he has also a strong faith in Indian philosophy and Indian religion. That Advaitism is the highest discovery in the domain of religion, the Professor has many times publicly admitted. That doctrine of reincarnation, which is a dread to the Christian who has identified the soul with the body, he firmly believes in because of his having found conclusive proof in his own personal experience. And what more, perhaps, his previous birth was in India; and lest by coming to India, the old frame may break down under the violent rush of a suddenly aroused mass of past recollections - is the fear in his mind that now stands foremost in the way of his visit to this country. Still as a worldly man, whoever he may be, he has to look to all sides and conduct himself accordingly. When, after a complete surrender of all worldly interests, even the Sannyasin, when performing any practices which he knows to be purest in themselves, is seen to shiver in fear of public opinion, simply because they are held with disapproval by the people among whom he lives; when the consideration of gaining name and fame and high position, and the fear of losing them regulate the actions of even the greatest ascetic, though he may verbally denounce such consideration as most filthy and detestable — what wonder then that the man of the world who is universally honoured, and is ever anxious not to incur the displeasure of society, will have to be very cautious in ventilating the views which he personally cherishes. It is not a fact that the Professor is an utter disbeliever in such subtle subjects as the mysterious psychic powers of the Yogis.

It is not many years since Professor Max Müller

---

1. "Paramahamsa Sreemat Ramakrishna" — Theistic Quarterly Review, October, 1879.

2. "A Modern Hindu Saint" — January, 1896.

3. "A Real Mahâtman."

"felt called upon to say a few words on certain religious movements, now going on in India"— "which has often and not unjustly, been called a country of philosophers"— which seemed to him "to have been very much misrepresented and misunderstood at home". In order to remove such misconceptions and to protest against "the wild and overcharged accounts of saints and sages living and teaching at present in India, which had been published and scattered broadcast in Indian, American, and English papers"; and "to show at the same time that behind such strange names as Indian Theosophy, and Esoteric Buddhism, and all the rest, there was something real something worth knowing" — or in other words, to point out to the thoughtful section of Europe that India was not a land inhabited only by "quite a new race of human beings who had gone through a number of the most fearful ascetic exercises", to carry on a lucrative profession by thus acquiring the powers of working such "very silly miracles" as flying through the air like the feathered race, walking on or living fishlike under the water, healing all sorts of maladies by means of incantations, and, by the aid of occult arts fabricating gold, silver, or diamond from baser materials, or by the power of Siddhis bestowing sturdy sons to rich families — but that men, who had actually realised in their life great transcendental truths, who were real knowers of Brahman, true Yogis, real devotees of God, were never found wanting in India: and, above all, to show that the whole Aryan population of India had not as yet come down so low as to be on the same plane as the brute creation, that, rejecting the latter, the living Gods in human shape, they "the high and the low" were, day and night, busy licking the feet of the first-mentioned performers of silly juggleries, — Professor Max Müller presented Shri Ramakrishna's life to the learned European public, in an article entitled "A Real Mahâtman", which appeared in The Nineteenth Century in its August number, 1896.

The learned people of Europe and America read the article with great interest and many have been attracted towards its subject, Shri Ramakrishna Deva, with the result that the wrong ideas of the civilised West about India as a country full of naked, infanticidal, ignorant, cowardly race of men who were cannibals and little removed from beasts, who forcibly burnt their widows and were steeped in all sorts of sin and darkness — towards the formation of which ideas, the Christian missionaries and, I am as much ashamed as pained to confess, some of my own countrymen also have been chiefly instrumental — began to be corrected. The veil of the gloom of ignorance, which was spread across the eyes of the Western people by the strenuous efforts of these two bodies of men, has been slowly and slowly rending asunder. "Can the country that has produced a great world-teacher like Shri Bhagavân Ramakrishna Deva be really full of such abominations as we have been asked to believe in, or have we been all along duped by interested organised bodies of mischief-makers, and kept in utter obscurity and error about the real India?"— Such a question naturally arises in the Western mind.

When Professor Max Müller, who occupies in the West the first rank in the field of Indian religion, philosophy, and literature, published with a devoted heart a short sketch of Shri Ramakrishna's life in The Nineteenth Century for the benefit of Europeans and Americans, it is needless to say that a bitter feeling of burning rancour made its appearance amongst those two classes of people referred to above.

By improper representation of the Hindu gods and goddesses, the Christian missionaries were trying with all their heart and soul to prove that really religious men could never be produced from among their worshippers; but like a straw before a tidal wave, that attempt was swept away; while that class of our countrymen alluded to above, which set itself to devise means for quenching the great fire of the rapidly spreading power of Shri Ramakrishna, seeing all its efforts futile, has yielded to despair. What is human will in opposition to the divine?

Of course from both sides, unintermittent volleys of fierce attack were opened on the aged Professor's devoted head; the old veteran, however, was not the one to turn his back. He had triumphed many times in similar contests. This time also he has passed the trial with equal ease. And to stop the empty shouts of his inferior opponents, he has published, by way of a warning to them, the book, Ramakrishna: His Life and Sayings, in which he has collected more complete information and given a fuller account of his life and utterances, so that the reading public may get a better knowledge of this great sage and his religious ideas — the sage "who has lately obtained considerable celebrity both in India and America where his disciples have been actively engaged in preaching his gospel and winning converts to his doctrines even among Christian audiences". The Professor adds, "This may seem very strange, nay, almost incredible to us. . . . Yet every human heart has its religious yearnings; it has a hunger for religion, which sooner or later wants to be satisfied. Now the religion taught by the disciples of Ramakrishna comes to these hungry souls without any untoward authority", and is therefore, welcomed as the "free elixir of life"... "Hence, though there may be some exaggeration in the number of those who are stated to have become converted to the religion of Ramakrishna, ... there can be no doubt that a religion which can achieve such successes in our time, while it calls itself with perfect truth the oldest religion and philosophy of the world, viz the Vedanta, the end or highest object of the Vedas, deserves our careful attention."

After discussing, in the first part of the book, what is meant by the Mahatman, the Four Stages of Life, Ascetic Exercises or Yoga, and after making some mention about Dayananda Sarasvati, Pavhâri Bâbâ, Debendranath Tagore, and Rai Shâligrâm Sâheb Bahadur, the leader of the Râdhâswami sect, the Professor enters on Shri Ramakrishna's life.

The Professor greatly fears lest the Dialogic Process — the transformation produced in the description of the facts as they really happened by too much favourableness or unfavourableness of the narrator towards them — which is invariably at work in all history as a matter of inevitable course, also influences this present sketch of life. Hence his unusual carefulness about the collection of facts. The present writer is an insignificant servant of Shri Ramakrishna. Though the materials gathered by him for Ramakrishna's life have been well-pounded in the mortar of the Professor's logic and impartial judgment, still he (Max Müller) has not omitted to add that there may be possible "traces of what I call the Dialogic Process and the irrepressible miraculising tendencies of devoted disciples" even in "his unvarnished description of his Master". And, no doubt, those few harsh-sweet words which the Professor has said in the course of his reply to what some people, with the Brâhmo-Dharma preacher, the Rev. Pratap Chandra Mazumdar, at their head, wrote to him in their anxiety to make out a "not edifying side" of Ramakrishna's character — demand thoughtful consideration from those amongst us of Bengal who, being full of jealousy, can with difficulty bear the sight of others' weal.

Shri Ramakrishna's life is presented in the book in very brief and simple language. In this life, every word of the wary historian is weighed, as it were, before being put on paper; those sparks of fire, which are seen here and there to shoot forth in the article, "A Real Mahatman", are this time held in with the greatest care. The Professor's boat is here plying between the Scylla of the Christian missionaries on the one hand, and the Charybdis of the tumultuous Brahmos on the other. The article, "A Real Mahatman" brought forth from both the parties many hard words and many carping remarks on the Professor. It is a pleasure to observe that there is neither the attempt made here to retort on them, nor is there any display of meanness — as the refined writers of England are not in the habit of indulging in that kind of thing — but with a sober, dignified, not the least malignant, yet firm and thundering voice, worthy of the aged scholar, he has removed the charges that were levelled against some of the uncommon ideas of the great-soured sage — swelling forth from a heart too deep for ordinary grasp.

And the charges are, indeed, surprising to us. We have heard the great Minister of the Brahmo Samaj, the late revered Âchârya Shri Keshab Chandra Sen, speaking in his charming way that Shri Ramakrishna's simple, sweet, colloquial language breathed a superhuman purity; though in his speech could be noticed some such words as we term obscene, the use of those words, on account of his uncommon childlike innocence and of their being perfectly devoid of the least breath of sensualism, instead of being something reproachable, served rather the purpose of embellishment — yet, this is one of the mighty charges!

Another charge brought against him is that his treatment of his wife was barbarous because of his taking the vow of leading a Sannyasin's life! To this the Professor has replied that he took the vow of Sannyasa with his wife's assent, and that during the years of his life on this earth, his wife, bearing a character worthy of her husband, heartily received him as her Guru (spiritual guide) and, according to his instructions, passed her days in infinite bliss and peace, being engaged in the service of God as a lifelong Brahmachârini. Besides, he asks, "Is love between husband and wife really impossible without the procreation of children?" "We must learn to believe in Hindu honesty" — in the matter that, without having any physical relationship, a Brahmachari husband can live a life of crystal purity, thus making his Brahmacharini wife a partner in the immortal bliss of the highest spiritual realisation, Brahmânanda — "however incredulous we might justly be on such matters in our own country". May blessings shower on the Professor for such worthy remarks! Even he, born of a foreign nationality and living in a foreign land, can understand the meaning of our Brahmacharya as the only way to the attainment of spirituality, and belies that it is not even in these days rare in India, whilst the hypocritical heroes of our own household are unable to see anything else than carnal relationship in the matrimonial union! "As a man thinketh in his mind, so he seeth outside."

Again another charge put forward is that "he did not show sufficient moral abhorrence of prostitutes". To this the Professor's rejoinder is very very sweet indeed: he says that in this charge Ramakrishna "does not stand quite alone among the founders of religion! " Ah! How sweet are these words — they remind one of the prostitute Ambâpâli, the object of Lord Buddha's divine grace, and of the Samaritan woman who won the grace of the Lord Jesus Christ.

Yet again, another charge is that he did not hate those who were intemperate in their habits. Heaven save the mark! One must not tread even on the shadow of a man, because he took a sip or two of drink — is not that the meaning? A formidable accusation indeed! Why did not the Mahâpurusha kick away and drive off in disgust the drunkards, the prostitutes, the thieves, and all the sinners of the world! And why did he not, with eyes closed, talk in a set drawl after the never-to-be-varied tone of the Indian flute-player, or talk in conventional language concealing his thoughts! And above all, the crowning charge is why did he not "live maritalement" all his life!

Unless life can be framed after the ideal of such strange purity and good manners as set forth by the accusers, India is doomed to go to ruin. Let her, if she has to rise by the help of such ethical rules!

The greater portion of the book has been devoted to the collection of the sayings, rather than to the life itself. That those sayings have attracted the attention of many of the English-speaking readers throughout the world can be easily inferred from the rapid sale of the book. The sayings, falling direct from his holy lips, are impregnate with the strongest spiritual force and power, and therefore they will surely exert their divine influence in every part of the world. "For the good of the many, for the happiness of the many" great-souled men take their birth; their lives and works are past the ordinary human run, and the method of their preaching is equally marvellous.

And what are we doing? The son of a poor Brahmin, who has sanctified us by his birth, raised us by his work, and has turned the sympathy of the conquering race towards us by his immortal sayings — what are we doing for him? Truth is not always palatable, still there are times when it has to be told: some of us do understand that his life and teachings are to our gain, but there the matter ends. It is beyond our power even to make an attempt to put those precepts into practice in our own lives, far less to consign our whole body and soul to the huge waves of harmony of Jnâna and Bhakti that Shri Ramakrishna has raised. This play of the Lord, those who have understood or are trying to understand, to them we say, "What will mere understanding do? The proof of understanding is in work. Will others believe you if it ends only in verbal expressions of assurance or is put forward as a matter of personal faith? Work argues what one feels; work out what you feel and let the world see." All ideas and feelings coming out of the fullness of the heart are known by their fruits — practical works.

Those who, knowing themselves very learned, think lightly of this unlettered, poor, ordinary temple-priest, to them our submission is: "The country of which one illiterate temple-priest, by virtue of his own strength, has in so short a time caused the victory of the ancient Sanâtana Dharma of your forefathers to resound even in lands far beyond the seas — of that country, you are the heroes of heroes, the honoured of all, mighty, well-bred, the learned of the learned — how much therefore must you be able to perform far more uncommon, heroic deeds for the welfare of your own land and nation, if you but will its Arise, therefore, come forward, display the play of your superior power within, manifest it, and we are standing with offerings of deepest veneration in hand ready to worship you. We are ignorant, poor, unknown, and insignificant beggars with only the beggar's garb as a means of livelihood; whereas you are supreme in riches and influence, of mighty power, born of noble descent, centres of all knowledge and learning! Why not rouse yourselves? Why not take the lead? Show the way, show us that example of perfect renunciation for the good of the world, and we will follow you like bond-slaves!"

On the other hand, those who are showing unjustified signs of causeless, rancorous hostilities out of absolute malice and envy — natural to a slavish race — at the success and the celebrity of Shri Ramakrishna and his name — to them we say, "Dear friends, vain are these efforts of yours! If this infinite, unbounded, religious wave that has engulfed in its depths the very ends of space — on whose snow-white crest shineth this divine form in the august glow of a heavenly presence — if this be the effect brought about by our eager endeavours in pursuit of personal name, fame, or wealth, then, without your or any others' efforts, this wave shall in obedience to the insuperable law of the universe, soon die in the infinite womb of time, never to rise again! But if, again, this tide, in accordance with the will and under the divine inspiration of the One Universal Mother, has begun to deluge the world with the flood of the unselfish love of a great man's heart, then, O feeble man, what power cost thou possess that thou shouldst thwart the onward progress of the Almighty Mother's will?"

THE PARIS CONGRESS OF THE HISTORY OF RELIGIONS[1]

In the Paris Exhibition, the Congress of the History of Religions recently sat for several days together. At the Congress, there was no room allowed for the discussions on the doctrines and spiritual views of any religion; its purpose was only to inquire into the historic evolution of the different forms of established faiths, and along with it other accompanying facts that are incidental to it. Accordingly, the representation of the various missionary sects of different religions and their beliefs was entirely left out of account in this Congress. The Chicago Parliament of Religions was a grand affair, and the representatives of many religious sects from all parts of the world were present at it. This Congress, on the other hand, was attended only by such scholars as devote themselves to the study of the origin and the history of different religions. At the Chicago Parliament the influence of the Roman Catholics was great, and they organised it with great hopes for their sect. The Roman Catholics expected to establish their superiority over the Protestants without much opposition; by proclaiming their glory and strength and laying the bright side of their faith before the assembled Christians, Hindus,

---

1. Translated from a Paris letter written to the *Udbodhana*.

Buddhists, Mussulmans, and other representatives of the world-religions and publicly exposing their weakness, they hoped to make firm their own position. But the result proving otherwise, the Christian world has been deplorably hopeless of the reconciliation of the different religious systems; so the Roman Catholics are now particularly opposed to the repetition of any such gathering. France is a Roman Catholic country; hence in spite of the earnest wish of the authorities, no religious congress was convened on account of the vehement opposition on the part of the Roman Catholic world.

The Congress of the History of Religions at Paris was like the Congress of Orientalists which is convened from time to time and at which European scholars, versed in Sanskrit, Pali, Arabic, and other Oriental languages, meet; only the antiquarianism of Christianity was added to this Paris Congress.

From Asia only three Japanese Pandits were present at the Congress. From India there was the Swami Vivekananda.

The conviction of many of the Sanskrit scholars of the West is that the Vedic religion is the outcome of the worship of the fire, the sun, and other awe-inspiring objects of natural phenomena.

Swami Vivekananda was invited by the Paris Congress to contradict this conviction, and he promised to read a paper on the subject. But he could not keep his promise on account of ill health, and with difficulty was only able to be personally present at the Congress, where he was most warmly received by all the Western Sanskrit scholars, whose admiration for the Swami was all the greater as they had already gone through many of his lectures on the Vedanta.

At the Congress, Mr. Gustav Oppert, a German Pandit, read a paper on the origin of the Shâlagrâma-Shilâ. He traced the origin of the Shalagrama worship to that of the emblem of the female generative principle. According to him, the Shiva-Linga is the phallic emblem of the male and the Shalagrama of the female generative principle. And thus he wanted to establish that the worship of the Shiva-Linga and that of the Shalagrama — both are but the component parts of the worship of Linga and Yoni! The Swami repudiated the above two views and said that though he had heard of such ridiculous explanations about the Shiva-Linga, the other theory of the Shalagrama-Shila was quite new and strange, and seemed groundless to him.

The Swami said that the worship of the Shiva-Linga originated from the famous hymn in the Atharva-Veda Samhitâ sung in praise of the Yupa-Stambha, the sacrificial post. In that hymn a description is found of the beginningless and endless Stambha or Skambha, and it is shown that the said Skambha is put in place of the eternal Brahman. As afterwards the Yajna (sacrificial) fire, its smoke, ashes, and flames, the Soma plant, and the ox that used to carry on its back the wood for the Vedic sacrifice gave place to the conceptions of the brightness of Shiva's body, his tawny matted-hair, his blue throat, and the riding on the bull of the Shiva, and so on — just so, the Yupa-Skambha gave place in time to the Shiva-Linga, and was deified to the high Devahood of Shri Shankara. In the Atharva-Veda Samhita, the sacrificial cakes are also extolled along with the attributes of the Brahman.

In the Linga Purâna, the same hymn is expanded in the shape of stories, meant to establish the glory of the great Stambha and the superiority of Mahâdeva.

Again, there is another fact to be considered. The Buddhists used to erect memorial topes consecrated to the memory of Buddha; and the very poor, who were unable to build big monuments, used to express their devotion to him by dedicating miniature substitutes for them. Similar instances are still seen in the case of Hindu temples in Varanasi and other sacred places of India where those, who cannot afford to build temples, dedicate very small temple-like constructions instead. So it might be quite probable that during the period of Buddhistic ascendancy, the rich Hindus, in imitation of the Buddhists, used to erect something as a memorial resembling their Skambha, and the poor in a similar manner copied them on a reduced scale, and afterwards the miniature memorials of the poor Hindus became a new addition to the Skambha.

One of the names of the Buddhist Stupas (memorial topes) is Dhâtu-garbha, that is, "metal-wombed". Within the Dhatu-garbha, in small cases made of stone, shaped like the present Shalagrama, used to be preserved the ashes, bones, and other remains of the distinguished Buddhist Bhikshus, along with gold, silver, and other metals. The Shalagrama-Shilas are natural stones resembling in form these artificially-cut stone-cases of the Buddhist Dhatu-garbha, and thus being first worshipped by the Buddhists, gradually got into Vaishnavism, like many other forms of Buddhistic worship that found their way into Hinduism. On the banks of the Narmadâ and in Nepal, the Buddhistic influence lasted longer than in other parts of India; and the remarkable coincidence that the Narmadeshvara Shiva-Linga, found on the banks of the Narmadâ and hence so called, and the Shalagrama-Shilas of Nepal are given preference to by the Hindus to those found elsewhere in India is a fact that ought to be considered with respect to this point of contention.

The explanation of the Shalagrama-Shila as a phallic emblem was an imaginary invention and, from the very beginning, beside the mark. The explanation of the Shiva-Linga as a phallic emblem was brought forward by the most thoughtless, and was forthcoming in India in her most degraded times, those of the downfall of Buddhism. The filthiest Tântrika literature of Buddhism of those times is yet largely found and practiced in Nepal and Tibet.

The Swami gave another lecture in which he dwelt on the historic evolution of the religious ideas in India, and said that the Vedas are the common source of Hinduism in all its varied stages, as also of Buddhism and every other religious belief in India. The seeds of the multifarious growth of Indian thought on religion lie buried in the Vedas. Buddhism and the rest of India's religious thought are the outcome of the unfolding and expansion of those seeds, and modern Hinduism also is only their developed and matured form. With the expansion or the contraction of society, those seeds lie more or less expanded at one place or more or less contracted at another.

He said a few words about the priority of Shri Krishna to Buddha. He also told the Western scholars that as the histories of the royal dynasties described in the Vishnu Purâna were by degrees being admitted as proofs throwing light on the ways of research of the antiquarian, so, he said, the traditions of India were all true, and desired that Western Sanskrit scholars, instead of writing fanciful articles, should try to discover their hidden truths.

Professor Max Müller says in one of his books that, whatever similarities there may be, unless it be demonstrated that some one Greek knew Sanskrit, it cannot be concluded that ancient India helped ancient Greece in any way. But it is curious to observe that some Western savants, finding several terms of Indian astronomy similar to those of Greek astronomy, and coming to know that the Greeks founded a small kingdom on the borders of India, can clearly read the help of Greece on everything Indian, on Indian literature, Indian astronomy, Indian arithmetic. Not only so; one has been bold enough to go so far as to declare that all Indian sciences as a rule are but echoes of the Greek!

On a single Sanskrit Shloka —

म्लेच्छा वै यवनाः तेषु एषा विद्या प्रतिष्ठिता। ऋषवित् तेऽपि पूज्यन्ते . . .

— "The Yavanas are Mlechchhas, in them this science is established, (therefore) even they deserve worship like Rishis, . . ." — how much the Westerners have indulged their unrestrained imagination! But it remains to be shown how the above Shloka goes to prove that the Aryas were taught by the Mlechchhas. The meaning may be that the learning of the Mlechchha disciples of the Aryan teachers is praised here, only to encourage the Mlechchhas in their pursuit of the Aryan science.

Secondly, when the germ of every Aryan science is found in the Vedas and every step of any of those sciences can be traced with exactness from the Vedic to the present day, what is the necessity for forcing the far-fetched suggestion of the Greek influence on them? "What is the use of going to the hills in search of honey if it is available at home?" as a Sanskrit proverb says.

Again, every Greek-like word of Aryan astronomy can be easily derived from Sanskrit roots. The Swami could not understand what right the Western scholars had to trace those words to a Greek source, thus ignoring their direct etymology.

In the same manner, if on finding mention of the word Yavanikâ (curtain) in the dramas of Kâlidâsa and other Indian poets, the Yâvanika (Ionian or Greek) influence on the whole of the dramatic literature of the time is ascertained, then one should first stop to compare whether the Aryan dramas are at all like the Greek. Those who have studied the mode of action and style of the dramas of both the languages must have to admit that any such likeness, if found, is only a fancy of the obstinate dreamer, and has never any real existence as a matter of fact. Where is that Greek chorus? The Greek Yavanika is on one side of the stage, the Aryan diametrically on the other. The characteristic manner of expression of the Greek drama is one thing, that of the Aryan quite another. There is not the least likeness between the Aryan and the Greek dramas: rather the dramas of Shakespeare resemble to a great extent the dramas of India. So the conclusion may also be drawn that Shakespeare is indebted to Kalidasa and other ancient Indian dramatists for all his writings, and that the whole Western literature is only an imitation of the Indian.

Lastly, turning Professor Max Müller's own premisses against him, it may be said as well that until it is demonstrated that some one Hindu knew Greek some time one ought not to talk even of Greek influence.

Likewise, to see Greek influence in Indian sculpture is also entirely unfounded.

The Swami also said that the worship of Shri Krishna is much older than that of Buddha, and if the Gitâ be not of the same date as the Mahâbhârata, it is surely much earlier and by no means later. The style of language of the Gita is the same as that of the Mahabharata. Most of the adjectives used in the Gita to explain matters spiritual are used in the Vana and other Parvans of the Mahabharata, respecting matters temporal. Such coincidence is impossible without the most general and free use of those words at one and the same time. Again, the line of thought in the Gita is the same as in the Mahabharata; and when the Gita notices the doctrines of all the religious sects of the time, why does it not ever mention the name of Buddhism?

In spite of the most cautious efforts of the writers subsequent to Buddha, reference to Buddhism is not withheld and appears somewhere or other, in some shape or other, in histories, stories, essays, and every book of the post-Buddhistic literature. In covert or overt ways, some allusion is sure to be met with in reference to Buddha and Buddhism. Can anyone show any such reference in the Gita? Again, the Gita is an attempt at the reconciliation of all religious creeds, none of which is slighted in it. Why, it remains to be answered, is Buddhism alone denied the tender touch of the Gita-writer?

The Gita wilfully scorns none. Fear? — Of that there is a conspicuous absence in it. The Lord Himself, being the interpreter and the establisher of the Vedas, never hesitates to even censure Vedic rash presumptuousness if required. Why then should He fear Buddhism?

As Western scholars devote their whole life to one Greek work, let them likewise devote their whole life to one Sanskrit work, and much light will flow to the world thereby. The Mahabharata especially is the most invaluable work in Indian history; and it is not too much to say that this book has not as yet been even properly read by the Westerners.

After the lecture, many present expressed their opinions for or against the subject, and declared that they agreed with most of what the Swami had said, and assured the Swami that the old days of Sanskrit Antiquarianism were past and gone. The views of modern Sanskrit scholars were largely the same as those of the Swami's, they said. They believed also that there was much true history in the Puranas and the traditions of India

Lastly, the learned President, admitting all other points of the Swami's lecture, disagreed on one point only, namely, on the contemporaneousness of the Gita with the Mahabharata. But the only reason he adduced was that the Western scholars were mostly of the opinion that the Gita was not a part of the Mahabharata.

The substance of the lecture will be printed in French in the General Report of the Congress.

KNOWLEDGE: ITS SOURCE AND ACQUIREMENT[1]

Various have been the theories propounded as regards the primitive source of knowledge. We read in the Upanishads that Brahmâ, who was the first and the foremost among the Devas, held the key to all knowledge, which he revealed to his disciples and which, being handed down in succession, has been bequeathed as a legacy to the subsequent age. According to the Jains, during an indefinite period of cycle of Time, which comprises between one thousand and two thousand billions of "oceans" of years, are born some extraordinary, great, perfected beings whom they call Jinas, and through them the door to knowledge is now and shell opened to human society. Likewise Buddhism believes in, and expects at regular intervals, the appearance of the Buddhas, that is, persons possessed of infinite universal wisdom. The same is the reason also of the introduction of Incarnations of God by the Paurânika Hindus, who ascribe to them, along with other missions, the special function of restoring the lost spiritual knowledge by its proper adjustment to the needs of the time. Outside India, we find the great-souled Zoroaster bringing down the light of knowledge from above to the mortal world. So also did Moses, Jesus, and Mohammed, who, possessed of heavenly authority, proclaim to fallen humanity the tidings of divine wisdom in their own unique ways.

Brahma is the name of a high position among the Devas, to which every man can aspire by virtue of meritorious deeds. Only a selected few can become Jinas, while others can never attain to Jinahood; but they can only go so far as to gain the state of Mukti. The state of being a Buddha is open to one and all without distinction. Zoroaster, Moses, Jesus, and Mohammed are great personalities who incarnated themselves for the fulfilment of some special mission; so also did the Incarnations of God mentioned by the Pauranika sages. For others to look up to that seat of these divine personages with a longing eye is madness.

Adam got his knowledge through the tasting of the forbidden fruit. Noah was taught social science by the grace of Jehovah. In India, the theory is that every science has its presiding deity; their founders are either Devas or perfected beings; from the most menial arts as that of a cobbler to the most dignified office of the spiritual guide, everything depends on the kind intervention of the gods or supreme beings. "No knowledge is possible without a teacher." There is no way to the attainment of knowledge unless it is transmitted through an apostolic succession from disciple to disciple, unless it comes through the mercy of the Guru and direct from his mouth.

Then again, the Vedantic and other philosophers of the Indian schools hold that knowledge is not to be acquired from without. It is the innate nature of the human soul and the essential birthright of every man. The human soul is the repository of infinite wisdom; what external agency can illuminate it? According to some schools, this infinite wisdom remains always the same and is never lost; and man is not ordinarily; conscious of this, because a veil, so to speak, has fallen over it on account of his evil deeds, but as soon as the veil is removed it reveals itself. Others say that this infinite wisdom, though potentially present in a human soul, has become contracted through evil deeds and it becomes expanded again by the mercy of God gained by good deeds. We also read in our scriptures various other methods of unfolding this inborn infinite power and knowledge, such as devotion to God, performance of work without attachment, practicing the eightfold accessories of the Yoga system, or constant dwelling on this knowledge, and so on. The final conclusion, however, is this, that through the practice of one or more or all of these methods together man gradually becomes conscious of his inborn real

---
1. Translated from a Bengali contribution by Swami Vivekananda to the *Udbodhana*, 12th February, 1899.

nature, and the infinite power and wisdom within, latent or veiled, becomes at last fully manifest.

On the other side, the modern philosophers have analysed the human mind as the source of infinitely possible manifestations and have come to the conclusion that when the individual mind on the one hand, and favourable time, place, and causation on the other can act and react upon one another, then highly developed consciousness of knowledge is sure to follow. Nay, even the unfavourableness of time and place can be successfully surmounted by the vigour and firmness of the individual. The strong individual, even if he is thrown amidst the worst conditions of place or time, overcomes them and affirms his own strength. Not only so, all the heavy burdens heaped upon the individual, the acting agent, are being made lighter and lighter in the course of time, so that any individual, however weak he may be in the beginning, is sure to reach the goal at the end if he assiduously applies himself to gain it. Look at the uncivilised and ignorant barbarians of the other day! How through close and studious application they are making long strides into the domains of civilisation, how even those of the lower strata are making their way and are occupying with an irresistible force the most exalted positions in it! The sons of cannibal parents are turning out elegant and educated citizens; the descendants of the uncivilised Santals, thanks to the English Government, have been nowadays meeting in successful competition our Bengali students in the Indian Universities. As such, the partiality of the scientific investigators of the present day to the doctrine of hereditary transmission of qualities is being gradually diminished.

There is a certain class of men whose conviction is that from time eternal there is a treasure of knowledge which contains the wisdom of everything past, present, and future. These men hold that it was their own forefathers who had the sole privilege of having the custody of this treasure. The ancient sages, the first possessors of it, bequeathed in succession this treasure and its true import to their descendants only. They are, therefore, the only inheritors to it; as such, let the rest of the world worship them.

May we ask these men what they think should be the condition of the other peoples who have not got such forefathers? "Their condition is doomed", is the general answer. The more kind-hearted among them is perchance pleased to rejoin, "Well, let them come and serve us. As a reward for such service, they will be born in our caste in the next birth. That is the only hope we can hold out to them." "Well, the moderns are making many new and original discoveries in the field of science and arts, which neither you dreamt of, nor is there any proof that your forefathers ever had knowledge of. What do you say to that?" "Why certainly our forefathers knew all these things, the knowledge of which is now unfortunately lost to us. Do you want a proof? I can show you one. Look! Here is the Sanskrit verse ......" Needless to add that the modern party, who believes in direct evidence only, never attaches any seriousness to such replies and proofs.

Generally, all knowledge is divided into two classes, the Aparâ, secular, and the Parâ, spiritual. One pertains to perishable things, and the other to the realm of the spirit. There is, no doubt, a great difference these two classes of knowledge, and the way to the attainment of the one may be entirely different from the way to the attainment of the other. Nor can it be denied that no one method can be pointed out as the sole and universal one which will serve as the key to all and every door in the domain of knowledge. But in reality all this difference is only one of degree and not of kind. It is not that secular and spiritual knowledge are two opposite and contradictory things; but they are the same thing — the same infinite knowledge which is everywhere fully present from the lowest atom to the highest Brahman — they are the same knowledge in its different stages of gradual development. This one infinite knowledge we call secular when it is in its lower process of manifestation, and spiritual when it reaches the corresponding higher phase.

"All knowledge is possessed exclusively by some extraordinary great men, and those special personages take birth by the command of God, or in conformity to a higher law of nature, or in some preordained order of Karma; except through the agency of these great ones, there is no other way of attaining knowledge." If such a view be correct and certain, there seems to be no necessity for any individual to strive hard to find any new and original truth — all originality is lost to society for want of exercise and encouragement; and the worst of all is that, society tries to oppose and stop any attempt in the original direction, and thus the faculty of the initiative dies out. If it is finally settled that the path of human welfare is for ever chalked out by these omniscient men, society naturally fears its own destruction if the least deviation be made from the boundary line of the path, and so it tries to compel all men through rigid laws and threats of punishment to follow that path with unconditional obedience. If society succeeds in imposing such obedience to itself by confining all men within the narrow groove of these paths, then the destiny of mankind becomes no better than that of a machine. If every act in a man's life has been all previously determined, then what need is there for the culture of the faculty of thought — where is the field for the free play of independent thought and action? In course of time, for want of proper use, all activity is given up, all originality is lost, a sort of Tâmasika dreamy lifelessness hovers over the whole nation, and headlong it goes down and down. The death of such a nation is not far to seek.

On the other hand, if the other extreme were true that that society prospers the most which is not guided by the injunctions of such divinely-inspired souls, then civilisation, wisdom, and prosperity — deserting the Chinese, Hindus, Egyptians, Babylonians, Iranians, Greeks, Romans, and other great nations of ancient and modern times, who have always followed the path laid down by their sages — would have embraced the Zulus, the Kafirs, the Hottentots, and the aboriginal tribes of the Andamans and the Australian islands who have led a life of guideless independence.

Considering all these points, it must be admitted that though the presence of knowledge everywhere in every individual is an eternal truism, yet the path pointed out by the great ones of the earth has the glory peculiar to it, and that there is a peculiar interest attached to the transmission of knowledge through the succession of teachers and their disciples. Each of them has its place in the development of the sum total of knowledge; and we must learn to estimate them according to their respective merits. But, perhaps, being carried away by their over-zealous and blind devotion to their Masters, the successors and followers of these great ones sacrifice truth before the altar of devotion and worship to them, and misrepresent the true meaning of the purpose of those great lives by insisting on personal worship, that is, they kill the principle for the person.

This is also a fact of common experience that when man himself has lost all his own strength, he naturally likes to pass his days in idle remembrance of his forefathers' greatness. The devoted heart gradually becomes the weakest in its constant attempt to resign itself in every respect to the feet of its ancestors, and at last a time comes when this weakness teaches the disabled yet proud heart to make the vainglory of its ancestors' greatness as the only support of its life. Even if it be true that your ancestors possessed all knowledge, which has in the efflux of time been lost to you, it follows that you, their descendants, must have been instrumental in this disappearance of knowledge, and now it is all the same to you whether you have it or not. To talk of having or losing this already lost knowledge serves no useful purpose at present. You will have to make new efforts, to undergo troubles over again, if you want to recover it.

True, that spiritual illumination shines of itself in a pure heart, and, as such, it is not something acquired from without; but to attain this purity of heart means long struggle and constant practice. It has also been found, on careful inquiry in the sphere of material knowledge, that those higher truths which have now and then been discovered by great scientific men have flashed like sudden floods of light in their mental atmosphere, which they had only to catch and formulate. But such truths never appear in the mind of an uncultured and wild savage. All these go to prove that hard Tapasyâ, or practice of austerities in the shape of devout contemplation and constant study of a subject is at the root of all illumination in its respective spheres.

What we call extraordinary, superconscious inspiration is only the result of a higher development of ordinary consciousness, gained by long and continued effort. The difference between the ordinary and the extraordinary is merely one of degree in manifestation. Conscious efforts lead the way to superconscious illumination.

Infinite perfection is in every man, though unmanifested. Every man has in him the potentiality of attaining to perfect saintliness, Rishihood, or to the most exalted position of an Avatâra, or to the greatness of a hero in material discoveries. It is only a question of time and adequate well-guided investigation, etc., to have this perfection manifested. In a society where once such great men were born, there the possibility of their reappearance is greater. There can be no doubt that a society with the help of such wise guides advances faster than the one without it. But it is equally certain that such guides will rise up in the societies that are now without them and will lead them to equally rapid progress in the future.

MODERN INDIA

Translated from a Bengali contribution to the Udbodhana, March 1899

The Vedic priests base their superior strength on the knowledge of the sacrificial Mantras[1]. By the power of these Mantras, the Devas are made to come down from their heavenly abodes, accept the drink and food offerings, and grant the prayers of the Yajamânas[2]. The kings as well as their subjects are, therefore, looking up to these priests for their welfare during their earthly life. Raja Soma[3] is worshipped by the priest and is made to thrive by the power of his Mantras. As such, the Devas, whose favourite food is the juice of the Soma plant offered in oblation by the priest, are always kind to him and bestow his desired boons. Thus strengthened by divine grace, he defies all human opposition; for what can the power of mortals do against that of the gods? Even the king, the centre of all earthly power, is a supplicant at his door. A kind look from him is the greatest help; his mere blessing a tribute to the State, pre-eminent above everything else.

Now commanding the king to be engaged in affairs fraught with death and ruin, now standing by him as his fastest friend with kind and wise counsels, now spreading the net of subtle, diplomatic statesmanship in which the king is easily caught — the priest is seen, oftentimes, to make the royal power totally subservient to him. Above all, the worst fear is in the knowledge that the name and fame of the royal forefathers and of himself and his family lie at the mercy of the priest's pen. He is the historian. The king might have paramount power; attaining a great glory in his reign, he might prove himself as the father and mother in one to his subjects; but if the priest is not appeased, his sun of glory goes down with his last breath for ever; all his worth and usefulness deserving of universal approbation are lost in the great womb of time, like unto the fall of gentle dew on the ocean. Others who inaugurated the huge sacrifices lasting over many years, the performers of the Ashvamedha and so on — those who showered, like incessant rain in the rainy season, countless wealth on the priests — their names, thanks to the grace of priests, are emblazoned in the pages of history. The name of Priyadarshi Dharmâshoka[4], the beloved of the gods, is nothing but a name in the priestly world, while Janamejaya[5], son of Parikshit, is a household word in every Hindu family.

To protect the State, to meet the expenses of the personal comforts and luxuries of himself and his long retinue, and, above all, to fill to overflowing the

---

1. Vedic hymns uttered by the priests to invoke the Devas at the time of sacrifice.

2. The men who perform sacrifices.

3. The name of the Soma plant as commonly found in the Vedas. The priests offered to the Devas the juice of this plant at the time of sacrifice.

4. The name given to the great king, Asoka, after he embraced Buddhism.

5. The performer of the great snake-sacrifice of Mahâbhârata.

coffers of the all-powerful priesthood for its propitiation, the king is continually draining the resources of his subjects, even as the sun sucks up moisture from the earth. His especial prey — his milch cows — are the Vaishyas.

Neither under the Hindu kings, nor under the Buddhist rule, do we find the common subject-people taking any part in expressing their voice in the affairs of the State. True, Yudhishthira visits the houses of Vaishyas and even Shudras when he is in Vâranâvata; true, the subjects are praying for the installation of Râmachandra to the regency of Ayodhyâ; nay, they are even criticising the conduct of Sitâ and secretly making plans for the bringing about of her exile: but as a recognised rule of the State they have no direct voice in the supreme government. The power of the populace is struggling to express itself in indirect and disorderly ways without any method. The people have not as yet the conscious knowledge of the existence of this power. There is neither the attempt on their part to organise it into a united action, nor have they got the will to do so; there is also a complete absence of that capacity, that skill, by means of which small and incoherent centres of force are united together, creating insuperable strength as their resultant.

Is this due to want of proper laws? — no, that is not it. There are laws, there are methods, separately and distinctly assigned for the guidance of different departments of government, there are laws laid down in the minutest detail for everything, such as the collection of revenue, the management of the army, the administration of justice, punishments and rewards. But at the root of all, is the injunction of the Rishi — the word of divine authority, the revelation of God coming through the inspired Rishi. The laws have, it can almost be said, no elasticity in them. Under the circumstances, it is never possible for the people to acquire any sort of education by which they can learn to combine among themselves and be united for the accomplishment of any object for the common good of the people, or by which they can have the concerted intellect to conceive the idea of popular right in the treasures collected by the king from his subjects, or even such education by which they can be fired with the aspiration to gain the right of representation in the control of State revenues and expenditure. Why should they do such things? Is not the inspiration of the Rishi responsible for their prosperity and progress?

Again, all those laws are in books. Between laws as codified in books and their operation in practical life, there is a world of difference. One Ramachandra is born after thousands of Agnivarnas[1] pass away! Many kings show us the life of Chandâshoka[2]; Dharmâshokas are rare! The number of kings like Akbar, in whom the subjects find their life, is far less than that of kings like Aurangzeb who live on the blood of their people!

Even if the kings be of as godlike nature as that of Yudhishthira, Ramachandra, Dharmashoka, or Akbar under whose benign rule the people enjoyed safety and prosperity, and were looked after with paternal care by their rulers, the hand of him who is always fed by another gradually loses the power of taking the food to his mouth. His power of self-preservation can never become fully manifest who is always protected in every respect by another. Even the strongest youth remains but a child if he is always looked after as a child by his parents. Being always governed by kings of godlike nature, to whom is left the whole duty of protecting and providing for the people, they can never get any occasion for understanding the principles of self-government. Such a nation, being entirely dependent on the king for everything and never caring to exert itself for the common good or for self-defence, becomes gradually destitute of inherent energy and strength. If this state of dependence and protection continues long, it becomes the cause of the destruction of the nation, and its ruin is not far to seek.

Of course, it can be reasonably concluded that, when the government a country, is guided by codes

---

1. Agnivarna was a prince of the Solar race, who never used to come out of the seraglio, and died of consumption due to excessive indulgence.

2. The great king Asoka was at first called Chandashoka, i.e. Fierce Asoka, because of his ascending the throne by killing his brother and his other cruel deeds. After nine years of reign he became a convert to Buddhism and his character underwent a complete transformation; he was thenceforth known for his good deeds by the name of Dharmashoka, Virtuous Asoka.

of laws enjoined by Shâstras which are the outcome of knowledge inspired by the divine genius of great sages, such a government must lead to the unbroken welfare of the rich and the poor, the wise and the ignorant, the king and the subjects alike. But we have seen already how far the operation of those laws was, or may be, possible in practical life. The voice of the ruled in the government of their land — which is the watchword of the modern Western world, and of which the last expression has been echoed with a thundering voice in the Declaration of the American Government, in the words, "That the government of the people of this country must be by the people and for the good of the people" — cannot however be said to have been totally unrecognised in ancient India. The Greek travellers and others saw many independent small States scattered all over this country, and references are also found to this effect in many places of the Buddhistic literature. And there cannot be the least doubt about it that the germ of self-government was at least present in the shape of the village Panchâyat[1], which is still to be found in existence in many places of India. But the germ remained for ever the germ; the seed though put in the ground never grew into a tree. This idea of self-government never passed beyond the embryo state of the village Panchayat system and never spread into society at large.

In the religious communities, among Sannyasins in the Buddhist monasteries, we have ample evidence to show that self-government was fully developed. Even now, one wonders to see how the power of the Panchayat system of the principles of self-government, is working amongst the Nâgâ Sannyasins — what deep respect the "Government by the Five" commands from them, what effective individual rights each Naga can exercise within his own sect, what excellent working of the power of organisation and concerted action they have among themselves!

With the deluge which swept the land at the advent of Buddhism, the priestly power fell into decay and the royal power was in the ascendant. Buddhist priests are renouncers of the world, living in monasteries as homeless ascetics, unconcerned with secular affairs. They have neither the will nor the endeavour to bring and keep the royal power under their control through the threat of curses or magic arrows. Even if there were any remnant of such a will, its fulfilment has now become an impossibility. For Buddhism has shaken the thrones of all the oblation-eating gods and brought them down from their heavenly positions. The state of being a Buddha is superior to the heavenly positions of many a Brahmâ or an Indra, who vie with each other in offering their worship at the feet of the Buddha, the God-man! And to this Buddhahood, every man has the privilege to attain; it is open to all even in this life. From the descent of the gods, as a natural consequence, the superiority of the priests who were supported by them is gone.

Accordingly, the reins of that mighty sacrificial horse — the royal power — are no longer held in the firm grasp of the Vedic priest; and being now free, it can roam anywhere by its unbridled will. The centre of power in this period is neither with the priests chanting the Sâma hymns and performing the Yajnas according to the Yajur-Veda; nor is the power vested in the hands of Kshatriya kings separated from each other and ruling over small independent States. But the centre of power in this age is in emperors whose unobstructed sway extend over vast areas bounded by the ocean, covering the whole of India from one end to the other. The leaders of this age are no longer Vishvâmitra or Vasishtha, but emperors like Chandragupta, Dharmashoka, and others. There never were emperors who ascended the throne of India and led her to the pinnacle of her glory such as those lords of the earth who ruled over her in paramount sway during the Buddhistic period. The end of this period is characterised by the appearance of Râjput power on the scene and the rise of modern Hinduism. With the rise of Rajput power, on the decline of Buddhism, the sceptre of the Indian empire, dislodged from its paramount power, was again broken into a thousand pieces and wielded by small powerless hands. At this time, the Brâhminical (priestly) power again succeeded in

---
1. Literally, "government by five", in which the village-men sit together and decide among themselves, all disputes.

raising its head, not as an adversary as before, but this time as an auxiliary to the royal supremacy.

During this revolution, that perpetual struggle for supremacy between the priestly and the royal classes, which began from the Vedic times and continued through ages till it reached its climax at the time of the Jain and Buddhist revolutions, has ceased for ever. Now these two mighty powers are friendly to each other; but neither is there any more that glorious Kshatra (warlike) velour of the kings, nor that spiritual brilliance which characterised the Brahmins; each has lost his former intrinsic strength. As might be expected, this new union of the two forces was soon engaged in the satisfaction of mutual self-interests, and became dissipated by spending its vitality on extirpating their common opponents, especially the Buddhists of the time, and on similar other deeds. Being steeped in all the vices consequent on such a union, e.g., the sucking of the blood of the masses, taking revenge on the enemy, spoliation of others' property, etc., they in vain tried to imitate the Râjasuya and other Vedic sacrifices of the ancient kings, and only made a ridiculous farce of them. The result was that they were bound hand and foot by a formidable train of sycophantic attendance and its obsequious flatteries, and being entangled in an interminable net of rites and ceremonies with flourishes of Mantras and the like, they soon became a cheap and ready prey to the Mohammeden invaders from the West.

That priestly power which began its strife for superiority with the royal power from the Vedic times and continued it down the ages, that hostility against the Kshatra power, Bhagavân Shri Krishna succeeded by his super-human genius in putting a stop to, at least for the tired being, during his earthly existence. That Brâhmanya power was almost effaced from its field of work in India during the Jain and Buddhist revolutions, or, perhaps, was holding its feeble stand by being subservient to the strong antagonistic religions. That Brahmanya power, since this appearance of Rajput power, which held sway over India under the Mihira dynasty and others, made its last effort to recover its lost greatness; and in its effort to establish that supremacy, it sold itself at the feet of the fierce hordes of barbarians newly come from Central Asia, and to win their pleasure introduced in the land their hateful manners and customs. Moreover, it, the Brahmanya; power, solely devoting itself to the easy means to dupe ignorant barbarians, brought into vogue mysterious rites and ceremonies backed by its new Mantras and the like; and in doing so, itself lost its former wisdom, its former vigour and vitality, and its own chaste habits of long acquirement. Thus it turned the whole Âryâvarta into a deep and vast whirlpool of the most vicious, the most horrible, the most abominable, barbarous customs; and as the inevitable consequence of countenancing these detestable customs and superstitions, it soon lost all its own internal strength and stamina and became the weakest of the weak. What wonder that it should be broken into a thousand pieces and fall at the mere touch of the storm of Mussulman invasions from the West! That great Brahmanya power fell — who knows, if ever to rise again?

The resuscitation of the priestly power under the Mussulman rule was, on the other hand, an utter impossibility. The Prophet Mohammed himself was dead against the priestly class in any shape and tried his best for the total destruction of this power by formulating rules and injunctions to that effect. Under the Mussulman rule, the king himself was the supreme priest; he was the chief guide in religious matters; and when he became the emperor, he cherished the hope of being the paramount leader in all matters over the whole Mussulman world. To the Mussulman, the Jews or the Christians are not objects of extreme detestation; they are, at the worst, men of little faith. But not so the Hindu. According to him, the Hindu is idolatrous, the hateful Kafir; hence in this life he deserves to be butchered; and in the next, eternal hell is in store for him. The utmost the Mussulman kings could do as a favour to the priestly class — the spiritual guides of these Kafirs — was to allow them somehow to pass their life silently and wait for the last moment. This was again sometimes considered too, much kindness! If the religious ardour of any king was a little more uncommon, there would immediately follow arrangements for a great Yajna by way of Kafir-slaughter!

On one side, the royal power is now centred in kings professing a different religion and given to different customs. On the other, the priestly power has been entirely displaced from its influential position as the controller and lawgiver of the society. The Koran and its code of laws have taken the place of the Dharma Shâstras of Manu and others. The Sanskrit language has made room for the Persian and the Arabic. The Sanskrit language has to remain confined only to the purely religious writings and religious matters of the conquered and detested Hindu, and, as such, has since been living a precarious life at the hands of the neglected priest. The priest himself, the relic of the Brahmanya power, fell back upon the last resource of conducting only the comparatively unimportant family ceremonies, such as the matrimonial etc., and that also only so long and as much as the mercy of the Mohammedan rulers permitted.

In the Vedic and the adjoining periods, the royal power could not manifest itself on account of the grinding pressure of the priestly power. We have seen how, during the Buddhistic revolution, resulting in the fall of the Brahminical supremacy, the royal power in India reached its culminating point. In the interval between the fall of the Buddhistic and the establishment of the Mohammedan empire, we have seen how the royal power was trying to raise its head through the Rajputs in India, and how it failed in its attempt. At the root of this failure, too, could be traced the same old endeavours of the Vedic priestly class to bring back and revive with a new life their original (ritualistic) days.

Crushing the Brahminical supremacy under his feet the Mussulman king was able to restore to a considerable extent the lost glories of such dynasties of emperors as the Maurya, the Gupta, the Andhra, and the Kshâtrapa[1].

Thus the priestly power — which sages like Kumârila, Shankara, and Râmânuja tried to re-establish, which for some time was supported by the sword of the Rajput power, and which tried to rebuild its structure on the fall of its Jain and Buddhist adversaries — was under Mohammedan rule laid to sleep for ever, knowing no awakening. In this period, the antagonism or warfare is not between kings and priests, but between kings and kings. At the end of this period, when Hindu power again raised its head, and, to some extent, was successful in regenerating Hinduism through the Mahrattas and the Sikhs, we do not find much play of the priestly power with these regenerations. On the contrary, when the Sikhs admitted any Brahmin into their sect, they, at first, compelled him publicly to give up his previous Brahminical signs and adopt the recognised signs of their own religion.

In this manner, after an age-long play of action and reaction between these two forces, the final victory of the royal power was echoed on the soil of India for several centuries, in the name of foreign monarchs professing an entirely different religion from the faith of the land. But at the end of this Mohammedan period, another entirely new power made its appearance on the arena and slowly began to assert its prowess in the affairs of the Indian world.

This power is so new, its nature and workings are so foreign to the Indian mind, its rise so inconceivable, and its vigour so insuperable that though it wields the suzerain power up till now, only a handful of Indians understand what this power is.

We are talking of the occupation of India by England.

From very ancient times, the fame of India's vast wealth and her rich granaries has enkindled in many powerful foreign nations the desire for conquering her. She has been, in fact, again and again conquered by foreign nations. Then why should we say that the occupation of India by England was something new and foreign to the Indian mind?

From time immemorial Indians have seen the mightiest royal power tremble before the frown of the ascetic priest, devoid of worldly desire, armed with spiritual strength — the power of Mantras (sacred formulas) and religious lore — and the weapon of curses. They have also seen the subject

---

1. The Persian governors of Âryâvarta and Gujarat.

people silently obey the commands of their heroic all-powerful suzerains, backed by their arms and armies, like a flock of sheep before a lion. But that a handful of Vaishyas (traders) who, despite their great wealth, have ever crouched awe stricken not only before the king but also before any member of the royal family, would unite, cross for purposes of business rivers and seas, would, solely by virtue of their intelligence and wealth, by degrees make puppets of the long-established Hindu and Mohammedan dynasties; not only so, but that they would buy as well the services of the ruling powers of their own country and use their valour and learning as powerful instruments for the influx of their own riches — this is a spectacle entirely novel to the Indians, as also the spectacle that the descendants of the mighty nobility of a country, of which a proud lord, sketched by the extraordinary pen of its great poet, says to a common man, "Out, dunghill! darest thou brave a nobleman?" would, in no distant future, consider it the zenith of human ambition to be sent to India as obedient servants of a body of merchants, called The East India Company — such a sight was, indeed, a novelty unseen by India before!

According to the prevalence, in greater or lesser degree, of the three qualities of Sattva, Rajas, and Tamas in man, the four castes, the Brahmin, Kashatriya, Vaishya, and Shudra, are everywhere present at all times, in all civilised societies. By the mighty hand of time, their number and power also vary at different times in regard to different countries. In some countries the numerical strength or influence of one of these castes may preponderate over another; at some period, one of the classes may be more powerful than the rest. But from a careful study of the history of the world, it appears that in conformity to the law of nature the four castes, the Brahmin, Kshatriya, Vaishya, and Shudra do, in every society, one after another in succession, govern the world.

Among the Chinese, the Sumerians, the Babylonians, the Egyptians, the Chaldeans, the Areas, the Iranians, the Jews, the Arabs — among all these ancient nations, the supreme power of guiding society is, in the first period of their history, in the hands of the Brahmin or the priest. In the second period, the ruling power is the Kshatriya, that is, either absolute monarchy or oligarchical government by a chosen body of men. Among the modern Western nations, with England at their head, this power of controlling society has been, for the first time, in the hands of the Vaishyas or mercantile communities, made rich through the carrying on of commerce.

Though Troy and Carthage of ancient times and Venice and similar other small commercial States of comparatively modern times became highly powerful, yet, amongst them, there was not the real rising of the Vaishya power in the proper sense of the term.

Correctly speaking, the descendants of the royal family had the sole monopoly of the commerce of those old days by employing the common people and their servants under them to carry on the trade; and they appropriated to themselves the profits accruing from it. Excepting these few men, no one was allowed to take any part or voice an opinion even in the government of the country and kindred affairs. In the oldest countries like Egypt, the priestly power enjoyed unmolested supremacy only for a short period, after which it became subjugated to the royal power and lived as an auxiliary to it. In China, the royal power, centralised by the genius of Confucius, has been controlling and guiding the priestly power, in accordance with its absolute will, for more than twenty-five centuries; and during the last two centuries, the all-absorbing Lamas of Tibet, though they are the spiritual guides of the royal family, have been compelled to pass their days, being subject in every way to the Chinese Emperor.

In India, the royal power succeeded in conquering the priestly power and declaring its untrammelled authority long after the other ancient civilised nations had done so; and therefore the inauguration of the Indian Empire came about long after the Chinese, Egyptian, Babylonian, and other Empires had risen. It was only with the Jewish people that the royal power, though it tried hard to establish its supremacy over the priestly, had to meet a complete defeat in the attempt. Not even the Vaishyas attained the ruling power with the Jews. On the other hand, the common subject people, trying to free themselves from the shackles of priestcraft, were crushed to death under the internal commotion of adverse religious movements like Christianity and the external pressure of the mighty Roman Empire.

As in the ancient days the priestly power, in spite of its long-continued struggle, was subdued by the more powerful royal power, so, in modern times, before the violent blow of the newly-risen Vaishya power, many a kingly crown has to kiss the ground, many a sceptre is for ever broken to pieces. Only those few thrones which are allowed still to exercise some power in some of the civilised countries and make a display of their royal pomp and grandeur are all maintained solely by the vast hordes of wealth of these Vaishya communities — the dealers in salt, oil, sugar, and wine — and kept up as a magnificent and an imposing front, and as a means of glorification to the really governing body behind, the Vaishyas.

That mighty newly-risen Vaishya power — at whose command, electricity carries messages in an instant from one pole to another, whose highway is the vast ocean, with its mountain-high waves, at whose instance, commodities are being carried with the greatest ease from one part of the globe to another, and at whose mandate, even the greatest monarchs tremble — on the white foamy crest of that huge wave the all-conquering Vaishya power, is installed the majestic throne of England in all its grandeur.

Therefore the conquest of India by England is not a conquest by Jesus or the Bible as we are often asked to believe. Neither is it like the conquest of India by the Moguls and the Pathans. But behind the name of the Lord Jesus, the Bible, the magnificent palaces, the heavy tramp of the feet of armies consisting of elephants, chariots, cavalry, and infantry, shaking the earth, the sounds of war trumpets, bugles, and drums, and the splendid display of the royal throne, behind all these, there is always the virtual presence of England — that England whose war flag is the factory chimney, whose troops are the merchantmen, whose battlefields are the market-places of the world, and whose Empress is the shining Goddess of Fortune herself! It is on this account I have said before that it is indeed an unseen novelty, this conquest of India by England. What new revolution will be effected in India by her clash with the new giant power, and as the result of that revolution what new transformation is in store for future India, cannot be inferred from her past history.

I have stated previously that the four castes, Brahmin, Kshatriya, Vaishya, and Shudra do, in succession, rule the world. During the period of supreme authority exercised by each of these castes, some acts are accomplished which conduce to the welfare of the people, while others are injurious to them.

The foundation of the priestly power rests on intellectual strength, and not on the physical strength of arms. Therefore, with the supremacy of the priestly power, there is a great prevalence of intellectual and literary culture. Every human heart is always anxious for communication with, and help from, the supersensuous spiritual world. The entrance to that world is not possible for the generality of mankind; only a few great souls who can acquire a perfect control over their sense-organs and who are possessed with a nature preponderating with the essence of Sattva Guna are able to pierce the formidable wall of matter and come face to face, as it were, with the supersensuous — it is only they who know the workings of the kingdom that bring the messages from it and show the way to others. These great souls are the priests, the primitive guides, leaders, and movers of human societies.

The priest knows the gods and communicates with them; he is therefore worshipped as a god. Leaving behind the thoughts of the world, he has no longer to devote himself to the earning of his bread by the sweat of his brow. The best and foremost parts of all food and drink are due as offerings to the gods; and of these gods, the visible proxies on earth are the priests. It is through their mouths that they partake of the offerings. Knowingly or unknowingly, society gives the priest abundant leisure, and he can therefore get the opportunity of being meditative and of thinking higher thoughts. Hence the development of wisdom and learning originates first with the supremacy of the priestly power. There stands the priest between the dreadful lion — the king — on the one hand, and the terrified flock of sheep — the subject people — on the other. The destructive leap of the lion is checked by the controlling rod of spiritual power in the hands of the priest. The flame of the despotic will of the king, maddened in the pride of his wealth and men, is able to burn into ashes everything that comes in his way; but it is only a word from the priest, who has neither wealth nor men behind him but whose sole strength is his spiritual power, that can quench the despotic royal will, as water the fire.

With the ascendancy of the priestly supremacy are seen the first advent of civilisation, the first victory of the divine nature over the animal, the first mastery of spirit over matter, and the first manifestation of the divine power which is potentially present in this very slave of nature, this lump of flesh, to wit, the human body. The priest is the first discriminator of spirit from matter, the first to help to bring this world in communion with the next, the first messenger from the gods to man, and the intervening bridge that connects the king with his subjects. The first offshoot of universal welfare and good is nursed by his spiritual power, by his devotion to learning and wisdom, by his renunciation, the watchword of his life and, watered even by the flow of his own life-blood. It is therefore that in every land it was he to whom the first and foremost worship was offered. It is therefore that even his memory is sacred to us!

There are evils as well. With the growth of life is sown simultaneously the seed of death. Darkness and light always go together. Indeed, there are great evils which, if not checked in proper time, lead to the ruin of society. The play of power through gross matter is universally experienced; everyone sees, everyone understands, the mighty manifestation of gross material force as displayed in the play of battle-axes and swords, or in the burning properties of fire and lightning. Nobody doubts these things, nor can there ever be any question about their genuineness. But where the repository of power and the centre of its play are wholly mental, where the power is confined to certain special words, to certain special modes of uttering them, to the mental repetition of certain mysterious syllables, or to other similar processes and applications of the mind, there light is mixed with shade, there the ebb and flow naturally disturb the otherwise unshaken faith, and there even when things are actually seen or directly perceived, still sometimes doubts arise as to their real occurrence. Where distress, fear, anger, malice, spirit of retaliation, and the like passions of man, leaving the palpable force of arms, leaving the gross material methods to gain the end in view which every one can understand, substitute in their stead the mysterious mental processes like Stambhana, Uchchâtana, Vashikarana, and Mârana[1] for their fructification — there a cloud of smoky indistinctness, as it were, naturally envelops the mental atmosphere of these men who often live and move in such hazy worlds of obscure mysticism. No straight line of action presents itself before such a mind; even if it does, the mind distorts it into crookedness. The final result of all this is insincerity — that very limited narrowness of the heart — and above all, the most fatal is the extreme intolerance born of malicious envy at the superior excellence of another.

The priest naturally says to himself: "Why should I part with the power that has made the Devas subservient to me, has given me mastery over physical and mental illnesses, and has gained for me the service of ghosts, demons, and other unseen spirits? I have dearly bought this power by the price of extreme renunciation. Why should I give to others that to get which I had to give up my wealth, name, fame, in short, all my earthly comforts and happiness?" Again, that power is entirely mental. And how many opportunities are there of keeping it a perfect secret! Entangled in this wheel of circumstances, human nature becomes what it inevitably would: being used to practice constant self-concealment, it becomes a victim of extreme selfishness and hypocrisy, and at last succumbs to the poisonous consequences which they bring in their train. In time, the reaction of this very desire to concealment rebounds upon oneself. All knowledge, all wisdom is almost lost for want of proper exercise and dif-

---
1. Suppression of any bodily faculty, thereby causing a person's ruin, removing him from a position, subduing and getting mastery over him, and killing him by means of magical incantations.

fusion, and what little remains is thought to have been obtained from some supernatural source; and, therefore, far from making fresh efforts to go in for originality and gain knowledge of new sciences, it is considered useless and futile to attempt even to improve the remnants of the old by cleansing them of their corruptions. Thus lost to former wisdom, the former indomitable spirit of self-reliance, the priest, now glorifying himself merely in the name of his forefathers, vainly struggles to preserve untarnished for himself the same glory, the same privilege, the same veneration, and the same supremacy as was enjoyed by his great forefathers. Consequently, his violent collision with the other castes.

According to the law of nature, wherever there is an awakening of a new and stronger life, there it tries to conquer and take the place of the old and the decaying. Nature favours the dying out of the unfit and the survival of the fittest. The final result of such conflict between the priestly and the other classes has been mentioned already.

That renunciation, self-control, and asceticism of the priest which during the period of his ascendancy were devoted to the pursuance of earnest researches of truth are on the eve of his decline employed anew and spent solely in the accumulation of objects of self-gratification and in the extension of privileged superiority over others. That power, the centralization of which in himself gave him all honour and worship, has now been dragged down from its high heavenly position to the lowest abyss of hell. Having lost sight of the goal, drifting aimless, the priestly power is entangled, like the spider, in the web spun by itself. The chain that has been forged from generation to generation with the greatest care to be put on others' feet is now tightened round its own in a thousand coils, and is thwarting its own movement in hundreds of ways. Caught in the endless thread of the net of infinite rites, ceremonies, and customs, which it spread on all sides as external means for purification of the body and the mind with a view to keeping society in the iron grasp of these innumerable bonds — the priestly power, thus hopelessly entangled from head to foot, is now asleep in despair! There is no escaping out of it now. Tear the net, and the priesthood of the priest is shaken to its foundation! There is implanted in every man, naturally, a strong desire for progress; and those who, finding that the fulfilment of this desire is an impossibility so long as one is trammelled in the shackles of priesthood, rend this net and take to the profession of other castes in order to earn money thereby — them, the society immediately dispossesses of their priestly rights. Society has no faith in the Brahminhood of the so-called Brahmins who, instead of keeping the Shikhâ[1], part their hair, who, giving up their ancient habits and ancestral customs, clothe themselves in semi European dress and adopt the newly introduced usages from the West in a hybrid fashion. Again, in those parts of India, wherever this new-comer, the English Government, is introducing new modes of education and opening up new channels for the coming in of wealth, there hosts of Brahmin youths are giving up their hereditary priestly profession and trying to earn their livelihood and become rich by adopting the callings of other castes, with the result that the habits and customs of the priestly class, handed down from their distant forefathers, are scattered to the winds and are fast disappearing from the land.

In Gujarat, each secondary sect of the Brahmins is divided into two subdivisions, one being those who still stick to the priestly profession, while the other lives by other professions. There only the first subdivisions, carrying on the priestly profession, are called "Brâhmanas", and though the other subdivisions are by lineage descendants from Brahmin fathers, yet the former do not link themselves in matrimonial relation with the latter. For example, by the name of "Nâgara Brâhmana" are meant only those Brahmins who are priests living on alms; and by the name "Nâgara" only are meant those Brahmins who have accepted service under the Government, or those who have been carrying on the Vaishya's profession. But it appears that such distinctions will not long continue in these days in Gujarat. Even the sons of the "Nagara Brahmanas" are nowadays getting English education, and entering into

---

1. The sacred tuft or lock of hair left on the crown of the head at tonsure.

Government service, or adopting some mercantile business. Even orthodox Pandits of the old school, undergoing pecuniary difficulties, are sending their sons to the colleges of the English universities or making them choose the callings of Vaidyas, Kâyasthas, and other non-Brahmin castes. If the current of affairs goes on running in this course, then it is a question of most serious reflection, no doubt, how long more will the priestly class continue on India's soil. Those who lay the fault of attempting to bring down the supremacy of the priestly class at the door of any particular person or body of persons other than themselves ought to know that, in obedience to the inevitable law of nature, the Brahmin caste is erecting with its own hands its own sepulchre; and this is what ought to be. It is good and appropriate that every caste of high birth and privileged nobility should make it its principal duty to raise its own funeral pyre with its own hands. Accumulation of power is as necessary as its diffusion, or rather more so. The accumulation of blood in the heart is an indispensable condition for life; its non-circulation throughout the body means death. For the welfare of society, it is absolutely necessary at certain times to have all knowledge and power concentrated in certain families or castes to the exclusion of others, but that concentrated power is focussed for the time being, only to be scattered broadcast over the whole of society in future. If this diffusion be withheld, the destruction of that society is, without doubt, near at hand.

On the other side, the king is like the lion; in him are present both the good and evil propensities of the lord of beasts. Never for a moment his fierce nails are held back from tearing to pieces the heart of innocent animals, living on herbs and grass, to allay his thirst for blood when occasion arises; again, the poet says, though himself stricken with old age and dying with hunger, the lion never kills the weakest fox that throws itself in his arms for protection. If the subject classes, for a moment, stand as impediments in the way of the gratification of the senses of the royal lion, their death knell is inevitably tolled; if they humbly bow down to his commands, they are perfectly safe. Not only so. Not to speak of ancient days, even in modern times, no society can be found in any country where the effectiveness of individual self-sacrifice for the good of the many and of the oneness of purpose and endeavour actuating every member of the society for the common good of the whole have been fully realised. Hence the necessity of the kings who are the creations of the society itself. They are the centres where all the forces of society, otherwise loosely scattered about, are made to converge, and from which they start and course through the body politic and animate society.

As during the Brâhminical supremacy, at the first stage is the awakening of the first impulse for search after knowledge, and later the continual and careful fostering of the growth of that impulse still in its infancy — so, during the Kshatriya supremacy, a strong desire for pleasure pursuits has made its appearance at the first stage, and later have sprung up inventions and developments of arts and sciences as the means for its gratification. Can the king, in the height of his glory, hide his proud head within the lowly cottages of the poor? Or can the common good of his subjects ever minister to his royal appetite with satisfaction?

He whose dignity bears no comparison with anyone else on earth, he who is divinity residing in the temple of the human body — for the common man, to cast even a mere glance at his, the king's, objects of pleasure is a great sin; to think of ever possessing them is quite out of the question. The body of the king is not like the bodies of other people, it is too sacred to be polluted by any contamination; in certain countries it is even believed never to come under the sway of death. A halo of equal sacredness shines around the queen, so she is scrupulously guarded from the gaze of the common folk, not even the sun may cast a glance on her beauty! Hence the rising of magnificent palaces to take the place of thatched cottages. The sweet harmonious strain of artistic music, flowing as it were from heaven, silenced the disorderly jargon of the rabble. Delightful gardens, pleasant groves, beautiful galleries, charming paintings, exquisite sculptures, fine and costly apparel began to displace by gradual steps the natural beauties of rugged woods and the rough and coarse dress of the simple rustic. Thousands of intelligent men left the toilsome task of the ploughman and turned their attention to the new field of fine arts, where they could display the finer play of their intellect in less laborious and easier ways. Villages lost their importance; cities rose in their stead.

It was in India, again, that the kings, after having enjoyed for some time earthly pleasures to their full satisfaction, were stricken at the latter part of their lives with heavy world-weariness, as is sure to follow on extreme sense-gratification; and thus being satiated with worldly pleasures, they retired at their old age into secluded forests, and there began to contemplate the deep problems of life. The results of such renunciation and deep meditation were marked by a strong dislike for cumbrous rites and ceremonials and an extreme devotion to the highest spiritual truths which we find embodied in the Upanishads, the Gita, and the Jain and the Buddhist scriptures. Here also was a great conflict between the priestly and the royal powers. Disappearance of the elaborate rites and ceremonials meant a death-blow to the priest's profession. Therefore, naturally, at all times and in every country, the priests gird up their loins and try their best to preserve the ancient customs and usages, while on the other side stand in opposition kings like Janaka, backed by Kshatriya prowess as well as spiritual power. We have dealt at length already on this bitter antagonism between the two parties.

As the priest is busy about centralising all knowledge and learning at a common centre, to wit, himself, so the king is ever up and doing in collecting all the earthly powers and focusing them in a central point, i.e. his own self. Of course, both are beneficial to society. At one time they are both needed for the common good of society, but that is only at its infant stage. But if attempts be made, when society has passed its infant stage and reached its vigorous youthful condition, to clothe it by force with the dress which suited it in its infancy and keep it bound within narrow limits, then either it bursts the bonds by virtue of its own strength and tries to advance, or where it fails to do so, it retraces its footsteps and by slow degrees returns to its primitive uncivilised condition.

Kings are like parents to their subjects, and the subjects are the kings' children. The subjects should, in every respect, look up to the king and stick to their king with unreserved obedience, and the king should rule them with impartial justice and look to their welfare and bear the same affection towards them as he would towards his own children. But what rule applies to individual homes applies to the whole society as well, for society is only the aggregate of individual homes. "When the son attains the age of sixteen, the father ought to deal with him as his friend and equal"[1] — if that is the rule, does not the infant society ever attain that age of sixteen? It is the evidence of history that at a certain time every society attains its manhood, when a strong conflict ensues between the ruling power and the common people. The life of the society, its expansion and civilisation, depend on its victory or defeat in this conflict.

Such changes, revolutionizing society, have been happening in India again and again, only in this country they have been effected in the name of religion, for religion is the life of India, religion is the language of this country, the symbol of all its movements. The Chârvâka, the Jain, the Buddhist, Shankara, Ramanuja, Kabir, Nânak, Chaitanya, the Brâhmo Samâj, the Arya Samaj — of all these and similar other sects, the wave of religion, foaming, thundering, surging, breaks in the front, while in the rear follows the filling-up of social wants. If all desires can be accomplished by the mere utterance of some meaningless syllables, then who will exert himself and go through difficulties to work out the fulfilment of his desires? If this malady enters into the entire body of any social system, then that society becomes slothful and indisposed to any exertion, and soon hastens to it, ruin. Hence the slashing sarcasm of the Charvakas, who believed only in the reality of sense-perceptions and nothing beyond. What could have saved Indian society from

---

1. Taken from one of the well-known didactic verses of the statesman-Pandit, Chânakya, which runs thus: "Let the father treat with tenderness the child till he is five, let him (the father) reprove him (the child) for the next ten years; when the son attains the age of sixteen, the father ought to deal with him as his friend."

the ponderous burden of omnifarious ritualistic ceremonialism, with its animal and other sacrifices, which all but crushed the very life out of it, except the Jain revolution which took its strong stand exclusively on chaste morals and philosophical truth? Or without the Buddhist revolution what would have delivered the suffering millions of the lower classes from the violent tyrannies of the influential higher castes? When, in course of time, Buddhism declined and its extremely pure and moral character gave place to equally bad, unclean, and immoral practices, when Indian society trembled under the infernal dance of the various races of barbarians who were allowed into the Buddhistic fold by virtue of its universal all-embracing spirit of equality — then Shankara, and later Ramanuja, appeared on the scene and tried their best to bring society back to its former days of glory and re-establish its lost status. Again, it is an undoubted fact that if there had not been the advent of Kabir, Nanak, and Chaitanya in the Mohammedan period, and the establishment of the Brahmo Samaj and the Arya Samaj in our own day, then, by this time, the Mohammedans and the Christians would have far outnumbered the Hindus of the present day in India.

What better material is there than nourishing food to build up the body composed of various elements, and the mind which sends out infinite waves of thought? But if that food which goes to sustain the body and strengthen the mind is not properly assimilated, and the natural functions of the body do not work properly, then that very thing becomes the root of all evil.

The individual's life is in the life of the whole, the individual's happiness is in the happiness of the whole; apart from the whole, the individual's existence is inconceivable — this is an eternal truth and is the bed-rock on which the universe is built. To move slowly towards the infinite whole, bearing a constant feeling of intense sympathy and sameness with it, being happy with its happiness and being distressed in its affliction, is the individual's sole duty. Not only is it his duty, but in its transgression is his death, while compliance with this great truth leads to life immortal. This is the law of nature, and who can throw dust into her ever-watchful eyes? None can hoodwink society and deceive it for any length of time. However much there may have accumulated heaps of refuse and mud on the surface of society — still, at the bottom of those heaps the life-breath of society is ever to be found pulsating with the vibrations of universal love and self-denying compassion for all. Society is like the earth that patiently bears incessant molestations; but she wakes up one day, however long that may be in coming, and the force of the shaking tremors of that awakening hurls off to a distance the accumulated dirt of self-seeking meanness piled up during millions of patient and silent years!

We ignore this sublime truth; and though we suffer a thousand times for our folly, yet, in our absurd foolishness, impelled by the brute in us, we do not believe in it. We try to deceive, but a thousand times we find we are deceived ourselves, and yet we do not desist! Mad that we are, we imagine we can impose on nature' With our shortsighted vision we think ministering to the self at any cost is the be-all and end-all of life.

Wisdom, knowledge, wealth, men, strength, prowess and whatever else nature gathers and provides us with, are all only for diffusion, when the moment of need is at hand. We often forget this fact, put the stamp of "mine only" upon the entrusted deposits, and pari passu, we sow the seed of our own ruin!

The king, the centre of the forces of the aggregate of his subjects, soon forgets that those forces are only stored with him so that he may increase and give them back a thousandfold in their potency, so that they may spread over the whole community for its good. Attributing all Godship to himself, in his pride, like the king Vena[1] he looks upon other people as wretched specimens of humanity who should grovel before him; any opposition to his will, whether good or bad, is a great sin on the part of his

---

1. His story occurs in the Bhâgavata. The King Vena thought himself higher than Brahmâ, Vishnu, and Maheshvara, and declared accordingly that all worship should be offered to him. The Rishis once sought him and tried by good advice to make him give up such egoism, but he in return insulted them and ordered them to worship him, whereupon, it is said, he was destroyed by the fire of the anger of the Rishis.

subjects. Hence oppression steps into the place of protection — sucking their blood in place of preservation. If the society is weak and debilitated, it silently suffers all ill-treatment at the hands of the king, and as the natural consequence, both the king and his people go down and down and fall into the most degraded state, and thus become an easy prey to any nation stronger than themselves. Where the society is healthy and strong, there soon follows a fierce contest between the king and his subjects, and, by its reaction and convulsion, are flung away the sceptre and the crown; and the throne and the royal paraphernalia become like past curiosities preserved in the museum galleries.

As the result of this contest — as its reaction — is the appearance of the mighty power of the Vaishya, before whose angry glance the crowned heads, the lords of heroes, tremble like an aspen leaf on their thrones — whom the poor as well as the prince humbly follow in vain expectation of the golden jar in his hands, that like Tantalus's fruit always recedes from the grasp.

The Brahmin said, "Learning is the power of all powers; that learning is dependent upon me, I possess that learning, so the society must follow my bidding." For some days such was the case. The Kshatriya said, "But for the power of my sword, where would you be, O Brahmin, with all your power of lore? You would in no time be wiped off the face of the earth. It is I alone that am the superior." Out flew the flaming sword from the jingling scabbard — society humbly recognised it with bended head. Even the worshipper of learning was the first to turn into the worshipper of the king. The Vaishya is saying, "You, madmen! what you call the effulgent all-pervading deity is here, in my hand, the ever-shining gold, the almighty sovereign. Behold, through its grace, I am also equally all-powerful. O Brahmin! even now, I shall buy through its grace all your wisdom, learning, prayers, and meditation. And, O great king! your sword, arms, valour, and prowess will soon be employed, through the grace of this, my gold, in carrying out my desired objects. Do you see those lofty and extensive mills? Those are my hives. See, how, swarms of millions of bees, the Shudras, are incessantly gathering honey for those hives. Do you know for whom? For me, this me, who in due course of time will squeeze out every drop of it for my own use and profit."

As during the supremacy of the Brahmin and the Kshatriya, there is a centralization of learning and advancement of civilization, so the result of the supremacy of the Vaishya is accumulation of wealth. The power of the Vaishya lies in the possession of that coin, the charm of whose clinking sound works with an irresistible fascination on the minds of the four castes. The Vaishya is always in fear lest the Brahmin swindles him out of this, his only possession, and lest the Kshatriya usurps it by virtue of his superior strength of arms. For self-preservation, the Vaishyas as a body are, therefore, of one mind. The Vaishya commands the money; the exorbitant interest that he can exact for its use by others, as with a lash in his hand, is his powerful weapon which strikes terror in the heart of all. By the power of his money, he is always busy curbing the royal power. That the royal power may not anyhow stand in the way of the inflow of his riches, the merchant is ever watchful. But, for all that, he has never the least wish that the power should pass on from the kingly to the Shudra class.

To what country does not the merchant go? Though himself ignorant, he carries on his trade and transplants the learning, wisdom, art, and science of one country to another. The wisdom, civilization, and arts that accumulated in the heart of the social body during the Brahmin and the Kshatriya supremacies are being diffused in all directions by the arteries of commerce to the different market-places of the Vaishya. But for the rising of this Vaishya power, who would have carried today the culture, learning, acquirements, and articles of food and luxury of one end of the world to the other?

And where are they through whose physical labour only are possible the influence of the Brahmin, the prowess of the Kshatriya, and the fortune of the Vaishya? What is their history, who, being the real body of society, are designated at all times in all countries as "baseborn"? — for whom kind India prescribed the mild punishments, "Cut out his tongue, chop off his flesh", and others of like nature, for such a grave offence as any attempt on their part to gain a share of the knowledge and wisdom monopolised by her higher classes — those "moving corpses" of India and the "beasts of burden" of other countries — the Shudras, what is their lot in life? What shall I say of India? Let alone her Shudra class, her Brahmins to whom belonged the acquisition of scriptural knowledge are now the foreign professors, her Kshatriyas the ruling Englishmen, and Vaishyas, too, the English in whose bone and marrow is the instinct of trade, so that, only the Shudra-ness — the-beast-of-burdenness — is now left with the Indians themselves.

A cloud of impenetrable darkness has at present equally enveloped us all. Now there is neither firmness of purpose nor boldness of enterprise, neither courage of heart nor strength of mind, neither aversion to maltreatments by others nor dislike for slavery, neither love in the heart nor hope nor manliness; but what we have in India are only deep-rooted envy and strong antipathy against one another, morbid desire to ruin by hook or by crook the weak, and to lick dog-like the feet of the strong. Now the highest satisfaction consists in the display of wealth and power, devotion in self-gratification, wisdom in the accumulation of transitory objects, Yoga in hideous diabolical practices, work in the slavery of others, civilisation in base imitation of foreign nations, eloquence in the use of abusive language, the merit of literature in extravagant flatteries of the rich or in the diffusion of ghastly obscenities! What to speak separately of the distinct Shudra class of such a land, where the whole population has virtually come down to the level of the Shudra? The Shudras of countries other than India have become, it seems, a little awake; but they are wanting in proper education and have only the mutual hatred of men of their own class — a trait common to Shudras. What avails it if they greatly outnumber the other classes? That unity, by which ten men collect the strength of a million, is yet far away from the Shudra; hence, according to the law of nature, the Shudras invariably form the subject race.

But there is hope. In the mighty course of time, the Brahmin and the other higher castes, too, are being brought down to the lower status of the Shudras, and the Shudras are being raised to higher ranks. Europe, once the land of Shudras enslaved by Rome, is now filled with Kshatriya valour. Even before our eyes, powerful China, with fast strides, is going down to Shudra-hood, while insignificant Japan, rising with the sudden start of a rocket, is throwing off her Shudra nature and is invading by degrees the rights of the higher castes. The attaining of modern Greece and Italy to Kshatriya-hood and the decline of Turkey, Spain, and other countries, also, deserve consideration here.

Yet, a time will come when there will be the rising of the Shudra class, with their Shudra-hood; that is to say, not like that as at present when the Shudras are becoming great by acquiring the characteristic qualities of the Vaishya or the Kshatriya, but a time will come when the Shudras of every country, with their inborn Shudra nature and habits — not becoming in essence Vaishya or Kshatriya, but remaining as Shudras — will gain absolute supremacy in every society. The first glow of the dawn of this new power has already begun to break slowly upon the Western world, and the thoughtful are at their wits' end to reflect upon the final issue of this fresh phenomenon. Socialism, Anarchism, Nihilism[1], and other like sects are the vanguard of the social revolution that is to follow. As the result of grinding pressure and tyranny, from time out of mind, the Shudras, as a rule, are either meanly senile, licking dog-like the feet of the higher class, or otherwise are as inhuman as brute beasts. Again, at all times their hopes and aspirations are baffled; hence a firmness of purpose and perseverance in action they have none.

In spite of the spread of education in the West, there is a great hindrance in the way of the rising of the Shudra class, and that is the recognition of caste as determined by the inherence of more or less good or bad qualities. By this very qualitative caste system which obtained in India in ancient

---

1. Socialism took its birth in 1835 A.D. The initiator of Anarchism was Bakunin, who was born in 1814 A.D. Nihilism was first inaugurated in Russia in 1862.

days, the Shudra class was kept down, bound hand and foot. In the first place, scarcely any opportunity was given to the Shudra for the accumulation of wealth or the earning of proper knowledge and education; to add to this disadvantage, if ever a man of extraordinary parts and genius were born of the Shudra class, the influential higher sections of the society forthwith showered titular honours on him and lifted him up to their own circle. His wealth and the power of his wisdom were employed for the benefit of an alien caste — and his own caste-people reaped no benefits of his attainments; and not only so, the good-for-nothing people, the scum and refuse of the higher castes, were cast off and thrown into the Shudra class to swell their number. Vasishtha, Nârada, Satyakâma Jâbâla, Vyâsa, Kripa, Drona, Karna, and others of questionable parentage[1] were raised to the position of a Brahmin or a Kshatriya, in virtue of their superior learning or valour; but it remains to be seen how the prostitute, maidservant, fisherman, or the charioteer[2] class was benefited by these upliftings. Again, on the other hand, the fallen from the Brahmin, the Kshatriya, or the Vaishya class were always brought down to fill the ranks of the Shudras.

In modern India, no one born of Shudra parents, be he a millionaire or a great Pandit, has ever the right to leave his own society, with the result that the power of his wealth, intellect, or wisdom, remaining confined within his own caste limits, is being employed for the betterment of his own community. This hereditary caste system of India, being thus unable to overstep its own bounds, is slowly but surely conducing to the advancement of the people moving within the same circle. The improvement of the lower classes of India will go on, in this way, so long as India will be under a government dealing with its subjects irrespective of their caste and position.

Whether the leadership of society be in the hands of those who monopolise learning or wield the power of riches or arms, the source of its power is always the subject masses. By so much as the class in power severs itself from this source, by so much is it sure to become weak. But such is the strange irony of fate, such is the queer working of Mâyâ, that they from whom this power is directly or indirectly drawn, by fair means or foul — by deceit, stratagem, force, or by voluntary gift — they soon cease to be taken into account by the leading class. When in course of time, the priestly power totally estranged itself from the subject masses, the real dynamo of its power, it was overthrown by the then kingly power taking its stand on the strength of the subject people; again, the kingly power, judging itself to be perfectly independent, created a gaping chasm between itself and the subject people, only to be itself destroyed or become a mere puppet in the hands of the Vaishyas, who now succeeded in securing a relatively greater co-operation of the mass of the people. The Vaishyas have now gained their end; so they no longer deign to count on help from the subject people and are trying their best to dissociate themselves from them; consequently, here is being sown the seed of the destruction of this power as well.

Though themselves the reservoir of all powers, the subject masses, creating an eternal distance between one another, have been deprived of all their legitimate rights; and they will remain so as long as this sort of relation continues.

A common danger, or sometimes a common cause of hatred or love, is the bond that binds people together. By the same law that herds beasts of prey together, men also unite into a body and form a caste or a nation of their own. Zealous love for one's own people and country, showing itself in bitter ha-

---

1. (1) Vasishtha's father was Brahmâ and mother unknown. (2) Narada's mother was a maidservant and father unknown. (3) Satyakama Jabala's mother was a maidservant, by name Jabâlâ, and father unknown. (4) Vyasa's father was a Brahmin sage Parâshara, and mother Matsyagandhâ, the virgin daughter of a fisherman. (5) Kripa s father was a Brahmin sage, Sharadvân Gautama, and mother the goddess Jânapadi. (6) Drona's father was the Brahmin sage, Bharadvâja, and mother the goddess Ghritâchi. (7) Karna's mother was Kunti, who conceived during her maidenhood, and father the god sun. For detailed information vide the accounts of their births: for (1), see chapter 174, Âdiparva, Mahabharata, or in Rigveda, 7, 33, 11-13; for (2), chapter 6, Skandha I, Srimad Bhagavata, for (3) section 4 Prapâthaka iv, Chhândogya Upanishad; for (4), (5), (6) and (7) chapters 105, 130, 130 and 111, respectively of the Âdiparva of the Mahabharata.

2. In her anxiety to save her reputation, Kunti threw the newborn child Karna, into water. A charioteer found the child in his pitiable condition and adopted him as his son.

tred against another — as of Greece against Persia, or Rome against Carthage, of the Arab against the Kafir, of Spain against the Moor, of France against Spain, of England and Germany against France, and of America against England — is undoubtedly one of the main causes which lead to the advancement of one nation over another, by way of uniting itself in hostilities against another.

Self-love is the first teacher of self-renunciation. For the preservation of the individual's interest only one looks first to the well-being of the whole. In the interest of one's own nation is one's own interest; in the well-being of one's own nation is one's own well-being. Without the co-operation of the many, most words can by no means go on — even self-defence becomes an impossibility. The joining of friendly hands in mutual help for the protection of this self-interest is seen in every nation, and in every land. Of course, the circumference of this self-interest varies with different people. To multiply and to have the opportunity of somehow dragging on a precarious existence, and over and above this, the condition that the religious pursuits of the higher castes may not suffer in any way, is of the highest gain and interest for Indians! For modern India, there is no better hope conceivable; this is the last rung of the ladder of India's life!

The present government of India has certain evils attendant on it, and there are some very great and good parts in it as well. Of highest good is this, that after the fall of the Pâtaliputra Empire till now, India was never under the guidance of such a powerful machinery of government as the British, wielding the sceptre throughout the length and breadth of the land. And under this Vaishya supremacy, thanks to the strenuous enterprise natural to the Vaishya, as the objects of commerce are being brought from one end of the world to another, so at the same time, as its natural sequence, the ideas and thoughts of different countries are forcing their way into the very bone and marrow of India. Of these ideas and thoughts, some are really most beneficial to her, some are harmful, while others disclose the ignorance and inability of the foreigners to determine what is truly good for the inhabitants of this country.

But piercing through the mass of whatever good or evil there may be is seen rising the sure emblem of India's future prosperity — that as the result of the action and reaction between her own old national ideals on the one hand, and the newly-introduced strange ideals of foreign nations on the other, she is slowly and gently awakening from her long deep sleep. Mistakes she will make, let her: there is no harm in that; in all our actions, errors and mistakes are our only teachers. Who commits mistaken the path of truth is attainable by him only. Trees never make mistakes, nor do stones fall into error; animals are hardly seen to transgress the fixed laws of nature; but man is prone to err, and it is man who becomes God-on-earth. If our every movement from the nursery to the death-bed, if our every thought from rising at day-break till retirement at midnight, be prescribed and laid down for us in minutest detail by others — and if the threat of the king's sword be brought into requisition to keep us within the iron grasp of those prescribed rules — then, what remains for us to think independently for ourselves? What makes a man a genius, a sage? Isn't it because he thinks, reasons, wills? Without exercise, the power of deep thinking is lost. Tamas prevails, the mind gets dull and inert, the spirit is brought down to the level of matter. Yet, even now, every religious preacher, every social leader is anxious to frame new laws and regulations for the guidance of society! Does the country stand in want of rules? Has it not enough of them? Under the oppression of rules, the whole nation is verging on its ruin — who stops to understand this?

In the case of an absolute and arbitrary monarchy, the conquered race is not treated with so much contempt by the ruling power. Under such an absolute government, the rights of all subjects are equal, in other words, no one has any right to question or control the governing authority. So there remains very little room for special privileges of caste and the like. But where the monarchy is controlled by the voice of the ruling race, or a republican form of government rules the conquered race, there a wide distance is created between the ruling and the ruled;

and the most part of that power, which, if employed solely for the well-being of the ruled classes, might have done immense good to them within a short time, is wasted by the government in its attempts and applications to keep the subject race under its entire control. Under the Roman Emperorship, foreign subjects were, for this very reason, happier than under the Republic of Rome. For this very reason, St. Paul, the Christian Apostle, though born of the conquered Jewish race, obtained permission to appeal to the Roman Emperor, Caesar, to judge of the charges laid against him[1] Because some individual Englishman may call us "natives" or "niggers" and hate us as uncivilized savages, we do not gain or lose by that. We, on account of caste distinctions, have among ourselves far stronger feelings of hatred and scorn against one another; and who can say that the Brahmins, if they get some foolish unenlightened Kshatriya king on their side, will not graciously try again to "cut out the Shudras' tongues and chop off their limbs"? That recently in Eastern Aryavarta, the different caste-people seem to develop a feeling of united sympathy amidst themselves with a view to ameliorating their present social condition — that in the Mahratta country, the Brahmins have begun to sing paeans in praise of the "Marâthâ" race — these, the lower castes cannot yet believe to be the outcome of pure disinterestedness.

But gradually the idea is being formed in the minds of the English public that the passing away of the Indian Empire from their sway will end in imminent peril to the English nation, and be their ruin. So, by any means whatsoever, the supremacy of England must be maintained in India. The way to effect this, they think, is by keeping uppermost in the heart of every Indian the mighty prestige and glory of the British nation. It gives rise to both laughter and tears simultaneously to observe how this ludicrous and pitiful sentiment is gaining ground among the English, and how they are steadily extending their modus operandi for the carrying out of this sentiment into practice. It seems as if the Englishmen resident in India are forgetting that so long as that fortitude, that perseverance, and that intense national unity of purpose, by which Englishmen have earned this Indian Empire — and that ever wide-awake commercial genius aided by science' which has turned even India, the mother of all riches, into the principal mart of England — so long as these characteristics are not eliminated from their national life, their throne in India is unshakable. So long as these qualities are inherent in the British character, let thousands of such Indian Empires be lost, thousands will be earned again. But if the flow of the stream of those qualifier be retarded, shall an Empire be governed by the mere emblazoning of British prestige and glory? Therefore when such remarkable traits of character are still predominant in the English as a nation, it is utterly useless to spend so much energy and power for the mere preservation of meaningless "prestige". If that power were employed for the welfare of the subject-people, that, would certainly have been a great gain for both the ruling and the ruled races.

It has been said before that India is slowly awakening through her friction with the outside nations; and as the result of this little awakening, is the appearance, to a certain extent, of free and independent thought in modern India. On one side is modern Western science, dazzling the eyes with the brilliancy of myriad suns and driving in the chariot of hard and fast facts collected by the application of tangible powers direct in their incision, on the other are the hopeful and strengthening traditions of her ancient forefathers, in the days when she was at the zenith of her glory — traditions that have been brought out of the pages of her history by the great sages of her own land and outside, that run for numberless years and centuries through her every vein with the quickening of life drawn from universal love — traditions that reveal unsurpassed valour, superhuman genius, and supreme spirituality, which are the envy of the gods — these inspire her with future hopes. On one side, rank materialism, plenitude of fortune, accumulation of gigantic power, and intense sense-pursuits have, through foreign literature, caused a tremendous stir; on the other, through the confounding din of all these discordant sounds, she hears, in low yet unmistakable ac-

---

1. The Acts, xxv. 11.

cents, the heart-rending cries of her ancient gods, cutting her to the quick. There lie before her various strange luxuries introduced from the West — celestial drinks, costly well-served food, splendid apparel, magnificent palaces, new modes of conveyance, new manners, new fashions dressed in which moves about the well-educated girl in shameless freedom — all these are arousing unfelt desires. Again, the scene changes, and in its place appear, with stern presence, Sitâ, Sâvitri, austere religious vows, fastings, the forest retreat, the matted locks and orange garb of the semi-naked Sannyasin, Samâdhi and the search after the Self. On one side is the independence of Western societies based on self-interest; on the other is the extreme self-sacrifice of the Aryan society. In this violent conflict, is it strange that Indian society should be tossed up and down? Of the West, the goal is individual independence, the language money-making education, the means politics; of India, the goal is Mukti, the language the Veda, the means renunciation. For a time, Modern India thinks, as it were, I am ruining this worldly life of mine in vain expectation of uncertain spiritual welfare hereafter which has spread its fascination over one; and again, lo! spellbound she listens —

इति संसारे स्फुटतरदोषः कथमिह मानव तव सन्तोषः
—"Here, in this world of death and change, O man, where is thy happiness?"

On one side, new India is saying, "We should have full freedom in the selection of husband and wife; because the marriage, in which are involved the happiness and misery of all our future life, we must have the right to determine according to our own free will." On the other, old India is dictating, "Marriage is not for sense-enjoyment, but to perpetuate the race. This is the Indian conception of marriage. By the producing of children, you are contributing to, and are responsible for, the future good or evil of the society. Hence society has the right to dictate whom you shall marry and whom you shall not. That form of marriage obtains in society which is conducive most to its well-being; do you give up your desire of individual pleasure for the good of the many."

On one side, new India is saying, "If we only adopt Western ideas, Western language, Western food, Western dress, and Western manners, we shall be as strong and powerful as the Western nations"; on the other, old India is saying, "Fools! By imitation, other's ideas never become one's own; nothing, unless earned, is your own. Does the ass in the lion's skin become the lion?"

On one side, new India is saving, "What the Western nations do is surely good, otherwise how did they become so great?" On the other side, old India is saying, "The flash of lightning is intensely bright, but only for a moment; look out, boys, it is dazzling your eyes. Beware!"

Have we not then to learn anything from the West? Must we not needs try and exert ourselves for better things? Are we perfect? Is our society entirely spotless, without any flaw. There are many things to learn, he must struggle for new and higher things till we die — struggle is the end of human life. Shri Ramakrishna used to say, "As long as I live, so long do I learn." That man or that society which has nothing to learn is already in the jaws of death. Yes, learn we must many things from the West: but there are fears as well.

A certain young man of little understanding used always to blame the Hindu Shâstras before Shri Ramakrishna. One day he praised the Bhagavad-Gita, on which Shri Ramakrishna said, "Methinks, some European Pandit has praised the Gita, and so he has also followed suit."

O India, this is your terrible danger. The spell of imitating the West is getting such a strong hold upon you that what is good or what is bad is no longer decided by reason, judgment, discrimination, or reference to the Shastras. Whatever ideas, whatever manners the white men praise or like are good; whatever things they dislike or censure are bad. Alas! what can be a more tangible proof of foolishness than this?

The Western ladies move freely everywhere, therefore that is good; they choose for themselves their husbands, therefore that is the highest step of advancement; the Westerners disapprove of our dress, decorations, food, and ways of living, therefore they must be very bad; the Westerners condemn image-worship as sinful, surely then, image-worship is the greatest sin, there is no doubt of it!

The Westerners say that worshipping a single Deity is fruitful of the highest spiritual good, therefore let us throw our gods and goddesses into the river Ganga! The Westerners hold caste distinctions to be obnoxious, therefore let all the different castes be jumbled into one! The Westerners say that child-marriage is the root of all evils, therefore that is also very bad, of a certainty it is!

We are not discussing here whether these customs deserve continuance or rejection; but if the mere disapproval of the Westerners be the measure of the abominableness of our manners and customs, then it is our duty to raise our emphatic protest against it.

The present writer has, to some extent, personal experience of Western society. His conviction resulting from such experience has been that there is such a wide divergence between the Western society and the Indian as regards the primal course and goal of each, that any sect in India, framed after the Western model, will miss the aim. We have not the least sympathy with those who, never leaving lived in Western society and, therefore, utterly ignorant of the rules and prohibitions regarding the association of men and women that obtain there, and which act as safeguards to preserve the purity of the Western women, allow a free rein to the unrestricted intermingling of men and women in our society.

I have observed in the West also that the children of weaker nations, if born in England, give themselves out as Englishmen, instead of Greek, Portuguese, Spaniard, etc., as the case may be. All drift towards the strong. That the light of glory which shines in the glorious may anyhow fall and reflect on one's own body, i.e. to shine in the borrowed light of the great, is the one desire of the weak. When I see Indians dressed in European apparel and costumes, the thought comes to my mind, perhaps they feel ashamed to own their nationality and kinship with the ignorant, poor, illiterate, downtrodden people of India! Nourished by the blood of the Hindu for the last fourteen centuries, the Parsee is no longer a "native"! Before the arrogance of the casteless, who pretend to be and glorify themselves in being Brahmins, the true nobility of the old, heroic, high-class Brahmin melts into nothingness! Again, the Westerners have now taught us that those stupid, ignorant, low-caste millions of India, clad only in loin-cloths, are non-Aryans. They are therefore no more our kith and kin!

O India! With this mere echoing of others, with this base imitation of others, with this dependence on others this slavish weakness, this vile detestable cruelty — wouldst thou, with these provisions only, scale the highest pinnacle of civilisation and greatness? Wouldst thou attain, by means of thy disgraceful cowardice, that freedom deserved only by the brave and the heroic? O India! Forget not that the ideal of thy womanhood is Sita, Savitri, Damayanti; forget not that the God thou worshippest is the great Ascetic of ascetics, the all-renouncing Shankara, the Lord of Umâ; forget not that thy marriage, thy wealth, thy life are not for sense-pleasure, are not for thy individual personal happiness; forget not that thou art born as a sacrifice to the Mother's altar; forget not that thy social order is but the reflex of the Infinite Universal Motherhood; forget not that the lower classes, the ignorant, the poor, the illiterate, the cobbler, the sweeper, are thy flesh and blood, thy brothers. Thou brave one, be bold, take courage, be proud that thou art an Indian, and proudly proclaim, "I am an Indian, every Indian is my brother." Say, "The ignorant Indian, the poor and destitute Indian, the Brahmin Indian, the Pariah Indian, is my brother." Thou, too, clad with but a rag round thy loins proudly proclaim at the top of thy voice: "The Indian is my brother, the Indian is my life, India's gods and goddesses are my God. India's society is the cradle of my infancy, the pleasure-garden of my youth, the sacred heaven, the Varanasi of my old age." Say, brother: "The soil of India is my highest heaven, the good of India is my good," and repeat and pray day and night, "O Thou Lord of Gauri, O Thou Mother of the Universe, vouchsafe manliness unto me! O Thou Mother of Strength, take away my weakness, take away my unmanliness, and make me a Man!"

THE EDUCATION THAT INDIA NEEDS[1]

In reply to your questions about the methods of work, the most important thing I have to say is that the work should be started on a scale which would be commensurate with the results desired. I have heard much of your liberal mind, patriotism, and steady perseverance from my friend Miss Müller; and the proof of your erudition is evident. I look upon it as a great good fortune that you are desirous to know what little this insignificant life has been able to attempt; I shall state it to you here, as far as I can. But first I shall lay before you my mature convictions for your deliberation.

We have been slaves for ever, i.e. it has never been given to the masses of India to express the inner light which is their inheritance. The Occident has been rapidly advancing towards freedom for the last few centuries. In India, it was the king who used to prescribe everything from Kulinism down to what one should eat and what one should not. In Western countries, the people do everything themselves.

The king now has nothing to say in any social matter; on the other hand, the Indian people have not yet even the least faith in themselves, what to say of self-reliance. The faith in one's own Self, which is the basis of Vedânta, has not yet been even slightly carried into practice. It is for this reason that the Western method — i.e. first of all, discussion about the wished-for end, then the carrying it out by the combination of all the forces — is of no avail even now in this country: it is for this reason that we appear so greatly conservative under foreign rule. If this be true, then it is a vain attempt to do any great work by means of public discussion. "There is no chance of a headache where there is no head" — where is the public? Besides, we are so devoid of strength that our whole energy is exhausted if we undertake to discuss anything, none is left for work. It is for this reason, I suppose, we observe in Bengal almost always — "Much cry but little wool."

Secondly, as I have written before, I do not expect anything from the rich people of India. It is best to work among the youth in whom lies our hope — patiently, steadily, and without noise.

Now about work. From the day when education and culture etc. began to spread gradually from patricians to plebeians, grew the distinction between the modern civilisation as of Western countries, and the ancient civilisation as of India, Egypt, Rome, etc. I see it before my eyes, a nation is advanced in proportion as education and intelligence spread among the masses. The chief cause of India's ruin has been the monopolising of the whole education and intelligence of the land, by dint of pride and royal authority, among a handful of men. If we are to rise again, we shall have to do it in the same way, i.e. by spreading education among the masses. A great fuss has been made for half a century about social reform. Travelling through various places of India these last ten years, I observed the country full of social reform associations. But I did not find one association for them by sucking whose blood the people known as "gentlemen" have become and continue to be gentlemen! How many sepoys were brought by the Mussulmans? How many Englishmen are there? Where, except in India, can be had millions of men who will cut the throats of their own fathers and brothers for six rupees? Sixty millions of Mussulmans in seven hundred years of Mohammedan rule, and two millions of Christians in one hundred years of Christian rule — what makes it so? Why has originality entirely forsaken the country? Why are our deft-fingered artisans daily becoming extinct, unable to compete with the Europeans? By what power again has the German labourer succeeded in shaking the many-century-grounded firm footing of the English labourer?

Education, education, education alone! Travelling through many cities of Europe and observing in them the comforts and education of even the poor people, there was brought to my mind the state of our own poor people, and I used to shed tears. What made the difference? Education was the answer I got. Through education comes faith in one's own Self, and through faith in one's own Self the

---
1. Written to Shrimati Saralâ Ghosal, B.A., Editor, *Bhârati*, from Darjeeling, 24th April, 1897. Translated from Bengali.

inherent Brahman is waking up in them, while the Brahman in us is gradually becoming dormant. In New York I used to observe the Irish colonists come — downtrodden, haggard-looking, destitute of all possessions at home, penniless, and wooden-headed — with their only belongings, a stick and a bundle of rags hanging at the end of it, fright in their steps, alarm in their eyes. A different spectacle in six months — the man walks upright, his attire is changed! In his eyes and steps there is no more sign of fright. What is the cause? Our Vedanta says that that Irishman was kept surrounded by contempt in his own country — the whole of nature was telling him with one voice, "Pat, you have no more hope, you are born a slave and will remain so." Having been thus told from his birth, Pat believed in it and hypnotised himself that he was very low, and the Brahman in him shrank away. While no sooner had he landed in America than he heard the shout going up on all sides, "Pat, you are a man as we are. It is man who has done all, a man like you and me can do everything: have courage!" Pat raised his head and saw that it was so, the Brahman within woke up. Nature herself spoke, as it were, "Arise, awake, and stop not till the goal is reached" (Katha Upanishad, I. ii. 4.)

Likewise the education that our boys receive is very negative. The schoolboy learns nothing, but has everything of his own broken down — want of Shraddhâ is the result. The Shraddha which is the keynote of the Veda and the Vedanta — the Shraddha which emboldened Nachiketâ to face Yama and question him, through which Shraddha this world moves the annihilation of that Shraddha!

अज्ञश्चाश्रद्दधानश्च संशयात्मा विनश्यति

— "The ignorant, the man devoid of Shraddha, the doubting self runs to ruin." Therefore are we so near destruction. The remedy now is the spread of education. First of all, Self-knowledge. I do not mean thereby, matted hair, staff, Kamandalu, and mountain caves which the word suggests. What do I mean then? Cannot the knowledge, by which is attained even freedom from the bondage of worldly existence, bring ordinary material prosperity? Certainly it can. Freedom, dispassion, renunciation all these are the very highest ideals, but

स्वल्पमप्यस्य धर्मस्य त्रायते महतो भयात्

— "Even a little of this Dharma saves one from the great fear (of birth and death)." Dualist, qualified-monist, monist, Shaiva, Vaishnava, Shâkta, even the Buddhist and the Jain and others — whatever sects have arisen in India — are all at one in this respect that infinite power is latent in this Jivatman (individualised soul); from the ant to the perfect man there is the same Âtman in all, the difference being only in manifestation. "As a farmer breaks the obstacles (to the course of water)" (Patanjali's Yoga-Sutra, Kaivalsapâda, 3). That power manifests as soon as it gets the opportunity and the right place and time. From the highest god to the meanest grass, the same power is present in all — whether manifested or not. We shall have to call forth that power by going from door to door.

Secondly, along with this, education has to be imparted. That is easy to say, but how to reduce it into practice? There are thousands of unselfish, kind-hearted men in our country who has renounced every thing. In the same way as they travel about and give religious instructions without any remuneration, so at least half of them can be trained as teachers or bearers of such education as we need most. For that, we want first of all a centre in the capital of each Presidency, from whence to spread slowly throughout the whole of India. Two centres have recently been started in Madras and Calcutta; there is hope of more soon. Then, the greater part of the education to the poor should be given orally, time is not yet ripe for schools. Gradually in these main centres will be taught agriculture, industry, etc., and workshops will be established for the furtherance of arts. To sell the manufactures of those workshops in Europe and America, associations will be started like those already in existence. It will be necessary to start centres for women, exactly like those for men. But you are aware how difficult that is in this country. Again, "The snake which bites must take out its own poison" — and that this is going to be is my firm conviction; the money required for these works would have to come from the West. And for that reason our religion should be preached in Europe and America. Modern science has undermined the basis of religions like Christianity. Over and above that, luxury is about to kill the religious instinct itself. Europe and America are now looking towards India with expectant ewes: this is the time for philanthropy, this is the time to occupy the hostile strongholds.

In the West, women rule; all influence and power are theirs. If bold and talented women like yourself versed in Vedanta, go to England to preach, I am sure that every year hundreds of men and women will become blessed by adopting the religion of the land of Bharata. The only woman who went over from our country was Ramâbâai; her knowledge of English, Western science and art was limited; still she surprised all. If anyone like you goes, England will be stirred, what to speak of America! If an Indian woman in Indian dress preach there the religion which fell from the lips of the Rishis of India — I see a prophetic vision — there will rise a great wave which will inundate the whole Western world. Will there be no women in the land of Maitreyi, Khanâ, Lilâvati, Sâvitri, and Ubhayabhârati, who will venture to do this? The Lord knows. England we shall conquer, England we shall possess, through the power of spirituality.

नान्यः पन्था विद्यतेऽयनाय

— "There is no other way of salvation." Can salvation ever come by getting up meetings and societies? Our conquerors must be made Devas by the power of our spirituality. I am a humble mendicant, an itinerant monk; I am helpless and alone. What can I do? You have the power of wealth, intellect, and education; will you forgo this opportunity? Conquest of England, Europe, and America — this should be our one supreme Mantra at present, in it lies the well-being of the country. Expansion is the sign of life, and we must spread over the world with our spiritual ideals. Alas! this frame is poor, moreover, the physique of a Bengali; even under this labour a fatal disease has attacked it, but there is the hope:

उत्पत्स्यतेऽस्ति मम कोऽपि समानधर्मा।
कालो ह्ययं निरवधिर्विपुला च पृथ्वी॥

—"A kindred spirit is or will be born out of the limitless time and populous earth to accomplish the work" (Bhavabhuti).

About vegetarian diet I have to say this — first, my Master was a vegetarian; but if he was given meat offered to the Goddess, he used to hold it up to his head. The taking of life is undoubtedly sinful; but so long as vegetable food is not made suitable to the human system through progress in chemistry, there is no other alternative but meat-eating. So long as man shall have to live a Râjasika (active) life under circumstances like the present, there is no other way except through meat-eating. It is true that the Emperor Asoka saved the lives of millions of animals by the threat of the sword; but is not the slavery of a thousand years more dreadful than that? Taking the life of a few goats as against the inability to protect the honour of one's own wife and daughter, and to save the morsels for one's children from robbing hands — which of these is more sinful? Rather let those belonging to the upper ten, who do not earn their livelihood by manual labour, not take meat; but the forcing of vegetarianism upon those who have to earn their bread by labouring day and night is one of the causes of the loss of our national freedom. Japan is an example of what good and nourishing food can do.

May the All-powerful Vishveshvari inspire your heart!

OUR PRESENT SOCIAL PROBLEMS[1]

स ईशोऽनिर्वचनीयप्रेमस्वरूपः

— "The Lord whose nature is unspeakable love."

That this characteristic of God mentioned by Nârada is manifest and admitted on all hands is the firm conviction of my life. The aggregate of many individuals is called Samashti (the whole), and each individual is called Vyashti (a part). You and I — each is Vyashti, society is Samashti. You, I, an animal, a bird, a worm, an insect, a tree, a creeper, the earth, a planet, a star — each is Vyashti, while this universe is Samashti, which is called Virât, Hiranyagarbha, or Ishvara in Vedânta, and Brahmâ, Vishnu, Devi, etc., in the Purânas. Whether or not Vyashti has individual freedom, and if it has, what should be its measure, whether or not Vyashti should completely sacrifice its own will, its own happiness for Samashti — are the perennial problems before every society. Society everywhere is busy finding the solution of these problems. These, like big waves, are agitating modern Western society. The doctrine which demands the sacrifice of individual freedom to social supremacy is called socialism, while that which advocates the cause of the individual is called individualism.

Our motherland is a glowing example of the results and consequence of the eternal subjection of the individual to society and forced self-sacrifice by dint of institution and discipline. In this country men are born according to Shâstric injunctions, they eat and drink by prescribed rules throughout life, they go through marriage and kindred functions in the same way; in short, they even die according to Shastric injunctions. The hard discipline, with the exception of one great good point, is fraught with evil. The good point is that men can do one or two things well with very little effort, having practiced them every day through generations. The delicious rice and curry which a cook of this country prepares with the aid of three lumps of earth and a few sticks can be had nowhere else. With the simple mechanism of an antediluvian loom, worth one rupee, and the feet put in a pit, it is possible to make kincobs worth twenty rupees a yard, in this country alone. A torn mat, an earthen lamp, and that fed by castor oil — with the aid of materials such as these, wonderful savants are produced in this country alone. An all-forbearing attachment to an ugly and deformed wife, and a lifelong devotion to a worthless and villainous husband are possible in this country alone. Thus far the bright side.

But all these things are done by people guided like lifeless machines. There is no mental activity, no unfoldment of the heart, no vibration of life, no flux of hope; there is no strong stimulation of the will, no experience of keen pleasure, nor the contact of intense sorrow; there is no stir of inventive genius, no desire for novelty, no appreciation of new things. Clouds never pass away from this mind, the radiant picture of the morning sun never charms this heart. It never even occurs to this mind if there is any better state than this; where it does, it cannot convince; in the event of conviction, effort is lacking; and even where there is effort, lack of enthusiasm kills it out.

If living by rule alone ensures excellence, if it be virtue to follow strictly the rules and customs handed down through generations, say then, who is more virtuous than a tree, who is a greater devotee, a holier saint, than a railway train? Who has ever seen a piece of stone transgress a natural law? Who has ever known cattle to commit sin?

The huge steamer, the mighty railway engine — they are non-intelligent; they move, turn, and run, but they are without intelligence. And yonder tiny worm which moved away from the railway line to save its life, why is it intelligent? There is no manifestation of will in the machine, the machine never wishes to transgress law; the worm wants to oppose law — rises against law whether it succeeds or not; therefore it is intelligent. Greater is the happiness, higher is the Jiva, in proportion as this will is more successfully manifest. The will of God is perfectly fruitful; therefore He is the highest.

---

1. Translated from a Bengali letter written to Shrimati Mrinalini Bose from Deoghar (Vaidyanâth), on 23rd December, 1898.

What is education? Is it book-learning? No. Is it diverse knowledge? Not even that. The training by which the current and expression of will are brought under control and become fruitful is called education. Now consider, is that education as a result of which the will, being continuously choked by force through generations, is well-nigh killed out; is that education under whose sway even the old ideas, let alone the new ones, are disappearing one by one; is that education which is slowly making man a machine? It is more blessed, in my opinion, even to go wrong, impelled by one's free will and intelligence than to be good as an automaton. Again, can that be called society which is formed by an aggregate of men who are like lumps of clay, like lifeless machines, like heaped up pebbles? How can such society fare well? Were good possible, then instead of being slaves for hundreds of years, we would have been the greatest nation on earth, and this soil of India, instead of being a mine of stupidity, would have been the eternal fountain-head of learning.

Is not self-sacrifice, then, a virtue? Is it not the most virtuous deed to sacrifice the happiness of one, the welfare of one, for the sake of the many? Exactly, but as the Bengali adage goes, "Can beauty be manufactured by rubbing and scrubbing? Can love be generated by effort and compulsion?" What glory is there in the renunciation of an eternal beggar? What virtue is there in the sense control of one devoid of sense-power? What again is the self-sacrifice of one devoid of idea, devoid of heart, devoid of high ambition, and devoid of the conception of what constitutes society? What expression of devotedness to a husband is there by forcing a widow to commit Sati? Why make people do virtuous deeds by teaching superstitions? I say, liberate, undo the shackles of people as much as you can. Can dirt be washed by dirt? Can bondage be removed by bondage? Where is the instance? When you would be able to sacrifice all desire for happiness for the sake of society, then you would be the Buddha, then you would be free: that is far off. Again, do you think the way to do it lies through oppression? "Oh, what examples or self-denial are our widows! Oh, how sweet is child-marriage! Is another such custom possible! Can there be anything but love between husband and wife in such a marriage!" such is the whine going round nowadays. But as to the men, the masters of the situation, there is no need of self-denial for them! Is there a virtue higher than serving others? But the same does not apply to Brâhmins — you others do it! The truth is that in this country parents and relatives can ruthlessly sacrifice the best interests of their children and others for their own selfish ends to save themselves by compromise to society; and the teaching of generations rendering the mind callous has made it perfectly easy. He, the brave alone, can deny self. The coward, afraid of the lash, with one hand wipes his eyes and gives with the other. Of what avail are such gifts? It is a far cry to love universal. The young plant should be hedged in and taken care of. One can hope gradually to attain to universal love if one can learn to love one object unselfishly. If devotion to one particular Ishta-Deva is attained, devotion to the universal Virat is gradually possible.

Therefore, when one has been able to deny self for an individual, one should talk of self-sacrifice for the sake of society, not before. It is action with desire that leads to action without desire. Is the renunciation of desire possible if desire did not exist in the beginning? And what could it mean? Can light have any meaning if there is no darkness?

Worship with desire, with attachment, comes first. Commence with the worship of the little, then the greater will come of itself.

Mother, be not anxious. It is against the big tree that the great wind strikes. "Poking a fire makes it burn better"; "A snake struck on the head raises its hood" — and so on. When there comes affliction in the heart, when the storm of sorrow blows all around, and it seems light will be seen no more, when hope and courage are almost gone, it is then, in the midst of this great spiritual tempest, that the light of Brahman within gleams. Brought up in the lap of luxury, lying on a bed of roses and never shedding a tear, who has ever become great, who has ever unfolded the Brahman within? Why do you fear to weep? Weep! Weeping clears the eyes and brings about intuition. Then the vision of diversity

— man, animal, tree — slowly melting away, makes room for the infinite realisation of Brahman everywhere and in everything. Then —

समं पश्यन् हि सर्वत्र समवस्थितमीश्वरम् ।

न हिनस्त्यात्मनात्मानं ततो याति परां गतिम् ॥

— "Verily, seeing the same God equally existent every where, he does not injure the Self by the self, and so goes to the Supreme Goal" (Gitâ, XIII. 28).

TRANSLATION: POEMS

To a Friend

Rendered from a Bengali poem composed by Swami Vivekananda

Where darkness is interpreted as light,
Where misery passes for happiness,
Where disease is pretended to be health,
Where the new-born's cry but shows 'tis alive;
Dost thou, O wise, expect happiness here?

Where war and competition ceaseless run,
Even the father turns against the son,
Where "self", "self"—this always the only note,
Dost thou, O wise, seek for peace supreme here?

A glaring mixture of heaven and hell,
Who can fly from this Samsâr[1] of Mâyâ?
Fastened in the neck with Karma's fetters,
Say, where can the slave escape for safety?

The paths of Yoga and of sense-enjoyment,
The life of the householder and Sannyâs,
Devotion, worship, and earning riches,
Vows, Tyâga, and austerities severe,
I have seen through them all. What have I known?

—Have known there's not a jot of happiness,
Life is only a cup of Tantalus;
The nobler is your heart, know for certain,

---

[1]. Samsâra, the world.

The more must be your share of misery.

Thou large-hearted Lover unselfish, know,
There's no room in this sordid world for thee;
Can a marble figure e'er brook the blow
That an iron mass can afford to bear?

Couldst thou be as one inert and abject,
Honey-mouthed, but with poison in thy heart,
Destitute of truth and worshipping self,
Then thou wouldst have a place in this Samsar.

Pledging even life for gaining knowledge,
I have devoted half my days on earth;
For the sake of love, even as one insane,
I have often clutched at shadows lifeless;

For religion, many creeds have I sought,
Lived in mountain-caves, on cremation-grounds,
By the Ganga and other sacred streams,
And how many days have I passed on alms!

Friendless, clad in rags, with no possession,
Feeding from door to door on what chance would bring,
The frame broken under Tapasyà's[1] weight;
What riches, ask thou, have I earned in life?

Listen, friend, I will speak my heart to thee;
I have found in my life this truth supreme—

---

1. Of austerities.

Buffeted by waves, in this whirl of life,
There's one ferry that takes across the sea[1].

Formulas of worship, control of breath,
Science, philosophy, systems varied,
Relinquishment, possession, and the like,
All these are but delusions of the mind—
Love, Love—that's the one thing, the sole treasure.

In Jiva and Brahman, in man and God,
In ghosts, and wraiths, and spirits, and so forth,
In Devas, beasts, birds, insects, and in worms,
This Prema[2] dwells in the heart of them all.

Say, who else is the highest God of gods?
Say, who else moves all the universe?
The mother dies for her young, robber robs—
Both are but the impulse of the same Love!

Beyond the ken of human speech and mind,
It dwells in weal and woe; 'tis that which comes
As the all-powerful, all-destroyer
Kâli, and as the kindliest mother.

Disease, bereavement, pinch of poverty,
Dharma[3], and its opposite Adharma[4],
Are but ITS worship in manifold modes;

---

1. The sea of Samsara.
2. Love.
3. Virtue.
4. Vice.

Say, what does by himself a Jiva do?

Deluded is he who happiness seeks,
Lunatic he who misery wishes,
Insane he too who fondly longs for death,
Immortality—vain aspiration!

For, far, however far you may travel,
Mounted on the brilliant mental car,
'Tis the same ocean of the Samsar,
Happiness and misery whirling on.

Listen O Vihangam[1], bereft of wings,
'Tis not the way to make good your escape;
Time and again you get blows, and collapse,
Why then attempt what is impossible?

Let go your vain reliance on knowledge,
Let go your prayers, offerings, and strength,
For Love selfless is the only resource;—
Lo, the insects teach, embracing the flame!

The base insect's blind, by beauty charmed,
Thy soul is drunken with the wine of Love;
O thou Lover true, cast into the fire
All thy dross of self, thy mean selfishness.

Say—comes happiness e'er to a beggar?
What good being object of charity?

---

1. Bird, here addressed to the bound soul.

Give away, ne'er turn to ask in return,
Should there be the wealth treasured in thy heart.

Ay, born heir to the Infinite thou art,
Within the heart is the ocean of Love,
"Give", "Give away"—whoever asks return,
His ocean dwindles down to a mere drop.

From highest Brahman to the yonder worm,
And to the very minutest atom,
Everywhere is the same God, the All-Love;
Friend, offer mind, soul, body, at their feet.

These are His manifold forms before thee,
Rejecting them, where seekest thou for God?
Who loves all beings without distinction,
He indeed is worshipping best his God.

The Hymn of Creation

Rendered from Bengali

One Mass, devoid of form, name, and colour,
Timeless, devoid of time past and future,
Spaceless, voiceless, boundless, devoid of all—
Where rests hushed even speech of negation[1].

From thence, down floweth the river causal,
Wearing the form of desire radiant,
Its heaving waters angrily roaring
The constant roar, "I am", "I am".

In that ocean of desire limitless,
Appear shining waves, countless, infinite,
Oh, of what power manifold they are,
Of what forms myriad, of what repose,
Of what movements varied, who can reckon?

Millions of moons, millions of suns,
Taking their birth in that very ocean,
Rushing headlong with din tumultuous,
Overspread the whole firmament, drowning
The points of heaven in light effulgent.

In it arise and reside what beings,
Quick with life, dull, and lifeless—unnumbered,
And pleasure and pain, disease, birth, and death!

---

[1] "Neti, Neti", "Not this, not this." Brahman cannot be described in any positive way.

Verily, the Sun is He, His the ray,
Nay, the Sun is He, and He is the ray.

The Hymn of Samadhi

Rendered from Bengali

Lo! The sun is not, nor the comely moon,
All light extinct; in the great void of space
Floats shadow-like the image-universe.

In the void of mind involute, there floats
The fleeting universe, rises and floats,
Sinks again, ceaseless, in the current "I".

Slowly, slowly, the shadow-multitude
Entered the primal womb, and flowed ceaseless,
The only current, the "I am", "I am".

Lo! 'Tis stopped, ev'n that current flows no more,
Void merged into void — beyond speech and mind!
Whose heart understands, he verily does.

A Hymn to the Divine Mother

अम्बास्तोत्रम्।

का त्वं शुभे श्रविकरे सुखदुःखहस्ते
आधूर्णितं भवजलं प्रबलोर्मिभङ्गैः।
शान्तिं विधातुमिह किं बहुधा विभिग्नाम्
मातः प्रयत्नपरमासि सदैव विश्वे॥

O Thou most beautiful! Whose holy hands
Hold pleasure and hold pain! Doer of good!
Who art Thou? The water of existence
By Thee is whirled and tossed in mighty waves.
Is it, O Mother, to restore again
This universe's broken harmony
That Thou, without cessation, art at work?

संपादयत्यविरतं त्वववरिमवृत्ता
या वै स्थिति कृतफलं त्वकृतस्य नेत्री।
सा मे भवत्वनुदिनं वरदा भवानी
जानाम्यहं ध्रुवमिदं धृतकर्मपाशा॥

Oh! May the Mother of the universe—
In whose activity no respite rests,
Incessantly distributing the fruits
Of action done, guiding unceasingly
All action yet to come—bestow Her boon
Of blessing on me, Her child, for evermore.
I realise, I know, that it is Thou
Who holdest in Thy hands dread Karma's rope.

को वा धर्मः किमकृतं कः कपालेखः
कविदृष्ट फलमिहास्ति हि यां विना भोः
इच्छापाशैर्नियमिति नियमाः स्वतन्त्रैः
यस्या नेत्री भवतु सा शरणं ममाद्या॥

Is it inherent nature? Something uncreate?
Or Destiny? Some unforeseen result?—
Who lacking nothing, is accountable,
Whose chain of will, untrammelled, grasps the laws,
May She, the Primal Guide, my shelter be!

सन्तानयन्ति जलधीं जनमृत्युजालं
सम्भावयन्त्यविकृतं विकृतं विभिन्नम्।
यस्या विभूतय इहामितशक्तिपालाः
नाश्रित्य तां वद कुतः शरणं व्रजामः॥

Manifestations of Her glory show
In power of immeasurable might,
Throughout the universe, powers that swell
The sea of birth and death, forces that change
And break up the Unchanged and changed again.
Lo! Where shall we seek refuge, save in Her?

मित्रे शत्रौ त्ववविषमं तव पद्मनेत्रम्
स्वस्थे दुःस्थे त्ववितथं तव हस्तपातः।
मृत्युच्छाया तव दया त्वमृतञ्च मातः
मा मां मुञ्चन्तु परमे शुभदृष्टयस्ते॥

To friend and foe Thy lotus-eyes are even;
Ever Thine animating touch brings fruit
To fortunate and unfortunate alike;
The shade of death and immortality—
Both these, O mother, are Thy grace Supreme!
Mother Supreme! Oh, may Thy gracious face
Never be turned away from me, Thy child!

क्वाम्बा सर्वा क्वा गृणनं मम हीनबुध्देः
धर्तत्तुं दोर्भ्यामवि मतिर्जगदेकधात्रीम्॥
श्रीसञ्चिन्त्यं सुचरणं अभयप्रतिष्ठं
सेवासारैरभिनुतं शरणं प्रपद्ये॥

What Thou art, the Mother! the All. How praise?
My understanding is so little worth.
'Twere like desire to seize with hands of mine
The sole Supporter of the universe!
So, at Thy blessed feet—contemplated
By the Goddess of Fortune Herself—the abode
Of fearlessness, worshipped by service true—
There, at those blessed feet, I take refuge!

या मामाजन्म वनियत्यतिदुःखमार्गैः
आसंसध्देः स्वकलितिललितैर्वलिासैः।
या मे बुध्दिं सुविदधे सततं धरणायां
साम्बा सर्वा मम गतिः सफलेऽफले वा॥

She who, since birth, has ever led me on
Through paths of trouble to perfection's goal,

Mother-wise, in Her own sweet playful ways,
She, who has always through my life inspired
My understanding, She, my Mother, She,
The All, is my resort, whether my work
O'erdow with full fruition or with none.

A Hymn to Shiva

शिवस्तोत्रम्।
ॐ नमः शिवाय।

नखिलिभुवनजन्मस्थेमभङ्गप्ररोहाः
अकलितमहिमानः कल्पिता यत्र तस्मिन्।
सुविमलगगनाभे ईशसंस्थेऽप्यनीशे
मम भवतु भवेऽस्मिन् भासुरो भावबन्धः॥

Salutation to Shiva! whose glory
Is immeasurable, who resembles sky
In clearness, to whom are attributed
The phenomena of all creation,
The preservation and dissolution
Of the universe! May the devotion,
The burning devotion of this my life
Attach itself to Him, to Shiva, who,
While being Lord of all, transcends Himself.

निहितनखिलमोहेऽधीशता यत्र रूढा
प्रकटितपरप्रेम्णा यो महादेवसंज्ञः।
अशिथिलपरिरम्भः प्रेमरूपस्य यस्य
प्रणयति हृदि विश्वं व्याजमात्रं विभुत्वम्॥

In whom Lordship is ever established,
Who causes annihilation of delusion,
Whose most surpassing love, made manifest,
Has crowned Him with a name above all names,

The name of "Mahâdeva", the Great God!
Whose warm embrace, of Love personified,
Displays, within man's heart, that all power
Is but a semblance and a passing show,

वहति विपुलवातः पूर्वसंस्काररूपः
परमथति बलवृन्दं धूर्णतिवोर्ममिला।
प्रचलति खलु युग्मं युष्मदस्मत्प्रतीतं
अतिविकलितरूपं नौमि चित्तं शिवस्थम्॥

In which the tempest of the whole past blows,
Past Samskâras[1], stirring the energies
With violence, like water lashed to waves;
In which the dual consciousness of "I" and "Thou"
Plays on: I salute that mind unstable,
Centred in Shiva, the abode of calm!

जनकजनितभावो वृत्तयः संस्कृताश्च
अगणनबहुरूपो यत्र एको यथार्थः।
शामतिविकृतिवाते यत्र नान्तर्बहिश्च
तमहह हरमीडे चेत्तवृत्तेर्निरोधम्॥

Where the ideas of parent and produced,
Purified thoughts and endless varied forms,
Merge in the Real one; where the existence ends
Of such conceptions as "within", "without"—
The wind of modification being stilled—
That Hara I worship, the suppression
Of movements of the mind. Shiva I hail!

---

1. The accumulated effects of past desires and action.

गलिततिमिरमालः शुभ्रतेजःप्रकाशः
धवलकमलशोभः ज्ञानपुञ्जाट्टहासः।
यमजिनहृदगिम्यः निष्कलं ध्यायमानः
प्रणतमवतु मां स मानसो राजहंसः॥

From whom all gloom and darkness have dispersed;
That radiant Light, white, beautiful
As bloom of lotus white is beautiful;
Whose laughter loud sheds knowledge luminous;
Who, by undivided meditation,
Is realised in the self-controlled heart:
May that Lordly Swan of the limpid lake
Of my mind, guard me, prostrate before Him!

दुरितदलनदक्षं दक्षजादत्तदोषं
कलितकलकिलङ्कं कम्रकह्लारकान्तं।
परहितकरणाय प्राणविच्छेदसूत्कं
नतनयननियुक्तं नीलकण्ठं नमामः॥

Him, the Master-remover of evil,
Who wipes the dark stain of this Iron Age;
Whom Daksha's Daughter gave Her coveted hand;
Who, like the charming water-lily white,
Is beautiful; who is ready ever
To part with life for others' good, whose gaze
Is on the humble fixed; whose neck is blue[1]
With the poison[2] swallowed:
Him, we salute!

---

1. Nilkantha, a name of Shiva.
2. The all-destructive evil.

A Hymn to the Divinity of Shri Ramakrishna

We salute Thee!
Lord! Adored of the world,
Samsâra's bondage breaker, taintless Thou,
Embodiment of blessed qualities,
Thou transcendest all Gunas; human form
Thus bearest.
Thee we salute and adore!

Refuge of mind and speech, Thou art beyond
The reach of either. Radiance art Thou
In all radiance that is. The heart's cave
Is by Thy visitance resplendent made.
Verily Thou art that which dispelleth
The densest darkness of Tamas in man.

Lo! In variety of melody
Forth-breaking in fine harmony most sweet,
Hymns of Thy devotees, accompanied
By Mridanga[1] playing with music's grace,
Fill the air, in evening worship to Thee.

One glancing vision at Thine eyes divine
Cleared by the collyrium of Jnâna
Defies delusion. O thou blotter-out
Of all the taints of sin, Intelligence
Pure, unmingled is Thy form. Of the world
Thou art embellisher. Self-luminous

---

1. A kind of drum.

Art Thou. O Ocean of feeling sublime,
And of Love Divine, O God-maddened One,
Devotees win Thy blessed feet and cross
Safely the swelling sea of Samsara.

O Lord of the world, though Thy Yoga power
Thou shinest as the Incarnation clear
Of this our time. O thou of strict restraint,
Only through Thine unstinted grace we see
The mind in Samâdhi completely merged ;
Mercy Incarnate! austere are Thy deeds.

Thou dealest to the evil of Misery
Destruction. Kali's[1] binding cords
Are cut by Thee asunder. Thine own life
Thou gavest freely, O sweet Sacrifice,
O best of men! O Saviour of the world!

Devoid wert Thou of the idea of sex,
Thought of possession charmed Thee not. To Thee
Obnoxious was all pleasure. Give to us,
O greatest among Tyâgis[2], love intense
Unto Thy sacred feet ; give, we implore!

Fearless art Thou, and past all gloom of doubt ;
Thy mind is wrapt in its own firm resolve ;
Thy lovers, whose devotion mounts above
The realm of reason, who renounce the pride

---

1. Of the Iron Age.
2. Renouncers.

Of caste and parentage, of name and fame—
Their safe refuge art Thou alone, O Lord!

My one true treasure is Thy blessed feet,
Reaching which the whole universe itself
Seems like a puddle in the hollow made
By hoof of passing cow.
O offering
To Love! O Seer of equality
In all! O verily, in Thee the pain
And evil of this mortal world escapes,
And vanishes, O cherished One.

"And Let Shyama Dance There"

Rendered from Bengali

Beaut'ous blossoms ravishing with perfume,
Swarms of maddened bees buzzing all around;
The silver moon—a shower of sweet smile,
Which all the dwellers of heaven above
Shed lavishly upon the homes of earth;
The soft Malaya[1] breeze, whose magic touch
Opens to view distant memory's folds;
Murmuring rivers and brooks, rippling lakes
With restless Bhramaras[2] wheeling over
Gently waving lotuses unnumbered;
Foaming flow cascades—a streaming music—
To which echo mountain caves in return;
Warblers, full of sweet-flowing melody,
Hidden in leaves, pour hearts out—love discourse;
The rising orb of day, the painter divine,
With his golden brush but lightly touches
The canvas earth and a wealth of colours
Floods at once o'er the bosom of nature,
—Truly a museum of lovely hues—
Waking up a whole sea of sentiments.

The roll of thunder, the crashing of clouds,
War of elements spreading earth and sky;
Darkness vomiting forth blinding darkness,

---

[1]. A fabulous Sandal-wood mountain in the South. Hence, Malaya breeze means a fragrant breeze from the South.

[2]. A beetle somewhat like a humble-bee, which lives solely on honey.

The Pralaya[1] wind angrily roaring;

In quick bursts of dazzling splendour flashes

Blood-red terrific lightning, dealing death;

Monster waves roaring like thunder, foaming,

Rush impetuous to leap mountain peaks;

The earth booms furious, reels and totters,

Sinks down to its ruin, hurled from its place;

Piercing the ground, stream forth tremendous flames.

Mighty ranges blow up into atoms.

A lovely villa, on a lake of blue—

Festooned with dusters of water-lilies;

The heart-blood of ripe grapes capped with white foam

Whispering softly tells tale of passion;

The melody of the harp floods the ears,

And by its air, time, and harmony rich,

Enhances desire in the breast of man ;

What stirring of emotions! How many

Hot sighs of Love! And warm tears coursing down!

The Bimba[2]-red lips of the youthful fair,

The two blue eyes—two oceans of feelings;

The two hands eager to advance—love's cage—

In which the heart, like a bird, lies captive.

The martial music bursts, the trumpets blow,

The ground shakes under the warriors' tread;

The roar of cannon, the rattle of guns,

Volumes of smoke, the gruesome battlefield,

The thundering artillery vomits fire

---

1. The time of cosmic destruction.

2. A kind of fruit of a rich red colour.

In thousand directions; shells burst and strike
Vital parts of the body; elephants
And horses mounted are blown up in space;
The earth trembles under this infernal dance;
A million heroes mounted on steeds
Charge and capture the enemy's ordnance,
Piercing through the smoke and shower of shells
And rain of bullets; forward goes the flag,
The emblem of victory, of heroism
With the blood, yet hot, streaming down the staff,
Followed by the rifles, drunk with war-spirit;
Lo! the ensign falls, but the flag proceeds
Onwards on the shoulder of another;
Under his feet swell heaps of warriors
Perished in battle; but he falters not.
The flesh hankers for contacts of pleasure,
The senses for enchanting strains of song,
The mind hungers for peals of laughter sweet,
The heart pants to reach realms beyond sorrow;
Say, who cares exchange the soothing moonlight
For the burning rays of the noontide sun?
The wretch whose heart is like the scorching sun,
—Even he fondly loves the balmy moon;
Indeed, all thirst for joy. Breathes there the wretch
Who hugs pain and sorrow to his bosom?
Misery in his cup of happiness,
Deadly venom in his drink of nectar,
Poison in his throat—yet he clings to hope!
Lo! how all are scared by the Terrific,

None seek Elokeshi[1] whose form is Death.

The deadly frightful sword, reeking with blood,

They take from Her hand, and put a lute instead!

Thou dreaded Kâli, the All-destroyer,

Thou alone art true; Thy shadow's shadow

Is indeed the pleasant Vanamâli[2].

O Terrible Mother, cut quick the core,

Illusion dispel—the dream of happiness,

Rend asunder the fondness for the flesh.

True, they garland Thee with skulls, but shrink back

In fright and call Thee, "O All-merciful!"

At Thy thunder peal of awful laughter,

At Thy nudeness—for space is thy garment—

Their hearts sink down with terror, but they say,

"It is the demons that the Mother kills!"

They only pretend they wish to see Thee,

But when the time comes, at Thy sight they flee.

Thou art Death! To each and all in the world

Thou distributest the plague and disease

—Vessels of venom filled by Thine own hands.

O thou insane! Thou but cheatest thyself,

Thou cost not turn thy head lest thou behold.

Ay, the form terrible of the Mother.

Thou courtest hardship hoping happiness,

Thou wearest cloak of Bhakti and worship,

With mind full of achieving selfish ends.

The blood from the severed head of a kid

---

1. She with untied hair, a name of Kâli, the Divine Mother of the Universe.

2. Literally, he who is garlanded with wild flowers. The Shepherd Krishna in His aspect of youthful sport.

Fills thee with fear—thy heart throbs at the sight—
Verily a coward! Compassionate?[1]
Bless my soul! A strange state of things indeed!
To whom shall I tell the truth?—Who will see?
Free thyself from the mighty attraction—
The maddening wine of love, the charm of sex.
Break the harp! Forward, with the ocean's cry!
Drink tears, pledge even life—let the body fall.
Awake, O hero! Shake off thy vain dreams,
Death stands at thy head—does fear become thee?
A load of misery, true though it is—
This Becoming[2]—know this to be thy God!
His temple—the Shmashân[3] among corpses
And funeral pyres; unending battle —
That verily is His sacred worship;
Constant defeat — let that not unnerve thee;
Shattered be little self, hope, name, and fame;
Set up a pyre of them and make thy heart
A burning-ground.
And let Shyâmâ[4] dance there.

---

1. The idea is that the brave alone can be compassionate, and not the coward.
2. The wheel of constant birth and death, hence the world.
3. The cremation-ground.
4. The Dark One, Kali.

A Song I Sing to Thee

Rendered from Bengali

A song I sing. A song I sing to Thee!
Nor care I for men's comments, good or bad.
Censure or praise I hold of no account.
Servant am I, true servant of Thee Both[1],
Low at Thy feet, with Shakti, I salute!

Thou standest steadfast, ever at my back,
Hence when I turn me round, I see Thy face,
Thy smiling face. Therefore I sing again
And yet again. Therefore I fear no fear;
For birth and death lie prostrate at my feet.

Thy servant am I through birth after birth,
Sea of mercy, inscrutable Thy ways;
So is my destiny inscrutable;
It is unknown; nor would I wish to know.
Bhakti, Mukti, Japa, Tapas, all these,
Enjoyment, worship, and devotion too—
These things and all things similar to these,
I have expelled at Thy supreme command.
But only one desire is left in me—
An intimacy with Thee, mutual!
Take me, O Lord across to Thee;
Let no desire's dividing line prevent.

---

1. Purusha and Prakriti together.

The eye looks out upon the universe,
Nor does it seek to look upon itself;
Why should it? It sees itself in others.
Thou art my eyes! Thou and Thou alone ;
For every living temple shrines Thy face.

Like to the playing of a little child
Is every attitude of mine toward Thee.
Even, at times, I dare be angered with Thee;
Even, at times, I'd wander far away:—
Yet there, in greyest gloom of darkest night,
Yet there, with speechless mouth and tearful eyes,
Thou standest fronting me, and Thy sweet Face
Stoops down with loving look on face of mine.
Then, instantly, I turn me back to Thee,
And at Thy feet I fall on bended knees.
I crave no pardon at Thy gentle hands,
For Thou art never angry with Thy son.
Who else with all my foolish freaks would bear?

Thou art my Master! Thou my soul's real mate.
Many a time I see Thee—I am Thee!
Ay, I am Thee, and Thou, my Lord, art me!
Thou art within my speech. Within my throat
Art Thou, as Vinâpâni,[1] learned, wise.
On the flow of Thy current and its force
Humanity is carried as Thou wilt.
The thunder of Thy Voice is borne upon the boom
Of crashing waves, of over-leaping seas;

---

1. Goddess of learning.

The sun and moon give utterance to Thy Voice;
Thy conversation, in the gentle breeze
Makes itself heard in truth, in very truth,
True! True! And yet, the while, these gross precepts
Give not the message of the Higher Truth
Known to the knower!
Lo! The sun, the moon,
The moving planets and the shining stars,
Spheres of abode by myriads in the skies,
The comet swift, the glimmering lightning-flash,
The firmament, expanded, infinite—
These all, observant watchful eyes behold,

Anger, desire, greed, Moha[1],and the rest[2]
Whence issues forth the waving of the play
Of this existence; the home wherein dwells
Knowledge, and non-knowledge—whose centre is
The feeling of small self, the "Aham!" "Aham!"
Full of the dual sense of pleasure and of pain,
Teeming with birth and life, decay and death,
Whose arms are "The External" and "The Internal",
All things that are, down to the ocean's depths,
Up to sun, moon, and stars in spanless space—
The Mind, the Buddhi, Chitta, Ahamkâr,
The Deva, Yaksha, man and demon, all,
The quadruped, the bird, the worm, all insect life,
The atom and its compound, all that is,
Animate and inanimate, all, all—

---

1. Delusion.

2. Such as pride and malice, the sixfold evil.

The Internal and the External—dwell
In that one common plane of existence!
This outward presentation is of order gross,
As hair on human brow, Ay! very gross.

On the spurs of the massive Mount Meru[1]
The everlasting snowy ranges lie,
Extending miles and miles beyond more miles.
Piercing through clouds into the sky above
Its peaks thrust up in hundreds, glorious,
Brilliantly glistening, countless, snowy-white:
Flash upon flash of vivid lightning fleet,
The sun, high in his northern solstice hung,
With force of thousand rays concentrating,
Pours down upon the mountain floods of heat,
Furious as a billion thunderbolts,
From peak to peak.
Behold! The radiant sun
Swoons, as it were, in each. Then melts
The massive mountain with its crested peaks!
Down, down, it falls, with a horrific crash!
Water with water lies commingled now,
And all has passed like to a passing dream.

When all the many movements of the mind
Are, by Thy grace, made one, and unified,
The light of that unfoldment is so great
That, in its splendour, it surpasses far
The brilliance of ten thousand rising suns.

---

1. The name of a fabulous mountain round which the planets are said to revolve.

Then, sooth, the sun of Chit[1] reveals itself.
And melt away the sun and moon and stars,
High heaven above, the nether worlds, and all!
This universe seems but a tiny pool
Held in a hollow caused by some cow's hoof.
This is the reaching of the region which
Beyond the plane of the External lies.
Calmed are the clamours of the urgent flesh,
The tumult of the boastful mind is hushed,
Cords of the heart are loosened and set free,
Unfastened are the bandages that bind,
Attachment and delusion are no more!
Ay! There sounds sonorous the Sound
Void of vibration. Verily! Thy Voice!
Hearing that Voice, Thy servant, reverently,
Stands ever ready to fulfil Thy work.

"I exist. When, at Pralaya time
This wondrous universe is swallowed up;
Knowledge, the knower and the known, dissolved;
The world no more distinguishable, now,
No more conceivable; when sun and moon
And all the outspent stars, remain no more—
Then is the state of Mahâ-Nirvâna,
When action, act, and actor, are no more,
When instrumentality is no more;
Great darkness veils the bosom of the dark —
There I am present.

---

1. Knowledge.

"I am present! At Pralaya time,
When this vast universe is swallowed up,
Knowledge, and knower, and the known
Merged into one.
The universe no more
Can be distinguished or can be conceived
By intellect. The sun and moon and stars are not.
Over the bosom of the darkness, darkness moves
Intense Devoid of all the threefold bonds,
Remains the universe. Gunas are calmed
Of all distinctions. Everything deluged
In one homogeneous mass, subtle,
Pure, of atom-form, indivisible—
There I am present.

"Once again, I unfold Myself—that 'I';
Of My 'Shakti' the first great change is Om;
The Primal Voice rings through the void;
Infinite Space hears that great vibrant sound.
The group of Primal Causes shakes off sleep,
New life revives atoms interminable;
Cosmic existence heaves and whirls and sways,
Dances and gyrates, moves towards the core,
From distances immeasurably far.
The animate Wind arouses rings of Waves
Over the Ocean of great Elements;
Stirring, falling, surging, that vast range of Waves
Rushes with lightning fury. Fragments thrown
By force of royal resistance through the path

Of space, rush, endless, in the form of spheres
Celestial, numberless. Planets and stars
Speed swift; and man's abode, the earth revolves.

"At the Beginning, I the Omniscient One,
I am! The moving and the un-moving,
All this Creation comes into being
By the unfoldment of My power supreme.
I play with My own Maya, My Power Divine.
The One, I become the many, to behold
My own Form.

"At the Beginning, I, the Omniscient One,
I am! The moving and the un-moving,
All this Creation comes into being
By the unfoldment of My power supreme.
Perforce of My command, the wild storm blows
On the face of the earth; clouds clash and roar;
The flash of lightning startles and rebounds;
Softly and gently the Malaya breeze
Flows in and out like calm, unruffled breath;
The moon's rays pour their cooling current forth;
The earth's bare body in fair garb is clothed,
Of trees and creepers multitudinous;
And the flower abloom lifts her happy face,
Washed with drops of dew, towards the sun."

Discovery Publisher is a multimedia publisher whose mission is to inspire and support personal transformation, spiritual growth and awakening. We strive with every title to preserve the essential wisdom of the author, spiritual teacher, thinker, healer, and visionary artist.

www.ingramcontent.com/pod-product-compliance
Lightning Source LLC
Chambersburg PA
CBHW080534170426
43195CB00016B/2553